Stealing Fire from Heaven

Stealing Fire from

Heaven

The Rise of Modern Western Magic

NEVILL DRURY

OXFORD
UNIVERSITY PRESS

OXFORD
UNIVERSITY PRESS

Oxford University Press, Inc., publishes works that further
Oxford University's objective of excellence
in research, scholarship, and education.

Oxford   New York
Auckland   Cape Town   Dar es Salaam   Hong Kong   Karachi
Kuala Lumpur   Madrid   Melbourne   Mexico City   Nairobi
New Delhi   Shanghai   Taipei   Toronto

With offices in
Argentina   Austria   Brazil   Chile   Czech Republic   France   Greece
Guatemala   Hungary   Italy   Japan   Poland   Portugal   Singapore
South Korea   Switzerland   Thailand   Turkey   Ukraine   Vietnam

Published by Oxford University Press, Inc.
198 Madison Avenue, New York, New York 10016

www.oup.com

Oxford is a registered trademark of Oxford University Press.

Library of Congress Cataloging-in-Publication Data
Drury, Nevill, 1947–
Stealing fire from heaven : the rise of modern Western magic / Nevill Drury.
    p.   cm.
Includes bibliographical references and index.
ISBN 978-0-19-975099-3; 978-0-19-975100-6 (pbk)
1. Magic—History—20th century. 2. Magic—Western countries—History—20th century. I. Title.
BF1595.D78   2011
133.4′30904—dc22   2010013324

9 8 7 6 5 4 3 2 1

Printed in the United States of America
on acid-free paper

For Lesley, who shares my journey in every way

Preface

This book is an extension of doctoral work undertaken in recent times at
the University of Newcastle in Australia, but in a sense has its origins
some forty years ago when, as an undergraduate student at the
University of Sydney, I first became interested in the Western magical
traditions. I was spurred on by reading a controversial, popular book
titled *The Dawn of Magic* (later retitled *The Morning of the Magicians*) by
Louis Pauwels and Jacques Bergier. The book had originally been
published in French and at the time of its release in England in 1963 had
already sold over a quarter of a million copies in Europe. It was here that
I learned for the first time about the Hermetic Order of the Golden
Dawn and many key figures in Western esotericism, and the book really
stirred my imagination! Around the same time I discovered the artworks
of the remarkable British trance artist Austin Osman Spare in a magazine
and subsequently researched his magical ideas in the British Museum for
my first book, *The Search for Abraxas*—co-authored with a university
friend, Stephen Skinner, who had introduced me to the Kabbalah. I
could not have known at the time that Austin Spare would eventually
emerge as one of the most significant influences on Western magic in the
latter part of the twentieth century, although I am hardly surprised in
retrospect, given his extraordinary brilliance both as an artist and as an
original magical thinker.

This book seeks to provide an overview of the modern magical
revival—that is to say, it focuses specifically on the resurgence of interest
in the Western esoteric tradition in the twentieth century. As one would

expect, the central themes revolve around the magic of the Golden Dawn, Aleister Crowley's cult of *Thelema*, the rise of Wicca and Goddess spirituality, and the subsequent emergence of more divergent occult groups like the Temple of Set and the practitioners of Chaos Magick. However I have also intentionally delved into areas of modern magical thought that are less well known, profiling several of contemporary magic's most fascinating individuals—like the Australian trance artist and witch Rosaleen Norton, Chicago-based Gnostic voodoo magician Michael Bertiaux, Left-Hand Path practitioner Michael Aquino, and Swiss fantasy artist H. R. Giger. These individuals, in their own unique, and sometimes eccentric, ways have also helped shape the modern magical imagination.

I am well aware that in compiling and writing an overview history like *Stealing Fire from Heaven* I am entering a field that has already been well served by some outstanding research and scholarship. Key titles like Margot Adler's *Drawing Down the Moon*, Ronald Hutton's *The Triumph of the Moon*, Hugh Urban's *Magia Sexualis*, and Andrei Znamenski's *The Beauty of the Primitive: Shamanism and the Western Imagination* come readily to mind. Nevertheless, the Hutton and Adler volumes focus primarily on the rise of twentieth-century pagan witchcraft—the latter dealing exclusively with neopaganism in the United States, and Hugh Urban's *Magia Sexualis* describes the esoteric groups that have been influenced by Aleister Crowley's controversial approach to sex magick (Crowley's unique spelling). Andrei Znamenski's *The Beauty of the Primitive*, meanwhile, explores the rise of neoshamanism in the West in all its myriad forms—in itself a vast undertaking. *Stealing Fire from Heaven* will, it is hoped, be seen as complementing these works rather than in any way endeavoring to compete with them. Austin Spare, in particular, has been ignored in most of the major overviews published to date, and I seek to redress that here.[1] Spare is now rightly regarded as one of the most significant figures in the twentieth-century magical revival, alongside MacGregor Mathers, Aleister Crowley, Dion Fortune, and Gerald Gardner.

Looking back on the lengthy period prior to my doctoral work, I can see in retrospect that certain events have greatly influenced my research interests. Prior to my more recent postgraduate studies I worked for many years in the international book-publishing industry, with occasional involvement in documentary films. I was fortunate in December 1984 to take part in the filming of an award-winning ninety-minute international television documentary, *The Occult Experience*—screened originally in Australia, where I live, and later released in the United States on Sony Home Video. My role as the co-producer, researcher, and interviewer for that documentary gave me direct personal access to several key figures in the Wicca and Goddess spirituality movements, and information acquired at that time proved invaluable by way of historical background. The most positive aspect of making this documentary—from my own personal perspective—was my direct contact with such pivotal figures as Michael Harner, Z. Budapest, Starhawk, Alex Sanders, Janet and Stewart Farrar, Michael Bertiaux, and H. R. Giger—all of whom feature in this book.

Finally, on a personal note, I would like to thank a small group of academic researchers at various universities around the world who have encouraged my esoteric research. They include Dr. Marguerite Johnson, from the University of Newcastle; Dr. Lynne Hume, Dr. Helen Farley, and Dr. Philip Almond from the University of Queensland; Dr. Michael Tucker from the University of Brighton in the UK; Dr. J. Gordon Melton and Dr. Lee Irwin in the United States, and "new religions" specialist Dr. James R. Lewis, who is currently based in Norway. I would also like to thank Cynthia Read, Molly Balikov, Tamzen Benfield, and Margaret Case from Oxford University Press, New York, for their valuable editorial and production assistance in preparing this book for publication.

Contents

Introduction, 3

1. Medieval Precursors, 7

2. Freemasons and the Rose Cross, 23

3. New Light: The Rise of the Golden Dawn, 43

4. Aleister Crowley and the Left-Hand Path, 77

5. Three Magical Visionaries, 127

6. The Rebirth of the Goddess, 175

7. Dark Forces: Contemporary Satanism and Black Magic, 205

8. Spirit, Myth, and Cosmos: From Shamanism to Chaos Magick, 225

9. Archetypes and Cyberspace: Magic in the Twenty-First Century, 257

Notes, 275

Bibliography, 335

Index, 351

Stealing Fire from Heaven

Introduction

Magical thought is commonly identified with superstition and regarded as a form of pre-science—an earlier and less sophisticated phase of human intellectual development. Indeed, elements of this perception have entered popular folklore. One thinks immediately of evil eye amulets, of black cats, or magic spells cast by wicked, toothless crones. However the sort of magic described in this book has little to do with superstition. As we will see, the magic of twentieth century occultism has an altogether different thrust. Here the concept of magical consciousness relates much more to the concept of will or intent—to the idea that one can bring about specific effects or changes within one's sphere of consciousness. This form of magic is basically about personal transformation—or more specifically, about the transformation of one's perception or state of awareness.

Some have regarded occult exploration as inherently dangerous—as a foray into uncharted waters. To some extent this fear is warranted, for modern Western magic is, by its very nature, an esoteric tradition and involves the exploration of relatively unexplored human potentials. As the English artist and occultist Austin Osman Spare once observed: the aim of magic is *to steal the fire from heaven.*[1] However, one of my aims in this book is to show that, for many practitioners, the practice of magic has an essentially spiritual intent. Its imaginal methods transport the visionary magician into transcendental realms of consciousness, facilitating direct experience of the sacred archetypes of the Western psyche.

The Concept of Magical Will

It is in relation to the issue of will that magic differs from mysticism and the more mainstream forms of religion. The magician, unlike the mystic or religious devotee, draws not so much upon the concept of grace bestowed by God as on the idea that one may alter one's state of consciousness magically at will—that the gods will respond if one undertakes certain ritual or visualization procedures. It may be that the magician dresses ceremonially to capture their likeness, and in so doing invokes their sacred and symbolic energy. Perhaps sacred god names are uttered or intoned—like those found in the Kabbalah, in the pagan traditions of contemporary witchcraft, and in certain Gnostic formulations. Here the core idea is that the name of the god or goddess embodies the very essence of the deity and that by invoking that sacred vibration one is not only tuning in to the archetypal level of awareness associated with these sacred beings but actually attaining mastery of them.

As will become evident in later chapters of this book, the idea of will is vital to the magical attitude. We find it in the magic of the Hermetic Order of the Golden Dawn, where focused intent enables the magician to rise through the planes of "inner space"—through the symbolic and mythological realms of the Tree of Life. We find it in the quest for the Higher Self—anthropomorphized in Aleister Crowley's writings as the Holy Guardian Angel. And we also find it in the controversial shamanic accounts of Carlos Castaneda, where the magical apprentice has to whirl his spirit catcher near the sacred water hole and concentrate on the "spaces" within the conjured sounds, in order to will a magical ally to appear. In all of these instances the idea of the magical will is central to the activity in question.

All of this, of course, is quite foreign to most established religious traditions. Prayer and supplication, offerings of thanks to a Savior god, and acts of worship in a church, are in no way intended to capture the god. Quite the reverse, in fact. Western religious devotion is an attitude of mind where one humbly submits oneself before God in the hope that He will bestow grace and salvation. There is no implied act of control or mastery here—no stealing fire from heaven. One waits, passively, until grace is received.

The magical attitude, on the other hand, is clearly more active—and often more assertive. The magician or witch is at the center of his or her own particular universe. With their sacred formulae, ritual invocations, and concentrated will-power, magicians and witches believe they can bring certain forces to bear. The magician believes that he or she can *will* to effect.

In one sense the "primitivism" of this approach has been legitimized by existential philosophy and the rise of the contemporary human potential or "personal growth" movement.[2] It has become common for recent interpreters of the Western magical tradition to regard the gods of High Magic as emanations of the creative imagination, as forces of the transcendent psyche. The noted authority on Western magic Israel Regardie—who was a practitioner of Reichian therapy as well as a member of the Stella Matutina, an offshoot of the Golden Dawn—employed the Jungian model of the archetypes of the collective unconscious to explain to his contemporary audience what he meant by invoking a god. For him it was nothing other than a ritual means of channeling into conscious awareness a specific archetypal energy-form from the universal or "collective" psyche.[3]

It is only fair to point out, however, that many modern magicians, witches, and occultists view their pantheon of gods and goddesses as existing in their own right—as beings beyond the human psyche, as entities belonging intrinsically to another plane of existence. For these devotees, magic becomes a vital means of communication. The gods and goddesses provide knowledge of these esoteric domains to the inquiring magician and thereby allow the devotee to grow in awareness. Several notable contemporary magicians, including Michael Aquino of the Temple of Set, the controversial Satanist Anton LaVey, and the Australian witch Rosaleen Norton, have held this view.

Nevertheless, most modern magicians—irrespective of the tradition they follow—do tend to share one feature in common, and that is the notion of a hierarchy of supernatural beings or "powers" with whom they can interrelate. These powers in turn provide sacred knowledge and wisdom—wisdom that allows the magical devotee special insights into the dynamics of the universe and the sacred potentials of humanity. In a sense, magic would make gods and goddesses of us all. Considered in this light, for many practitioners magic is essentially about growth and renewal on an archetypal level of being, and also about transforming one's perception of the world from one that is profane and devalued to one that is sacred. This type of magic is about vision and deep, insightful, spiritual knowledge. This is High Magic, or *gnosis*.

The modern magical revival has been unfolding for over a century. As a spiritual movement committed to the development of esoteric knowledge or gnosis in the West, the occult resurgence first began to gather momentum in the final decade of the nineteenth century and has since seeded itself around the world in fascinating ways, spawning divergent esoteric groups and organizations. In terms of actual historical beginnings, however, the story of the twentieth-century magical revival commences with the Hermetic Order of the Golden Dawn, arguably the most influential esoteric organization in modern history.[4] All modern occult perspectives—including Wicca, Goddess spirituality, and the Thelemic magick of Aleister Crowley—owe a debt to the Golden Dawn for gathering together the threads of the Western esoteric tradition and initiating a transformative process that continues in the twenty-first century.

Established in England in 1888, the Hermetic Order of the Golden Dawn drew on a range of ancient and medieval cosmologies and incorporated them into a body of ceremonial practices centered on the Kabbalistic Tree of Life, an important motif within the Jewish mystical tradition.[5] In addition to revitalizing the use of the Kabbalah, which occupied a central position in the cosmology of the Golden Dawn, its members believed they were building on the Hermetic tradition, which had its roots in Neoplatonism and underwent a revival during the Renaissance. Alchemy, the Tarot, Rosicrucianism, and the ritual grades of nineteenth-century Freemasonry were also important elements. I will discuss the historical influence of Rosicrucianism and Freemasonry on the Hermetic Order of the Golden Dawn later in this book, but it is appropriate in the first instance to consider the key esoteric source-traditions that provide the foundations on which the structures of twentieth-century occultism have been built. These key traditions are the medieval Kabbalah, the Hermetica, Alchemy, and the Tarot—and this is where the story of the modern magical revival really begins.

In later chapters we will discuss some of the occasionally brilliant, and often eccentric, byways of the twentieth-century occult revival—including the highly distinctive cosmologies of esoteric practitioners like Austin Osman Spare, Rosaleen Norton, Michael Aquino, and Michael Bertiaux. But if we are to consider the nature of contemporary magical consciousness we must first explore the Kabbalistic Tree of Life—for this is the symbol that establishes the matrix of the modern magical imagination.

1

Medieval Precursors

According to Gershom Scholem, one of the preeminent authorities on Jewish mysticism, the medieval Kabbalah belongs to an emanationist cosmological tradition that has its origins in Gnosticism.[1] Indeed, Scholem has referred to the Kabbalah as a form of Jewish Gnosticism.[2] In its most fundamental sense, the Kabbalah can be defined as a mystical commentary on the Pentateuch: the written Torah, or "five books of Moses."[3] The Hebrew word *Kabbalah*—which translates as "that which has been received"–refers to an oral or secret tradition, and as Scholem has observed, the *Zohar*, the central text of the medieval Kabbalah, compiled in written form by the Spaniard Moses de Leon circa 1280 CE, has spiritual links with earlier schools of Gnosticism and Neoplatonism.[4] In all three, there are references to the concept of sacred emanations from the Godhead, to the idea of the preexistence of the soul and its descent into matter, and to the sacred names of God.

Although the Kabbalah did not exist in written form until the Middle Ages, it is thought that the *Sefer Yetzirah*, or *Book of Creation*, was composed in Palestine between the third and sixth centuries CE. The *Sefer Yetzirah* descibes how God created the world by means of the twenty-two letters of the Hebrew alphabet and the ten *sefirot*—a term that appears for the first time in Hebrew literature.[5] The ten *sefirot* of the Tree of Life (also spelled *sephiroth*) are a central symbolic aspect of the Kabbalah.

Another early Kabbalistic text, *Sefer ha-Bahir*, emerged in Provence—where there was a Jewish community—between 1150 and 1200.

Interest in the Kabbalah subsequently spread across the Pyrenees into Catalonia and then to Castile. In about 1280, the Spanish Jewish mystic Moses de Leon (1238–1305) began circulating booklets among his fellow Kabbalists. These texts were written in Aramaic, and de Leon claimed that he had transcribed them from an ancient book of wisdom composed in the circle of Rabbi Shim'on bar Yohai, a famous disciple of Rabbi Akiva, who lived and taught in Israel in the second century. These booklets gradually formed the text known as *Ha-Zohar ha-Qadosh*, usually referred to as the *Zohar* (The Book of Splendor). Although Moses de Leon may have drawn on early material received through the secret oral tradition, it is now thought that he himself was probably the author of the *Zohar*.

According to the *Zohar*, God first taught the doctrines of the Kabbalah to a select group of angels. After the creation of the Garden of Eden, these angels shared the secret teachings with the first man, Adam. They were then passed to Noah, and subsequently to Abraham, who took them to Egypt. Moses was initiated into the Kabbalah in Egypt, the land of his birth, and King David and King Solomon were also initiated. No one, however, dared write them down until Rabbi Shim'on bar Yohai.[6]

In the Kabbalah, all aspects of manifested form, including the sacred archetypes or manifestations of the Godhead, are said to have their origin in *Ain Soph Aur*—also referred to as *En-Sof* or *Ein-Sof*—"the limitless light," a realm of being entirely beyond form and conception which "has neither qualities nor attributes."[7] In Kabbalistic cosmology, the subsequent emanations that emerge from this profound Mystery, and that constitute the spheres upon the Tree of Life (*Otz Chiim*), reveal different aspects of the sacred universe but are nevertheless considered as part of a divine totality. *Ain Soph Aur*, writes Scholem, "manifests . . . to the Kabbalist under ten different aspects, which in turn comprise an endless variety of shades and gradations."[8] These emanations nevertheless reflect the essential unity of the Godhead, and because the human form is said to have been created "in the image of God," the spheres on the Tree of Life are also spheres within the body of Adam Kadmon, the archetypal human being.[9] In the Kabbalah, the quest for mystical self-knowledge is therefore regarded essentially as a process of regaining undifferentiated Oneness with the Divine.

According to the Kabbalah, the mystical universe is sustained by the utterance of the Holy Names of God: the ten emanations or *sephiroth* on the Tree of Life are none other than "the creative names which God called into the world, the names which He gave to Himself."[10] According to the *Zohar*:

> In the Beginning, when the will of the King began to take effect, he
> engraved signs into the divine aura. A dark flame sprang forth from the
> innermost recess of the mystery of the Infinite, *En-Sof* [*Ain Soph Aur*]

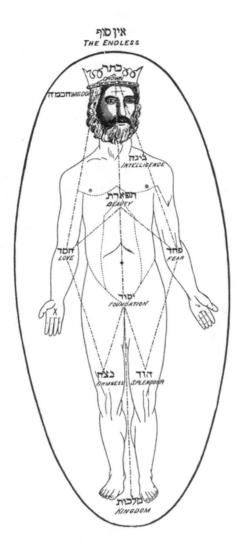

FIGURE 1.1. Adam Kadmon, the archetypal human being. His body contains the ten *sephiroth*, or emanations from the Godhead.

like a fog which forms out of the formless, enclosed in the ring of this aura, neither white nor black, neither red nor green, and of no color whatever. But when this flame began to assume size and extension it produced radiant colors. For in the innermost center of the flame a well sprang forth from which flames poured upon everything below, hidden in the mysterious secrets of *En-Sof*. The well broke through, and yet did not entirely break through, the ethereal aura which surrounded it. It was entirely unrecognizable until the impact of its breakthrough a hidden supernal point shone forth. Beyond this point nothing may be known or understood, and therefore it is called *Reshith*, that is "Beginning," the first word of Creation.[11]

Scholem writes that the "Primordial Point" was thought of by the majority of Kabbalists not as Kether, the Crown (normally considered the first emanation upon the Tree of Life) but as the Great Father, Chokmah or Wisdom, which is the second *sephirah*. In Kabbalistic cosmology, the energy of the Great Father unites with that of Binah, the Great Mother (Understanding), and from her womb all archetypal forms come forth.[12] As Christian Ginsburg notes in his seminal book *The Kabbalah: Its Doctrines, Development and Literature*, "It is not the *En-Sof* who created the world, but this Trinity . . . the world was born from the union of the crowned King and Queen . . . who, emanated from the *En-Sof*, produced the Universe in their own image."[13] In a symbolic sense, the seven subsequent emanations beneath the trinity of Kether, Chokmah, and Binah constitute the seven days of Creation.[14] The Tree of Life, with its ten *sephiroth* or emanations of divine consciousness, therefore encompasses a symbolic process by which the Infinite becomes tangible.[15] The ten spheres on the Tree of Life are as follows:

Kether	The Crown
Chokmah	Wisdom (The Father)
Binah	Understanding (The Mother)
Chesed	Mercy
Geburah	Severity, or Strength
Tiphareth	Beauty, or Harmony (The Son)
Netzach	Victory
Hod	Splendor
Yesod	The Foundation
Malkuth	Kingdom, or Earth (The Daughter)

These emanations align themselves into three pillars, the outer two being the Pillar of Mercy headed by Chokmah (symbolizing light and purity) and the Pillar of Severity headed by Binah (symbolizing darkness and impurity). Beneath them lies the Garden of Eden, with its four rivers Chesed, Geburah, Netzach, and Hod converging in Tiphareth, which is located at a central point on the Middle Pillar. The occult historian A. E. Waite—a leading member of the Golden Dawn—has suggested that the Middle Pillar can be regarded as the Perfect Pillar, for it reaches to the Crown, Kether.[16] The other two pillars provide a duality of opposites and represent the Tree of Knowledge of Good and Evil. The sixth emanation on the Tree of Life, Tiphareth, is associated symbolically with the divine Son and is regarded in the Western esoteric tradition as the sphere of spiritual rebirth. The final emanation on the Tree of Life, Malkuth, The World, is represented symbolically by the Daughter, Shekinah, who in turn is a reflection of the Great Mother, Binah.[17]

In addition to recognising ten *sephiroth* upon the Tree of Life, the medieval Kabbalists also divided the Tree into "four worlds" of creative manifestation. God was said to be present in each of these four worlds, and each in turn was represented symbolically by a letter in the Tetragrammaton, the sacred name JHVH (consisting of the four Hebrew letters *Yod, He, Vau, He*) usually translated as Jehovah, or Yahweh, meaning Lord.[18] The four worlds are as follows:

Atziluth, the Archetypal World

This level of existence is closest to the unmanifested realm of *Ain Soph Aur* and contains only one *sephirah*, Kether, which is described as "the hidden of the hidden. It is the emergence of God's Will, His creative urge. It is the infinite, the initiation of all that can and will be. It is infinity."[19]

Briah, the World of Creation

This world contains two *sephiroth*, Chokmah and Binah, representing the Great Father and the Great Mother and reflecting the highest expression of the sacred male and female principles. Their union gives rise to the World of Formation.[20]

Yetzirah, the World of Formation

This world contains the *sephiroth* Chesed, Geburah, Tiphareth, Netzach, Hod, and Yesod. As indicated by its name, Yesod literally provides the "foundation"' for all that has preceded it in the creative process of sacred emanation from the highest realms of the Tree of Life.

Assiah, the Physical World

This world represents the final materialization of God's Will in the sphere of Malkuth on the Tree of Life and is represented by Shekinah, the Daughter, who is spoken of variously as "the Bride of the Divine Son in Tiphareth," "the Bride of Kether," and the "Daughter of Binah." Shekinah personifies the Divine Feminine on Earth.[21]

Each *sephirah* is also said to contain an entire Tree of Life. The "Malkuth" of the first *sephirah* emanates the "Kether" of the following *sephirah*, and so on, through the ten emanations on the Tree. Each of these ten spheres is therefore considered a mirror of the Divine. According to the Jewish mystical tradition, nothing exists beyond God, and as John Ferguson has observed in relation to the spiritual quest in the Kabbalah: "We must see God as the First Cause, and the universe as an emanation from his Will or Wisdom. The finite has no existence except in the light of the Infinite, which contracted so that the finite might be. . . . Man is the highest point of the created world, and his soul contains animal and moral elements, but also an element of pure spirit, which in the righteous ascends to God."[22]

The Hermetic Tradition

During the fifteenth and sixteenth centuries the Hermetica, or Hermetic tradition, gained intellectual and philosophical influence in Europe. Hermetic philosophy has its roots in Hellenism.[23] During the Renaissance, Florence became a cultural center where esoteric and metaphysical perspectives were strongly supported, and it was in the royal courts under the rule of Cosimo and Lorenzo de Medici that the Hermetic tradition received significant endorsement. In 1460, a monk named Leonardo da Pistoia brought with him to Florence a collection of Greek manuscripts that had been discovered in Macedonia and that would later become known as the *Corpus Hermeticum*, or *Hermetica*. These texts were presented to Cosimo de Medici (1389–1464), the Italian merchant prince who ruled Florence and who was also a noted collector of Greek manuscripts. In 1462, Cosimo passed the Hermetic texts to his young court scholar, Marsilio Ficino (1433–1499), requesting that he translate them into Latin. This work was completed in 1463, and Cosimo was able to read the translation before his death the following year.[24]

The Hermetic material was essentially a body of Greek mystical and philosophical writings that drew on Platonism, Stoicism, and Neoplatonism, and then subsequently emerged within a Gnostic-Egyptian context. The Hermetic texts date from the latter half of the second century CE through to the end of the third century.[25] In these writings the central figure, Hermes Trismegistus (Thrice Greatest Hermes) is presented as a wise spiritual teacher, a Gnostic master who is a composite of Hermes and Thoth.[26] In the Hermetic model of the universe, all things were believed to have come from God, and the world was therefore part of a sacred Unity. The universe itself was divided into three worlds, or emanations. The lowest sphere was the world of Nature, which in turn received divine influences from the more sanctified realms above. At the next level were the stars, spirits, and "guardians." Higher still was the supercelestial world of *nous*, the world of angelic spirits who were thought to have a superior knowledge of reality because they were closer to the Godhead, the sacred source of Creation. According to the Hermetic perspective, the transcendent act of achieving a state of Oneness with God entailed liberating oneself from the constrictions of temporal life and entering the realm of pure and divine Thought.[27]

Ficino's work on the *Corpus Hermeticum* was developed by Giovanni Pico, Count of Mirandola (1463–1494). Pico combined Ficino's Hermetic Neoplatonism with an extensive knowledge of astrology, the Kabbalah, Christianity, and "high magic" (*mageia*).[28] Like Ficino, Pico conceived of a universe that emanated from the Godhead. However, Pico's conception was not simply that of the devotional mystic. According to Pico, not only could man come to know God but he could also become a type of god himself—an attitude to divinity also found among some contemporary magical practitioners:

> He who knows himself in himself knows all things, as Zoroaster first wrote. When we are finally lighted in this knowledge, we shall in bliss be addressing the true Apollo on intimate terms. . . . And, restored to health, Gabriel "the strength of God," shall abide in us, leading us through the miracles of Nature and showing us on every side the merit and the might of God.[29]

According to Pico, *mageia* or high magic could provide humanity with access to the inner workings of Nature and the cosmos. *Mageia* could be employed "in calling forth into the light, as if from their hiding places, the powers scattered and sown in the world by the loving-kindness of God."[30] The role of the sacred magician, the practitioner of *mageia*, was to raise earth (matter) to the level of heaven (spirit). In the *Asclepius*, Hermes Trismegistus similarly urges his followers to become "god-like":

> He takes in the nature of a god as if he were himself a god. . . . He is united to the gods because he has the divinity pertaining to gods. . . . He takes the earth as his own, he blends himself with the elements by the speed of thought, by the sharpness of spirit he descends to the depths of the sea. Everything is accessible to him; heaven is not too high for him, for he measures it as if he were in his grasp by his ingenuity. What sight the spirit shows to him, no mist of the air can obscure; the earth is never so dense as to impede his work; the immensity of the sea's depths do not trouble his plunging view. He is at the same time everything as he is everywhere.[31]

It was primarily the high magic or *mageia* of the Hermetic tradition that attracted the founding members of the Golden Dawn because, at its most profound level, high magic (or "'theurgy'") proposed an archetypal process of mythic renewal.

The magical quest, as delineated within the Hermetic and Gnostic traditions, was to be "reborn" from the limited and restricted world of material form into the realm of Spirit.[32]

The Spiritual Dimension in Alchemy

Western alchemy dates from the beginning of the second century CE and flourished in Hellenistic Egypt, where there was a high level of proficiency in metalworking skills, especially in relation to silver and copper alloys that resembled gold. Two papyri found in a gravesite in Thebes, the so-called Leiden and Stockholm papyri that date from around 300 CE, include recipes for changing the color of a metal so that it would resemble gold or silver, a fascinating precursor, perhaps, of the metaphysical concept of the transmutation of base metals into gold. The word "alchemy" itself is thought to derive from an Egyptian word, *chem* or *qem*, meaning "black," a reference to the black alluvial soils bordering the Nile. The fourth-century alchemical writer Zosimos of Panopolis (Akhmim) in Egypt maintained that a person named Chemes had given rise to the quest for gold and had authored a book of supernaturally inspired instruction called *Chema*, but proof of Chemes's historical existence has not been established. It is thought, however, that the Greek word *chyma*, meaning to fuse or cast metals, established itself in Arabic as *al kimia*, from which the more familiar term "alchemy" is in turn derived.

As a pagan practice, the study of alchemy thrived in Alexandria in buildings adjacent to the famous Temple of Serapis, but this temple (the Serapeum), together with numerous statues and works of art, was destroyed in 391 on the orders of the Christian archbishop of Alexandria, Theophilus. The persecuted alchemical scholars then withdrew to Athens, where the Thracian Neoplatonist Proclus was teaching, and in this way a more comprehensive knowledge of Egyptian alchemy was introduced to Greece. Although pagan traditions were finally suppressed by Emperor Justinian in 529, interest in alchemy was rekindled in the seventh century when Stephanos of Alexandria dedicated his *Nine Lessons in Chemia* to the Byzantine emperor Heraclitus, and in the eleventh century when Psellus revived Platonism. According to Kurt Seligmann, the writings of Stephanos inspired a number of medieval alchemical poets, and these writers also extolled the virtues of the Hermetic philosophy.[33]

Like their Neoplatonic and Hermetic counterparts, the medieval alchemists believed in the unity of the cosmos and maintained that there was a clear correspondence between the physical and spiritual realms, with comparable laws operating in each domain. As the sixteenth-century Moravian alchemist Michael Sendivogius writes in *The New Chemical Light*:

The Sages have been taught of God that this natural world is only an image and material copy of a heavenly and spiritual pattern; that the very existence of this world is based upon the reality of its celestial archetype; and that God has created it in imitation of the spiritual and invisible universe, in order that men might be the better enabled to comprehend His heavenly teaching and the wonders of His absolute and ineffable power and wisdom. Thus the Sage sees heaven reflected in Nature as in a mirror; and he pursues this Art, not for the sake of gold or silver, but for the love of the knowledge which it reveals; he jealously conceals it from the sinner and the scornful, lest the mysteries of heaven should be laid bare to the vulgar gaze.[34]

The alchemists adopted the Hermetic concept that the universe and humanity reflect each other, which in essence is the core meaning behind the idea of the macrocosm and microcosm and the dictum "as above, so below." It was assumed by the alchemists that whatever existed in the universe must also, to some degree, be latent or present in every human being. A Syriac Hermetic text affirms this point emphatically:

What is the adage of the philosophers? Know thyself! This refers to the intellectual and cognitive mirror. And what is this mirror if not the Divine and original Intellect? When a man looks at himself and sees himself in this, he turns away from everything that bears the name of gods or demons, and, by uniting himself with the Holy Spirit, becomes a perfect man. He sees God within himself.[35]

In medieval alchemical thought, each individual person consisted of spirit, soul, and body, and to this extent contained the very essence of the universe as a whole. Alchemy affirmed, as the Hermetic texts had similarly conveyed, that the Universal Mind is indivisible and unites all things in the material universe. The various metals, always a specific alchemical concern, were similarly one in essence, and had sprung from the same seed in the womb of Nature. Indeed, as historian E. J. Holmyard observes in his pioneering study of alchemy, it was assumed by the medieval European alchemists that because the world was permeated by a universal spirit, this meant that "every object in the universe possessed some sort of life. Metals grew, as did minerals, and were even attributed sex. A fertilized seed of gold could develop into a nugget, the smoky exhalation was masculine and the vaporous one feminine, and mercury was a womb in which embryonic metals could be gestated."[36]

However, the alchemists did not regard all of the metals as equally mature or "perfect." Gold symbolized the highest development in Nature, and as an element came to personify human renewal, or regeneration. A "golden" human being was one who was resplendent with spiritual beauty and who had triumphed over temptations and the lurking power of evil. By way of contrast, the most base of all the metals, lead, represented the sinful and unrepentant individual who continued to wallow in sin and was readily overcome by the forces of darkness. The Philosopher's Stone, said to be capable of bringing about a state of alchemical transmutation, was associated by some Christian alchemists with the figure of Jesus himself. Here alchemical transmutation was considered as a type of spiritual redemption, and the imagery of base and precious metals provided a metaphor for personal transformation. As H. Stanley Redgrove has noted, "Alchemy was an attempted application of the principles of mysticism to the things of the physical world."[37]

According to the medieval alchemists, all aspects of matter were a reflection of God, and matter itself consisted of four elements—earth, fire, air, and water—which in turn proceeded from the *quinta essentia*, or "quintessence." The alchemists also associated certain metals with the astrological "planets": Sun—gold; Moon—silver; Mercury—quicksilver; Venus—copper; Mars—iron; Jupiter—tin; Saturn—lead.

The alchemists believed, however, that the process of transmutation from a base metal into silver or gold was not possible without the metal first being reduced to its *materia prima*, or fundamental substance. This, in effect, involved an attempt to reduce the base metal to a state of "soul" or "essence." According to the alchemists, the soul, in its original state of pure receptivity, is fundamentally one with the *materia prima* of the whole world. In one way, this is but a restatement of the theoretical premise of all alchemy, namely, that macrocosm and microcosm correspond to one another. At the same time, it is also an expression of the goal of the alchemical work.[38]

The idea of the *materia prima* itself referred to the potential of "soul" to take a material form. At this level, one could consider a metal to be latent, or "unrealized." A metal in this condition was considered "uncongealed"—free of specific qualities. By contrast, specific metals were normally, and by definition, rigid, restricted, or "coagulated." Alchemical transformation therefore involved a shift from the initial coagulation through such processes as burning, dissolving, and purification, in order to produce a new outcome: a quite different reformulation from the original substance. However, although many alchemists believed that amorphous *materia* could be burnt, dissolved, and purified and then subsequently "coagulated" into the form of a perfect metal like gold (a literal symbol of wholeness), those alchemists who were more mystically inclined also believed that this process could be applied to the mystical quest for Oneness with God. As Titus Burckhardt has written:

The form of the soul thus "born again" is nevertheless distinguishable from the all-embracing Spirit, as it still belongs to conditioned existence. But at the same time it is transparent to the undifferentiated Light of the Spirit and its vital union with the primordial *materia* of all souls, for the "material" or "substantial" ground of the soul, just like its essential or active ground, has a unitary nature. . . . The highest meaning of alchemy is the knowledge that all is contained in all.[39]

The Early Renaissance Tarot

Court records dating from 1392 CE indicate that King Charles VI of France made a payment to a painter named Jacquemin Gringonneur for three packs of cards that were described as "gilded and coloured, and ornamented with various devices, supplied to the King for his amusement."[40] It has not been established whether these were early Tarot cards or hand-painted playing cards: the cards themselves have not been located. The Bibliothèque Nationale collection, however, includes seventeen cards, sixteen of which are identifiable as Tarot cards. These cards were originally thought to have been those created for Charles VI by Gringonneur, but they have now been identified as Venetian in origin, and date from about 1470.[41]

The earliest specific references to Tarot cards date back to 1442 and the d'Este court of Ferrara, although Tarot cards may have been invented a few years earlier, originating in northern Italy between 1410 and 1425.[42] It seems likely that the earliest Tarot cards were associated with the aristocratic courts of either Ferrara or Milan; most of the Tarot decks that survive from fifteenth-century Italy reflect the style and fashion of the nobility from that era.[43] Interest in the Tarot subsequently spread from Italy to France and Switzerland. The modern Tarot deck is descended from the Piedmontese Tarot, which was widely known in northern Italy and France by the beginning of the sixteenth century. This pack consisted of seventy-eight cards divided into twenty-two cards of the Major Arcana and fifty-six cards of the Minor Arcana.[44] The Major Arcana are the so-called court or mythological cards, while the Minor Arcana consists of four basic suits—swords, wands, cups, and pentacles—which parallel the four suits in the modern (early twentieth-century) Rider-Waite Tarot deck.[45]

The widespread belief that the Tarot cards conceal a hidden symbolic language based on esoteric themes has led to a plethora of fanciful explanations relating to the Tarot's actual origins and purpose. Even today, some enthusiasts continue to claim that the Tarot cards originated in ancient Egypt and are associated with an esoteric wisdom tradition dating back thousands of years.[46] Such a view was first proposed by French theologian Antoine Court de Gébelin (1725–1784), author of *Le monde primitif* (nine volumes), published in Paris between 1775 and 1784. His essay on the Tarot is included in volume 8 of this work, published in 1781.[47]

Court de Gébelin felt assured that his "discovery" of the Egyptian origin of the Tarot would be well received, and he made brief mention of the Tarot in volume 4 of *Le monde primitif*, published in 1776: "We were convinced that the public would take pleasure in a discovery and a gift of such a kind, an Egyptian Book escaped from barbarism, from the ravages of time."[48] According to Court de Gébelin, the Tarot cards had been invented by ancient Egyptian priests; their seventy-eight-page book, disguised as a pack of playing cards, escaped the fire that destroyed their ancient libraries:

> If one heard it announced that there still exists in our days a work of the ancient Egyptians, one of their books that had escaped the flames that devoured their magnificent libraries, that contained in a pure form their doctrines concerning interesting subjects, everyone would without doubt be eager to come to know so precious and so remarkable a book. . . . The fact is, however, quite true. This Egyptian Book, the only remnant of their magnificent libraries, exists in our day. . . . This Book is, in a word, the game of TAROTS.[49]

Citing evidence of the Tarot's alleged Egyptian origin, Court de Gébelin identified Trump VII (The Chariot) with "Osiris triumphant"; Trump XV (The Devil) as Typhon, a Greek mythical being associated with the Egyptian figure of Set, enemy of Osiris; and Trump XVII (The Star) with Sirius the Dog-Star.[50] He also took the word "tarot" itself to be Egyptian, giving its derivation as *tar*, meaning road or way, and *ro*, meaning a king, or royal. The word "tarot" could therefore be translated as the "royal road" or "the royal road of life." According to Court de Gébelin, the symbolic wisdom of the Tarot had subsequently been introduced to Europe by wandering gypsies, themselves of Egyptian origin.[51]

One of Court de Gébelin's followers, a wigmaker named Jean-Baptiste Alliette (1738–1791), reversed his name to Etteilla, and in 1783 published a book titled *Manière de se récréer avec le jeu de cartes nommées tarots* (A Way to Entertain One-self with the Pack of Cards called Tarots).[52] In this book he claimed that the Tarot, otherwise known as *The Book of Thoth* (after the ancient Egyptian god of wisdom), had been created by seventeen Magi, 171 years after the Deluge. He further claimed that one of these Magi, Athotis, was descended from Mercury and Noah.[53] Alliette associated the Tarot with the Hermetic tradition, maintaining that it had been conceived by Hermes Trismegistus, and that the text of *The Book of Thoth* had been written on leaves of gold in a temple three leagues from Memphis.[54] Alliette also emphasized the role of the Tarot in fortunetelling, creating a deck of cards and an accompanying book titled *Manière de tirer: Le Grand Etteilla ou tarots égyptiens*, specifically for the purpose of divination.[55]

While Court de Gébelin and Alliette promoted the concept of an Egyptian origin for the Tarot, the French ceremonial magician Eliphas Lévi (Alphonse-Louis Constant, 1810–1875) maintained that the origins of the Tarot could be traced to an even earlier cultural epoch. Lévi possessed a copy of the *Grand Etteilla* Tarot deck,

FIGURE 1.2. French ceremonial magician Alphonse-Louis Constant, better known as Eliphas Lévi

FIGURE 1.3. Dr. Gerard Encausse, also known as Papus, amid his occult regalia

but believed that the Tarot cards represented a secret esoteric alphabet that had links with the ancient Jewish mystical tradition.[56] According to Lévi, the Tarot originated with Enoch, the oldest son of Cain, and provided the universal key to the Kabbalah.[57] In one of his major works, *Dogme et rituel de la haute magie* (1856), Lévi proclaimed that the twenty-two cards of the Major Arcana (the mythological cards of the Tarot) could be directly attributed to the twenty-two letters of the Hebrew alphabet and therefore linked to the Tree of Life.[58] He also believed that he had found the key to the sacred origins of the Tarot:

> When the Sovereign Priesthood ceased in Israel, when all the oracles of the world became silent in presence of the Word which became Man, and speaking by the mouth of the most popular and gentle of sages, when the Ark was lost, the sanctuary profaned, and the Temple destroyed, the mysteries of the Ephod and Theraphim, no longer recorded on gold and precious stones, were written or rather figured by certain wise kabbalists first on ivory, parchment, on gilt and silvered leather, and afterwards on simple cards, which were always objects of suspicion to the Official Church as containing a dangerous key to its mysteries. From these have originated those tarots whose antiquity was revealed to the learned Court de Gébelin through the sciences of hieroglyphics and of numbers, and which afterwards severely exercised the doubtful perspicacity and tenacious investigations of Etteilla.[59]

Lévi's concept of merging the Kabbalistic Tree of Life with the Major Arcana of the Tarot was developed by the French physician Dr. Gerard Encausse (1865–1916), who wrote under the name of Papus.

In 1889, Papus published an influential work titled *The Tarot of the Bohemians* which was illustrated with images from the Tarot of Marseilles.[60] Papus provided a text-commentary on the symbolism of each letter of the Hebrew alphabet in direct association with the Tarot cards of the Major Arcana, and his Tarot card images incorporated letters of the Hebrew alphabet next to their titles, thereby reinforcing the idea that the Tarot and the Jewish mystical tradition were symbolically interconnected.[61] The concept of mapping the Major Arcana of the Tarot as a network of symbolic pathways upon the Tree of Life was subsequently adopted by the ceremonial magicians of the Hermetic Order of the Golden Dawn and the Fraternity of the Inner Light, whose philosophy and occult practices are described in later chapters.[62] Two Golden Dawn members, Arthur Edward Waite (*Frater Sacramentum Regis*) and Pamela Colman Smith (*Soror Quod Tibi id Aliis*), created the well-known Rider-Waite Tarot deck (first published by Rider & Co., London, in 1910), which has remained one of the most popular Tarot decks up to the present day.

The key precursors of the modern magical revival, then, are the medieval Kabbalah, the Hermetic tradition, alchemy, and the Tarot. All of these elements were in turn embraced by a group of nineteenth-century Freemasons and Rosicrucians who would lay the basis for the rebirth of Western magic. Freemasonry and Rosicrucianism build on mystical themes of spiritual transformation and renewal that have become an intrinsic component of modern magical perspectives; it is to them that we now turn.

2

Freemasons and the Rose Cross

Freemasonry has been defined as "a system of morality veiled in allegory and illustrated by symbols" and as "a science which is engaged in the search after divine truth."[1] In his influential study of Freemasonry, *The Builders: A Story and Study of Masonry* (1914), Joseph Fort Newton acknowledges the widespread perception of Freemasonry as a secret society "based on the secret rites used in its initiations and the signs and grips by which its members recognize each other" but notes emphatically that "*its one great secret is that it has no secret. Its principles are published abroad in its writings; its purposes and laws are known . . . if it still adheres to secret rites it is not in order to hide the truth, but the better to teach it more impressively, to train men in its pure service, and to promote union and amity upon earth.*"[2] According to the prescripts established by the Grand Lodge of England, Freemasons are expected to believe in a Supreme Being, use a holy book appropriate to the religion of the lodge's members, and maintain a vow of secrecy concerning the order's ceremonies.[3]

Modern Freemasonry has eighteenth-century origins. The Masonic Grand Lodge of England was established in London in 1717.[4] According to Dr. James Anderson, who published an account of the historical inaugural meeting in *The New Book of Constitutions* (London 1738), members of four London Lodges met in the Apple-Tree Tavern in Covent Garden, and these lodge members constituted themselves "A Grand Lodge pro Tempore [for the time being] in *Due Form* and . . . resolv'd to hold the Annual Assembly and Feast, and then to chuse [*sic*] a Grand Master from among themselves, till they should have the Honour of a Noble Brother at their Head."[5] At a subsequent meeting, which took place on St. John Baptist's Day (24 June), 1717, at the Goose and Gridiron Ale-house in St. Paul's Church Yard, London, Mr. Anthony Sayer, Gentleman, was duly elected Grand Master of Masons.[6] All forms of modern English Freemasonry can be traced to these two meetings, which resulted in the constitution of the Grand Lodge of England. Since 1721, when the Duke of Montague was appointed to the position, the Grand Master has been a person of noble or royal birth.

The formation of the Grand Lodge of England in 1717 represented the beginning of what is known as "speculative" Freemasonry, the present-day fraternal order which does not require that its members should be working stonemasons.[7] Freemasonry as a tradition, however, derives originally from the practices of the highly skilled stonemasons and cathedral builders who worked on large-scale constructions in Italy, France, Spain, Germany, and England during the early Middle Ages.[8] As early as the fourteenth century, these so-called Operative or Working Masons formed lodges and recognized "degrees" in order to maintain their professional skills and standards. An itinerant builder was required to answer veiled questions and respond to special signs and passwords in order to establish his credentials as a Master Mason. In due course, an elaborate system of masonic rituals developed, sheathed in secrecy and maintained by oaths of fidelity and fraternity.

By 1723, there were approximately thirty lodges in England; the Grand Lodge of England developed rapidly into the central governing body overseeing these lodges, thereby bringing a sense of coherence and stability to British Masonry. By the end of the eighteenth century, there were also Masonic lodges in most European countries. However, there was no central authority overseeing the rise of European Masonry. Historian Christopher McIntosh notes that it was in France that Masonry first took hold outside of Britain: "The earliest French lodges appear to have been formed in the 1720s; in 1756, a Grand Lodge of France was founded. The progress of the craft of Masonry as a British export was facilitated by the presence on the Continent of Scottish and Irish Jacobite exiles."[9]

One of these Jacobite exiles was the Scotsman Andrew Michael Ramsay (1696–1743), an active Freemason who became chancellor of the Grand Lodge of France. Ramsay supported the idea that the Masons had been active in the Crusades and had sought to restore the Temple of the Christians in the Holy Land. According to Ramsay, they therefore developed a series of signs and symbolic words "to recognise themselves amongst the heathen and Saracens."[10] Later, Ramsay maintained, the Masons formed a union with the Knights of St. John of Jerusalem. This alleged connection with the Knights of St. John led some to speculate that the Masons were also allied to the heretical Order of Knights Templar.[11]

Ramsay's theories gave rise to what became known as Scottish Masonry, and along with orthodox Masonry, Scottish Masonry spread from France to many regions of Europe. McIntosh notes that although Masonry was originally a British creation, it was the French variant that gained the largest following on the Continent.[12] Freemasonry also developed a strong representation in Germany, giving rise in 1757 to the influential Gold-und Rosenkreuz Order, a Masonic/Rosicrucian organization that in many respects can be viewed as an earlier, Germanic counterpart of the Hermetic Order of the Golden Dawn.[13] Freemasonry also spread to the United States. The first American lodge was founded in Philadelphia in 1730 and included the prominent statesman Benjamin Franklin (1706–1790) among its members.[14]

Symbolic Aspects of Freemasonry

Despite its secret rituals, Freemasonry is not in itself a religion. As Newton has noted, Masonic membership is "open to men of all faiths, Catholic and Protestant, Hebrew and Hindu."[15] According to Newton, the spiritual roots of Freemasonry lie not in specific religious doctrines but in the mystical appreciation of architecture, the nature of architecture encompassing both physical necessity and spiritual aspiration:

> Of course, the first great impulse of all architecture was need, honest response to the demand for shelter; but this demand included a Home for the Soul, not less than a roof over the head. . . . The story of the Tower of Babel is more than a myth. Man has ever been trying to build to heaven, embodying his prayer and his dream in brick and stone. For there are two sets of realities—material and spiritual—but they are so interwoven that all practical laws are exponents of moral laws.[16]

According to Masonic mythology, whose central themes were first enunciated by Dr. James Anderson in the first edition of *The Book of Constitutions* (London 1723), the medieval stone masons derived their secret signs and passwords from the builders of the Temple of Solomon.[17] Traditionally, Masonic lodges include figures representing the steps that led to Solomon's Temple as well as symbolic motifs derived from ancient Egypt. All lodges have a vaulted ceiling, painted blue and covered with golden stars to represent the heavens. The floor is mosaic, its variegated colors representing the earth covered with flowers after the withdrawal of the waters of the Nile. In the modern Masonic lodge, two bronze pillars are located in the west, inscribed J and B (representing Jachin and Boaz and, symbolically, the summer and winter solstices), and there are ten other pillars connected to them by an architrave.[18]

Masonic initiatory ritual also focuses on the figure of Hiram Abiff, the architect who was slain during the building of the Temple of Solomon.[19]

According to Masonic tradition, when Solomon decided to build the Temple in Jerusalem, the king of Tyre sent cedar trees cut from the forests of Lebanon in exchange for corn, wine, and oil. He also offered the services of a skilled artisan—Hiram Abiff (*Abiff* : Hebrew, "father")—as superintending architect, and also to make the two bronze pillars Jachin and Boaz as well as various metal ornaments.[20] Eighty-five thousand workmen were employed in building the Temple, and the construction process took seven years. Those who labored diligently were promised the status of Master Mason on completion. Some workers, however, demanded recognition of higher status, and also higher wages, before completion. When Hiram Abiff refused their request, three of the workers killed him in the unfinished Temple and buried his body on a solitary hill, planting a sprig of acacia over the grave. King Solomon sent a search party to look for him and the body was discovered after fourteen days. The heads of the three murderers were presented to the king. As a martyr, Hiram Abiff came to embody the human values that Masons should strive to attain, especially virtue and integrity. For some Masons, Hiram is also the symbolic counterpart of Osiris, the ancient Egyptian deity associated with vegetation and fertility who was slain by Set and restored to life by Isis. In a Masonic context, Hiram similarly symbolizes death and spiritual rebirth.[21]

Despite its symbolic references to the Temple of Solomon and the mythology of ancient Egypt, Freemasonry does not limit its conception of the Divine; as mentioned earlier, it requires only a statement of religious faith from its members. Adherents are now asked only to confess their faith in "God the Father Almighty, the Architect and Master-builder of the Universe." Dr. James Anderson's *The Book of Constitutions* (London 1723) contains a statement that is read at the admission of a new Brother: "Adam, our first parent, created after the Image of God, the great Architect of the Universe, must have had the Liberal Sciences, particularly Geometry, written in his Heart; for ever since the Fall, we find the Principles of it in the Heart of his Offspring."[22]

Freemasonry appears to contain both pantheistic and transcendental elements within its overriding philosophy. According to Joseph Fort Newton:

> Out of this simple faith grows, by inevitable logic, the philosophy which Masonry teaches in signs and symbols, in pictures and parables. Stated briefly, stated vividly, it is that behind the pageant of Nature, in it and over it, there is a Supreme Mind which initiates, impels and controls all. That behind the life of man and its pathetic story in history, in it and over it, there is a righteous Will, the intelligent Conscience of the Most High. In short, that the first and last thing in the universe is mind, that

the highest and deepest thing is conscience, and that the final reality is the absoluteness of love. Higher than that faith cannot fly; deeper than that thought cannot dig.[23]

Winwood Reade in *The Veil of Isis* (1861) similarly emphasises love and tolerance as key aspects of ethical practice in Freemasonry: "Love is the key-stone which supports the entire edifice of this mystic science. Love one another, teach one another, help one another. That is all our doctrine, all our science, all our law. We have no narrow-minded prejudices; we do not debar from our society this sect or that sect; it is sufficient for us that a man worships God, no matter under what name or in what manner."[24]

The Rosicrucian Fraternity

Virtually unknown until the second decade of the seventeenth century, the Rosicrucian fraternity announced their existence in Germany with the release of four pamphlets in 1614–1616. The first of these documents was the *Fama Fraternitatis, dess Löblichen Ordens des Rosenkreutzes* (The Declaration of the Worthy Order of the Rosy Cross) issued in Kassel in 1614, together with a satirical work by the Italian writer Trajano Boccalini titled *Allgemeine und General Reformation, der gantzen weiten Welt* (The Universal and General Reformation of the Whole Wide World).[25] In 1615 an anti-Papal document entitled the *Confessio Fraternitatis* also appeared in Kassel, published in Latin. This in turn was followed by a fourth work published in Strasbourg in the German language in 1616, titled *Die Chymische Hochzeit Christiani Rosenkreutz* (The Chemical Marriage of Christian Rosencreutz [or Rosycross]). The last of these, an allegorical rather than a polemical work, is especially important in the context of contemporary magical thought because of its alchemical themes and spiritual rebirth symbolism, and its direct later influence on the Inner Order ritual grades of the Hermetic Order of the Golden Dawn.[26]

Both the *Fama* and the *Confessio* contained brief information on the life of the mythical figure Christian Rosencreutz and the formation of his Order.

The *Fama* was translated into English by the alchemist and mystic Thomas Vaughan (1622–1665) and published in 1652 under Vaughan's nom de plume, Eugenius Philalethes.[27] The *Fama* begins by declaring that God has revealed a more profound understanding of Jesus Christ and Nature because there are now men of wisdom who understand the Microcosmus. The reader is then introduced to the person who may initiate such "a general Reformation, the most godly and highly illuminated Father, our Brother C. R., a German, the chief and original of our Fraternity." The *Fama* goes on to relate that Brother C. R. has traveled extensively and received the wisdom of the East. The text also presents the view that in Germany today there are many learned magicians, Kabbalists, physicians, and philosophers who should collaborate with each other because until now they have kept "their secrets close only to themselves." The writer explains how the "faults of the Church and the whole *Philosophia Moralis* [can] be amended" and reformed through this new sacred knowledge, and goes on to explain how the Rosicrucian fraternity came into existence, initially with four members and later with a much expanded following.[28] The text also mentions that members of the Brotherhood meet annually in the House of the Holy Spirit (a building called Sancti spiritus) and that a vault has been discovered where the original Brother Rosencreutz is buried.[29]

The vault containing the body of Brother Rosencreutz had seven sides and was said to have been illuminated by an inner sun. In the vault there was also a round altar, covered with a plate of brass on which was engraved these words: *A.C.R.C. Hoc universi compendium unius mili sepulchrum feci* ("This compendium of the Universe I made in my lifetime to be my tomb"). Around the rim were inscribed the words: *Jesus mihi omnia* ("Jesus is all things to me"). There were also lamps, magical mirrors, and bells, geometrical figures on the walls, and writings by *Theoph: Par. Ho* (the Swiss alchemist Theophrastus Paracelsus of Hohenheim, 1493–1541).[30] Perhaps most significant of all, when the altar was moved aside by the brethren and the brass plate lifted, the brethren found a "fair and worthy body, whole and unconsumed. . . . In his hand he held a parchment book, called *T* . . . which next unto the Bible is our greatest treasure, which ought not lightly be delivered to the censure of the world." The *Fama* also states that at the end of the mysterious book *T* was an *Elogium* providing a spiritual profile of R. C. himself: a man, according to the text, "admitted into the Mysteries and secrets of heaven and earth" and "summoned by the Spirit of God" to "construct a microcosm corresponding in all motions to the Macrocosm." The *Elogium* ends with a statement that the uncorrupted body of R. C. has lain in the vault "hidden here by his disciples for 120 years."[31]

The discovery of the vault, said to have taken place in the year 1604, was proclaimed in the *Fama* as the symbolic beginning of a new era of spiritual reformation: "We know," announced the anonymous author of the tract, "that there will now be a general reformation, both of divine and human things, according to our desire and the expectations of others."[32] For English hermetic philosopher and physician Robert Fludd (1574–1637), who soon became a Rosicrucian apologist and sought to join the Brotherhood in 1616, the discovery of the vault of Christian Rosencreutz represented nothing less than the quest for spiritual perfection:[33]

> Some writers have dealt with this mystery in dark sayings and methinks
> the great Rosarius hath described it shrouded in sacred symbols. For here

we see a corpse, buried, wherefrom the soul hath gone and seemeth to soar heavenward. The body duly prepared for burial, or even now decaying; yet we see the soul that belongeth thereto, clothed with greater powers, descending to its body. We see a light, as if it were the Sun, yet winged and exceeding the Sun of our heaven, arising from the tomb. We see displayed with wondrous courage, a picture of the making of the perfect man.[34]

The *Fama* was published in German, but the first edition of the *Confessio* was in Latin, implying that it was aimed at a more learned audience. The *Confessio* boldly declared that the pope of Rome was the Antichrist and, like the *Fama*, it urged readers of the tract to cooperate with the Order in bringing about a new spiritual orientation, equivalent to the state of Adam in Paradise. It claimed that God would allow light and truth to flood the land and that the pope would be overthrown. New stars had appeared in the constellations of Serpentarius and Cygnus as omens of what was to come.[35]

Many who read the Rosicrucian pamphlets sought to contact the Fraternity without success: "The Brothers, if they existed seemed invisible and impervious to entreaties to make themselves known."[36] This lack of public response intensified interest in the Rosicrucian mystery, especially since the pamphlets were anonymous and the identity of the Brothers unknown.[37]

Christopher McIntosh, author of a recent history of the Rosicrucians, believes that the author of *Die Chymische Hochzeit Christiani Rosenkreutz* was "almost certainly" the Tübingen-based Protestant theologian Johann Valentin Andreae (1586–1654), and that Andreae may possibly have authored, or co-authored, the *Fama* as well. The author of the *Confessio* remains unknown.[38] Renaissance scholar Frances A. Yates believes that the *Monas Hieroglyphica*, published in 1564 by the Elizabethan philosopher Dr. John Dee (1527–1608), exerted a significant influence on the Rosicrucian writers. According to Yates, Dee's text, a fusion of Kabbalah, alchemy, and mathematics, represented the "secret philosophy" behind the antipapal movement.[39]

Of all the Rosicrucian documents, however, *Die Chymische Hochzeit Christiani Rosenkreutz* is the most intriguing, because of its highly symbolic and allegorical content. The narrator, who is portrayed as Christian Rosencreutz himself, describes his experiences as a guest at the wedding of a king and queen who live in a mysterious palace.[40] During the wedding, the guests undergo various ordeals: many are killed, and some are brought back to life in what would appear to be an alchemical operation.[41] The earliest English translation of *The Chemical Marriage*, by Ezechiel Foxcroft, was published in 1690, seventy-five years after its first appearance in Germany.[42]

FIGURE 2.1.   Johann Valentin Andreae

The Chemical Marriage of Christian Rosencreutz is an allegorical narrative spanning seven richly symbolic days.[43] Just prior to Easter, Christian Rosencreutz is
summoned by a female angelic being to attend a royal wedding. The summons
includes the symbol of a cross with a solar disc and lunar crescent.[44] The next day,
Christian Rosencreutz wakes early and prepares for his journey. He is wearing four
red roses in his hat and carrying with him bread, salt, and water. When he finally
departs on his journey and ventures through a forest he discovers that four different

FIGURE 2.2.   Dr. John Dee

roads lead to the palace of the king. Only one of these is the Royal Road, but which-
ever he chooses is a road he must persist with, because to turn back will result in
his death. Initially Christian Rosencreutz cannot decide which road to take, but
after offering bread to a snow-white dove who is being tormented by a black raven,
he finds himself before a large gate inscribed with various "noble figures" and devices. Christian Rosencreutz is asked to give his name and replies that he is a
"Brother of the *Red-Rosie Cross.*"[45] In exchange for water, he is given a gold token
and now comes to a second gate, which is similarly inscribed with mystical symbols
and is guarded by a lion. He is allowed through after giving the gift of salt.[46] Christian Rosencreutz ventures through a third gate and is just in time for the wedding
feast. In the wedding hall, he discovers a "great multitude of guests," including
emperors, kings, princes, and lords, and also poor and "ignoble" people. After the
feast, the guests are told that the following day they will be weighed in the Scales of
Judgment.

Most of the guests fail this test and are given a potion that dissolves their
memory of the event. They are then turned away from the palace. However,
Christian Rosencreutz and a few others continue. Each member of this group is
presented with a Golden Fleece and Medal of Gold surmounted with the Sun
and Moon, before being summoned to a banquet and shown various mysteries
of the palace, including a Great Phoenix.[47] The next day, the candidates attend
the banquet, but after they have removed their white garments and replaced

them with black ones, a black man appears, beheads the king and queen and places them in coffins.

Christian Rosencreutz and his colleagues now journey with a guide called the Virgin to a seven-storied Tower of the Gods, where they prepare material for the Great Work, the supreme achievement of the alchemists.[48] Employing the blood of the phoenix, they bring the king and queen back to life and in turn are proclaimed by the Virgin to be Knights of the Golden Stone. In the sumptuous processions that follow, Christian Rosencreutz rides with the king, "each of us bearing a snow-white ensign with a Red Cross."[49] A page from the royal court then reads aloud a series of articles binding the Knights of the Golden Stone to a code of ethical and spiritual behavior:

1. You my Lords the Knights, shall swear that you shall at no time ascribe your order either unto any Devil or Spirit, but only to God your Creator, and his hand-maid Nature.
2. That you will Abominate all Whoredom, Incontinency, and Uncleanness and not defile your order with such Vices.
3. That you through your Talents will be ready to assist all that are worthy, and have need of them.
4. That you desire not to employ this honor to worldly Pride and high Authority.
5. That you shall not be willing to live longer than God will have you.[50]

As Frances Yates observes, there is a clear connection here between the Brothers of the Rosy Cross and the medieval Knights of the Golden Stone with their code of chivalry, for both are engaged in a spiritual quest:

In the manifestos, Christian Rosencreutz was associated with an order of benevolent brethren; in the wedding, he is associated with an order of chivalry. The R. C. Brothers were spiritual alchemists; so are the Knights of the Golden Stone. The activities of the R. C. Brothers were symbolized through the treasures in their vault; similar activities are symbolized through the treasures in the castle. In fact, the theme of the vault containing a tomb actually occurs in the *Wedding* [i.e., the text of *The Chemical Marriage*, which is also often referred to as *The Chemical* (or *Chymical*) *Wedding*], surely an allusion to the famous vault in the *Fama*. . . . Though *Fama* and *Confessio* may not be written by the same hand as the *Wedding*, the plan of the allegories in all three works bears the stamp of minds working in concert, bent on sending out into the world their myth of Christian Rosencreutz, a benevolent figure, center of brotherhoods and orders.[51]

Yates also writes that *The Chemical Marriage* is "an alchemical fantasia, using the fundamental image of elemental fusion, the marriage, the uniting of the *sponsus* and the *sponsa*, touching also on the theme of death, the *nigredo* through which the elements must pass in the process of transmutation." She notes that "the allegory is of course also a spiritual one, typifying processes of regeneration and change within the soul."[52]

Historian Christopher McIntosh believes that the Rosicrucianism of "the Andreae era," that is to say, the first half of the seventeenth century, was only partly concerned with alchemy, but that later developments within the Rosicrucian movement placed greater emphasis on the alchemical secrets of transmutation and knowledge of the Philosopher's Stone or the Elixir of Life.[53] Michael Maier (1568–1622), a Lutheran physician with a strong interest in the Hermetica, was one of the first writers to emphasize the alchemical aspects of Rosicrucianism through such publications as *Symbola Aureae Mensae* (1617) and *Themis Aurea* (1618).[54] Maier also defended the authenticity of the Rosicrucian brotherhood, even though he claimed at the time that he was not a member.[55] Dr. Lyndy Abraham describes the Philosopher's Stone in her *Dictionary of Alchemical Imagery* (1998) as "the most famous of all alchemical ideas. The Stone is the arcanum of all arcana, possessing the power to perfect imperfection in all things, able to transmute base metals into pure gold and transform earthly man into an illumined philosopher." The Philosopher's Stone also had a Christian dimension that Maier would have found especially relevant. Abraham writes: "It [i.e., the Stone] is the figure of light veiled in dark matter, that divine love essence which combines divine wisdom and creative power, often identified with Christ as creative Logos."[56]

Several eighteenth-century Rosicrucian publications similarly reflect an understanding of both inner and outer alchemy. One such work is *Geheime Figuren der Rosenkreuzer* (*The Secret Symbols of the Rosicrucians*), published in Altona in 1785 and included in a collection of facsimile documents titled *A Christian Rosenkreutz Anthology* (1968).[57]

One of the illustrations in this work is a complex Hermetic composition that provides a visual interpretation of the famous *Tabula Smaragdina* or "Emerald Tablet" of Hermes Trismegistus.[58] This illustration depicts a circular medallion on which are three shields chained together and bearing an eagle, a star, and a lion: there are also two globes representing the Earth and the heavens, an orb, two arms emerging from clouds at the side of the medallion, and symbols of the seven planets, with the Sun and Moon pouring two streams of liquid into a cup. An accompanying prose poem explains that the eagle, the lion, and the star represent, respectively, salt, sulphur, and mercury, as well as body, soul, and spirit.[59]

FIGURE 2.3.   A Rosicrucian medallion depicting Hermetic and alchemical motifs

A Fusion of Masonry, Rosicrucianism, and Alchemy

As mentioned earlier, the Masonic Gold-und Rosenkreuz Order was established in Germany in 1757, following the introduction of British Masonry to Europe. This particular esoteric Order is of historical interest as a precursor of the Hermetic Order of the Golden Dawn, but is also significant because its members were interested both in alchemy and the Rosicrucian mythology of spiritual renewal. The Gold-und Rosenkreuz Order had centers in Vienna, Frankfurt-am-Main, Marburg, Kassel, Regensburg, and Prague, as well as in Sulzbach in the Upper Palatinate. Duke Christian August (1622–1702), one of the rulers of the Upper Palatinate, was deeply interested in the mystical traditions and encouraged the presence of like-minded thinkers.[60] Scholars who gathered at his court included the Kabbalist Knorr von Rosenroth (1636–1689), whose *Kabbala Denudata* would subsequently be translated from Latin into English by Golden Dawn magician S. L. MacGregor

Mathers, and Francis Mercurius van Helmont (1618–1699), who was a Kabbalist and alchemist as well as a skilled chemist and physician.[61] According to Christopher McIntosh, alchemy was also practiced at the Sulzbach court.[62]

In addition to its branches in Vienna, Prague, and Germany, the Gold-und Rosenkreuz Order also had a circle in Warsaw, founded in the 1770s by Count Karl Adolf von Brühl, as well as a branch in Moscow; the Russian membership included the writer and publisher I. V. Lopuchin, who published Russian-language editions of mystical authors such as Jakob Boehme and Louis-Claude de Saint-Martin.[63]

With regard to the late nineteenth-/early twentieth-century magical revival, however, a crucial aspect of the Gold-und Rosenkreuz Order was its ritual grade structure which, with some variations, would be mirrored in the ritual grades of the Hermetic Order of the Golden Dawn over a century later.[64] The ritual grades of the Gold-und Rosenkreuz Order are described in an Order document dating from 1767 that is included in a pamphlet written by I. A. Fessler titled *Rosenkreuzery* (1805–1806). Fessler's pamphlet was published privately by Friedrich Ludwig Schröder, a prominent German Freemason. There were nine grades in the Gold-und Rosenkreuz Order—Junior, Theoreticus, Practicus, Philosophus, Minor, Major, Adeptus Exemptus, Magister, and Majus—and these grades form a nearly exact parallel with the ritual grades of the Hermetic Order of the Golden Dawn: Neophyte, Zelator, Theoricus, Practicus, Philosophus, Adeptus Minor, Adeptus Major, Adeptus Exemptus, Magister Templi, Magus, and Ipsissimus.[65]

A key explanatory point that throws light on this surprising parallel is that descriptions of the grades of the Gold-und Rosenkreuz Order were apparently copied by the English Freemason Kenneth Mackenzie (1833–1886) and included in his influential *Royal Masonic Cyclopaedia* (1877).[66] Mackenzie is, in his own right, a pivotal figure connecting the nineteenth-century esoteric traditions of Britain and Europe. Mackenzie had a celebrated meeting with the famous French Kabbalist Eliphas Lévi in Paris in December 1861, during which a broad range of esoteric subjects were discussed in depth (including the Tarot, Kabbalah, Theosophy, and the prophecies of Paracelsus).[67] He also claimed that he had been initiated into the Austrian Rosicrucian brotherhood by Count Apponyi, for whom he worked as an English-language tutor.[68] More specifically, Mackenzie helped co-founder Robert Wentworth Little develop the ritual grades employed in the Societas Rosicruciana in Anglia (SRIA).[69] The SRIA was itself a key precursor of the Hermetic Order of the Golden Dawn, established in February 1888, and it is significant that the three founding members of the Golden Dawn, S. L. MacGregor Mathers, Dr. Wynn Westcott, and Dr. W. R. Woodman, were all SRIA members.[70] This may well explain the clear parallels between the ritual grades of the Gold-und Rosenkreuz Order and those utilized by Westcott and Mathers in the Hermetic Order of the Golden Dawn.

Interestingly, the mythic theme of "coming forth into the light," referred to in chapter 3 as a key ritual aim of the "high magic" practiced in the Golden Dawn, was also a ceremonial function of the Gold-und Rosenkreuz Order. In his book *Starke Erweise*, the eighteenth-century writer J. J. Bode drew on details contained in a Gold-und Rosenkreuz manual titled *Eingang zur ersten Classe des preisswürdigsten Ordens vom Goldenen Rosen Creutze nach der letzten Haupt- und Reformations-Convention* (1788), noting that the "ultimate purpose" of the Order was "to make effective the hidden forces of nature, to release nature's light which has become deeply buried beneath the dross resulting from the curse, and thereby to light within every brother a torch by whose light he will be able better to recognize the hidden God . . . and thereby become more closely united with the original source of light."[71] Both the Golden Dawn members and those of the Gold-und Rosenkreuz were, in their own way, seeking the light, "as if it were the Sun, yet winged and exceeding the Sun of our heaven," in order to make the perfect man.

The Nineteenth-Century French Magical Revival

In addition to the teachings and ritual activities of the Gold-und Rosenkreuz Order, esoteric practices in fin-de-siècle Europe were also influenced by modern Kabbalists such as Eliphas Lévi (Alphonse-Louis Constant, 1810–1875), Stanislas de Guaita (1861–1897), and Joséphin Péladan (1858–1918), all of whom are major figures in the nineteenth-century French magical revival.[72] The Golden Dawn's Official History Lecture, thought to have been written about 1892 by the Order's co-founder, Dr. Wynn Westcott, described Lévi as "the greatest of modern Magi'" and identified him as "prominent among the Adepts of our Order."[73] The author of the History Lecture was not, however, referring to Lévi as an "inner-plane" inspirational Adept or Secret Chief, but acknowledging him as a major guiding influence on the membership of the Golden Dawn; in the same document the author also refers to the contribution of Robert Wentworth Little, co-founder of the Societas Rosicruciana in Anglia, describing him as a "student of the Mysteries," an "eminent Freemason" and, most specifically, "a student in the school of Lévi."[74]

Lévi's influence on the Golden Dawn derived primarily from his principal writings on the Kabbalah and magic: *Dogme et rituel de la haute magie* (1856),[75] *Histoire de la magie* (1860),[76] and *La Clé des grandes mystères* (1861),[77] all of which were translated from French into English by one-time members of the Golden Dawn. A. E. Waite translated the first two works, *Transcendental Magic, Its Doctrine and Ritual* (1896) and *The History of Magic* (1913),[78] and Aleister Crowley translated *The Key of the Mysteries*.[79] Crowley's enthusiasm for Lévi as a ceremonial magician was so pronounced that the controversial British occultist claimed to be a reincarnation of the French sage.[80]

It was Eliphas Lévi who had first proposed the symbolic connection between the Major Arcana of the Tarot and the letters of the Hebrew alphabet. As already mentioned, S. L. MacGregor Mathers, co-founder of the Golden Dawn, accepted Lévi's proposal that because the paths linking the ten *sephiroth* on the Kabbalistic Tree of Life were associated with specific Hebrew letters, the Major Arcana linked to these Hebrew letters could be used to gain meditative access to paths on the Tree.[81]

Mathers's Golden Dawn colleague, A. E. Waite (*Frater Sacramentum Regis*) also praised Lévi for emphasising the importance of the "magical will."' In the *Biographical and Critical Essay* that Waite prepared as an introduction to his digest of Lévi's major writings, *The Mysteries of Magic* (1886), Waite assesses Lévi's contribution to esoteric thought in the following terms: "the true greatness of Eliphas Lévi consists in his revelation for the first time to the modern world of the great Arcanum of will-power, which comprises in one word the whole history and mystery of magical art. Doctrine and theory are nothing—all magic is in the will, that secret of universal power in heaven and on earth."[82] Waite then goes on to consider Lévi's contribution to alchemical and Hermetic thought in recognizing that "the transmutation of the philosophical metals is not . . . a chemical process; rather, it is a process of transcendental and mystical chemistry by the application of the purified and emancipated will to the psycho-chemical instrument of a diaphanous imagination." Waite also extends due credit to Lévi for originating what he describes as "a new departure in Kabbalistic exegesis." According to Waite, Lévi's intrepretations "have infused new life into old symbolism, and his doctrine of the transfiguration of dogmas—whatever may be its ultimate value—casts much light on comparative theology."[83] Waite's introductory essay ends in a paean of generous acclaim: "The noble and generous spirit of Eliphas Lévi has passed behind the veil, and has doubtless achieved the immortality he aspired to, and the Absolute which he sought in life. May the benediction of Azoth be upon him, and the Crown of Life reward him."[84]

With the death of Eliphas Lévi in 1875, the mantle of esoteric leadership passed to the Marquis Stanislas de Guaita (1861–1897) and Joséphin Péladan (1858–1918), who together in 1888 founded L'Ordre Kabbalistique de la Rose Croix, the Kabbalistic Order of the Rosy Cross. This Order, established in Paris, essentially involved gatherings of like-minded friends.[85] Just two years later, in 1890, de Guaita claimed that the Order had over a hundred adherents, but this figure appears greatly exaggerated.[86] Both de Guaita and Péladan were interested in Kabbalah and high magic, and their Order attracted members such as astrologer and alchemy enthusiast Alfred Faucheux, the writer Paul Adam, Abbé Melinge, and Dr. Gérard Encausse

FIGURE 2.4A AND B.   A. E. Waite (*Frater Sacramentum Regis*), an enthusiastic supporter of Eliphas Lévi, photographed in 1892, a few years before he joined the Golden Dawn (a), and in 1920 (b).

FIGURE 2.5. Marquis Stanislas de Guaita

(better known as Papus, author of *The Tarot of the Bohemians*, referred to earlier).[87] De Guaita and Péladan's L'Ordre Kabbalistique de la Rose Croix had three grades of initiation.[88] Its members were primarily engaged in studying the classics of occultism and "entering into spiritual communion with the Divine through meditation." De Guaita and Péladan later had an intense disagreement over Péladan's strong commitment to Roman Catholicism, and in 1890 Péladan founded his own L'Ordre de la Rose Croix Catholique, du Temple et du Graal, which he hoped would "bring

FIGURE 2.6. Joséphin Péladan

occultism back under the wing of the Church."[89] Péladan's order had three grades—
equerries, knights, and commanders, the commanders being assigned to different
sephiroth on the Kabbalistic Tree of Life. De Guaita and Péladan became increasingly hostile toward each other, and after unsuccessful attempts to resolve their differences, de Guaita finally denounced Péladan, declaring him "a schismatic and
apostate Rosicrucian."[90]

Péladan's practice of assigning ritual grades to the Kabbalistic Tree of Life parallels the approach adopted around the same time in England in the Hermetic Order of the Golden Dawn, but the magical activities pursued in the Golden Dawn were more far-ranging and their impact in esoteric circles much greater than those of its French counterpart. Unlike L'Ordre de la Rose Croix Catholique, whose esoteric influence was largely confined to France, the Hermetic Order of the Golden Dawn, which is described in the following chapter, established the basis for the twentieth-century magical revival—which would in turn become an international phenomenon, extending from Britain to the United States and subsequently to many other countries around the world.

3

New Light

The Rise of the Golden Dawn

Now widely acknowledged as the key source of the modern magical revival, the Hermetic Order of the Golden Dawn was formally established in London on 12 February 1888, when its three founding figures, Samuel Liddell MacGregor Mathers (1854–1918), Dr. William Wynn Westcott (1848–1925), and Dr. William Robert Woodman (1828–1891), signed a document headed "Order of the G.D." All three were members of the Societas Rosicruciana in Anglia (SRIA) and it was through this esoteric Masonic organisation that they had met each other.[1] The first official document defined the purpose of the Golden Dawn as a secret society dedicated to the pursuit of "occult science." The text began as follows:

> For the purpose of the study of Occult Science, and the further investigation of the Mysteries of Life and Death, and our Environment, permission has been granted by the Secret Chiefs of the R.C. to certain Fratres learned in the Occult Sciences, (and who are also members of the Soc. Ros. in Ang.) to work the Esoteric Order of the G.D. in the Outer; to hold meetings thereof for Study and to initiate any approved person *Male* or *Female*, who will enter into an Undertaking to maintain strict secrecy regarding all that concerns it. Belief in One God necessary. No other restrictions.[2]

Several points in this document will be discussed in more detail later in this chapter. The first is the reference to "Secret Chiefs": from the very establishment of the Order it was claimed that these mysterious personages provided the spiritual authority for the Golden Dawn, and this would prove to be a point of contention in later years. The second is that the founders of the Golden Dawn had decided to admit both male and female members, thus differentiating the new organization from mainstream Freemasonry; this is significant because, in addition to being members of the Societas Rosicruciana in Anglia, Mathers, Westcott, and Woodman were all Freemasons, and traditionally Freemasonry admitted only male members.[3] The third is that the new magical order required its members to believe in "One God." The inference here was that the Golden Dawn would be grounded philosophically in a monotheistic spiritual tradition. This was further clarified in the text of the new Golden Dawn "pledge form," which specified that the preferred religion should be Christianity: "Belief in a Supreme Being, or Beings, is indispensable. In addition, the Candidate, if not a Christian, should be at least prepared to take an interest in Christianity."[4]

The latter document also clarified the earlier statement that the Golden Dawn was dedicated to the "investigation of the Mysteries of Life and Death" by confirming that it was not prepared to admit candidates to the Order who were Mesmerists or Spiritualists, "or who habitually allow[ed] themselves to fall into a completely passive condition of Will."[5] This, too, is a crucial point. Central to the development of the Golden Dawn as a magical organization would be the development of the "magical will," sometimes capitalized as Will to connote a higher spiritual purpose. As noted earlier, development of the magical will is itself a defining characteristic of the Western magical tradition.

The Cipher Manuscript and Fraulein Sprengel

Even if the signing of the Golden Dawn charter in February 1888 can be said to have defined its formal status and identified its founders, it was not in itself the event that had brought the magical organization into being. A year earlier, Westcott had acquired a manuscript in cipher form that contained five Masonic rituals. How this manuscript was originally discovered remains a matter of conjecture. According to one account, the Masonic papers were obtained by another member of the SRIA, a clergyman named Alphonsus F. A. Woodward, who had in turn found them in a London bookshop in 1884.[6] Another explanation was that the manuscript had been discovered by Woodward in the papers of a deceased SRIA member, Frederick Hockley, while a third explanation was that the papers were ritual grades from a German Rosicrucian society, the Gold and Rosy Cross, into which SRIA member Kenneth Mackenzie, a friend of Hockley's, had been initiated.[7] Westcott further complicated the situation by claiming that he had found among the leaves of the

FIGURE 3.1A, B, AND C. Dr. William Wynn Westcott (a) with pages from the cipher document (b and c)

cipher manuscript the name and address of a certain Fraulein Anna Sprengel, a resident of Stuttgart, said to be an eminent Rosicrucian adept (*Soror Sapiens Dominabitur Astris*) and a leading member of an organization known as Die Goldene Dammerung.[8] On her authority, and following a lengthy correspondence, Westcott announced in Masonic and Theosophical circles that he had been instructed to found an English branch of her German occult group, calling it the Hermetic Order of the Golden Dawn.

Recent research into the history of the Order suggests that the correspondence with Fraulein Sprengel was fictitious, although it appears that she was a real person with genuine esoteric connections.[9] It seems likely that Westcott concocted the correspondence in an effort to compete with the esoteric school that Madame Helena Blavatsky had established within the Theosophical Society four years after bringing her organization to London in 1884.[10] Blavatsky claimed to be inspired by Mahatmas, or spiritual Masters, living in Tibet, with whom she had psychic rapport, and this had widespread appeal to devotees seeking some sense of mystical authority. While Westcott was not at this stage claiming such exalted metaphysical inspiration for his new Hermetic Order, he was nevertheless appealing, through the persona of Fraulein Sprengel, to a sense of authentic occult lineage. It is conceivable that he proposed the notion of Secret Chiefs to rival Madame Blavatsky's Mahatmas.

Establishment of the Golden Dawn Temples

Westcott invited his colleague from the SRIA, Samuel Liddell Mathers, to expand the cipher material so that it could form the basis of a "complete scheme of initiation," and this proposal had a positive outcome.[11] Mathers developed the five Masonic grades into a workable system suitable for the practice of ceremonial magic, and as a result the Isis-Urania Temple of the Golden Dawn was established in London on 1 March 1888, with Mathers, Westcott, and Woodman as leaders of the Order.[12] In a relatively short time it would be followed by other branches: the Osiris Temple in Weston-super-Mare, the Horus Temple in Bradford, the Amen-Ra Temple in Edinburgh, and the Ahathoor Temple in Paris.[13]

In due course, the Hermetic Order of the Golden Dawn would attract a distinguished membership, including such figures as Arthur Edward Waite, an authority on the Kabbalah, Rosicrucianism, and the Holy Grail legends; the distinguished poet William Butler Yeats, who would later win the Nobel prize; well-known physician and pioneer of tropical medicine, Dr. R. W. Felkin; the noted homeopath Dr. Edward Berridge; the Scottish Astronomer Royal, William

FIGURE 3.2.   Samuel Liddell MacGregor Mathers, co-founder of the Golden Dawn

Peck; lawyer John W. Brodie-Innes; the well-known fantasy novelists Arthur
Machen and Algernon Blackwood; and the controversial ritual magician and adventurer Aleister Crowley. The Order also included within its membership several notable women, among them Annie Horniman, later a leading patron of
Irish theater; artist Moina Bergson, sister of the influential French philosopher
Henri Bergson and future wife of Samuel Mathers; Celtic revivalist Maud Gonne;
actress Florence Farr; and in later years Violet Firth, better known as the magical
novelist Dion Fortune.[14]

FIGURE 3.3A, B, AND C.   Women of the Golden Dawn: Maud Gonne (a), Florence Farr
(b), and Moina Bergson (c). Bergson married MacGregor Mathers in 1890.

Ritual Degrees and the Tree of Life

As Freemasons, Westcott and Mathers were strongly attracted to the concept of
ritual degrees, and the grades of the Hermetic Order of the Golden Dawn were
formulated in a manner that would align them symbolically with the *sephiroth*, or
levels of mystical consciousness upon the Kabbalistic Tree of Life. Four of the five
ritual grades had Latin names: Zelator (corresponding to the *sephirah* Malkuth on
the Tree of Life), Theoricus (corresponding to Yesod), Practicus (corresponding to
Hod), and Philosophus (corresponding to Netzach).[15] There was also a "Neophyte"
grade which, in a symbolic sense, was located below the Kabbalistic Tree of Life
because at this stage the candidate who had just entered the Golden Dawn had not
yet embarked on the magical exploration of the higher spheres on the Tree. Occult
historian Francis King notes that immediately after admission to the grade, the
Neophyte was given the first Knowledge Lecture, a document that contained various Hermetic teachings together with instructions on the meditations the candidate was to perform as part of his psycho-spiritual training. The Neophyte was also
given the rubric of the "Qabalistic Cross and the Lesser Ritual of the Pentagram,"
so that he or she might copy, learn, and practice it, "thus arriving at some . . . com-
prehension of the way to come into contact with spiritual forces."[16]

When Westcott, Mathers, and Woodman established the Isis-Urania Temple
in London in 1888, they conferred upon themselves a Second Order ritual grade,
which implied that they were the Secret Chiefs incarnate: the grade 7°=4° corresponded to the *sephirah* Chesed, the fourth emanation on the Tree of Life and the
sphere symbolically associated with the Ruler of the Universe (represented cosmo-
logically by Jehovah/Yahweh in Judaism, Zeus in ancient Greece, and Jupiter in
ancient Rome).[17] As the leaders of the Isis-Urania Temple, Westcott, Mathers, and
Woodman interacted with incoming members by using secret magical names, for
as a matter of principle Golden Dawn members could only be allowed to know the
magical names of their peers and those with lower grades beneath them. Mathers
was known as *Deo Duce Comite Ferro* and later *'S Rioghail Mo Dhream*, Westcott
was *Non Omnis Moriar* and *Sapere Aude*, and Woodman *Magna est Veritas et Prae-
valebit* and *Vincit Omnia Veritas*.[18]

Three years later, after the birth of the Isis-Urania Temple, however, the "correspondence" between Westcott and Fraulein Anna Sprengel ceased suddenly, following a suggestion from Germany that "no further information would be given to
the English students [and that] if they wished to establish a link with the Secret
Chiefs of the Order they must do it themselves."[19] Westcott was clearly interested
in establishing a series of Second Order ritual workings within the Golden Dawn.[20]
However, such a process would have required spiritual "guidance" from the Secret

FIGURE 3.4. The symbol of the Rosae Rubeae et Aureae Crucis (the Red Rose and the Cross of Gold)

Chiefs, and according to Francis King it was Mathers who claimed to have established the crucial link with the Secret Chiefs in 1892 by supplying actual rituals for the Second Order (or Inner Order) of the Golden Dawn, otherwise known as the Rosae Rubeae et Aureae Crucis (the Red Rose and the Cross of Gold), based on the legend of Christian Rosencreutz.[21] Interestingly, Mathers's biographer, Ithell Colquhoun, maintains that the ritual content of the Inner Order was formulated not by Mathers alone but in partnership with his wife Moina, who was one of the first Golden Dawn initiates.[22] According to Colquhoun, it was Moina's "arduous sessions of clairvoyance [that] . . . brought through material from the inner planes which [helped] form the basis of the Second Order a few years later."[23]

The three grades of the Second Order were Adeptus Minor (corresponding to Tiphareth on the Tree of Life), Adeptus Major (corresponding to Geburah), and Adeptus Exemptus (corresponding to Chesed).[24] By passing through the 5°=6° ritual grade of Adeptus Minor, the ceremonial magician entered what Mathers called the Vault of the Adepts.[25] The candidate was bound symbolically on the "Cross of Suffering" while also witnessing "the resurrection of the Chief Adept, who represented Christian Rosencreutz, from a tomb within an elaborately painted, seven-sided vault."[26]

The Spiritual Realm of the Secret Chiefs

As mentioned in my summary description of the medieval Kabbalah, the fourth emanation on the Kabbalistic Tree (Chesed) lies just below the supernal triad of Kether, Chokmah, and Binah. Between the supernal triad and the seven lower *sephiroth* upon the Tree is a symbolic divide associated with a transitional *sephirah* known as Daath (knowledge), which is often referred to by magical practitioners as the Abyss.[27] The Abyss symbolically distinguishes the transcendent nature of the Godhead (above) from the domain of Creation (below). In the Jewish mystical tradition, symbolic forms are rarely ascribed to levels of mystical reality above the Abyss because, essentially, they lie beyond the realm of Creation. Despite the transcendental nature of the supernal triad on the Kabbalistic Tree of Life, Mathers and his wife conceived of a mystical Third Order that corresponded to the exalted levels of spiritual awareness above the Abyss. They proposed the ritual grades of Magister Templi (corresponding to Binah), Magus (corresponding to Chokmah), and Ipsissimus (corresponding to Kether), and declared that the sacred domain of the Third Order was also the spiritual home of the Secret Chiefs referred to in the founding charter of the Golden Dawn. Mathers spoke of "the Great White Lodge of the Adepti," but was less than forthcoming when it came to describing how contact with the Secret Chiefs could actually be achieved.[28] Nevertheless, he did take the credit for establishing the inspirational connection that sustained the Golden Dawn:

Prior to the establishment of the Vaults of the Adepts in Britannia (the First of the Golden Dawn in the Outer being therein actively working) . . .

it was found absolutely and imperatively necessary that there should be
some eminent Member especially chosen to act as the link between the
Secret Chiefs and the more external forms of the Order. It was requisite
that such Member should be me, who, while having the necessary and
peculiar educational basis of critical and profound occult archaeological
knowledge should at the same time not only be ready and willing to
devote himself in every sense to a blind and unreasoning obedience to
those Secret Chiefs—to pledge himself to the fidelity of those to whom
this Wisdom was to be communicated: to be one who would shrink
neither from danger physical, astral or spiritual, from privation or
hardship, nor from terrible personal and psychic responsibility. . . . He
must further pledge himself to obey in everything the commands of the
aforesaid Secret Chiefs "perinde ac cadaver," body and soul, without
question and without argument whether their commands related to:
Magical Action in the External World; or to Psychic Action in Other
Worlds, or Planes, whether Angelic, Spiritual or Demonic, or to the
Inner Administration of the Order to which so tremendous a knowledge
was to be communicated.[29]

However, Mathers was unable to supply his followers with any detailed information about the actual identity of the mysterious Secret Chiefs who represented the
source of his magical authority: "I do not even know their earthly names. I know
them only by certain secret mottoes. I have *but very rarely* seen them in the physical
body; and on such rare occasions *the rendezvous was made astrally by them* at the
time and place which had been astrally appointed beforehand. For my part I believe
them to be human and living upon this earth but possessing terrible superhuman
powers."[30]

By claiming exclusive access to the Secret Chiefs, Mathers was acting in a way
that would have a substantial impact on the future development of the Golden
Dawn: he was effectively claiming privileged access to a unique source of sacred
power. And Mathers would soon be able to exert his total authority over the Golden
Dawn in a more literal and specific way. Woodman had died in 1891, and Westcott
had already begun to redirect his attention away from the Golden Dawn toward the
Societas Rosicruciana in Anglia, which became his administrative responsibility
from 1892 onward.[31] Westcott finally resigned from the Golden Dawn in 1897
because rumors relating to his involvement in the Golden Dawn were affecting his
professional career as Crown Coroner.[32] The death of Woodman and the resigna-
tion of Westcott left Mathers effectively in control of both the Inner and Outer
Orders of the Golden Dawn, even though he and his wife were now based in Paris,
having moved there in 1894.

Mathers's Autocratic Leadership and Its Consequences

At the time of his assumption of total control of the Golden Dawn, Mathers was engaged in literary research at the Bibliothèque de l'Arsenal, where there was a large occult archive, and much of his time was taken up translating the French manuscript of a lengthy and important fifteenth-century grimoire (textbook of magic) titled *The Sacred Magic of Abramelin the Mage*.[33] Mathers had also begun to cultivate certain social pretensions and was now referring to himself as MacGregor Mathers, MacGregor of Glenstrae, and Count of Glenstrae to feign some sense of rank and importance.[34] Supported financially by wealthy Golden Dawn member Annie Horniman (*Soror Fortiter et Recte*), a tea heiress and key senior member of the London Isis-Urania Temple, Mathers was presiding over the Ahathoor Temple in Paris while simultaneously attempting to maintain dominance over the various Golden Dawn branches across the Channel.[35] When Annie Horniman queried various aspects of the funding of Mathers's stay in Paris, however, Mathers responded to her in an authoritarian manner by reaffirming that his unique and privileged relationship with the Secret Chiefs had to be maintained.[36] Annie Horniman eventually withdrew her financial assistance, and Mathers had to turn to other means of means of support while endeavoring to consolidate his position of authority.[37] Ruling in absentia from Paris proved to be a difficult task, however. As early as 29 October 1896, Mathers had sought to quell a potential uprising among senior Golden Dawn members of the Isis-Urania Temple in London by insisting that they should "send [him] a written statement of voluntary submission in all points regarding the Orders of the G . . . D . . . in the Outer and the R . . . R . . . et A . . . C . . . [at the same time undertaking to] refrain from stirring up any strife or schism hereon in the First and Second Orders."[38] Five weeks later, on 3 December 1896, just a few months after Annie Horniman had cut off his Paris allowance, Mathers wrote her a vitriolic letter, accusing her of insubordination. Part of Mathers's text read as follows: "In my letter to you . . . I insisted upon your complete and absolute submission to my authority as regards the *management as well as the teaching* of both the First and Second orders . . . I do not care one atom what you *think* but I refuse absolutely to permit open criticism of, or any argument concerning my action in either order from you or any other member" (emphasis in the original text).[39] Mathers concluded the letter by advising Annie Horniman that she would forthwith be expelled from the Order.

Mathers's autocratic style and the expulsion of Annie Horniman from the Golden Dawn caused considerable disquiet among Order members, and he caused even more consternation the following year when, in a letter to senior Order member Mrs. Florence Farr Emery (*Soror Sapientia Sapienti Dono Data*) dated 16 February

FIGURE 3.5A AND B. MacGregor Mathers (a) and his wife Moina (b), in ritual attire. The portrait of Mathers was painted by Moina.

1897, he charged her with "attempting to make a schism" in the Golden Dawn and accused Wynn Westcott, the acting head of the Golden Dawn in London, of forging his correspondence with Fraulein Anna Sprengel. In the same letter, Mathers denied that Westcott had ever been in contact with the Secret Chiefs and added, *"every atom* of the knowledge of the Order has come *through me alone* from 0°=0° [i.e., the Neophyte grade] to 5°=6° [i.e., Tiphareth, Second Order grade] inclusive."[40] On 23 March 1897, Mathers wrote a further letter to Mrs. Emery expelling her from the Order, as well.[41] The expulsion of Annie Horniman and Mrs. Emery from the Golden Dawn would lead to three years of internal bickering and dissension among Order members.

A crucial confrontation occurred in April 1900, when another Golden Dawn member, Aleister Crowley, a perceived ally of Mathers, arrived in London from Paris, where he had been initiated by Mathers into the 5°=6° degree.[42] On 17 April, Crowley (*Frater Perdurabo*) and a Golden Dawn colleague, Miss Elaine Simpson (*Soror Donorum Dei Dispensatis Fidelis*), broke into the Second Order members' meeting rooms in an effort to seize Order property, acting on Mathers's direct authority. Two days later, Crowley was involved in a direct confrontation with Second Order members William Butler Yeats (*Frater Daemon Est Deus Inversus*) and Edward A. Hunter (*Frater Hora et Semper*) at the same meeting rooms. Hunter later provided a statement, describing Crowley's somewhat melodramatic performance: "About 11:30 Crowley arrived in Highland dress, a black mask over his face, and a plaid thrown over his head and shoulders, an enormous gold or gilt cross on his breast, and a dagger by his side."[43] Yeats and Hunter barred Crowley from access to the Order's premises, and Crowley subsequently called for a constable to intervene; the constable in turn advised Crowley to "place the matter in the hands of a lawyer."[44]

The upshot of this dramatic confrontation was that on 21 April 1900, at a meeting of twenty-two Second Order members of the Isis-Urania Temple, a resolution was passed expelling Mathers and Miss Simpson from the Order of the Golden Dawn and also refusing admission to Crowley, whose 5°=6° degree initiation in Paris had not been recognized by the London Second Order members.[45] Mathers's exclusive hold on the Order of the Golden Dawn had effectively come to an end.

Golden Dawn Splinter Groups

In spite of the reaction against Mathers's autocratic rule, several members of the Golden Dawn formed splinter groups inspired by their own versions of the Secret Chiefs. Mrs. Florence Farr Emery headed a Golden Dawn Second Order offshoot known as the Sphere Group, that at first was said to be controlled by an Egyptian

Adept and later drew on the inspirational symbolism of the Cup of the Stolistes, an image of the Holy Grail.[46] Much of the Sphere Group's activities were devoted to inner plane work, including astral explorations, skrying, color meditation, and spirit communication.[47] Meanwhile, Dr. R. W. Felkin (*Frater Finem Respice*), together with several members of the London Isis-Urania Temple and the Edinburgh Amen-Ra Temple, founded the Order of the Stella Matutina (Morning Star) and continued to strive for contact with the Secret Chiefs, even though they had broken their allegiance to their former leader. Felkin had named his Order the Stella Matutina because Venus (the Morning Star) was believed to be the guardian planet of the Isis-Urania Temple.[48] Prominent members of the Amoun Temple of the Stella Matutina in London included John W. Brodie-Innes (formerly a leading member of Amen-Ra Temple in Edinburgh, where he was known as *Frater Sub Spe*), Annie Horniman, Percy Bullock, Arthur Edward Waite, and William Butler Yeats.[49] In its later years, Israel Regardie, editor of the major four-volume source-work, *The Golden Dawn*, would also join the Stella Matutina.[50]

In May 1902, Felkin wrote to his colleagues: "We beg to assure you that we are in entire sympathy with the view that if in fact the Order is without the guidance and inspiration of higher intelligences its rationale is gone," and he went on to acknowledge that some members of the Golden Dawn thought it might be possible, by reverting to the original constitution, to reestablish a link with the Third Order. Felkin would later maintain that he had made spiritual contact with a mysterious being named Ara Ben Shemesh, whom he described as a "discarnate Arab [with a] Temple in the Desert where the Sons of Fire live [who] are personal communication with the Divine and are no longer bound in the flesh so that their material life is a matter of will." Felkin's wife, in a Stella Matutina history lecture, claimed that the Chiefs of their Order (who included Felkin and his wife) had visited the "great secret hidden Temple" of the Hidden Masters on the astral plane, and that this Temple had twenty-two chapels "representing the twelve Zodiacal signs, the seven planets known to the ancients, and the elements of fire, water and air."[51]

There is also evidence that William Butler Yeats believed in the existence of the Secret Chiefs. In his essay "Is the Order of the R.R. & A.C. to Remain a Magical Order?," written in 1901, Yeats refers to "the stream of lightning awakened in the Order, and the Adepti of the Third Order and of the Higher Degrees of the Second Order summoned to our help."[52]

Malkuth, Yesod, Hod, and Netzach

The desire to maintain contact with the Secret Chiefs, or their counterparts, was primarily an issue for the Second Order members because they were more concerned with the administration of the various Golden Dawn branches and the ongoing problem of spiritual authority. The majority of Golden Dawn members, however, remained within the confines of the Outer Order, and their spiritual endeavors focused ritually and meditatively on the four *sephiroth* Malkuth, Yesod, Hod, and Netzach located at the lower levels of the Tree of Life.

The first stage of the magical process, however, was the Neophyte degree. This was not assigned a position on the Tree of Life as such, but was nevertheless considered a vital symbolic milestone. Francis King has described this degree as "unquestionably the most important, since it gave [the individual] not only a glimpse of the Light to be experienced in the future but a key (albeit in an embryonic and undeveloped form) to the inner and hidden significance of the entire Order."[53] This view is also endorsed by Israel Regardie, who was himself a member of the Stella Matutina in its later years:

> If one idea more than any other is persistently stressed from the
> beginning that idea is the word *Light*. From the candidate's first
> reception in the Hall of the Neophytes when the Hierophant adjures him
> with these words—"Child of Earth, long hast thou dwelt in darkness.
> Quit the night and seek the day"—to the transfiguration in the [Second
> Order] Vault Ceremony, the whole system has as its objective the
> bringing down of the Light.[54]

As a Neophyte, the aspirant was instructed in the First Knowledge Lecture, which provided details of the four elements of the Ancients (Fire, Earth, Air, and Water) and the twelve signs of the zodiac. The correlations between these signs and the elements were also explained, so that Aries, Leo, and Sagittarius were said to be Fire signs; Taurus, Virgo, and Capricorn Earth signs, and so on. Some elementary Hebrew was also included in a table that provided the letter of the alphabet, its English equivalent, its name, and its meaning. Finally, the elementary symbolism of the *sephiroth* upon the Tree of Life was also explained. On the practical side, the Neophyte was expected to know how to perform the Lesser Ritual of the Pentagram, an occult exercise designed to "clear the air" of minor malevolent forces surrounding the magician during ritual invocations.[55]

In the Zelator grade (1°=10°), corresponding to Malkuth on the Kabbalistic Tree, members were taught aspects of alchemical symbolism and provided with details of the Order of Elemental Spirits (gnomes—Earth; sylphs—Air; undines—Water; and salamanders—Fire) and also instructed in the links between the *sephiroth* and the planets. In the latter case, each *sephirah* was said to be associated with specific gods that could be drawn from any of the great pantheons and charted as Correspondences.[56]

The candidate for Theoricus (2°=9°), corresponding to Yesod, was taught the Kabbalistic division of the soul: *Neschamah* ("answering to the Three Supernals");

Ruach ("answering to the six *sephiroth* from Chesed to Yesod, inclusive") and *Nephesch* ("the lowest, answering to Malkuth"). It was emphasized, also, that *Neschamah* was associated with "the higher aspirations of the soul," *Ruach* with "the mind and reasoning powers," and *Nephesch* with "the animal instincts." Other correlations taught in the Theoricus grade included the symbolic relationship between the suits in the Tarot deck (wands, cups, swords, pentacles), the four worlds of the Kabbalistic Tree of Life (Atziluth, Briah, Yetzirah, Assiah), and the four letters of the Tetragrammaton (the sacred four-letter name of God, *Yod, Heh, Vau, He*: Yahweh), as well as the connection between the symbol of the caduceus and the Tree of Life (the tip of the caduceus reaching to the supernals, Chokmah and Binah, the lower seven *sephiroth* entwined by the coiled serpents).[57]

In the Practicus grade (3°=8°), corresponding to Hod, members were instructed in the relationship between figures of geomancy, or earth divination, and their zodiacal attributes.[58] Practicus candidates also learned the symbolism of the Major Arcana of the Tarot (the twenty-two mythological or "court" cards) and their association with the twenty-two paths linking the ten *sephiroth* upon the Tree of Life.[59] Finally, the Philosophus (4°=7°) grade, corresponding to Netzach, completed the Outer Order of the Golden Dawn.[60] An important theme here was the concept of "god-names"—attributions of the archetypal Great Father and Great Mother—as well as links between alchemy and astrology. Details were also provided of the so-called *Qliphoth* upon the Tree of Life: the negative cosmic energy centers that were the "reverse" equivalents of the ten *sephiroth*. Lilith was one such example for, as the "Queen of the Night and of Demons," she was correlated with Malkuth—the Divine Daughter—and was thus the dark equivalent of Persephone, daughter of Demeter, queen of the Underworld and embodiment of the harvest. Philosophus candidates also learned the Hebrew names, associated Archangels, and Elementals for each of the traditional elements (Earth, Air, Water, and Fire), as well the astrological symbols of the planets.[61]

Magical Symbolism in the Golden Dawn

As Israel Regardie notes in relation to the Neophyte grade, for the Golden Dawn magician the ultimate mythic attainment was to come forth ritually into the Light, for this was the very essence of spiritual rebirth.[62] The process of ascending the Kabbalistic Tree of Life by means of visualization and ceremonial magic involved powerful acts of creative imagination: the magician had to feel that he or she was fully engaging with each sphere of consciousness in turn. However, the monotheistic nature of the Kabbalistic Tree of Life presented the Golden Dawn occultists with a paradox, for while they acknowledged the sacred unity of the Tree of Life in all its emanations, they also believed that they had to focus their creative awareness upon a sequence of specific archetypal images if they were to "ascend" to the Light. Their solution was to regard the Kabbalistic Tree of Life as a matrix upon which the archetypes of the great Western mythologies could be charted and interrelated as part of a sacred unity. It then became possible to correlate the major deities from the pantheons of ancient Egypt, Greece, Rome, and Celtic Europe in what was effectively a cumulative approach to the Western mythological imagination. In due course, other magical objects would also be charted symbolically upon the Tree, including various precious stones, perfumes, minerals, and sacred plants—each being assigned to specific gods and goddesses in a ceremonial context. These charted mythological images were known to the Golden Dawn magicians as "magical correspondences."

Ithell Colquhoun notes that S. L. Mathers and Wynn Westcott began compiling the lists of magical correspondences during the 1890s, but this work would subsequently be commandeered by Aleister Crowley and published under his own name:

> A manuscript arranged in tabular form and known as *The Book of Correspondences*, the compilation of which Mathers and Wynn Westcott had together begun in the early days of their association, was circulated by them among their more promising students during the 1890s. Allan Bennett had a copy which he passed on to [Aleister] Crowley, or allowed him to copy again. Years later Crowley, while convalescing in Bournemouth, had the bright idea of adding a few columns to it. He then gave it the title of *Liber 777*, wrote an introduction and notes and, in 1909, published the whole as his own work, "privately," under the imprint of the Walter Scott Publishing Co. Ltd., London and Felling-on-Tyne. This is the explanation of Crowley's claim to the feat of composing the whole within a week and without reference books. Certain of the columns were repeated in his *Magick in Theory and Practice* (1929) and in Regardie's *The Golden Dawn*. A new impression of the original was *Liber 777 Revised*, brought out in by the Neptune Press, London in 1955 . . . the authorship of Mathers, who had done most of the initial work, went unrecognised.[63]

The listings in *Liber 777* included references to ancient Egyptian and Roman deities as well as listings for Western astrology, plants, precious stones, and perfumes. Selected listings from Crowley's version of Mathers's and Westcott's *Book of Correspondences* published in Table 1 in *Liber 777* are shown in table 3.1.[64]

The perfumes, precious stones, and plants listed in table 3.2 were considered appropriate in rituals corresponding to the invoked god or goddess for each of the ten *sephiroth* and are also listings from Crowley's Table 1.[65]

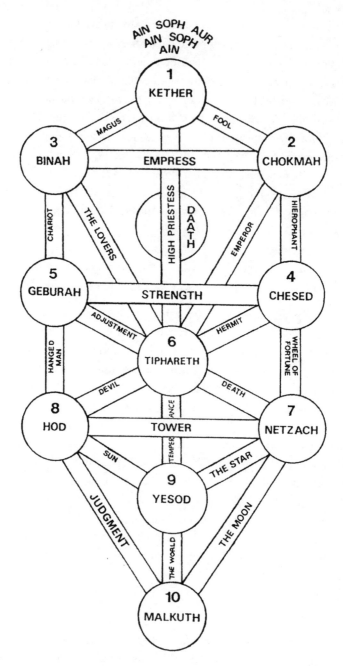

FIGURE 3.6. The Kabbalistic Tree of Life as it was conceived in the Hermetic Order of the Golden Dawn. The Major Arcana of the Tarot—the so-called mythological cards—were assigned to the twenty-two connecting paths linking the *sephiroth*.

TABLE 3.1. Table of Correspondences

Level	Kabbalah	Astrology	Egyptian	Roman
1	Kether	Primum Mobile	Ptah, Hadith	Jupiter
2	Chokmah	Zodiac/Fixed Stars	Amoun, Thoth	Janus
3	Binah	Saturn	Isis, Nephthys	Juno, Cybele, Hecate
4	Chesed	Jupiter	Amoun	Jupiter
5	Geburah	Mars	Horus	Mars
6	Tiphareth	Sol (Sun)	Ra	Apollo
7	Netzach	Venus	Hathoor	Venus
8	Hod	Mercury	Anubis	Mercury
9	Yesod	Luna	Shu	Diana
10	Malkuth	The Elements	Seb	Ceres

TABLE 3.2. Table of Correspondences, con'd

Level	Precious Stones	Perfumes	Plants
1	Diamond	Ambergris	Almond in flower
2	Star Ruby, Turquoise	Musk	Amaranth
3	Star Sapphire, Pearl	Myrrh, Civet	Cypress, Opium Poppy
4	Amethyst, Sapphire	Cedar	Olive, Shamrock
5	Ruby	Tobacco	Oak. Nux Vomica, Nettle
6	Topaz	Olibanum	Acacia, Bay, Laurel, Vine
7	Emerald	Benzoin, Rose, Sandalwood	Rose
8	Opal	Storax	Moly, *Anhalonium lewinii*
9	Quartz	Jasmine	Mandrake, Damiana
10	Rock Crystal	Dittany of Crete	Willow, Lily, Ivy

Liber 777 and its precursor, *The Book of Correspondences*, helped codify the modern magical imagination. The listings themselves are of historic significance because they represent an early attempt to systematize archetypal images and "mythic" levels of consciousness at a time when psychology itself was still in its infancy. *Liber 777* and *The Book of Correspondences* predate by well over a decade Carl Jung's work with the "primordial images" of the unconscious mind, later referred to as the "archetypes of the collective unconscious."[66]

From a psychological perspective, it is clear that the magicians of the Golden Dawn regarded the Tree of Life as a complex symbol representing the realm of sacred inner potentialities. To simulate the gods and goddesses through acts of magic was to become like them. The challenge was to identify oneself with the mythological and archetypal images of the psyche through a process of direct encounter: the act of engaging the gods, whether through ritual or by some other means like visualization, meditation, or magical trance, was essentially a process of discovering one's inner potential. As Aleister Crowley observed in *Magick in Theory and Practice* (1929): "the Gods are but names for the forces of Nature themselves" and "the true God is man. In man are all things hidden."[67]

The magicians in the Golden Dawn had therefore to imagine that they were partaking of the nature of each of the gods in turn, embodying within themselves the very essence of the deity. Their rituals were designed to control all the circumstances that might assist them in their journey through the subconscious mind and the mythic imagination. They included all the symbols and colors of the god, the utterance of magical names of power, and the burning of incense or perfume appropriate to the deity concerned. In Golden Dawn ceremonial workings, the ritual magician imagined that he or she had become the deity whose forms were imitated in ritual. The traditional concept of the gods (or God) ruling humanity was reversed so that it was now the ritual magician who controlled the gods, uttering the sacred names that sustained the universe. As Eliphas Lévi had stated in his seminal text *The Key of the Mysteries*, "All magic is in a word, and that word pronounced Kabbalistically is stronger than all the powers of Heaven, Earth and Hell. With the name of *Yod, He, Vau, He*, one commands Nature."[68]

Ritual Magic and the Senses

In passing through the ritual grades from Malkuth to Netzach, the Outer Order members of the Golden Dawn focused their magical activities on the mythic levels associated with the lower *sephiroth* of the Tree of Life, specifically the spheres of Malkuth, Yesod, Hod, and Netzach.[69] In doing so, they developed specific techniques for the expansion of spiritual awareness. These included a rich application of magical symbols and mythic imagery in their ritual adornments, ceremonial procedures, and invocations, all of which were intended to focus the imagination during the performance of a given magical ritual. In one of his most important books, Israel Regardie describes magical ritual as "a deliberate exhilaration of the Will and the exaltation of the Imagination, the end being the purification of the personality and the attainment of a spiritual state of consciousness, in which the ego enters into a union with either its own Higher Self or a God."[70]

In Aleister Crowley's essay "The Initiated Interpretation of Ceremonial Magic," which was included in S. L. MacGregor Mathers's edition of *The Goetia: The Lesser Key of Solomon the King* (1889), specific mention is made of the fact that magical ritual is intended to stimulate each and every one of of the physical senses. "Magical phenomena," writes Crowley, "are willed, and their cause is the series of 'real' phenomena called the operations of ceremonial Magic. These consist of 1) Sight: The circle, square, triangle, vessels, lamps, robes, implements etc. 2) Sound: The invocations. 3) Smell: The Perfumes. 4) Taste: The Sacraments. 5) Touch: As under (1). 6) Mind: The combination of all these and reflection on their significance."[71]

Crowley's list can be expanded as follows:

Sight

The ritual robes, actions, and implements are a visual representation relevant to the specific end that is sought (e.g., invoking a particular deity). In this drama, carefully chosen colors and symbols play a paramount role. The ritual magician's vestments, and also the motifs mounted upon the wall of the Temple, are intended to stimulate the mythic imagination and help consolidate the spiritual connection with the gods and goddesses to whom the ritual is addressed.

Sound

This involves the vibration of sacred god-names, chants, or invocations (predominantly derived from the Kabbalah) whose auditory rhythms have a profound impact on the consciousness of the participant.

Taste

This can take the form of a sacrament that relates symbolically to the nature of the god or goddess in the ritual.

Smell

Incense and perfumes (e.g., those listed in *Liber 777* and identified with specific spheres on the Tree of Life) are used to increase the sense of rapport with a specific deity within the magical cosmology.

Touch

The magician endeavors to develop a sense of tactile awareness beyond the normal functions of the organism, since assimilation with "god-forms" involves a heightened state of awareness. When states of trance are utilized (see below), the magician "wills" the dissociated "soul body" to perform ritual functions on the inner planes, parallel to those undertaken in a physical context within the Golden Dawn Temple (e.g., the visit to the "astral Temple" undertaken by senior members of the Stella Matutina, referred to earlier).

The Power of the Sacred Name

In the Western esoteric tradition, the magical power of the sacred word or name is widely recognized. From a Kabbalistic perspective, the Word, or Logos, was said to permeate the entire mystical act of Creation, and ritual magicians both within the Golden Dawn and also in other magical orders have held similar views on the intrinsic power of the magical utterance.[72] According to the influential Czechoslovakian ritual magician Franz Bardon (1909–1958), "the divine names are symbolic designations of divine qualities and powers," and Crowley makes a similar point when he writes: "Every true name of God gives the formula of the invocation of that God."[73] In many ancient religious traditions the sacred name was regarded as the very essence of being. According to the Ethiopian Gnostic text *Lefefa Sedek*, God created Himself and the Universe through the utterance of His own name and therefore "the Name of God was the essence of God [and] was not only the source of His power but also the seat of His very Life, and was to all intents and purposes His Soul."[74] Similarly, in the *Egyptian Book of the Dead* the deceased newcomer to the Hall of Maat (Hall of Judgment) says to the presiding deity, Osiris: "I know thee. I know thy name. I know the names of the two-and-forty gods who are with thee."[75] For it follows that he who knows the secret name strikes home to the very heart of the matter, and has the ability to liberate his soul: he is in control, for the essence of the god is within his very grasp. According to the distinguished Egyptologist Sir E.A. Wallis Budge, in ancient Egypt "the knowledge of the name of a god enabled a man not only to free himself from the power of that god, but to use that name as a means of obtaining what he himself wanted without considering the god's will."[76]

In the Hermetic Order of the Golden Dawn, Aleister Crowley related his designated magical name, *Perdurabo* ("I will endure to the end"), to the expression of his magical will. As Crowley notes in *Book Four* [1913]: "Words should express will; hence the Mystic Name of the Probationer is the expression of his highest Will."[77] In a comparable manner, trance magician Dion Fortune, a one-time member of the Golden Dawn Alpha and Omega Temple in London, found that she was more readily able to project her "body of light" when she uttered her magical name. In her book *Applied Magic* she writes: "In my own experience of the operation, the utterance to myself of my Magical name led to the picturing of myself in an idealised form, not differing in type, but upon an altogether grander scale, superhuman in fact, but recognisable as myself, as a statue more than life-size may yet be a good likeness. . . . I could not identify myself with it unless I uttered my Magical name."[78]

The Symbols of Ritual Magic

Specific ritual symbols were incorporated into Golden Dawn magical practice. They include some of the universal elements found within the broader Western esoteric tradition. The first of these was the temple itself.

In a symbolic context, the temple contains all magical activities; it represents the entire operative Universe and, by inference, the figure of the magician as well, because of the perceived relationship between microcosm and macrocosm.[79] On the walls are mounted banners decorated with sacred symbols and colors appropriate to the mythic imagery of the ritual, and on the floor of the temple are certain inscriptions, the most important of which is the circle.

The circle incorporates many symbolic meanings. As a symbol of containment and Oneness it represents the Infinite Godhead, the Alpha and Omega, the sacred source of self-knowledge to which the magician aspires. As Aleister Crowley notes in his book on practical ceremonial magic, *Book Four* (1913): "The Circle announces the Nature of the Great Work."[80] As a symbol of holistic spiritual aspiration, the circle is utilized in ritual acts of invocation.[81] Within the circle, the magician assumes a role of authority by seeking to subject the invoked deity to his or her will. The sacred god-names inscribed around the periphery of the circle stipulate the exact nature of the ritual working.[82] In addition, the circle may be circumscribed by an equal-sided geometric figure whose number of sides corresponds to the pertinent *sephirah* upon the Tree of Life. For example, a six-sided geometric figure like a hexagram would be employed to invoke Osiris, because as a god of rebirth Osiris is symbolically associated with Tiphareth, the sixth emanation upon the Tree.

In the Golden Dawn system, the ceremonial circle also contains a Tau cross which, as an assertive masculine symbol, balances the receptive role of the circle itself, the two together producing an appropriate balance of opposites. The Tau is made up of ten squares, one for each *sephirah*, and is vermillion in color, as are the inscribed god-names.[83] The circle area is complementary green. Nine equidistant pentagrams, each containing a small glowing lamp, surround the circle, and a tenth hangs above the center as a symbol of mystical aspiration. From a practical perspective, the circle needs to be large enough for the ritual magician, or in many cases a small group of ritual practitioners, to move around in. The magician remains within the circle for the duration of the ritual. It is also required that the sacred nature of the circle be ritually reaffirmed in the mind of the magician, for otherwise the circle remains a purely profane or secular symbol. The presiding magician therefore traces over its inscribed form with his ritual sword or outstretched hand, at the same time carefully reflecting upon the symbolic meaning of his action.

Some magical rituals utilize a triangle as a symbol of containment, but this ritual motif serves a purpose entirely different from that of the circle. Unlike the circle, which symbolises infinite sacred potential and is used to invoke higher spiritual beings such as gods, goddesses, and archangels, the triangle is employed for evocation, the magical act of summoning lesser (and sometimes evil) spirits through spells or words of power.[84] The ritual purpose of the triangle is to restrain the evoked entity.[85] The Golden Dawn magicians believed that if they were to lose control of an evoked spirit they could actually become possessed by it. The magical talisman placed in the center of the triangle incorporates the seal, or magical sigil, of the spirit and provides the focus of the ritual.[86] Evocation is usually associated with low magic rather than the high magic associated with archetypal aspiration and spiritual transformation, and was not a central feature of the magic of the Golden Dawn temples. As previously mentioned, however, MacGregor Mathers was fascinated by medieval magical grimoires dealing with the evocation of spirits, and several such documents gained currency through his translations.[87] Aleister Crowley was also an enthusiastic practitioner of magical evocation.[88]

During Golden Dawn rituals involving magical invocation, various implements were employed by the magician within the circle. Most of these objects were placed upon the central altar, which symbolized the foundation of the ritual itself.

Consisting of a double cube of wood, usually made of acacia or oak, the altar has ten exposed faces, corresponding with the ten *sephiroth* upon the Tree of Life. The lowest face is Malkuth, symbolizing the World, which represents things as they are in the manifested universe. The upper face represents Kether, the Crown, the First-Manifest. Aleister Crowley recommended that it be plated with gold, the metal of perfection. Upon the sides of the altar, wrote Crowley, one could inscribe "the sigils of the holy Elemental Kings."[89]

Placed upon the altar are symbolic implements whose ritual purpose is to focus the imagination of the ceremonial magician on the sacred nature of the specific function being performed.

The holy oil

This golden fluid is ideally contained in a vessel of rock crystal. In using it, the magician anoints the Four Points of the Microcosm (Kether, Chesed, Geburah, and Malkuth) upon his forehead, left and right shoulders, and solar plexus, respectively, at the same time reflecting on the sacred task ahead. The holy ointment consists of the oils of olive, myrrh, cinnamon, and galangual, corresponding in turn to Chokmah (Wisdom), Binah (Understanding), Tiphareth (Harmony/Spiritual Awakening), and Kether-Malkuth (the so-called Greater and Lesser Countenance, the Union of Being and Creation upon the Tree of Life).[90]

The wand

This ritual implement symbolizes the pursuit of higher wisdom (Chokmah), achieved through the magical Will.[91] Symbolically, the tip of the wand is in Kether, the first *sephirah* of the Tree of Life, which contains the "union of opposites" and represents the transcendence of duality in all its forms. In the Golden Dawn, a lotus wand was used that was multicolored, with its upper end white and its lower black. In between were twelve bands of color corresponding to the different signs of the zodiac:[92]

White	—
Red	Aries
Red-orange	Taurus
Orange	Gemini
Amber	Cancer
Lemon-yellow	Leo
Yellow-green	Virgo
Emerald	Libra
Green-blue	Scorpio
Blue	Sagittarius
Indigo	Capricorn
Violet	Aquarius
Crimson[93]	Pisces
Black	—

A lotus flower, with three whorls of petals, was placed on the tip of the wand, the white end used for magical invocation, the black end for "banishing," or removing, malevolent forces.[94]

The wand represents the first letter, *Yod*, of the Tetragrammaton JHVH and also the element Fire.[95] Three other ritual implements, the cup, sword, and disc (also known as the pentacle), complete the Sacred Name of God and represent the elements Water, Air, and Earth, respectively.

The cup

As a feminine, receptive symbol, the cup is associated with Netzach, the goddess Venus, and the element Water.[96] Made of glass, and ideally shaped in the form of a eight-petaled crocus, the ceremonial cup is a symbol of containment.[97] It was not used in Golden Dawn rituals of invocation, but rather in ceremonies related to acts of manifestation.

The sword

Indicative of the magician's mastery over both evoked and invoked powers, the sword (which symbolizes human force) complements the wand, which represents divine power. Associated with the element Air, the sword is regarded symbolically as the embodiment of Wisdom and Understanding (Chokmah and Binah) and is therefore attributed to Tiphareth, the sphere of harmony. The symmetry of the Sword is correspondingly appropriate. According to Aleister Crowley, the guard should consist of two moons, waxing and waning, affixed to the back (Yesod), and the blade should be made of steel (corresponding to Mars). The hilt should be constructed of copper (the metal symbolically associated with Venus), indicating that ultimately the sword is subject to the rule of love. When the sword is placed symbolically upon the Tree of Life, its pommel rests in Daath, the "sphere" associated with the Abyss beneath the Trinity, and the points of the guard lie in Chesed and Geburah. The tip rests in Malkuth. Crowley makes the observation that "the Magician cannot wield the Sword unless the Crown is on his head," that is to say, force and aspiration without inspiration are of no avail.[98]

The disc (pentacle)

In the same way that the sword is paired with the wand, both being symbolically masculine, the disc is paired with the cup as a feminine symbol. Fashioned from a disc of wood and then polished, the disc is associated with Malkuth, the element Earth, and also the Heavenly Daughter Shekinah, goddess of the manifested universe.[99] The disc also represents the body of the magician who wishes to be filled with the Holy Ghost.[100] It therefore symbolizes the magician's personal state of being prior to attaining a state of spiritual transformation in the Second Order 5°=6° ritual grade of Tiphareth.

The ceremonial magician wears upon his head the crown, or headband, representative of Kether. Golden in color, it is a symbol of aspiration toward the Divine. Over his body falls the robe, whose function is to protect the magician from adverse astral influences. Hooded, and normally black in color, the robe symbolizes anonymity and silence, and is the dark vessel into which Light will be poured. Attached to it, or sewn across the chest, is the lamen, or breastplate, which protects the heart (Tiphareth). The lamen also has inscribed upon it symbols that relate to all aspects of the magical purpose. Considered an "active" form of the passive disc, the lamen represents strength and purpose. So too does the magical book, which the magician holds in his hands. This book contains all the details of one's ritual aims and practice, and therefore represents the unfolding "history" of the effects of the magical Will. As such, the magical book constitutes a steadfast symbol of power and resolve.[101]

In addition, the ceremonial magician sometimes employs the use of a bell, worn on a chain around the neck. Representative of a state of alertness, it is said to be the bell that sounds "at the elevation of the Host" and thus alludes to the sublime music of the higher spheres. In this respect, the symbolism of the bell parallels that of the sacred lamp, which as "the light of the pure soul" is positioned above the ritual implements on the altar and represents the descent of spirit into form, light into darkness, the Godhead into humanity. It stands for all that is eternal and unchanging, and also represents the first swirlings of the Primal Energy in the Universe ("Let there be Light . . ." Genesis 1:3). "Without this Light," notes Aleister Crowley, "the magicians could not work at all; yet few indeed are the magicians that have known of it, and far fewer they that have beheld its brilliance."[102]

Magical Trance

Magicians in the Golden Dawn often described the inner journeys of the psyche by referring to such terms as "astral projection," "pathworkings," and the "Body of Light." Essentially, the trance meditation techniques utilized by the Golden Dawn magicians involved a transfer of focused awareness to the visionary world of symbols, through an act of willed imagination.

The Golden Dawn technique of magical trance combined bodily relaxation with a state of mental acuity, in which the magician focused increasingly on inner psychic processes. Usually magical meditation of this type took place in the dark, enabling the meditator to shift attention away from external visual stimuli to an inner perspective. The trance magician then attempted to reinforce the sense of the "alternative reality" provided by the mythological images or visionary landscapes that arise as a result of willed imagination.

Personal accounts of magical trance are contained in a series of papers prepared by leading members of the Golden Dawn. These papers were known as Flying Rolls, and they include the magical records of *Frater Sub Spe* (John W. Brodie-Innes), who was a prominent figure in the Golden Dawn's Amen-Ra Temple in Edinburgh prior to joining the Stella Matutina after the split with Mathers. *Frater Sub Spe* provides us with a graphic account of the switch in consciousness that takes place as the magician switches the field of awareness from the outer to the inner world:

> Gradually the attention is withdrawn from all surrounding sights and
> sounds, a grey mist seems to swathe everything, on which, as though
> thrown from a magic lantern on steam, the form of the symbol is
> projected. The Consciousness then seems to pass through the symbol to

realms beyond . . . the sensation is as if one looked at a series of moving pictures. . . . When this sensitiveness of brain and power of perception is once established there seems to grow out of it a power of actually going to the scenes so visionary and seeing them as solid, indeed of actually *doing things* and producing effects there.[103]

The Golden Dawn magicians also used the so-called Tattva symbols of the five elements as meditative "doorways" to magical visions.[104] The Tattvas derive from the Hindu tradition of Kundalini Yoga and are one of the few Eastern components directly incorporated within the Western esoteric tradition. In their basic form they are as follows:

Tejas, a red equilateral triangle	Fire
Apas, a silver crescent	Water
Vayu, a blue circle	Air
Prithivi, a yellow square	Earth
Akasha, a black, indigo or violet egg	Spirit

Golden Dawn *Flying Roll XI* describes a Tattva vision by Mrs. Moina Mathers (*Soror Vestigia*) as she sat meditating in her ceremonial robes, contemplating a Tattva card combining *Tejas* and *Akasha*, a violet egg within a red triangle (Spirit within Fire). The symbol seemed to grow before her gaze, enabling her to pass into a "vast triangle of flame." She felt herself to be in a harsh desert of sand. Intoning the god-name *Elohim*, she perceived a small pyramid in the distance and, drawing closer, she then noticed a small door on each face. She then vibrated the magical formula *Sephariel*, and a warrior appeared, leading a procession of guards. After a series of tests involving ritual grade signs, the guards knelt before her and she passed inside:

> dazzling light, as in a Temple. An altar in the midst—kneeling figures surround it, there is a dais beyond, and many figures upon it—they seem to be Elementals of a fiery nature. . . . She sees a pentagram, puts a Leo in it [i.e., a Fire sign], thanks the figure who conducts her—wills to pass through the pyramid, finds herself out amid the sand. Wills her return— returns—perceiving her body in robes.[105]

In this account and others like it, it is clear that the visionary landscape derives specifically from the meditative symbol. The intangible aspect of the vision, Spirit, seems to be reflected in the mysterious and sanctified nature of the inner temple, which in this case the magician was privileged to enter. The beings that Moina Mathers perceived, however, were fire elementals which, within the order of the occult hierarchy, are considered far beneath the level of gods. This particular visionary experience, while interesting, apparently provided no profound or trans- formative insights. On another occasion, however, Moina Mathers was able to con- jure beings of a more archetypal nature. Here she made use of the Tattva combinations Water and Spirit. Her account not only shows the link between the magical symbol and the visionary beings that appear but also indicates the role of focused imagination:

> A wide expanse of water with many reflections of bright light, and occasionally glimpses of rainbow colours appearing. When divine and other names were pronounced, elementals of the mermaid and merman type [would] appear, but few of the other elemental forms. These water forms were extremely changeable, one moment appearing as solid mermaids and mermen, the next melting into foam.
>
> Raising myself by means of the highest symbols I had been taught, and vibrating the names of Water, I rose until the Water vanished, and instead I beheld a mighty world or globe, with its dimensions and divisions of Gods, Angels, elementals and demons—the whole Universe of Water. I called on HCOMA and there appeared standing before me a mighty Archangel, with four wings, robed in glistening white and crowned. In one hand, the right, he held a species of trident, and in the left a Cup filled to the brim with an essence which he poured down below on either side.[106]

In this example, the perception of a hierarchy of magical beings and symbols produced a notable shift in magical awareness. According to her account, Moina Mathers was able to use a range of magical names to invoke beyond the level of the initial elemental symbols, causing an archangel to appear in her visions. She was also employing a technique known within the Golden Dawn as "rising in the planes," a method of willing oneself to rise meditatively from one sphere to another on the Tree of Life. In *Flying Roll XI*, MacGregor Mathers provides specific instruc- tions on how this is achieved:

> Rising in the Planes is a spiritual process after spiritual conceptions and higher aims; by concentration and contemplation of the Divine, you formulate a Tree of Life passing from you to the spiritual realms above and beyond you. Picture to yourself that you stand in Malkuth—then by use of the Divine Names and aspirations you strive upward by the Path

of Tau towards Yesod, neglecting the crossing rays which attract you as
you pass up. Look upwards to the Divine Light shining down from
Kether upon you. From Yesod leads up the Path of Temperance,
Samekh, the arrow cleaving upwards leads the way to Tiphareth, the
Great Central Sun of Sacred Power.[107]

Here Mathers is describing a twofold path on the Tree of Life extending from Malkuth to Yesod and then from Yesod to Tiphareth: the mystical ascension upon the
so-called Middle Pillar of the Tree. There were other meditative paths upon the
Tree of Life, however, specifically the paths connecting each of the ten *sephiroth*
with each other. Numbering twenty-two paths in all, they were symbolized by the
Major Arcana of the Tarot.

The Meditative Doorways of the Tarot

While Tattva meditations could clearly induce specific visionary states, the Golden
Dawn magicians discovered that a more complete transformational process was
possible using the Major Arcana of the Tarot in conjunction with the Tree of Life.
The Major Arcana are the twenty-two mythological cards of the Tarot deck as distinct from the fifty-six standard cards of the four suits, and their ascriptions upon
the Tree of Life are as follows:

The World	Malkuth-Yesod
Judgment	Malkuth-Hod
The Moon	Malkuth-Netzach
The Sun	Yesod-Hod
The Star	Yesod-Netzach
The Tower	Hod-Netzach
The Devil	Hod-Tiphareth
Death	Netzach-Tiphareth
Temperance	Yesod-Tiphareth
The Hermit	Tiphareth-Chesed
Justice	Tiphareth-Geburah
The Hanged Man	Hod-Geburah
Wheel of Fortune	Netzach-Chesed
Strength	Geburah-Chesed
The Chariot	Geburah-Binah
The Lovers	Tiphareth-Binah
The Hierophant	Chesed-Chokmah

The Emperor	Tiphareth-Chokmah
The Empress	Binah-Chokmah
The High Priestess	Tiphareth-Kether
The Magus	Binah-Kether
The Fool	Chokmah-Kether

MacGregor Mathers ascribed Kabbalistic "names of power" to each of the ten sephiroth and noted that different letters of the Hebrew alphabet could be visualized upon each of the Tarot paths, thereby intensifying and authenticating the trance visions as they arose:

> There are three special tendencies to error and illusion which assail the Adept in these studies. They are Memory, Imagination and actual Sight. These elements of doubt are to be avoided by the Vibration of Divine Names, and by the Letters and Titles of the "Lords Who Wander"—the Planetary Forces, represented by the Seven double letters of the Hebrew alphabet.
>
> If the Memory entice thee astray, apply for help to Saturn, whose Tarot Title is the "Great One of the Night of Time." Formulate the Hebrew letter *Tau* in whiteness.
>
> If the Vision change or disappear, your memory has falsified your efforts. If Imagination cheat thee, use the Hebrew letter *Kaph* for the Forces of Jupiter, named "Lord of the Forces of Life." If the Deception be of Lying—intellectual untruth—appeal to the Force of Mercury by the Hebrew letter *Beth*. If the trouble be of Wavering of Mind, use the Hebrew letter *Gimel* for the Moon. If the enticement of pleasure be the error, then use the Hebrew letter *Daleth* as an aid.[108]

A Tarot-based trance vision recorded in November 1892 by *Soror Sapientia Sapienti Dona Data* (Florence Farr Emery) and *Soror Fidelis* (Elaine Simpson) survives in *Flying Roll IV*. It is of particular interest because it indicates the trance magician's direct sense of encounter with the deities upon the Tree of Life. A blend of Christian and Egyptian elements is apparent, the Grail Mother being regarded here as an aspect of Isis. A ritual gesture appropriate to the Roman goddess Venus is also included, reflecting the eclectic blend of cosmologies found in Golden Dawn magical visualization:

> The Tarot Trump *The Empress* was taken; placed before the persons and contemplated upon, spiritualised, heightened in colouring, purified in design and idealised.

In vibratory manner, pronounced *Daleth*. Then, in spirit, saw a greenish blue distant landscape, suggestive of medieval tapestry. Effort to ascend was then made; rising on the planes; seemed to pass up through clouds and then appeared a pale green landscape and in its midst a Gothic Temple of ghostly outlines marked with light.

Approached it and found the temple gained in definiteness and was concrete, and seemed a solid structure. Giving the signs of the Netzach Grade (because of Venus) was able to enter; giving also Portal signs and 5°=6° signs in thought form.[109] Opposite the entrance perceived a Cross with three bars and a dove upon it; and beside this were steps leading downwards into the dark, by a dark passage. Here was met a beautiful green dragon, who moved aside, meaning no harm, and the spirit vision passed on. Turning a corner and still passing on in the dark emerged from the darkness onto a marble terrace brilliantly white, and a garden beyond, with flowers, whose foliage was of a delicate green kind and the leaves seemed to have a white velvety surface beneath. Here there appeared a woman of heroic proportions, clothed in green with a jewelled girdle, a crown of stars on her head, in her hand a sceptre of gold, having at one apex a lustrously white closed lotus flower; in her left hand an orb bearing a cross.

She smiled proudly, and as the human spirit sought her name, replied:

"I am the mighty Mother Isis; the most powerful of all the world, I am she who fights not, but is always victorious, I am that Sleeping Beauty who men have sought, for all time; and the paths which lead to my castle are beset with dangers and illusions. Such as fail to find me sleep—or may ever rush after the Fata Morgana leading astray all who feel that illusory influence—I am lifted up on high and do draw men unto me. I am the world's desire, but few there be who find me. When my secret is told, it is the secret of the Holy Grail."

Asking to learn it, [she] replied:

"Come with me, but first clothe in white garments, put on your insignia, and with bared feet follow where I shall lead."

Arriving at length at a Marble Wall, pressed a secret spring and entered a small compartment where the spirit seemed to ascend through a dense vapour, and emerged upon a turret of a building. Perceived some object in the midst of the place, but was forbidden to look at it until permission was accorded. Stretched out the arms and bowed the head to the Sun which was rising a golden orb in the East. Then turning, knelt with the face towards the centre, and being permitted to raise the eyes beheld a cup with a heart and the sun shining upon these; there seemed a clear ruby coloured fluid in the cup. Then "Lady Venus" said:

"This is love, I have plucked out my heart and have given it to the world; that is my strength. Love is the mother of the Man-God, giving the Quintessence of her life to save mankind from destruction and, and show forth the path to life eternal. Love is the mother of Christ.

"Spirit, and this Christ is the highest love—Christ is the heart of love, the heart of the Great Mother Isis—the Isis of Nature. He is the expression of her power—she is the Holy Grail, and He is the life blood of spirit, that is found in this cup."

After this, being told that man's hope lay in following her example, we solemnly gave our hearts to the keeping of the Grail; then, instead of feeling death, as our human imagination led us to expect, we felt an influx of the highest courage and power, for our own hearts were to be henceforth in touch with hers—the strongest force in all the world.

So then we went away, feeling glad that we had learned that "He who gives away his life, will gain it." For *that* love which is power, is given unto him—who hath given away his all for the good of others.[110]

This particular Golden Dawn trance experiment resulted in a visionary episode containing ancient Egyptian, Roman, Christian, and Celtic elements. Such syncretism was a characteristic of several of the Golden Dawn Flying Roll accounts, reflecting the diverse nature of the mythological pantheons charted in the *Book of Correspondences* by Mathers and Westcott during the 1890s. These trance journeys are of particular interest, however, because they demonstrate that some of the Golden Dawn magicians, most notably Moina Mathers, Florence Farr Emery, and Elaine Simpson, were able to convert an essentially eclectic listing of gods and goddesses into an experiential reality on the "inner planes."

4

Aleister Crowley and
the Left-Hand Path

Following the fragmentation of the Hermetic Order of the Golden Dawn during the period between 1900 and the end of World War I, the practice of ceremonial magic in the West became increasingly dominated by Aleister Crowley's doctrine of *Thelema* (Greek: will).[1] The teachings of *Thelema* were introduced initially into Crowley's own magical order, Argenteum Astrum (The Silver Star, established 1907), and later into the Ordo Templi Orientis, which Crowley headed from 1922 onward, as we shall discuss below. Wicca would emerge as a major esoteric movement later, in the 1950s and 1960s, following the repeal in 1951 of the British Witchcraft Act forbidding the practice of witchcraft.[2]

Since the 1960s, Western magical practice in Britain and the United States has been polarized, producing two major streams of occult thought led, on the one hand, by Crowleyan *Thelema* and its various derivative offshoots and affiliated movements, and by Wicca and Goddess spirituality, on the other.[3] The latter was exported to the United States by the Gardnerian initiate Raymond Buckland in 1964 (later to merge with various forms of Goddess spirituality through the activities of influential American feminists such as Starhawk, Z. Budapest, and Margot Adler). Other branches of magic such as the Dion Fortune-inspired Fraternity of the Inner Light and its more recent derivative, Servants of the Light (currently headed by Dolores Ashcroft-Nowicki), and revivalist movements like Druidry, Odinism, and Celtic neoshamanism remain very much minority practices within the contemporary occult spectrum.[4] Modern Western magic continues to be dominated by the legacy of Aleister Crowley, who has become an iconic personality in popular culture, featured on the cover of the Beatles' famous *Sergeant Pepper's* rock album (1967) and inspiring a number of novels and plays by other writers, as well as influencing leading rock stars such as David Bowie and Led Zeppelin's Jimmy Page.[5]

Crowley has been branded by many as a "black" magician: he was widely known in the mainstream British media as the Great Beast 666—that is, as the Antichrist—and was described by London's *John Bull* magazine as "the wickedest man in the world."[6] Within the context of modern esotericism, however, the familiar—and somewhat clichéd—notion of magic as either "black" or "white" is clearly in need of revision. When one considers the spectrum of modern magical practices established in the West during the twentieth century and still current today, it would seem appropriate, at least in part, to employ the terminology used by many of the actual magical practitioners themselves to distinguish between the various forms of occult practice dating from the post-Crowley period. Increasingly, many of these contemporary magical practitioners identify themselves as belonging either to the Left-Hand or Right-Hand Path in Western magic rather than identifying themselves, or allowing themselves to be labeled, as black or white magicians, respectively. Making the distinction between Left-Hand Path and Right-Hand Path magic instead of categorizing magic rigidly as black or white lessens the automatic stereotyping tendency of "black = evil" and "white = good" that has existed since ancient times.

Left-Hand Path / Right-Hand Path

Some writers maintain that the demarcation between the so-called Left-Hand or Right-Hand Path in Western magic has an exclusively Eastern origin. The anthropologist Richard Sutcliffe, who has studied contemporary Left-Hand Path magic in Britain, states quite specifically in a recently published article that "the notion of the Left-Hand Path is derived from the Tantric term *vama-marga* ('left path') i.e., the Left-Hand Path in Tantrism." Sutcliffe identifies the core practices of this occult path as the so-called five m's: *madya*, *mamsa*, *matsya*, *mudra*, and *maithuna*, that is, wine, flesh, fish, parched grain, and intercourse, and notes that these "involve the ritual transgression of certain taboos and incorporate ritual sexual intercourse."[7] He also notes that contemporary occultism has incorporated many ideas and techniques from both Tantrism and Yoga.[8] Sutcliffe is undoubtedly correct in stating that Eastern mystical terms and concepts have been introduced to the Western esoteric tradition—a case in point is Crowley's visit to Ceylon in 1901, where he was introduced to Tantric practices by his former Golden Dawn associate Allan Bennett.[9] It is also true that the Theosophist Madame H. P. Blavatsky referred to practitioners of the Left-Hand Path when introducing Hindu and Buddhist spiritual concepts to the West in the late nineteenth century.[10] However, the symbolic distinction between right and left as good and evil, respectively, also has ancient Western origins that are quite distinct from the *vama-marga*.

The Latin term for "left," *sinister*, was traditionally associated with evil, and this connotation has persisted into modern times, supported by Christian cosmology. The Gospel of Matthew locates God's followers (the sheep) on the right and non-followers (the goats) on the left-hand side, and in pictures of the Last Judgment the Christian God shows his disciples their heavenly abode with his right hand and points with his left hand to Hell.[11] The Left-Hand Path is therefore considered demonic—"the diabolical and the Earthly path to Hell."[12]

In a comparable manner, a quotation from the Classical period in ancient Greece referring to the hero Asclepius (later considered the founder and god of medicine and healing) employs a similar left/right distinction: "after he (Ascelepius) had become a surgeon, bringing that art to great perfection, he not only saved men from death, but even raised them up from the dead. He received from Athena blood from the veins of the Gorgon. He used blood from the left side for plagues of mankind, and he used that from the right side for healing and to raise up men from the dead."[13]

Occult historian and leading member of the Golden Dawn, Arthur Edward Waite (1857–1942), was one of the first writers to refer to the Brothers of the Left-Hand Path and the Brothers of the Right-Hand Path in modern occult literature. Waite, who was both a devout Roman Catholic and also a practitioner of Kabbalistic ritual theurgy, refers in his *Book of Black Magic and Pacts* (1898) to "the sovereign horror of the Brothers of the Left-Hand Path."[14] He later makes the observation in his *Book of Ceremonial Magic* (1911) that "occult life has been entered by two classes of adepts, who have sometimes been fantastically distinguished as the Brothers of the Right and the Brothers of the Left, transcendental good and transcendental evil being specified as their respective ends."[15] Whether Waite himself subscribed to this viewpoint is uncertain. However, the inference is that the Left-Hand Path in magic has been regarded by many with horror and is best avoided.

Despite the lingering association of the Left-Hand Path with evil, many practitioners aligned with this branch of modern Western magic—namely, Thelemites, Satanists, and also practitioners of contemporary Chaos Magick—nevertheless seem willing to apply this terminology to themselves.[16] The contemporary British-born, German-based Satanist Vexen Crabtree maintains that "the term 'Left-Hand Path' has become an umbrella term of self-designation used by certain contemporary ritual magicians and is usually taken to incorporate practitioners of Thelemic magick (beginning with Aleister Crowley), Tantrik magick and Chaos Magick (inspired by both Crowley and the magickal techniques devised by the occult artist

Austin O. Spare, 1886–1956)."[17] Elsewhere Crabtree adds: "I think all forms of Satanism are [also] considered Left Hand Path," and he quotes contemporary American Satanist Anton LaVey (1930–1997): "Satanism is not a white light religion; it is a religion of the flesh, the mundane, the carnal—all of which are ruled by Satan, the personification of the Left Hand Path."[18]

It has to be acknowledged that there are certain points in common between Crowley's advocacy of libertine individualism and Thelemic sex magick on the one hand, and LaVey's doctrine of carnality on the other (see chapter 7). However, contemporary Satanism and the other branches of the Left-Hand Path are by no means identical to each other, and certain distinctions need to be made. It is significant that Crabtree himself does not identify carnality per se as a key characteristic of Left-Hand Path magic: "The Left Hand Path is solitary, individualistic, personal, based on *self* development, *self* analysis, *self* empowerment [italics in the text]. . . . Frequently called 'evil' and 'dark' by non-Satanic religions, the followers of the Left Hand Path often have to remain in the darkness or face severe persecution from the religions that ironically call themselves 'good.'"[19] The magical aspects identified by Crabtree as characteristic of the Left-Hand Path include an emphasis on free thought (as distinct from dogma), a focus on individualism, the rejection of absolutes and moralism, and an emphasis on the personal rather than the universal.[20]

The contemporary Nordic order Dragon Rouge (founded in 1989), which aligns itself with the so-called Draconian path in magick and shares many points in common with Kenneth Grant's Typhonian branch of the Ordo Templi Orientis in England (see below), similarly identifies itself as belonging to the Left-Hand Path. Dragon Rouge refers to the Left-Hand Path as "the dark side of magic": "The darkness is a mirror of the depths of the soul. All that is hidden inside us, our desires and our fears, is projected on the darkness. . . . We are exploring the nightside tradition on many different levels. . . . Dragon Rouge is a practical magical order in which the individual experience is pivotal. We are focusing on an empirical occultism and a knowledge about the unknown based on experience."[21]

The members of Dragon Rouge also make a clear distinction between the magical paths of Right and Left:

> The philosophy of the dark side is represented by the Left-Hand Path and
> its ideology. The Left-Hand Path is founded around a philosophy which
> defines two main spiritual paths. One is the Right-Hand Path. It is
> evident in most forms of religion and mass movements. Its method is the
> magic of the light and its goal [is] that *the individual melts together with*
> *God* [emphasis added]. The other path is the Left-Hand Path. It
> emphasizes the unique, the deviant and the exclusive. Its method is dark
> magic and antinomianism (going against the grain). The goal is to

become a god. . . . The goal of the . . . magic of Dragon Rouge is self-deification. . . . To become a god means that one has transformed life from being predetermined and predestined by outer conditions, to the stage where one reaches a truly free will. Man becomes a god when he ceases to be a creation and instead becomes a creator.[22]

Dr. Stephen Flowers, a leading member of the Temple of Set in the United States—an offshoot of the Church of Satan—similarly emphasizes self-deification and antinomianism as key characteristics of the Left-Hand Path. Flowers defines self-deification as the "attainment of enlightened (or awakened), independently existing intellect and its relative immortality." This in turn depends on a heightened sense of individualism and "the strength . . . necessary for the desired state of evolution of self . . . attained by means of stages created by the will of the magician, not because he or she was 'divine' to begin with."[23] According to Flowers, antinomianism is also an important characteristic of the Left-Hand Path because magicians following this path have to have "the spiritual courage to identify [themselves] with the cultural norms of 'evil.' There will be an embracing of the symbols of . . . whatever quality the conventional culture fears and loathes."[24]

As noted earlier, it was the controversial magician and former Golden Dawn member Aleister Crowley who first brought these controversial matters to a head through his proclamation of the doctrine of *Thelema*. Crowley's teachings would polarize the Western esoteric tradition from this time onward, seeking to shift the pursuit of ceremonial magic away from the quest for mystical transcendence (or, as the members of the Dragon Rouge express it, "melting into God"), toward the affirmation of the individual human will through acts of sacred sex magic. It was indeed a radical departure although, as I will seek to demonstrate below, some aspects of his doctrine reflect cosmological concepts dating back to the time of the fourth-century Gnostics.

Aleister Crowley and the Magick of the New Aeon

Born at Leamington Spa, Warwickshire, on 12 October 1875, Edward Alexander Crowley was raised in a fundamentalist Plymouth Brethren home and soon developed an antipathy toward Christian belief and morality that would remain with him for his entire life.[25] His father was a prosperous brewer who had retired to Leamington to study the Christian scriptures. Crowley came to despise the Plymouth Brethren primarily on the basis of his unfortunate experiences at the special sect school in Cambridge that he was obliged to attend, which was run by an especially cruel headmaster. Much of his school education was unhappy—marked by poor health and vulnerability to bullying attacks—but after he went up to Trinity College, Cambridge, in 1895 he was able to spend much of his time reading poetry and classical literature as well as confirming his well-earned reputation as a champion chess player. Crowley had an adventurous spirit and would later become an enthusiastic mountaineer, joining an expedition in 1902 to scale the mountain known as Chogo Ri (Mount Godwin-Austin, also referred to as K2)—at the time the highest peak in the world open to European climbers.

Crowley's direct association with the Western esoteric tradition began in London in 1898 with his introduction to George Cecil Jones, a member of the Golden Dawn. By the following year Crowley had also become a close friend of magical initiate Allan Bennett, who for a time rivaled MacGregor Mathers as a dominant figure among the English occultists of the period. Within the Golden Dawn, Bennett had taken the magical name *Frater Iehi Aour* (Hebrew: "Let there be Light"), and he became a mentor to Crowley. For a time Bennett and Crowley shared the latter's Chancery Lane flat in London.[26] It was here that Bennett tutored Crowley on applied Kabbalah and the techniques of magical invocation and evocation, as well as showing him how to create magical talismans.

Crowley quickly grasped the fundamentals of magic—or *magick*, as he would later spell it in his own writings on the subject. In one of his most influential books—*Magick in Theory and Practice*, first published in 1929 and frequently reprinted since—Crowley outlined the basic philosophy of magic as he had come to see it, which in essence involved the process of making man godlike, both in vision and in power. Crowley's magical dictums are instructive because they reveal the particular appeal that magic had for him:

> A man who is doing his True Will has the inertia of the Universe to assist him.[27]
>
> Man is ignorant of the nature of his own being and powers. Even his idea of his limitations is based on an experience of the past and every step in his progress extends his empire. There is therefore no reason to assign theoretical limits to what he may be or what he may do.[28]
>
> Man is capable of being and using anything which he perceives, for everything that he perceives is in a certain sense a part of his being. He may thus subjugate the whole Universe of which he is conscious to his individual will.[29]
>
> The Microcosm is an exact image of the Macrocosm; the Great Work is the raising of the whole man in perfect balance to the power of Infinity.[30]
>
> There is a single main definition of the object of all magical Ritual. It is the uniting of the Microcosm with the Macrocosm. The Supreme and

Complete Ritual is therefore the Invocation of the Holy Guardian Angel, or, in the language of Mysticism, Union with God.[31]

Crowley was initiated as a Neophyte in the Golden Dawn on 18 November 1898. He soon came to appreciate that those with the loftiest ritual grades in the Order (especially Mathers and Westcott—see chapter 2) were able to wield profound spiritual influence over their followers by claiming rapport with the so-called Secret Chiefs, whose authority was said to emanate from higher planes of spiritual reality.[32] Keen to ascend to as high a rank as possible, Crowley took the grade of Zelator and then Theoricus and Practicus in the following two months. Initiation into the grade of Philosophus followed in May 1899. Greatly enthused by his magical research under the tutelage of Allan Bennett, Crowley also began making preparations for a substantial magical working based on the fifteenth-century rituals of Abramelin the Mage, described in a grimoire that had been translated from French into English by MacGregor Mathers and that George Cecil Jones had introduced him to a year earlier.[33] Apart from allegedly providing the magician with the services of 316 spirit-advisers, the Abramelin system of magic was also said to grant the practitioner communion with the Holy Guardian Angel, an embodiment in visionary form of one's higher spiritual self. However, Crowley believed there was another potential benefit: such an experience would enable him to claim spiritual parity with Mathers in the Golden Dawn hierarchy.

Crowley delayed the actual performance of his Abramelin operation but, after attaining the grade of Philosophus within the Golden Dawn, contacted Mathers in Paris and requested ritual entry into the Second Order—the Red Rose and the Cross of Gold. In January 1900, under Mathers's direct supervision, Crowley was admitted "to the Glory of Tiphareth"—the 5°= 6° Adeptus Minor ritual grade associated with the experience of spiritual rebirth. He then returned to England, where he challenged the authority of William Butler Yeats, who at the time was the leader of the Golden Dawn in England. As mentioned earlier, Yeats was unimpressed by this effrontery, and Crowley was unsuccessful in his bid for ritual supremacy. The dispute, however, caused a rift in loyalties among the Golden Dawn membership, since Crowley had apparently been sent by Mathers—and Mathers, in a letter to influential Golden Dawn member Annie Horniman, had earlier claimed spiritual autocracy and infallibility over the Order as his right.

Having failed to dislodge Yeats as the head of the Golden Dawn, Crowley now suddenly switched course. Unpredictably and apparently acting on pure impulse, he withdrew from the dispute altogether and in June 1900 embarked upon a series of travels through Mexico, the United States, France, Ceylon, and India before finally arriving in Cairo with his wife Rose on 9 February 1904.[34] Crowley's entire conception of the magical universe was about to be dramatically transformed.

FIGURE 4.1. Crowley with his first wife, Rose, and daughter, Lola Zaza,
photographed in 1910

Crowley's Thelemic Revelation

The Thelemic practice of sex magick derives specifically from a transformative
spiritual event that occurred during Crowley's visit to Cairo in 1904. Crowley
would come to believe that the revelatory communication itself emanated from
the ancient Egyptian gods, via an entity named Aiwass (or Aiwaz) whom Crowley believed to be a messenger from Horus.[35] Paradoxically, Crowley's personal

revelation would also come to acquire a quasi-biblical orientation, for it led him to regard himself henceforth as the Beast 666 referred to in the Book of Revelation.[36] Crowley's life and career as a ceremonial magician would subsequently focus on the ongoing personal quest to find the ideal Whore of Babalon (Crowley's variant spelling) or Scarlet Woman, with whom to enact the philosophy of *Thelema*, or magical will.[37] According to the doctrine of *Thelema*, Crowley's sex-magick encounters with his Scarlet Women—there would be many more than one!—were sacramental acts confirming Crowley's role as Lord of the New Aeon.

On 17 March 1904, Crowley performed a magical ceremony in his apartment in Cairo, invoking the Egyptian deity Thoth, god of wisdom.[38] Crowley's wife Rose appeared to be in a dazed, mediumistic state of mind and, the following day, while in a similar state of drowsiness, she announced that Horus was waiting for her husband. Crowley was not expecting such a statement from his wife, but according to his diary she subsequently led him to the nearby Boulak Museum, which he had not previously visited.[39] Rose pointed to a statue of Horus, or Ra-Hoor-Khuit, and Crowley was intrigued to discover that the exhibit was numbered 666, the number of the Great Beast in the Book of Revelation. Crowley regarded this as an omen. He returned to his hotel and invoked Horus:

> Strike, strike the master chord!
> Draw, draw the Flaming Sword!
> Crowning Child and Conquering Lord,
> Horus, avenger![40]

On 20 March 1904, Crowley received a mediumistic communication through Rose stating that "the Equinox of the Gods had come,"[41] and he arranged for an assistant curator at the Boulak Museum to make notes on the inscriptions from Stele 666. Rose continued to fall into a passive, introspective state of mind and advised her husband that precisely at noon on April 8, 9, and 10 he should enter the room where the transcriptions had been made, and for exactly an hour on each of these three days he should write down any impressions received. The resulting communications, allegedly dictated by a semi-invisible Egyptian entity named Aiwass—said to be a messenger of Horus—resulted in a document that Crowley later titled *Liber Al vel Legis* (The Book of the Law).[42]

The pronouncements contained in *Liber Al vel Legis* became a turning point in Crowley's magical career. Crowley was specifically commanded by Aiwass to put aside the Kabbalistic ceremonial magic he had learned in the Hermetic Order of the Golden Dawn and was instructed to pursue the magic of sexual partnership instead: "Now ye shall know that the chosen priest and apostle of infinite space is the prince-priest The Beast, and in his woman called The Scarlet Woman is all power given. They shall gather my children into their fold: they shall bring the glory of the stars into the hearts of men. For he is ever a sun and she a moon."[43]

Crowley would soon come to believe that his magical destiny was inextricably connected to the Horus figure Ra-Hoor-Khuit whose statue he had seen in the Boulak Museum. In Egyptian mythology, the deities Nuit (female-the circle-passive) and Hadit (male-the point-active) were said to have produced a divine child, Ra-Hoor-Khuit, through their sacred union. According to Crowley, this combination of the principles of love and will brought into incarnation the "magical equation known as the Law of Thelema."[44] *Thelema* is the Greek word for "will," and the principal magical dictum contained in *Liber Al vel Legis* is "Do what thou wilt shall be the whole of the Law." The concluding instruction in *Liber Al vel Legis* reads as follows: "There is no law beyond Do what thou wilt. Love is the law, love under will."[45]

Crowley's notion of the will, or Will—he usually capitalized it to denote its special significance—is central to his magical philosophy. Crowley understood that one should live according to the dictates of one's true Will because "A man who is doing his True Will has . . . the Universe to assist him."[46] An individual's True Will is that person's authentic spiritual purpose, and it also confers a sense of identity. "The first principle of success in evolution," wrote Crowley in *Magick in Theory and Practice*, "is that the individual should be true to his own nature."[47]

Crowley believed that in terms of his own individual spiritual purpose, his unique personal destiny had been made manifestly clear by the communications received from Aiwass in *Liber Al vel Legis*. As Crowley's magical disciple Kenneth Grant has written, from a Thelemic perspective the revelations in Cairo in 1904 represented nothing less than the birth of a new Aeon in the history of humanity's spiritual evolution:

> According to Crowley the true magical revival occurred in 1904, when an occult current of cosmic magnitude was initiated on the inner planes. Its focus was Aiwaz and it was transmitted through Crowley to the human plane. . . . The initiation of this occult current created a vortex, the birth-pangs of a New Aeon, technically called an Equinox of the Gods. Such an event recurs at intervals of approximately 2000 years. Each such revival of magical power establishes a further link in the chain of humanity's evolution, which is but one phase only of the evolution of Consciousness.[48]

In cosmological terms, Crowley believed he had now been recognized by the transcendent powers of the ancient Egyptian pantheon as the "divine child" brought into being through the sacred union of Nuit and Hadit. There could be no doubting the importance of this event and its dramatic outcome. In *Liber Al vel*

Legis we read, "Ra-Hoor-Khuit hath taken his seat in the East at the Equinox of the Gods."[49] Previously, according to Crowley, there had been two other Aeons: one associated with the Moon and the other with the Sun. The first of these, the Aeon of Isis, was a matriarchal age characterized by the worship of lunar deities; the second epoch, the Aeon of Osiris, was a patriarchal age associated with incarnating demigods or divine kings. John Symonds, Crowley's principal biographer and literary executor, describes this historical process in his introduction to Crowley's *Confessions*:

> The cosmology of *The Book of the Law* is explained by Crowley thus:
> there have been, as far as we know, two aeons in the history of the world.
> The first, that of Isis, is the aeon of the woman; hence matriarchy, the
> worship of the Great Mother and so on. About 500 B.C. this aeon was
> succeeded by the aeon of Osiris, that is the aeon of the man, the father,
> hence the paternal religions of suffering and death—Judaism, Buddhism,
> Christianity and Mohammedanism. This aeon came to an end in 1904
> when Aleister Crowley received *The Book of the Law*, and the new aeon,
> that of Horus, the child, was born. In this aeon the emphasis is on the
> true self or will, not on anything external such as gods or priests.[50]

There can be no doubting the position of *Liber Al vel Legis* with regard to the religious traditions that preceded the 1904 revelation. "With my Hawk's head," proclaims Ra-Hoor-Khuit (i.e., Horus) in stanzas III: 51–54 "I peck at the eyes of Jesus as he hangs upon the Cross. I flap my wings in the face of Mohammed and blind him. With my claws I tear out the flesh of the Indian and the Buddhist, Mongol and Din. Bahlasti! Ompedha! I spit on your crapulous creeds."[51]

Quite apart from the iconoclastic tone adopted by *Liber Al vel Legis* in dismissing earlier such religious traditions as Christianity, Buddhism, and Islam, the sexual implications of the revelation were also made clear. The received doctrine of the Aeon of Horus would now supersede Christianity and all the other outmoded religions that had constructed barriers to spiritual freedom, and the way this would be achieved was through the power of sexuality. *Liber Al vel Legis* summons the Scarlet Woman to "raise herself in pride!" and calls for uninhibited sexual freedom: "Let her work the work of wickedness! Let her kill her heart! Let her be loud and adulterous; let her be covered with jewels, and rich garments, and let her be shameless before all men. Then will I lift her to the pinnacles of power: then will I breed from her a child mightier than all the kings of the earth. I will fill her with joy."[52]

As Kenneth Grant has explained with reference to *Liber Al vel Legis* and its call for sexual freedom, Crowley came to believe that the so-called Great Work—sacred union, or the attainment of Absolute Consciousness—would be achieved through the sexual union of the Great Beast with the Whore of Babalon: "The Beast, as the

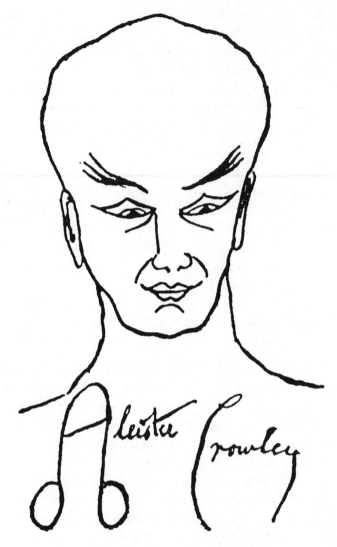

FIGURE 4.2. A Crowley self-portrait, with his phallic signature

embodiment of the Logos (which is Thelema, Will) symbolically and actually incarnates his Word each time a sacramental act of sexual congress occurs, i.e., each time love is made under Will."[53] A review of Crowley's subsequent career shows that he would spend much of his life from this time onward seeking lovers and concubines who could act as his Divine Whore. Although he would be frustrated in his numerous attempts to find a suitable and enduring partner, there were many who filled the role temporarily.[54]

In relation to the practice of sex magic, quite apart from defining Crowley's spiritual destiny as the high priest of *Thelema*, *Liber Al vel Legis* also contained instructions relating to ceremonial offerings associated with sacramental sex magic, specifically the preparation of what later came to be known as "cakes of light." Preparation of this ritual offering as specified by Ra-Hoor-Khuit, is outlined in III: 23–25 of *Liber Al vel Legis*:

> For perfume mix meal and honey and thick leavings of red wine: then oil
> of Abramelin and olive oil, and afterward soften and smooth down with
> rich fresh blood. The best blood is of the moon, monthly: then the fresh
> blood of a child, or dropping from the host of heaven: then of enemies;
> then of the priest or of the worshippers; last of some beast, no matter
> what. This burn: of this make cakes and eat unto me.[55]

As one of Crowley's most recent biographers, Lawrence Sutin, has noted: "There is no evidence that Crowley ever used the fresh blood of a child or an enemy in preparing the cakes. Indeed, in his comment on this verse, written during the period, Crowley was careful to specify that the 'child' was 'Babalon and the Beast conjoined'—that is, the elixir of sexual magic."[56] The magical elixir itself consisted of the "ingredients" of sexual congress itself: semen from the male, gluten from the woman's vagina, and preferably fresh menstrual blood, as specified in stanza 24 of Book III of *Liber Al vel Legis*. These ingredients were included in the preparation of the "cakes of light," which were then consumed by participants as a ritual offering to Ra-Hoor-Khuit.

It is clear that Crowley placed great emphasis on the magical elixir because it is later referred to as "the germ of life" in *The Book of the Unveiling of Sangraal*, which was part of the "Secret Instruction of the Ninth Degree" in the Ordo Templi Orientis (O.T.O.)—a European sex magic organization which Crowley was able to gradually transform into a Thelemite order after joining it in 1910 (see below).[57] In the Ninth degree of the Ordo Templi Orientis, which employs veiled sexual references, the candidate is instructed as follows:

> Now then, entering the privy chapel [the vagina], do thou bestow at least
> one hour in adoration at the altar, exalting thyself in love toward God,

and extolling Him in strophe and antistrophe [sexual lovemaking]. Then
do thou perform the Sacrifice of the Mass [ejaculation of semen]. The
Elixir [a mixture of semen and female sexual secretions] being then
prepared solemnly and in silence, do thou consume it utterly.[58]

The ritual consumption of a sexual magical elixir was not part of the magical
teachings of the Hermetic Order of the Golden Dawn, which tended to downplay
any references to sexual symbolism in its rituals.[59] And since Crowley had established his own unique connection with Aiwass and Ra-Hoor Khuit in 1904, he had
little need for an ongoing relationship with the Golden Dawn after his revelation in
Cairo. In deciding to enact the magical procedures dictated by *Liber Al vel Legis*,
Crowley had, in any case, already laid the foundation for a quite different sort of
magical practice based not on advancing through the *sephiroth* of the Kabbalistic
Tree of Life but instead on utilizing the magical energies of sexuality.

The Argenteum Astrum and Victor Neuburg

In 1907, Crowley established his own magical order, the Argenteum Astrum, or
Silver Star.[60] Two years later he commenced production of a semi-annual period-
ical titled *The Equinox* as its official publishing arm. Some of the early issues of *The
Equinox* contained Crowley's first writings on sex magic rituals.[61] In these writings,
Crowley identified three types of sexual activity—autoerotic, heterosexual, and
homosexual—as a way of raising magical energy, and he also formulated the notion
that sex magic rituals could be dedicated to achieving specific results like financial
gain, attaining personal creative success, and so forth. His central idea was that sex
magic could enable the practitioner to focus on a specific goal or outcome. The
magician would dedicate the sexual activity to the goal of the magical ritual and
would hold the image of that goal in his mind at the moment of sexual climax: at
that very moment the energy raised during the ritual would be directed to the goal
by the magical will. In this way, the sex magic practitioner would be able to "wed
the image and the magical power."[62]

Initially, the Argenteum Astrum drew primarily on borrowed sources from the
Hermetic Order of the Golden Dawn. Crowley had began rewriting MacGregor
Mathers's Kabbalistic rituals, employing an amended form of the Golden Dawn
grades as well as including some yogic and oriental material of his own. He also
published the secret rituals of Mathers's Second Order, the Red Rose and Cross of
Gold, in *The Equinox*.[63] Interestingly, although Crowley had made a commitment
to the sex magic proclaimed in *Liber Al vel Legis*, he did not initially include it
within the grades of his new magical order.[64] Nevertheless, the Argenteum Astrum

would gradually develop as a vehicle for Crowley's increasingly explicit bisexuality, thereby complicating the apparently clear sex-role distinction between the Beast and the Scarlet Woman delineated in *Liber Al vel Legis*.[65]

One of the early members of the Argenteum Astrum was Victor Neuburg (1883–1940), a young poet who, like Crowley, had studied at Trinity College, Cambridge. Crowley heard about Neuburg from another A.A. member, Captain J.F.C. Fuller, and invited him to his magical retreat in Boleskine, Scotland. Crowley quickly recognized in Neuburg a kindred spirit, and they would soon enter into a homosexual magic liaison tinged with sado-masochistic tendencies, which would last until 1914.[66]

Following a painful divorce from his wife Rose in 1909, Crowley went with Neuburg to Algeria, where they intended to explore the Enochian magic of the sixteenth-century Elizabethan occultists Dr. John Dee and Edward Kelley.[67] This process involved the magical evocation of thirty so-called Aethyrs or Aires—a group of metaphysical spirit-entities that included Choronzon, the demon of Chaos. Deep in the Algerian desert—at such locations as Aumale, Ain El Hajel, Bou-Saada, Benshrur, Tolga, and Biskra—Crowley summoned the different Aethyrs in turn. Crowley was carrying with him a large golden topaz set in a wooden rose-cross decorated with ritual symbols. Choosing a place of solitude, Crowley would recite the required Enochian conjuration and then use his topaz as a focusing glass to concentrate his attention on the visionary landscape as it unfolded before his gaze. As a result of his Enochian "calls," Crowley had a number of visionary experiences that were then transcribed by Neuburg as they took place.[68]

While in the Algerian desert, Crowley and Neuburg also engaged in an act of ritual sex magic. Crowley writes in his *Confessions* that on one occasion they climbed a mountain named Da'leh Addin and felt an intuitive command to perform a magical ceremony on the summit:

> We accordingly took loose rocks and built a great circle, inscribed with
> the words of power; and in the midst we erected an altar and there I
> sacrificed myself [submitted to anal sex]. The fire of the all-seeing sun
> [Neuburg's penis] smote down upon the altar, consuming every particle
> of my personality. I am obliged to write in hieroglyph of this matter,
> because it concerns things of which it is unlawful to speak openly under
> penalty of the most dreadful punishment.[69]

After Crowley returned to England, the Argenteum Astrum began to grow modestly, building on its core membership, which included Captain J.F.C. Fuller and Crowley's Golden Dawn teacher George Cecil Jones. The Argenteum Astrum would in due course initiate around a hundred of Crowley's followers, among them Neuburg's friend and fellow poet Pamela Hansford Johnson, Australian violinist

Leila Waddell, mathematics lecturer Norman Mudd from Bloemfontein, and the visionary English artist Austin Osman Spare.[70]

Events took a strange turn in London in May 1912, when Crowley was contacted one evening at his Fulham flat by a man named Theodor Reuss. Reuss identified himself as Brother Merlin, head of the German branch of the Ordo Templi Orientis. Crowley would already have been familiar with the O.T.O. because, according to occult historian Francis King, he had been admitted to its lower grades a year earlier.[71] What surprised the British occultist was Reuss's claim that Crowley had published a statement which revealed the most prized secret of the Order's ninth degree—the sacrament of sex magic.[72] Crowley was initially perplexed by Reuss's accusation and wondered which publication he was referring to. Reuss then reached across to Crowley's bookshelf and pulled down a copy of his recently published work *The Book of Lies*, a collection of magical commentaries and reflections. The offending lines were contained in Chapter XXXVI titled "The Star Sapphire," which begins with the words: "Let the Adept be armed with his Magick Rood and provided with his Mystic Rose." Further on, Crowley's text reads as follows: "Let him drink of the Sacrament and let him communicate the same."[73]

Crowley pointed out to Reuss that he had not yet been admitted to the ninth degree of the O.T.O, so he was not in a position to reveal its secrets. In "The Star Sapphire," Crowley had used the Old English word *rood* to mean a cross, and Reuss had assumed that he was referring to the phallus. Reuss had also assumed that the Mystic Rose was a reference to the vagina.[74] Then there was the issue of what "drinking the Sacrament" could actually be referring to. As they were speaking, Crowley realized intuitively that sexual intercourse between priest and priestess must be a culminating event in the ritual of the O.T.O's ninth degree, and he now engaged Reuss in a discussion about sex magic that lasted for several hours. The outcome was that Crowley would in due course become the head of a new magical order to be called the Mysteria Mystica Maxima, effectively an English subsidiary of the German Ordo Templi Orientis.[75] Much later, in 1922—following Reuss's retirement—Crowley would replace Reuss as the head of the O.T.O. itself, a position he held until his death in 1947.[76]

The Rise of the Ordo Templi Orientis

Although the practice of sex magic was central to Aleister Crowley's doctrine of *Thelema*, it did not originate with him. In recent times, the rise of the O.T.O and the history of sex magic as a branch of Western esotericism have been documented by a small group of specialist academic scholars, among them Peter R. Koenig in

Switzerland, Hugh B. Urban, Joscelyn Godwin, John Deveney and J. Gordon Melton in the United States, and Henrik Bogdan in Sweden.

From a historical perspective it is clear that the two key figures in the early development of the O.T.O in Europe were Carl Kellner and Crowley's German O.T.O. contact, Theodor Reuss. Kellner (1851–1905) was a wealthy Austrian chemist and industrialist and also a Freemason—he was a member of the Humanitas Lodge, established in Neuhäusl, Austria, in 1871 under the constitution of the Grand Lodge of Hungary. Reuss (1855–1923) was an Anglo-German Freemason who specialized in buying and selling Masonic charters, even though he was not recognized by any authentic lodges in Craft Masonry. According to Koenig, Reuss invented an organization known as the Order of the Illuminati as well as several Rosicrucian societies. While it is evident that Kellner was a businessman and inventor of considerable integrity, Reuss's reputation was more dubious, and some historians consider him a swindler. Nevertheless, it was through their joint efforts that the organization known as the Ordo Templi Orientis (O.T.O.) would eventually emerge.[77]

Around 1895, Kellner had the idea of forming a private group that could explore various "Tantric" exercises within a Hatha Yoga circle.[78] Kellner had a long-standing interest in both the Western esoteric tradition and Eastern mysticism. According to Urban, Kellner is said to have studied with three Eastern masters—a Sufi and two Hindu Tantrikers—and was also in touch with an American esoteric order known as the Hermetic Brotherhood of Light (an offshoot of the Hermetic Brotherhood of Luxor), which in turn drew on the sex magic ideas of the influential American occultist Paschal Beverly Randolph (see below).[79] Kellner and Reuss had in mind that they would form a new esoteric order that would fuse Craft Masonry, Rosicrucianism, and Hindu Tantra.[80] Urban maintains that at the time Kellner was one of the few Western figures with a detailed knowledge of Yoga, and that he regarded "white sexual magic" as a source of godlike power. Kellner performed Tantric rites with his wife and a small group of disciples in order to produce the so-called divine Elixir—an amalgam of male and female sexual fluids.[81]

Like Kellner, Reuss was also interested in phallic cults and Tantra, and would later produce a treatise on sexual worship titled *Lingam-Yoni*.[82] He believed that sexual congress mirrored the cosmic act of creation and that the lingam, or phallus, was a key symbol of the creator of the universe.[83] Urban argues that it was Reuss who incorporated sexual magic into the upper grades of the O.T.O.[84] Unfortunately, Kellner did not live to see the actual establishment of the new esoteric organization. He became terminally ill in 1904 and died the following year. Reuss was forced to act on his own, recruiting a range of "Oriental Freemasons" for the new Order and eventually naming it the Order of Oriental Templars (Ordo Templi Orientis).[85] With the assistance of Franz Hartmann and Heinrich Klein, Reuss prepared a constitution for the O.T.O. in 1906.[86]

Koenig maintains that Reuss never intended that the O.T.O would become a vehicle for Crowley's doctrine of *Thelema*.[87] However, Reuss was sufficiently impressed by Crowley's ideas that he translated the latter's sex-magick ritual, the *Gnostic Mass* (composed 1913), into German and had it recited at a special O.T.O congress at Monte Verità.[88] Reuss also announced at the same congress that he was translating Crowley's *Book of the Law* into German. Crowley reciprocated the gesture by publishing several major O.T.O. documents in *The Equinox*, among them *Liber LII: the Manifesto of the O.T.O.*[89]

In his *Confessions*, Crowley states that Reuss "resigned the office [of the Outer Head of the Order] in 1922 in my favour," although even in the official O.T.O History it is conceded that that no evidence or letter from Reuss has ever been found confirming this claim.[90] Nevertheless, Crowley succeeded Reuss as O.H.O. (Outer Head of the Order) in 1922 and would hold this position until his death in 1947.

Under Crowley, the O.T.O.'s original nine degrees were expanded to eleven. The eighth, ninth, and eleventh degrees focused on non-reproductive sexual acts including masturbation, the consumption of sexual fluids (referred to above as the "magical elixir"), and homosexual intercourse.[91] Koenig notes that other elements of Crowleyan sex magic, in addition to the ritual consumption of semen and vaginal fluids, were incorporated into the rites of the O.T.O. at this time. They included various forms of sexual visualization and the act of masturbating on magical sigils:

> Crowley's VIIIth degree unveiled . . . that masturbating on a sigil of a
> demon or meditating upon the image of a phallus would bring power or
> communication with a [or one's own] divine being. . . . The IXth degree
> was labelled heterosexual intercourse where the sexual secrets were
> sucked out of the vagina and when not consumed . . . put on a sigil to
> attract this or that demon to fulfil the pertinent wish. . . . In the XIth
> degree, the mostly homosexual degree, one identifies oneself with an
> ejaculating penis. The blood (or excrements) from anal intercourse
> attract the spirits/demons while the sperm keeps them alive.[92]

Crowley's Writings on Sex Magic

Crowley produced several short texts on sex magic, some of which are written in veiled symbolic language. These texts include *De Arte Magica* (written in 1914 and also translated and published in Reuss's German-language O.T.O. magazine, *Oriflamme*, in the same year); *Liber Agape*; *Energized Enthusiasm: A Note on Theurgy*; and the notorious, but blandly titled *Emblems and Modes of Use*. Crowley's *Gnostic Mass* and the *Mass of the Phoenix* also contain sex magic references. Despite their often discursive language and veiled symbolism, these texts provide intriguing insights into Crowley's philosophy and practice of sex magic.

De Arte Magica was intended as a document for Ninth degree O.T.O candidates. After reminding the reader that "the Phallus is the physiological basis of the Oversoul"—a statement with which Reuss would surely have agreed—Crowley goes on to describe sex magic methods drawn from both the Jewish Kabbalah and the Hindu spiritual tradition.[93] With regard to the former, Crowley states that "in the semen itself . . . lies a creative life which cannot be baulked." According to Jewish teachings, says Crowley, conjugal love should be a holy act, preceded by ablutions and prayer: "All lustful thoughts must be rigidly excluded, the purpose must be solely that of procreation [and] the blessing of God must be most earnestly invoked."[94] However, Crowley was also interested in the magical consequences of other types of sexual act:

> All other sexual acts involving emission of semen . . . attract other spirits,
> incomplete and therefore evil . . . nocturnal pollutions bring succubi,
> which are capable of separate existence and of vampirising their creator.
> But voluntary sterile acts create demons, and (if done with concentration
> and magical intention) such demons . . . may subserve that intention.[95]

Crowley also makes reference to the Hindu concept that *prana* or life-force "resides in the *Bindu*, or semen." Certain yogic practitioners, writes Crowley, are able to

> stimulate to the maximum its [i.e., the sperm's] generation, and at the
> same time vigorously withhold by will. After some little exercise they
> claim that they can deflower as many as eighty virgins in a night without
> losing a single drop of the Bindu. Nor is this ever to be lost, but
> reabsorbed through the tissues of the body. The organs thus act as a
> siphon to draw constantly fresh supplies of life from the cosmic
> reservoir, and flood the body with their fructifying virtue . . . in the
> semen itself exists a physical force which can be turned to [the] magical
> or mystical ends of the Adept.[96]

Here we have a clear expression of the concept that the individual human will can harness the life-force in semen and direct it to a specific magical purpose. Writings like *Liber Agape* and *Energized Enthusiasm: A Note on Theurgy*, on the other hand, are much more obscure: they contain veiled symbolism and require more detailed scrutiny. *Liber Agape* is also known as *The Book of the Unveiling of the Sangraal* and was intended as "a secret instruction of the Ninth degree" in the O.T.O.[97]

Liber Agape begins with a prayer, a salutation to Baphomet, and a statement implying that the Ninth degree of the O.T.O. will reveal occult secrets hitherto associated with the Knights of the Temple (Knights Templar) and the "Brethren of the Rose Crosse."[98] The rite itself is described as a "High Mass to be celebrated in the Temple of the Holy Ghost." Crowley also employs alchemical imagery in his text, making reference to the Medicine of Metals, the Philosopher's Stone, Tinctures White and Red, and the Elixir of Life. The latter two are clearly intended as sexual images. As mentioned earlier, the Elixir of Life refers to the sexual fluids produced and comingled in the vagina through sexual intercourse. The white tincture is also described elsewhere in Crowley's sex magic writings as the "Gluten of the White Eagle" and is a reference to the sexual fluids (and sometimes also the menstrual blood) of the female participant in sex magic.[99] The red tincture is the "Blood of the Red Lion," a reference to the semen generated by the male participant (Crowley often linked blood symbolically with semen).[100]

Interestingly, *Liber Agape* incorporates within its structure the text of *The Star Sapphire* (previously published as chapter 36 of *The Book of Lies*)—the short work which Theodor Reuss believed betrayed the innermost secret of the Ninth degree of the O.T.O. (see above). We are fortunate that a commentary on *The Star Sapphire* has recently been made available by American ceremonial magician Frater Osiris, a former member of the O.T.O., who was privy to the inner-Order Thelemic interpretation of the text.[101]

While it is clear at the outset that *The Star Sapphire* is intended as a sex-magic tract, and it comes as no surprise that the *Magick Rood* is the phallus, and the *Mystic Rose* is the vagina, it is perhaps less obvious that the reference to "make the Holy Hexagram" is an instruction that the man and woman should interlock their heads and bodies in a mutual oral sex position to form the shape of a hexagram.[102] Crowley provides a clue in the aptly numbered chapter 69 of *The Book of Lies*, where he refers to the Holy Hexagram and the "Double Gift of Tongues."[103] Frater Osiris explains that "Making the Rosy Cross" is also a reference to sexual intercourse and the participants should utter the magical exclamation *Ararita* three times at the moment of orgasm. The instruction "Let him drink of the Sacrament and let him communicate the same" is an instruction that the "sacrament"—the "elixir" or fluids arising from sexual intercourse—should be consumed by both participants, each providing this elixir to the other. As Frater Osiris notes, "It is suggested elsewhere in Crowley's writings that the Sacrament be dissolved and absorbed in the mouth to obtain the fullest effect."[104]

Energized Enthusiasm: A Note on Theurgy (Liber DCCCLX)—a work dedicated to "IAO, the supreme One of the Gnostics, the true God"[105]—is one of Crowley's most interesting writings on sex magic, combining didactic content with a seemingly autobiographical, yet highly symbolic, narrative written in the first person. Crowley begins by introducing the reader to the idea that divine consciousness is "reflected and refracted" in works of Genius (capitalized in Crowley's text) and in turn feeds on "a certain secretion . . . analogous to semen, but not identical to it."[106] Later Crowley claims that he can always trace a connection between his sexual state and "the condition of [his] artistic creation" and that what he calls "energized enthusiasm" is "the lever that moves God." In other words, there is a technique of ecstasy, heightened by sexuality, which is directly related to artistic creativity and Genius, and this is a technique that subjects God to the artistic intent and human will. We will encounter a similar concept in the artistic and magical trance-method of Austin Osman Spare, which is described in chapter 5. Spare was briefly a member of Crowley's O.T.O. circa 1910, but seems to have formulated his ideas independently. Both men believed that they could use the transcendent power of the sexual orgasm to subject the visionary universe to their own individual will in order to bring about a desired result—artistic or otherwise. In *Energized Enthusiasm*, Crowley writes quite specifically that through "the sacramental and ceremonial use of the sexual act, the divine consciousness may be attained."[107]

Later in the same work (which consists of sixteen short chapters), Crowley describes a sex-magick ceremony of the Rose Croix. The ceremony—which is presented in Crowley's text as taking place in a mystical vision—is a High Mass and is conducted in a private chapel. The altar is covered by a cloth which displays the symbols of the Rose and Cross, and at the entrance of the chapel stand a young man and woman "dressed in simple robes of white silk embroidered with gold, red and blue." The high priest presiding over the ceremony is a man of about sixty, with a white beard, and he is accompanied by a high priestess. Both wear richly ornamented robes, have a "stately" presence, and embrace each other. Knights and dames make up the congregation. The chapel is consecrated, the litany begins, and the high priest takes from the altar a flask that resembles a phallus—an indication that the ceremony about to be performed has a sexual orientation. The high priestess then kneels and presents a boat-shaped cup of gold (the cup, as a receptive vessel, being traditionally perceived in the Western esoteric tradition as a female symbol, especially in the sexual sense). The high priest's flask contains wine that looks like fire but which is cool to drink. Crowley somehow receives this as a sacrament—he is an onlooker at the ceremony and feels he is experiencing this sacred rite while in a mystical out-of-the-body state.[108] Crowley writes that he trembles as he consumes this sacred drink, as do other members of the congregation—for the ritual is charged with sacred meaning. In due course the celebrants move down the chapel aisle, and the knights and dames rise up and give the secret sign of the Rose Croix. The high priestess discards her robe, stands naked before the congregation, and begins to sing: "Io Paian! Io Pan! . . ." A sacred mist now rises up around the participants, heightening the sense of mystery as organ music wafts through the chapel, and the high priest joins his partner at the altar of the Rose Croix, where they both lie down. The celebrants, meanwhile, stretch forth their arms in the shape of a cross.

Presumably the "Great Rite" is about to be performed by the high priest and high priestess—Crowley does not provide us with the details of what happens next. However, given (as Frater Osiris has already explained above) that in the O.T.O. "Making the Rosy Cross" is a reference to ritual sexual intercourse, it would seem that Crowley's High Mass of the Rose Croix is analogous to the mystic marriage of the alchemical King Sol and Queen Luna, who consummate their sacred union and thereby create the "Elixir of Life."[109]

Crowley's Thelemic sex-magick ritual, the *Gnostic Mass* (*Liber XV, Ecclesiae Gnosticae Catholicae Canon Missae*), composed in 1913, is linked thematically to *Energized Enthusiasm* and was written around the same time. The *Gnostic Mass*— Crowley's Thelemic (and perhaps also blasphemous) response to the Roman Catholic Eucharist—employs specific sexual motifs and draws on the theme of transubstantiation. Although other minor characters play a part, the Mass focuses on two central figures, the priest, who bears the Sacred Lance (a symbol of the phallus) and the priestess, who in this ritual context is deemed to be Virgo Intacta and is identified symbolically with the Holy Graal (the sacred Cup). During the Consecration of the Elements, the priest gives a blessing and oversees the transubstantiation of the cakes of light ("By the virtue of the Rod / Be this bread the Body of God!") and wine ("By the virtue of the Rod / Be this wine the Blood of God"), and during the Mystic Marriage and Consummation the priest and priestess jointly lower the Sacred Lance into Cup in a symbolic expression of sexual union. All congregants then partake of the consecrated cakes of light, which contain the sexual elixir and which are said to embody "the essence of the life of the Sun."[110]

The Mass of the Phoenix (*Liber XLIV*), by way of contrast, is a simplified form of the Eucharist intended for daily life by the practicing Thelemic magician.[111] Despite its simpler form, Crowley nevertheless considered it to be just as significant as the *Gnostic Mass*.[112] *The Mass of the Phoenix* derives its name from the mythical phoenix, an alchemical symbol of transmutation and resurrection. The phoenix was said to feed its young on blood drawn from its own breast. First published as chapter 44 of *The Book of Lies* (1912), the Mass is performed only at sunset and is undertaken as a solitary ceremonial activity. At the climax of the ritual, the magician makes the Mark of the Beast on his (or her) breast, either drawing blood directly with a burin (a small sharp knife) or by cutting a finger and inscribing the sign in blood.[113] A cake of light is used to staunch the blood and is then ritually consumed.[114]

Crowley's most controversial work on sex magic, however, is a short four-page article titled *Emblems and Modes of Use*, which was intended as a secret text for the Ninth degree of the O.T.O.[115] Once again, Crowley utilizes alchemical imagery, writing that the Egg (Emblem 1) is borne by the "menstruum [that] the Alchemists call the Gluten [capitals in Crowley's text]." The Egg will be fertilized by the Serpent

(Emblem 2). Crowley says that the Serpent is "the principle of immortality, the self renewal through incarnation, of persistent will, inherent in the 'Red Lion' *who is, of course, the operator*."[116] Crowley writes that "both Lion and Eagle must be robust, in good health ... overflowing with energy, magnetically attracted to one another, and in absolute understanding [and] harmony about the object of the operation."[117]

According to Crowley, the sex magick operation has to be sufficiently intense that it creates a state of Black-Out where "the Ego-consciousness itself is abolished." This is remarkably similar to Austin Spare's notion of the "Void moment," which is described in chapter 5. At this stage, notes Crowley:

> the Will should still continue to create, stopping only when "the blood of the Red Lion" [i.e., semen] is one with the "Gluten of the White Eagle" and the "Serpent" and the "Egg" have fused completely. The result of this fusion is called the Elixir—and numerous other names, for example, The Stone of the Philosophers, the Medicine of the Metals, and so forth, especially the Quintessence.[118]

It would seem from this statement that Crowley believes that the symbolism of medieval Alchemy—a key branch of the Western esoteric tradition—should be interpreted primarily in sexual terms. For him, the elixir itself has innate magical potency. From a purely pragmatic point of view, it can be used to achieve specific magical outcomes and therefore becomes useful in the practice of sorcery:

> The Lion must collect it—the best method is by suction [i.e., sucking it out of his partner's vagina] so as to avoid waste, and share it with the Eagle. It should be absorbed by the mucous membrane [i.e., through the upper palate of the mouth, rather than swallowed]. A portion is reserved and placed in physical contact with the magickal link, or with a talisman specially prepared for the Operation, and consecrated accordingly. At the very least, some suitable symbol, e.g., if you are making an opus for $$ smear the Elixir on a gold coin, or ring; if for health, touch the bare earth, or the patient with it. In any case, be careful to consume it by absorption for it restores with interest any virtue that may have been expended in the work itself.[119]

This is not the only occasion where Crowley refers to the idea of the elixir, or semen, being used to achieve specific magical outcomes. In another short text, *Liber A'Aash vel Capricorni Pneumatici (Liber CCCLXX)*—which is recognized as a major (Class A) sex magic document by members of the O.T.O.—Crowley makes a veiled reference to masturbating on demonic sigils by using the magical utterance as a metaphor for ejaculation: "Let him sit and conjure; let him draw back the hood from his head and fix his basilisk eye upon the sigil of the demon. Then let him sway the force of him to and fro like a satyr in silence, until the Word burst from his throat . . . that which floodeth him is the infinite mercy of the Genitor-Genitrix of the Universe, whereof he is the Vessel."[120]

Sex Magic and "Spermo-Gnosis" prior to the O.T.O.

As mentioned above, within the context of the Western esoteric tradition the practice of sex magic precedes both Carl Kellner and Theodor Reuss and the establishment of the O.T.O. Several scholars, among them Hugh B. Urban (2006), John Deveney (1997), Joscelyn Godwin (1995), and J. Gordon Melton (1985), have drawn attention to the unique contribution made by the influential American occultist Paschal Beverly Randolph (1825–1875). Randolph is significant because, as Melton puts it: "Like Crowley, Randolph discovered the essential aspect of sex magick by suddenly combining long-term interests in sexuality and the occult."[121] The bridging link between Randolph and the O.T.O. is provided by two American esoteric orders, the Hermetic Brotherhood of Luxor and Randolph's Brotherhood of Eulis.

Born in New York in 1825, Paschal Beverly Randolph was the son of a wealthy Virginian named William Randolph, and a slave woman named Flora Beverly, who was of mixed East Indian, European, and Madagascan descent. Flora raised her son by herself in a "gloomy old stone house on Manhattan Island." When Randolph was five, however, his mother died during an epidemic and he was placed in an orphanage. Essentially growing up on his own, Randolph taught himself to read and write by copying letters from printed posters and billboards.[122] Classified as a "free man of color," he trained as a natural physician and also studied spiritualism and Franz Anton Mesmer's theory of animal magnetism, a precursor of modern hypnosis. Randolph worked for the Abolitionist cause before the Civil War and helped raise money for the Black Militias of Louisiana. He also gained a reputation as a trance speaker and spiritualist medium.[123] During the late 1840s, he traveled widely in Europe, visiting England, Scotland, Ireland, France, and Malta as well as Egypt, Turkey, and Palestine.[124]

Intent on seeking out the sources of esoteric wisdom wherever he could find them, Randolph maintained that he received many high initiations while he was in Europe. During his travels he met the famous French Kabbalist and magician Eliphas Lévi, whose writings and occult ideas would later greatly influence the Hermetic Order of the Golden Dawn. He also met the notable Rosicrucian occultists Kenneth R. H. Mackenzie and Edward Bulwer-Lytton and the eccentric cleric and Rosicrucian historian Hargrave Jennings (1817–1890), who was interested in ancient phallic worship.[125] After returning to the United States, Randolph founded

FIGURE 4.3.   Paschal Beverly Randolph

the Fraternitas Rosae Crucis in 1858, the oldest Rosicrucian organization in North America (currently headquartered in Beverly Hall, Quakertown, Pennsylvania).[126] In 1861, after returning to Europe, Randolph was initiated into the Order of the Rose, a group headed by Hargrave Jennings. He then traveled on to Syria, where he was inducted as a hierarch of the Ansaireh before returning to the United States in 1863.[127]

Randolph explored clairvoyant scrying with magic mirrors and also wrote a treatise on the use of hashish as an aid to trance possession (1860).[128] He became a controversial figure, however, largely because of his ideas on occult sexuality, expressed publicly at a time when such issues were largely a taboo subject. Randolph's Rosicrucian activities were interrupted during the Civil War period, but in 1870 he re-established his Rosicrucian organization in Boston, calling it the Brotherhood of Eulis and using it as a vehicle to explore sex magic.[129] Three years later, Randolph published one of his best-known and most controversial books, *Eulis! The History of Love: Its Wondrous Magic, Chemistry, Rules, Laws, Modes, Moods and Rationale, Being the Third Revelation of Soul and Sex.*[130]

In *Eulis!*—which derives its title ultimately from the Greek *eos*, meaning "the dawn, the gate of light"[131]—Randolph provides an account of how he was first initiated into the mysteries of sex magic while traveling in the Middle East:

> One night—it was in far-off Jerusalem or Bethlehem, I really forget
> which—I made love to . . . a dusky maiden of Arabic blood. I of her and
> that experience learned . . . the fundamental principle of the White Magic
> of Love; subsequently I became affiliated with some dervishes and fakirs
> by whom . . . I found the road to other knowledges . . . I am became
> practically . . . a mystic and in time chief of the lofty brethren . . .
> discovering the ELIXIR OF LIFE, the universal Solvent . . . and the
> philosopher's stone.[132]

Basing his ideas substantially on the ritual sex practices of the Islamic Nusairi sect in Syria, Randolph came to believe that the sexual instinct was a fundamental force in the cosmos. Randolph maintained that "the pellucid aroma of divinity" suffuses the sex act but he also believed that sexual union could become a metaphysical and sacred ritual *only* between married loving couples and *only* when it resulted in full and complete orgasms for both partners.[133] Many years before Crowley and Austin Spare, Randolph proposed that the sexual orgasm could be used to gain practical and tangible outcomes, that is to say, subject to willed intent, the power of sexuality could be harnessed to produce specific magical results:[134]

> It follows that as are the people at *that moment* [orgasm] so will be that
> which enters into them from the regions above, beneath, and round
> about; wherefore, whatsoever male or female shall truly will for,
> hopefully pray for, and earnestly yearn for, when love, pure and holy,
> is in the nuptive ascendent, in form, passional, affectional, divine and
> volitional, that prayer will be granted, and the boon given. *But the prayer
> must preceed* [the moment of orgasm].[135]

In another text, *The Ansairetic Mystery: A New Revelation Concerning Sex!* (circa 1873–1874), which was circulated privately to his Rosicrucian followers, Randolph lists over a hundred outcomes that he believed could be achieved or resolved through this type of sex magic. They include topics and issues relating to money matters, marital discord, prolonging life, eliminating disease, and charging amulets with life-force.[136] Randolph was unstinting in proclaiming the potency of sexuality but warned that it could lead to both highs and lows in the quest for spiritual awakening:

> The ejective moment . . . is the most divine and tremendously important
> one in the human career as an independent entity, for not only may we
> launch Genius, Power, Beauty, Deformity, Crime, Idiocy, Shame or
> Glory on the world's great sea of Life, in the person of the children we
> may then produce, but we may plunge our own souls neck-deep in Hell's
> horrid slime, or else mount the Azure as coequal associate Gods; for then
> the mystic Soul swings wide its Golden gates, opens its portals to the
> whole vast Universe and through them come trooping either Angels
> of Light or the Grizzly Presence from the dark corners of the Spaces.
> Therefore, human copulation is either ascentive and ennobling, or
> descensive and degrading.[137]

Superficially, Randolph's theories of sex magic and tangible outcomes seem to mirror those of Aleister Crowley, described earlier. However, Randolph's inter-pretation of sex magic was actually very different from Crowley's. Randolph deplored masturbation and homosexuality and other forms of non-reproductive sexuality and believed that sacred sex could only occur between a loving hetero-sexual husband and wife.[138] Randolph's approach essentially involved love among equals, whereas Crowley sometimes employed prostitutes or other available women who were not personally committed to his magical purpose and who were used purely for sex.[139] Crowley's magical episode with Victor Neuburg in Algeria involving homosexual anal sex, referred to earlier, was also an act of ritual sexual submission by Crowley and would therefore have failed Randolph's criteria on at least two counts.

Randolph seems to have been far more averse than Crowley to the negative (or *Qliphothic*) realms of primal consciousness that could be unleashed through what Randolph regarded as misplaced acts of sex magic. Nevertheless, Randolph and Crowley would certainly have agreed that the orgasm itself was among the most powerful and profound of all human experiences.[140] Randolph would also have agreed with Crowley's statement in *Energized Enthusiasm* (1913) that through "the sacramental . . . use of the sexual act, the divine consciousness may be attained."[141] For both men, sexuality was a vital key to potency and transcendence.

Robert North, who contributed an introduction to the 1988 edition of Randolph's *Sexual Magic*, maintains that Carl Kellner derived many of the O.T.O. teachings directly from Randolph's instructions for the Brotherhood of Eulis.[142] However, other writers, including T. Allen Greenfield (2003), Samuel Scarborough (2001), and Joscelyn Godwin (1994), believe it was the Hermetic Brotherhood of Luxor—which in turn drew on Randolph's sex magic teachings—that was probably the specific connecting link between Randolph, Kellner, and Reuss.

The Hermetic Brotherhood of Luxor was founded in 1870 by the Polish mystic Max Théon (1848–1927). Théon was interested in Hermeticism and looked to ancient Egypt as the source of the Western esoteric tradition. However, he was also highly eclectic, embracing the Kabbalah, the Rig Veda, Tantrism, and elements of Freemasonry. For a time he lived in Algeria, where he formulated what he referred to as the Cosmic Tradition and took the mystical name Aia Aziz ("the beloved").[143] In 1873, Théon recruited the Scottish occultist and Freemason Peter Davidson (1837–1915), a close friend and colleague of Dr. Gerard Encausse, also known as Papus, to join him in administering the Brotherhood. As an initiatory organization, the Hermetic Brotherhood of Luxor first became public in London in 1884, even though it had been in existence since 1870 and its initiations—based on Rosicrucian and Masonic principles—resembled those of the Hermetic Order of the Golden Dawn, established several years later.[144] Théon took the role of Grand Master of the Exterior Circle of the Order, while Davidson was appointed Provincial Grand Master of the North (Scotland) and later also the Eastern Section (America). Together, Théon and Davidson made extensive use of ancient Egyptian symbolism in their magical ceremonies. This symbolic emphasis was further developed by Thomas H. Burgoyne (1855–1895), who joined the Hermetic Brotherhood of Luxor in 1883 and helped Théon and Davidson run the organization from this time on. The early curriculum of the Hermetic Brotherhood also included selections from the writings of the Rosicrucian author Hargrave Jennings as well as Paschal Beverly Randolph.[145] During the 1880s and 1890s, Davidson and Burgoyne adapted Randolph's *The Mysteries of Eros* and *Eulis!*, thereby placing more emphasis on practical sex magic in the Brotherhood's curriculum.[146] It seems likely that it is through the reworking of Randolph's sex magic concepts in the Hermetic Brotherhood of Luxor, and in particular through Davidson's close association with Papus in Europe, that Randolph's sex magic teachings eventually attracted the attention of Reuss and Kellner.[147] According to P-R. Koenig, Reuss first made contact with Papus in 1901.[148]

Nevertheless, as indicated earlier, there is something of a gulf between Randolph's version of sex magic as the "White Magic of Love" and the homoerotic approach to sex magic advocated by Reuss and Crowley in the O.T.O. Clearly, Randolph cannot be considered the only major precursor of Crowley's Thelemic sex magick, since there are major aspects of Crowley's occult doctrine that are entirely absent in Randolph's writings and philosophy. It is necessary to explore other sources entirely—sources much closer to the origins of the Western esoteric tradition itself—and it comes as no surprise that some of Crowley's libertine mystical and sex-magick ideas mirror quite specifically the ritual practices of certain heretical Gnostic sects whose origins date back to the early centuries of the Christian era.[149] These include the Gnostic sects that Mircea Eliade refers to as *Pneumatikoi* and O.T.O. historian P.-R. Koenig calls "Spermo-Gnostics."[150]

One of the most intriguing elements in the rise of Gnosticism during the early Christian era was the concept that spiritual redemption could be attained by collecting, salvaging, and carrying to heaven the sparks of divine light that were buried in living matter—primarily within the human body. Eliade notes that

> the equation divine light = *pneuma* [Greek: "spirit"] = semen plays a
> central role only among the Phibionites (and sects related to them) and
> among the Manichaeans. But while the latter, on the ground of this very
> equation, scorned the sexual act and exalted a severe asceticism, the
> Phibionites extolled the most abject sexual orgies and practiced the
> sacramental absorption of *semen virile* and menstrual fluids, careful only
> to avoid pregnancy.[151]

Despite the overt sensuality of their sexual rituals, the Syrian Phibionites regarded themselves as Christian Gnostics: they believed that the divine power of the crucified Son had been trapped within the physical confines of the material world. The Phibionites also believed they were giving true expression to their Christian beliefs by releasing this spiritual power during their sacred rituals without creating more children in the process—from their perspective, pregnancy and the act of giving birth would trap more souls within the painful constrictions of physical existence. For them, consuming semen and menstrual blood during the Eucharist was a purer form of ritual communion than the more conventional symbolism of blood and wine.

The practices of the Phibionites are described in the *Panarion*, written by the fourth-century Christian writer Epiphanius: "The power, which is in menstruation and in the sperm they called *psyche*, which would be gathered and eaten. And whatever we eat, flesh or vegetables or bread or anything else, we do a favor to the creatures because we gather the psyche from everything. . . . And they say that it is the same psyche which is dispersed in animals and beasts, fishes, snakes, men, vegetables, trees and anything that is produced."[152]

Epiphanius was clearly horrified by what he describes as the "shameless" sexual practices of the Phibionites:

> they serve rich food, meat, and wine even if they are poor. When they
> thus ate together and so to speak filled up their veins, from the surplus of

their strength they turn to excitements. The man, leaving his wife, says to his own wife: "Stand up and make love with the brother" ("Perform the *agapē* with the brother"). Then the unfortunates unite with each other, and as I am truly ashamed to say the shameful things that are being done by them . . . nevertheless I will not be ashamed to say those things which they are not ashamed to do, in order that I may cause in every way a horror in those who hear about their shameful practices. After they have intercourse in the passion of fornication they raise their own blasphemy toward heaven. The woman and the man take the fluid of emission of the man into their hands, they stand, turn toward heaven, their hands besmeared with the uncleanness, and pray as the people called *Stratiotikoi* and *Gnostikoi*, bringing to the Father of the Nature of All, that which they have on their hands, and they say: "We offer to thee this gift, the body of Christ." And then they eat it, their own ignominy, and say: "This is the body of Christ and this is the Passover for the sake of which our bodies suffer and are forced to confess the suffering of Christ." Similarly also with the woman: when she happens to be in the flowing of the blood they gather the blood of menstruation of her uncleanness and eat it together and say: "This is the blood of Christ."[153]

The Phibionite ritual of consuming menstrual blood and semen is mirrored in Crowley's sex magick practice of consuming cakes of light, which contained precisely the same key ingredients (on the basis of the instructions conveyed to Crowley by Aiwass in 1904, as recorded in *The Book of the Law*). As with the Phibionites, Crowley included the consumption of sacramental cakes of light in both his *Gnostic Mass* and also in the *Mass of the Phoenix* (see above), and it is clear that Crowley intended that in these magickal ceremonies the cakes of light should serve as an alternative to the Body of Christ consumed by congregants during Christian communion. Although Crowley does not mention the Phibionites specifically in his writings, he nevertheless believed he was perpetuating the Gnostic tradition through such ceremonies, and for him the ritual consumption of blood and semen was a sacred act. According to the text of the *Gnostic Mass*, consecrated cakes of light contain the sexual elixir and therefore embody "the essence of the life of the Sun."[154]

The surviving papers of Theodor Reuss show that the sex magic practices incorporated within the O.T.O. by its founder also had an essentially "Spermo-Gnostic" orientation, and that this was linked to the mystical legend of the Holy Grail. According to P-R. Koenig,

> The whole body was considered divine (the Temple of the Holy Ghost) and the sexual organs were meant to fulfil a peculiar function: a Holy

Mass was the symbolic act of re-creating the universe. The root belief is
that only by co-operation between man and woman can either advance
spiritually. Sexually joining is a shadow of the cosmic act of creation.
Performed by adepts, the union of male and female approaches more
closely the primal act and partakes of its divine nature. . . . The central
secret of his Ordo Templi Orientis was built around Richard Wagner's
Parsifal. The spear became the phallus while the Graal, of course, was
the vagina which contained the "Grals-speise" (sperm and vaginal
fluids).[155]

The O.T.O. after Crowley

When Crowley died in 1947, he was succeeded as head of the O.T.O. by his former
representative in Germany, Karl Germer (1885–1962). At this time the focus of the
O.T.O. had already begun to shift to the United States, the organization of its European affiliates having become fragmented and dispersed as a result of the impact of
World War II.[156] At the end of the war in 1945, only the Agapé Lodge of the O.T.O.
in Pasadena was still actively functioning; this was a lodge established in the 1930s
by Wilfred Talbot Smith (1885–1957), a loyal Thelemite who had first met Crowley
in Vancouver in 1915, and Jane Wolfe (1875–1958), who had stayed at Crowley's
sex-magick Abbey at Cefalu, Sicily, in the early 1920s.[157] After Crowley's will was
probated, Germer received most of the materials from Crowley's estate and took
them to his home in Westpoint, California.[158] Various court proceedings have since
determined that Crowley's copyrights are held legally by the U.S. Grand Lodge of
the O.T.O., which now seeks to control publication of Crowley's works around the
world.[159]

In Britain, the thrust of Crowley's Thelemic teachings continued under the
enthusiastic leadership of Kenneth Grant (1924–). Following Crowley's death,
Germer charted a British branch of the O.T.O. under Grant but then expelled him
in July 1955 for associating with a rival O.T.O. offshoot, the Fraternitas Saturni, and
circulating a new, unauthorized O.T.O. manifesto.[160] Grant now heads the so-called
Typhonian O.T.O., which is not legally connected to the American O.T.O. and has
since become very much a rival occult organization.[161]

Grant first met Crowley at Netherwood, Hastings (UK), in December 1944 and
worked with him for a brief period as his secretary.[162] Grant has since emerged as
one of Crowley's most notable Thelemic disciples. A prolific author in his own
right, Grant has released a number of important volumes on the Western esoteric
tradition, several of which provide important insights into the magic of the Left-
Hand Path and cover such subject areas as the *Qliphothic* realms of the Kabbalistic

Tree of Life, Tantric sex magic, and the practical applications of Kundalini yoga.[163] Grant has also produced important publications on the visionary artist Austin Osman Spare (1886–1956), whom he knew personally, from 1949 onward.[164]

Grant's occult perspective is especially significant because it affirms the esoteric connection between Indian Tantra, Gnosticism, and what he calls the Draconian, Ophidian, and Typhonian currents in modern sex magick.[165] In 1948, Grant published a *Manifesto of the British Branch of the Ordo Templi Orientis* in which he claimed that the Order promulgated a range of esoteric practices spanning both the Western and Eastern esoteric traditions:

> In the O.T.O. are promulgated the essential teachings of the Draconian
> Tradition of Ancient Egypt; the teachings of the Indian Shakta Tantra
> Shastra; the teachings of the pre-Christian Gnosis; the Initiated Western
> Tradition as enshrined in the mysteries of the Holy Qabalah, and the
> Alchemical Mystical and Magical Formulae of the Arcane Schools of the
> age long past, as well as the mode of applying practically the essential
> principles underlying the Spagyric or Hermetic Sciences, the Orphic
> Mysteries and the use of the Ophidian Current.[166]

Crowley was sufficiently impressed by Grant's research into the subject of sex magick that he admitted him to the Ninth degree of the O.T.O., and this initiation was complemented by secret Tantric instructions from another occultist, David Curwen, who had become a Ninth degree member of the Order in 1945. It was Curwen who provided Grant with a full initiation into the Tantric *vama-marg* (the Left-Hand Path). According to Grant, Curwen's instructions convinced him that Crowley did not fully appreciate the significance of the female sexual fluids (*kalas*) which, together with the male fluids, form the basis of the "elixir" in Thelemic sex magick.[167] The contemporary Thelemic practitioner Frater Zephyros elaborates on this theme in a recent article titled "The Ophidian Current," which fuses the sex-magick doctrines of Grant and Crowley with references to the chakras, or spiritual energy centers in the body, which are awakened by the Kundalini serpent in Tantric yoga (see below for a description of chakras):

> The formula and function of the Scarlet Woman starts with zones of
> occult energy intimately related to the network of nerves and plexuses
> associated with the endocrine glands. Kundalini energy affects the
> chakras in her body . . . and its vibrations influence the chemical
> composition of her glandular secretions. Such fragrances are devoured
> by the Priest and transmuted into magickal energy. . . .
>   *Kalas* [genital secretions] may only be evoked into a chakra that has
> been properly prepared. . . . Consuming the kalas charged with the

upwardly directed currents (nectar) transforms consciousness and makes it possible to contact and communicate with transcendental entities. . . .

For the female to arouse the Kundalini, she visualizes the Serpent in phallic form in the Muladhara chakra and inflames herself to the point of orgasm. Yet before orgasm, she must move to the Ajna chakra. Then she must maintain the image until consummation occurs. The male must proceed by identifying Kundalini with Hadit and the Cerebral Centre with Nuit [the Egyptian deities involved in Crowley's *Thelemic* revelation]. The Hadit force is awakened and forces its way up the spinal column past all the sealed chakras into the cerebral centre [i.e., Ajna].[168]

The significance of Grant's Typhonian O.T.O. is that through its occult doctrines and practices it seeks to reaffirm the importance of the Tantric tradition both within Western sex magick specifically, and also within the Western esoteric tradition as a whole.

Kundalini Yoga and Tantra

The word "yoga" derives from the Sanskrit *yuj*, meaning "to bind" or "to yoke," and the essential aim of yoga is union with the Godhead, Brahman.[169] The Sanskrit word *kundalini* translates literally as "of spiral nature," while the Sanskrit word *tantra* (weft, context, continuum) refers to the nature of energy and power in the universe.[170] In *Tantra: The Yoga of Sex*, Omar Garrison provides a concise overview of the philosophy associated with Tantra:

The broad, underlying foundation of Tantra philosophy may be summarized briefly as follows: The universe and everything in it is permeated by a secret energy or power, emanating from the single Source of all being. This power, although singular in essence, manifests in three ways, namely, as static inertia, dynamic inertia or mental energy, and as harmonious union of these reacting opposites. The universe or macrocosm through which these modalities of cosmic force function is exactly duplicated by the human form as microcosm. The Tantrik [sic] seeks, therefore, by mystic formularies, rites and symbols, to identify the corresponding centers of his own body with those of the macrocosm. Ultimately, he seeks union with God Himself.[171]

Agehananda Bharati, an authority on the different branches of Tantra, distinguishes between guru-oriented, meditative yoga and Tantra per se, by drawing attention to the focus on a sexual partner in the Tantric tradition:

Orthodox yoga, that is the system of Patanjali and his protagonists, teaches the ascent of the dormant, coiled-up force as a process induced in the individual adept after due instruction by his own guru, and as a procedure in which the adept practices in solitude. The tantric's practice, however, is undertaken in conjunction with a partner of the other sex. She is considered as the embodiment of Sakti [Shakti], the active principle conceived as female, by the Hindus.[172]

In the Tantric tradition of Kundalini Yoga, this sexual partnership is expressed as the merging of two opposites—Shiva and Shakti—who represent the male and female polarities of existence, respectively. While the Higher Self (Atman) is represented in Kundalini Yoga as male, all created forms, all manifestations of life energy—intelligence, will, thoughts, and feelings—are considered to be female, and as such are aspects of Shakti. As the Great Goddess, Shakti encompasses three *gunas*, or characteristics of creation, known as *sattva* (purity), *rajas* (activity), and *tamas* (inertia) as well as the five elements from which the universe is formed. Swami Sivananda Sarasvati provides an eloquent summation: "She [Shakti] is the primal force of life that underlies all existence. She vitalises the body through her energy. She is the energy in the Sun, the fragrance in the flowers, the beauty in the landscape . . . the whole world is her body. Mountains are her bones. Rivers are her veins. Ocean is her bladder. Sun and Moon are her eyes. Wind is her breath. Agni is her mouth."[173]

Kundalini Yoga encompasses many different techniques, including the use of mantras, visualization, and breath control, in order to activate specific chakras [*chakra*: Sanskrit, "wheel"] or spiritual centers, in the body. These chakras can be listed as follows:

First chakra: Muladhara, located at the base of the spine, near the coccyx
Second chakra: Svadisthana, located below the navel in the sacral region
Third chakra: Manipura, located above the navel in the lumbar region
Fourth chakra: Anahata, located near the heart
Fifth chakra: Visuddha, located in the throat
Sixth chakra: Ajna, located between the eyebrows
Seventh chakra: Sahasrara, located above the crown of the head[174]

Different goddess-manifestations of Shakti are ascribed to the first six chakras.[175] In addition, Kundalini Yoga assigns the so-called Tattva motifs associated with each of the elements—Earth, Water, Fire, Air, and Spirit—to the first five chakras.[176]

Kundalini Yoga identifies a potentially cosmic process within every yogic practitioner: manifestations of the Hindu gods and goddesses are said to lie within the energy matrices of the human organism, and the purpose of Kundalini Yoga is to bring them to life, unleashing their energy through the nadis [*nadi*: Sanskrit, "tube," "vessel"], or spiritual channels in the body. The principal channel through which the Shakti energy can be awakened is via a nadi that passes through each of the seven chakras referred to above, extending from Muladhara at the base of the spine to Sahasrara located just above the crown of the head. This energy-channel is known in Kundalini Yoga as Sushumna and corresponds to the central nervous system in the human body. Around the Sushumna are coiled two other major channels: Pingala, which is symbolically masculine and associated with the heat of the Sun, and Ida, which is symbolically feminine and is represented by the cool, reflected light of the Moon. As Ida and Pingala coil themselves around the Sushumna, they meet in the lowest chakra energy center in the body, Muladhara, and again in the sixth center, Ajna. The essential meditative task in Kundalini Yoga is to "raise" the energy of the Goddess Shakti so she may once again be united with her consort Lord Shiva in the supreme bliss of Samadhi.[177] This occurs in the supreme chakra, Sahasrara, which is considered Shiva's domain.[178] This chakra is associated with the experience of Brahman or "Oneness."[179]

The Tantric practice of Kundalini Yoga focuses on the mystical properties of energy, and this in turn is reflected in the ritual use of mantras (energy as sound) and in meditations employing specific colors in relation to each chakra (energy as light). It is also demonstrated by the symbolic dance of Shiva and Shakti as they unite one with the other, dissolving old forms and creating the universe anew (energy as movement). The chakras themselves are conceived as sources of subtle energy depicted as "wheels" (the literal meaning of the Sanskrit word *chakra*) or as lotuses (*padma*). As yogic practitioner Madhav Pandit has noted, the meditative process in Kundalini Yoga involves "flowing" from one chakra to the next by visualizing each Tattva (or element) in turn, dissolving it in the associated mantra vibration, and then merging it with the next Tattva in sequence.[180] The five Tattva elements—Earth, Water, Fire, Air, and Spirit—are associated with the first five chakras. No element is ascribed to the transcendent sixth chakra, Ajna, which is considered the seat of all spiritual knowledge.[181] Shakti is united with her consort, Lord Shiva, in the seventh chakra, Sahasrara, which is located above the crown of the head, just outside the physical body and beyond the realm of human awareness. This is a sacred union represented by the symbolism of mystical androgyny for, as Swami Sivananda Radha notes: "In the Kundalini symbolism, the union of Siva [Shiva] and Sakti [Shakti] is presented in one body, not as two bodies united. Lord Siva ultimately becomes half-man and half-woman indicating that power and its manifestations are inseparable."[182]

The sacred union of Shiva and Shakti within the Oneness of Brahman can also be considered a mystery for, according to the Tantric tradition, at this point all aspects of form and creative manifestation are transcended. As the psychologist C. G. Jung has written, Sahasrara represents a "philosophical concept with no substance whatever for us—it is beyond any possible experience."[183]

Tantra and Thelemic Sex Magick

Lawrence Sutin, author of a recent biography of Aleister Crowley, believes that Crowley's first reference to sex magic is recorded in a diary titled *The Writings of Truth*, which was later published in a modified form in his *Temple of Solomon the King*. It was while visiting his friend and former Golden Dawn colleague Allan Bennett (*Frater Iehi Aour*) in Ceylon in 1901 that Crowley was tutored for the first time in yoga. Bennett had left the world of ceremonial magic behind in England and had come to Ceylon to become a Buddhist monk. Bennett was willing to share his practical knowledge of yoga with his friend, and together they rented a furnished bungalow in the hills near Kandy for a period of several months so Crowley could be shown the yogic techniques.[184]

Crowley's diary entries in *The Writings of Truth* record that during his stay in Kandy he practiced yogic *pranayama* (control of prana, or life-energy, utilizing breathing techniques) and that he had also been exploring *vamacharya*, a form of Left-Hand Path Tantra devoted to licentious rites and sexual debauchery.[185] Sutin writes:

> This reference to *vamacharya* is most important, as it documents his [i.e., Crowley's] first known foray into ritual sexual magic. This Sanskrit term refers to a Hindu tantric practice of sexual intercourse that could— if the spiritual aspirations were untainted by lust—re-enact the cosmic coupling of Shiva and Shakti. . . . In tantric tradition *vamacharya* is the "left-hand path" that involves physical intercourse with a woman (*vama*) as partner, while the "right-hand path" of *dakshinachara* enacts a symbolic intercourse.[186]

In *Tantra: The Way of Action*, occult historian and ceremonial magician Francis King describes the ritual procedure adopted in left-handed Tantra:

> The rite proper begins with the worshipers gathered in a circle, seated on the ground, man alternating with woman, the woman on the left of each man being his intended sexual partner—hence, of course, the term left-handed Tantra. At the center of the circle stands the male adept who will conduct the ceremony, the "priest," and near him sits or lies a naked woman, or "priestess." For tantrics all women are holy—as one text has

it "every woman is your image, O Shakti, you reside in the forms of all women in this world"—but for the duration of the rite the priestess, the woman at the center of the circle who is to be the sexual partner of the officiating adept, is considered especially holy, a particular manifestation of Shakti. As such her vulva is peculiarly sacred, a symbol of her creative power which sustains the universe, and it is displayed as fully as possible to the assembled congregation, the priestess lying or sitting with her legs held wide apart.[187]

Before the Tantric rite itself can commence, however, certain purificatory procedures have to take place:

the body of the priestess is ritually cleansed by being sprinkled with wine and consecrated "holy water," and then Shakti is invoked into that body by the priest. This latter is done by the priest gently caressing her head, trunk and limbs while muttering or chanting invocations. Almost every part of the body receives these caresses but particular attention is paid to the vulva, which has an aromatic sandalwood paste applied to it, is lightly kissed, and is then, as the supreme expression of the nature of the Goddess, the recipient of symbolic sacrifice—that is to say libations of water, wine, or coconut milk are poured over it or on the ground beneath it. . . . The priestess is now looked upon as being deified, for the time being an avatar of Shakti.[188]

Within this ritual context, the Shakti priestess is venerated by the entire assembled group but the priest himself has a specific sexual role: "The ritual worship of the priestess is often immediately followed by her copulation with the priest, the assembled worshipers devoutly observing what is regarded as a sacred action, a physical expression of the eternal embrace of Shiva and Shakti. The sexual coupling is regarded as holy and so are the participants, *but only as manifestations of Shiva and Shakti* [King's emphasis]."[189]

King also comments further on the distinction between left-handed and right-handed Tantra, noting that in the first instance the ritual sexual coupling actually takes place, whereas in the latter case it is symbolic. Left-handed Tantra is also more exuberant and spontaneous:

In right-handed Tantra the woman sits to the right side of the man; if the rite is left-handed, one which culminates in physical sexuality, the opposite is the case. . . . In either case the practitioners now endeavor to think of each other as the God and Goddess, Shiva and Shakti. In right-handed worship this "divine identification" remains on a fairly abstract level, but in left-handed rites it is very specific, the woman regarding her partner as "the phallus of Shiva," while she is thought of as being not only Shakti but the living altar on which sacrifice is offered to herself—in the words of one text, held in high regard by many schools of Tantra, "Her belly is the sacrificial altar, her pubic hairs the sacred grass-mat . . . the lips of her vagina are the sacrificial fire." . . .

In left-handed working . . . fervor and spontaneity are the essence of the rite. The participants not only identify themselves with the God and Goddess, but they give the divine forces full play, letting themselves improvise, as the divine polarities inspire them, the feasting, the love play and the copulation of Shiva and Shakti. Within the boundaries of the Temple there are no hard and fast rules—"Exceed, exceed" are the key words, and the Road to Excess leads to the Palace of Wisdom and Understanding and to that Greater Palace which subsumes them.[190]

King maintains that Hindu tantrics allow the ritual ejaculation of semen, whereas Buddhist tantrics try to avoid it.[191] On this point, however, he is contradicted by Agehananda Bharati, who writes: "The central rule behind the left-handed rites, both Hindu and Buddhist, is the retention of semen during the sexual act [i.e., during *maithuna*, ritualistic copulation].The man who discharges semen is a *pasu*, an "animal" in the Mahanirvana and the Yogini Tantra, whereas he who retains it during maithuna is *divya*, "divine."[192]

Because of Crowley's fascination with the magical potency of semen and his emphasis in Thelemic magical practice on the ritual consumption of sexual secretions as part of the "magical elixir," it is possible that even if he was following a practice of retaining semen during his exploration of *vamacharya* in 1901 he was prepared to abandon this aspect of Tantra after his transformative revelations in Cairo, just three years later.

In his article, "The Origins of Modern Sex Magick" (1985), J. Gordon Melton points out that there were certain aspects of Hindu Tantra that would definitely not have been to Crowley's liking after1904. Commenting on the traditional concept of Shakti as "Goddess" or "'power," Melton notes that

> while variously understood by different tantrics, an understanding of
> the role of the female and her energy is central to all Hindu tantrism,
> but is absent from Crowley's treatment of sex magick. As John
> Woodroofe would write just a few years after Crowley finished the new
> O.T.O. rituals, Hindu tantrism teaches that "Śakti [Shakti] in the
> highest causal sense is God as Mother, and in another sense it is the
> universe which issues from Her Womb." . . . Such concepts are quite
> foreign to and stand in stark contrast to the O.T.O. teaching of God as
> Sun and phallus.[193]

Melton also rightly observes that Crowley's notion of the Scarlet Woman as a sexual consort is based on the biblical Book of Revelation and has nothing whatever to do with the Tantric tradition. "Crowley's Scarlet Woman," he writes, bears "no substantive resemblance to Shakti in any of her forms, including Kali."[194]

Kenneth Grant, meanwhile, provides an important insight into the connection between the practice of Left-Hand Path sex magic and the image of the Kundalini serpent—or "fire-snake":

> The ability to function on the inner, or astral planes, and to travel freely in the realms of light or inner space, derived from a special purification and storage of vital force. This force in its densest form is identical with sexual energy. In order to transform sexual energy into magical energy (*ojas*), the dominant Fire Snake at the base of the spine is awakened. It then purges the vitality of all dross by the purifying virtue of its intense heat. Thus the function of the semen—in the tantras is to build up the body of light [the astral body], the inner body of man. As the vital fluid accumulates in the testicles it is consumed by the heat of the Fire Snake, and the subtle fumes or "perfumes" of this molten semen go to strengthen the inner body. The worship of *shakti* means in effect the exercise of the Fire Snake, which not only fortifies the body of light but gradually burns away all impurities in the physical body and rejuvenates it.[195]

Grant has also argued that arousing the Kundalini can stimulate "artistic or inventive creativity." In *The Magical Revival* (1972), he refers to the Kundalini as "the serpentine or spiral power of creative consciousness," and he goes on to emphasize that this type of occult exploration has the potential to bestow profound spiritual insights: "Men will become as gods, because the power of creation (the prerogative of gods) will be wielded by them through the direction of forces at present termed 'occult' or hidden."[196]

Variations within the Left-Hand Path

Aleister Crowley's doctrine of *Thelema*—and the related practice of sex magick—was clearly a radical departure from the Hermetic magic of the Golden Dawn and moved twentieth-century Western esotericism in the direction of the so-called Left-Hand Path, whose key characteristics I have already described. As noted earlier, many modern and contemporary occult practitioners regard themselves as belonging to the Left-Hand Path; these practitioners are members of organizations that have emerged in Crowley's wake and have been strongly influenced by

him—among them Kenneth Grant's Typhonian O.T.O., Anton LaVey's Church
of Satan, and the Temple of Set, headed by Michael Aquino. The principal philosophical elements associated with the Left-Hand Path are as follows:

> A focus on the "solitary, individualistic, and persona," based on "*self*-
>   development, *self*-analysis, and *self*-empowerment"; an emphasis also
>   on the "unique, deviant, and exclusive"
> An emphasis on the "dark" side of magic, and an exploration of "hidden
>   desires and fears"
> An acknowledgement of "antinomianism" as an overriding and defining
>   magical principle and a willingness to have the "spiritual courage" to
>   embrace symbols "feared and loathed by conventional culture"
> An emphasis on the spiritual quest for "self-deification" or the act of
>   "becoming a god"

During his exotic magical career, Crowley was very much an iconoclast,
introducing most of these specific elements into the Western esoteric tradition
following his Thelemic "revelation" in 1904. Crowley's cult of *Thelema* focused on
the unique role played by the Beast 666 (Crowley himself) and the Whore of
Babalon (Crowley's sexual partner) in heralding the sex-magick of the New Aeon
("love under Will").

We can summarize Crowley's Left-Hand Path tendencies as follows: In *Liber Al
vel Legis*—the key document announcing the New Aeon—Horus (regarded here as
an incarnation of the Divine Child) declares his opposition to all the major religious traditions that have preceded the Thelemic revelation: "I peck at the eyes of
Jesus . . . I flap my wings in the face of Mohammed . . . I tear at the flesh of the
Indian and Buddhist . . . I spit on your crapulous creeds."[197] Crowley also highlights
his antinomian credentials through the ceremonial consumption of cakes of light
containing semen and vaginal fluids: from a Christian perspective his *Gnostic Mass*
and *Mass of the Phoenix* could reasonably be regarded as a blasphemous parody of
the Eucharist. Further, as I have noted earlier, Crowley's *Gnostic Mass* has a specific
precursor in the consumption of menstrual blood and semen by the Gnostic Phibionites, whose ceremonial rituals were deplored by the fourth-century Church
Father Epiphanius and denounced as heresy in his *Panarion*.

In his doctrine of *Thelema*, Crowley emphasizes spiritual communication
with the Holy Guardian Angel, a spiritual being whom he personally associated
with the figure of Aiwass, the mysterious entity who had dictated the *Book of the
Law* (*Liber Al vel Legis*). Although we do not find the same emphasis on "self-
deification" in Crowley's teachings that we find, for example, in the Dragon
Rouge and the Temple of Set (see chapter 7), Crowley's approach to magic was

nevertheless highly individualistic, and he believed he could employ the techniques of magick to attain godlike powers and subjugate the universe to his Will, an approach later mirrored in the Temple of Set.[198]

Although there is clear agreement among many of the subgroups associated with the Left-Hand Path with regard to the principles and practices that unite them, it is also apparent that there are significant differences as well. As we will see in chapter 7, Anton LaVey emphasized sensual indulgence and carnality as the path to self-empowerment in the Church of Satan, whereas the Temple of Set has always been more philosophical and restrained in its approach and has moved away from hedonistic and libertine sexuality toward a more meditative and inner-directed association with the Prince of Darkness. According to Zeena Schreck, a one-time high priestess of the Temple of Set, the practice of sex magic is not specified within the curriculum of the temple, and no emphasis is placed upon it, thus differentiating the approach of Aquino and his associates from the sex-magick of *Thelema* and the Typhonian O.T.O.[199] Meanwhile, the Dragon Rouge and Kenneth Grant's Thelemic practitioners emphasize the significance of the so-called "Draconian current," in which sexual energies are awakened through Tantra and Kundalini Yoga—thereby introducing a notably Eastern influence to the Western esoteric tradition. This is in stark contrast to the Temple of Set, which directs its spiritual focus specifically toward the ancient Egyptian figure of Set, who is perceived as the Principle of Isolate Intelligence and "the patron of the magician who seeks to increase his existence through expansion."[200]

Chthonic Elements in Modern Western Magic

The term "chthonic" (Greek: *khthōn*, "earth") refers to deities and ritual artefacts symbolically associated with the Earth. In ancient Greece, the term *khthōn* referred to the interior of the soil, rather than its surface, and for this reason the word "chthonic" is generally used with reference to the gods, goddesses, and spirits of the Underworld, especially in the context of ancient Graeco-Roman religion. Typically, chthonic deities are associated with agriculture and the fertility of the land (e.g., the Greek goddesses Demeter and Persephone) or are directly associated with the Underworld itself (e.g., Hekate, Aidoneus/Hades). Chthonic deities are frequently represented by snakes, and some, like Attis and Adonis, are associated with ancient mystery cults of death and rebirth.[201]

Contemporary Thelemic writer Vadge Moore has recently suggested that the term "chthonic" may be used to refer generally to deities either *of the earth or under the earth*—including Pan, Dionysus, and Bacchus, as well as non-Hellenic deities such as Set and Abraxas.[202] He also relates their symbolic attributes to the occult quest for spiritual transcendence. Moore associates chthonic deities primarily with sexuality and the cycles of Nature:

> The chthonic gods represent the primal instincts that come to us directly through Nature. The Greek god Dionysus is certainly one of these. . . . Representative of the creative and destructive aspects of Nature, Dionysus is the ultimate chthonic figure. He can inspire the most beautiful, delirious sexual activity and the most degrading, violent, murderous activity. Dionysus' mother, Semele, has been described variously as a Moon-Goddess and as a mortal woman. His father was the leader of the Greek gods, Zeus. His mother as mortal then combines the earthly with the divine . . . bringing the balance that chthonic more deeply represents.[203]

Moore maintains that chthonic deities, by their very nature, provide the basis for magical transformation and spiritual transcendence:

> The chthonic process is an occult "awakening" that includes the very lowest instinctual elements of the human psyche leading to the very highest elements. It is the base, primordial material that the psyche needs in order to evolve and grow. Chthonic is the soil, the fertilizer, and the dark, primitive unconscious material *that can turn the beast into a god.*"[204]

For Moore, potent chthonic images can be found ranging from the depths of the mythic unconscious through to the pure light of transcendence, and can be quite varied in form. For example, Moore claims that dragons are regarded as symbols of magical transformation because they combine the chthonic serpent with the wings of a bird and therefore range symbolically "from earth to 'divinity.'" He also maintains that the Gnostic archon Abraxas, who was often depicted on ancient Middle Eastern amulets with serpentine legs and the head of a rooster, "is an ideal chthonic representation, embracing the depths symbolized by the serpents rising to the human, and achieving solar transcendence as depicted by the rooster head." Moore supports French decadent writer Georges Bataille, who similarly explores chthonic themes and emphasizes their potential for transcendence: "In opposition to the ancient sky and sun gods, Bataille proposes a worship of the gods of darkness and of the earth: Demeter, Hecate and Dionysus. . . . We must not forget that it is just this sinking into the underworld of the id and the dark unconscious that helps to plant the roots for our ascent."[205]

If Moore's chthonic approach is to be regarded as a model for spiritual rebirth and transformation, however, it is clear that some form of "ascent" has to actually occur—for without an ascent, according to Moore's chthonic conception, there can be no experience of transcendence. This in turn begs the question of what is

FIGURE 4.4. The Gnostic archon Abraxas, a characteristically chthonic deity

meant or implied, within a magical context, by the nature of the visionary "ascent" itself.

A carefully considered understanding of magical ascent requires an exploration of altered states of consciousness and if we are to consider the implications of Moore's Thelemic concept of ascent, we are in turn required to explore the role of altered states of consciousness within the Western esoteric tradition itself—which takes us into territory rarely accessed by academic enquiry.[206] Significant questions then arise: how have modern magical practitioners described their experiences of these altered states of consciousness, and what techniques have they employed in order to bring them about?

Altered States of Consciousness in Modern Magical Practice

As noted earlier, within the context of the twentieth-century magical revival, the Hermetic Order of the Golden Dawn provides extensive documentation of modern magical techniques involving altered states of consciousness (i.e., trance states, mystical experiences, and out-of-the-body experiences).[207] These magical techniques are described in a series of semi-official documents known as Flying Rolls which, according to occult historian Francis King, were privately circulated "among the Adepti of the pre-1900 Golden Dawn."[208] The Flying Rolls themselves were written by high-ranking members of the Golden Dawn but were not included in Israel Regardie's monumental four-volume collection of Golden Dawn rituals (first published 1937–1940), and did not become widely known in magical circles until the early 1970s.[209]

The Golden Dawn magicians employed a technique of willed imagination utilizing what was known as the body of light. The body of light has been described within an occult context as a "magical personality" that is "deliberately built for a purpose [and] acquired through practice and concentration." In a magical context, it is the vehicle of conscious awareness through which the magician interacts with "thought-forms," spirit-entities, and archetypal beings on the inner, or astral, planes.[210] Temple of Set magician Dr. Michael Aquino has described the role of this "magical double" in quasi-Egyptian terms as follows:

> The magician constructs within his subjective universe a magical double or *ka* (Goethe's *Doppelgänger*). This is an idealized entity whose precise characteristics may vary from Working to Working. He then, by an act of Will, transfers his soul or *ba* to the vehicle of this *ka* and then executes his Will in the subjective universe. This may be completely dissociated from the physical body of the magician, or it may be closely aligned with it. . . . At the conclusion of the Working, the *ba* is redirected to the physical body and the *ka* is disintegrated. The elements of the subjective universe specifically summoned for the Working are released into their normal contexts, there to influence their objective counterparts.[211]

Transferring consciousness to a magical simulacrum or body of light through willed concentration and visualization is central to the practice of visionary magic in the Western esoteric tradition, and the experience of "consciousness-transfer" is described in *Flying Roll XXV*, written by *Frater Sub Spe*—Dr. John W. Brodie-Innes—who was a prominent figure in the Golden Dawn's Amen-Ra Temple in Edinburgh.[212] *Frater Sub Spe* describes the shift in consciousness that occurs when a practitioner focuses meditatively on a Major Arcana Tarot card or one of the Tattva symbols of the elements, thereby switching personal awareness to the inner world of magical perception:

> Gradually the attention is withdrawn from all surrounding sights and sounds, a grey mist seems to swathe everything, on which, as though

thrown from a magic lantern on steam, the form of the symbol is
projected. The Consciousness then seems to pass through the symbol to
realms beyond . . . the sensation is as if one looked at a series of moving
pictures. . . . When this sensitiveness of brain and power of perception is
once established there seems to grow out of it a power of actually going
to the scenes so visionary and seeing them as solid, indeed of actually
doing things and producing effects there. . . . The sensation . . . is first
to become, as it were, dimly conscious of a figure walking among the
scenes of the new country—or the Astral Plane—gradually to become
conscious that it is my own figure that I am looking at—gradually, as it
were, to be able to look through the eyes—and feel with the sensations
of this *doppelganger*. Further to be able consciously to direct its motions,
to control it, to inhabit it. . . . It is as though my Consciousness had
extruded from my own body to take possession of a body which I had
either created for the purpose, or invoked out of the Astral Sphere as a
vehicle for myself.[213]

The key elements in this process include concentrating the mind on a specific
magical symbol, such as a Major Arcana Tarot card image or a Tattva symbol, and
then using it to bring about a transfer of consciousness to the inner, imaginal
realm of perception. Sometimes the magician also uses various utterances (pro-
nouncement of sacred god-names or one's personal magical name) to reinforce
the sense of a transfer of awareness. According to Dion Fortune, who was a member of the Alpha and Omega Temple of the Golden Dawn, the act of projecting
her body of light was greatly assisted by uttering her magical name.[214] As she
notes in *Applied Magic*: "Once perceived, I could re-picture this idealised version
of my body and personality at will, but I could not identify myself with it unless I
uttered my Magical name. Upon my affirming it as my own, identification was
immediate."[215]

Following the transfer of consciousness, the magician then experiences the
contents of the visionary realm as perceptually "real"—including mythic landscapes populated by gods, spirit-beings, and various other entities. According to
Frater Sub Spe:

At first it seems as though everything thus perceived were just the
product of one's own imagination. . . . But a little further experience
generally convinces one that the *new country one has become conscious of*
has its inviolable natural laws just as the physical world has: that one
cannot make or unmake at will, that the same causes produce the same
results, that one is in fact merely a spectator and in no sense a creator.
The conviction then dawns on one that one is actually perceiving a new and

much extended range of phenomena; that in fact, which is known as the Astral World or Astral Plane [emphasis added].[216]

When one considers that the symbols of the Major Arcana of the Tarot were employed in the Golden Dawn as meditative pathways connecting all ten *sephiroth* on the Tree of Life—resulting in a total of twenty-two interconnecting pathways on the Tree—it becomes clear that the Kabbalistic Tree of Life, itself a symbol of the Body of God, was regarded by the members of the Golden Dawn as nothing less than a map of the "'terrain" accessed through visionary magical consciousness. For them, the Body of God represented the operative magical territory, and what Vadge Moore has referred to as "ascent" and what the Golden Dawn magicians referred to as "rising in the planes" could be achieved by "rising" or "ascending"' meditatively from one *sephirah* to the next, on a path culminating eventually in the spiritual experience of *Kether* and mystical union with the Godhead.

There can be little doubt that the spiritual purpose associated in the Golden Dawn with "rising in the planes" was ultimately a quest for spiritual transcendence and union with the Godhead, which in turn aligns the Golden Dawn with the Right-Hand Path rather than the Left-Hand Path in the Western esoteric tradition.[217] A Golden Dawn document on the *Qliphoth* or negative energies of the Kabbalistic Tree of Life titled *The Book of the Black Serpent* (circa 1900) encourages its initiates to "banish thou therefore the Evil and seek the Good . . . let thy countenance be raised up towards the Light of the Holy One to invoke the Divine Brightness."[218]

Dan Merkur, a scholar well known for his study of Hermeticism and Gnosticism, argues that "ascension" is a key element in the Hermetic tradition (which in turn was an important precursor of modern Western esotericism as practiced in the Golden Dawn). Merkur also describes Hermetic "ascension" in terms that resemble the Golden Dawn conception of "rising in the planes":

> In the Hermetic literature . . . different varieties of mystical experience were each associated with a specific celestial region on the trajectory of ascension. . . . A single region of the sky might be termed the seven planetary heavens or the twelve zodiacal mansions. . . . The ascension was literal, but mental rather than bodily. The ascent beyond the seven planetary zones of the sensible world was a motion of the mind [and involved] an experiential sense of the mind's detachment from the body.[219]

In *Corpus Hermeticum XIII*, Hermes explains to his son Tat that in the course of Seeing, "I went out of myself into an immortal body, and now I am not what I was before. I have been born in mind."[220] Elsewhere in the *Corpus Hermeticum*, the sense of mystical ascent achieved during an out-of-the-body state is specifically associated with the spiritual will:

> Command your soul to travel to India, and it will be there faster than your command. Command it to cross over to the ocean, and again it will quickly be there, not as having passed from place to place but simply as being there. Command it even to fly up to heaven, and it will not lack wings. Nothing will hinder it, not the fire of the sun, nor the aether, nor the swirl nor the bodies of the other stars . . . You must think of god in this way, as having everything—the cosmos, himself [the] universe—like thoughts within himself. Thus, unless you make yourself equal to god, you cannot understand god.[221]

According to Merkur, for the Hermetic initiate the visionary or "imaginal" realm was located in the Eighth celestial region, in a "dimension" beyond the seven planetary heavens; however, in due course the initiate had to ascend still further, rising eventually to the Ninth cosmic region and achieving union with the pure Mind of the Creator. "The Hermetic God," writes Merkur, "was the Mind that contains the cosmos as its thoughts," and the Hermetic initiate had to proceed "from vision to *union*," thereby experiencing the sacred realization that "both the universe and self were located in the mind of God."[222]

On the Kabbalistic Tree of Life, the first three *sephiroth* (i.e., emanations from the Godhead) similarly transcend the imaginal realm of forms, because they are located above the Abyss that separates the seven lower *sephiroth* associated with Creation. MacGregor Mathers makes it clear that the initiate's task in "rising in the planes" is to "Look upwards to the Divine Light shining down from Kether."[223] The spiritual aspiration of the Hermetic magician is ultimately toward the highest point on the Kabbalistic Tree of Life and transcendent union with the Godhead.

If Hermetic "ascent" is characteristic of Right-Hand Path magic as practiced in the Golden Dawn, where does this leave the "ascent" advocated by Thelemic occultist Vadge Moore, who clearly aligns his magical philosophy with Aleister Crowley and the chthonic realms of the Left-Hand Path? The answer is by no means obvious. Both Vadge Moore and Bataille maintain that it is "the dark unconscious that helps to plant the roots for our ascent."[224] Other contemporary occultists associated with the Left-Hand Path, however, appear to have an entirely different focus. As mentioned earlier, the Temple of Set emphasises the role of the dark god Set as the "Principle of Isolate Intelligence," a magical concept vastly different from the Hermetic assertion that both the universe and self are located within the mind of God.[225] The antinomianism and self-deification associated with the Left-Hand Path are similarly far removed from the Hermetic perspective.

The *Qliphothic* orientation of the Typhonian O.T.O. and Scandinavian Dragon Rouge is also quite specific. In *Cults of the Shadow* (1975), Kenneth Grant makes specific reference to the *Qliphoth* in distinguishing the path of the mystic (Right-Hand Path) from that of the Typhonian magician (Left-Hand Path):

> The ascent of the Tree of Life is achieved by "rising on the planes" until consciousness is merged with the Highest (i.e., Kether). In order to reify this state in Malkuth (i.e., to "earth" magical consciousness) the process has to be reversed and the Tree descended *via* the *back* of the Middle Pillar. . . . The Mystic retains consciousness in the *Brahmarandra* (the topmost *chakra*, at the region of the cranial suture) but the Magician brings it down again to earth. It is the formula of Prometheus, who brought down fire from heaven. . . . Thus also the Tantric Adept brings down the Light to manifest in Maya—the shadow-world of illusory images. . . . The Secret Pathway through the realms of the *Qliphoth* at the back of the Tree follows the downward path and comports the assumption of animal forms which correspond to the "gods" of the Qabalistic [Kabbalistic] system. This is a valid explanation of the *were-animal* and its relation to pre-human atavisms.[226]

While Grant perceives the grounding of mystical consciousness via the *Qliphoth* essentially as a redirected flow of Tantric energy, the Dragon Rouge is somewhat more assertive in proclaiming the strengths and virtues of the *Qliphoth*. According to the Dragon Rouge, "the Qliphothic Qabalah [Kabbalah] uses the forces of destruction to free the adept from the limitations of creation" and its Draconian initiations have the potential to lead the adept "down into the darkness where he or she can become a god."[227] In contradistinction to the principle of Hermetic transcendence and union with the Divine Mind mentioned earlier, the Dragon Rouge maintains that the "dark forces [of the *Qliphoth*] . . . make a free will and *an individual existence outside God possible*" [emphasis added]. As a magical organization that openly aligns itself with what it calls the "nightside tradition," the Dragon Rouge also supports the practice of Goetic magic through which "the magician conjures and evokes personified dark forces in the shape of different demons."[228]

The demonic aspects of the *Qliphoth* are similarly addressed in the Golden Dawn document *The Book of the Black Serpent*, mentioned earlier, although the purpose and intent of this magical text is quite different. Here the *Qliphoth* are described as "unclean and evil," and the *Qliphothic* planetary rulers and their "archdaemon servitors" are identified as evil spirits similar to those associated with the *Goetia* and medieval grimoires.[229] However, the message to members of the Isis Urania Temple of the Golden Dawn in *The Book of the Black Serpent* is both clear and emphatic: "Banish thou therefore the Evil and seek the Good."[230]

So how can we identify the key characteristics of the Left-Hand Path in modern Western magic?

First, there is an emphasis in all forms of Left-Hand Path magic on individual mastery and self-empowerment. The focus in Crowley's magick is on individual communication with the Holy Guardian Angel—one's higher self. In Left-Hand Path occult practice it is the self that is finally triumphant, as in the Dragon Rouge, where the "created" becomes the "creator," or in the Temple of Set, where the "isolated psyche" achieves immortality. This magical self does not merge or experience union with the Godhead, as in the Hermetic and mystical traditions, but remains distinct and separate from God, and may even become a god in its own right (see also *self-deification* below).

Second, there is a distinct orientation toward the "dark" side of magic. Goetic (demonic) evocation may be employed to conquer fears and limitations (as in the Dragon Rouge), and Greater Black Magic may be practiced in order to subjugate the universe to the will of the individual in his or her quest for "infinite potential" (as in the Temple of Set). The Kabbalistic *Qliphoth* can also be considered potentially demonic.

Third, antinomianism, or the act of going against the grain, is an overriding defining principle of the Left-Hand Path. In the modern magical context, this includes heretical or blasphemous ritual acts (e.g., Crowley's *Gnostic Mass* or LaVey's naked female "altar"—see chapter 7), or the use of ritual elements feared and loathed by conventional culture (e.g., the consumption of semen, vaginal secretions, and menstrual blood as advocated by Crowley and practiced in the O.T.O.). Most modern magical or "occult" groups, by their very nature, would be regarded in Christian circles as heretical, heathen, or demonic and therefore, by definition, antinomian.

A fourth characteristic of Left-Hand Path magic is its emphasis on the spiritual quest for self-deification or the act of becoming a god. This magical aspiration is most clearly articulated in the Temple of Set and the Dragon Rouge. However, it is also less obvious but nevertheless present in Wicca—where the high priestess incarnates the Goddess within a ceremonial context by "Drawing down the Moon."

Finally, the Left-Hand Path is clearly associated with chthonic elements in magic—with pagan gods and goddesses of the Underworld and deities associated with fertility, lust, ecstasy, and the primal forces of the id. Vadge Moore and Georges Bataille propose a worship of the gods and goddesses of darkness and the earth—including such deities as Demeter, Hecate, and Dionysus—because it is "the underworld of the id and the dark unconscious that helps to plant the roots for our ascent." The Ophidian nature of O.T.O. Tantric sex-magick, with its emphasis on the arousal of the Kundalini serpent energy from the base of the spine, similarly has chthonic overtones: traditionally chthonic deities are symbolized by, or associated with, serpents.

5

Three Magical Visionaries

While Aleister Crowley polarized twentieth-century occultism by establishing his cult of *Thelema*—thereby consolidating what would become recognized as the Left-Hand Path—he was not alone in exploring the potentials of visionary magic. Dion Fortune, a member of the Golden Dawn, and later the founder of her own magical organization, would bring a new emphasis to feminine mythological archetypes—especially variants like the Green and Black Isis—and would also help develop the magical concept of "pathworkings," a method of using guided imagery to explore the mythic imagery associated with the Kabbalistic Tree of Life. Meanwhile, the gifted British artist Austin Osman Spare would develop a unique approach to trance consciousness that involved the use of magical sigils. And during the 1940s and 1950s, the controversial Australian witch, Rosaleen Norton, would attract both acclaim and notoriety for her fusion of esoteric imagery and pagan, visionary art. All three have made their mark on contemporary occult perspectives and all three can be regarded as key bridging figures linking earlier generations of magical practitioners with the contemporary neopagan movement.

Dion Fortune

Dion Fortune was born Violet Mary Firth on 6 December 1890 at Bryn-y-Bia, in Llandudno, Wales. Her father, Arthur Firth, was a solicitor, but for her own reasons Violet liked to emphasize a close connection with the better-known Firth family of Sheffield, a leading steel-producing company, and she would later take its family motto as her own.

By the time she had reached her teenage years, Violet Firth had already acquired a Christian Science orientation—it is likely that her parents were also devotees, although this has not been established—and she seems to have had an early inclination toward psychism and metaphysics. One of her poems, titled "Angels," which appeared in the *Christian Science Journal* in April 1908, alludes to an empty tomb in a garden, and to thoughts of mortality and the fragility of love.[1]

Although details of her early professional life are scanty, it is known that she worked as a therapist in a medico-psychological clinic in East London and later studied psychoanalysis in classes held at the University of London by a Professor Flugel, who was also a member of the Society for Psychical Research.[2] Strongly influenced by the theories of Freud, Adler, and Jung, Firth became a lay psychoanalyst in 1918. In Jung's thought, especially, she found correlations between the archetypes of the collective unconscious and a realm of inquiry that would increasingly fascinate her: the exploration of sacred mythological images invoked by occultists during their rituals and visionary encounters.

According to Fortune's principal biographer, Alan Richardson, her first contact with occult perspectives seems to have come through her association with an Irish Freemason, Dr. Theodore Moriarty. Firth probably met Moriarty at the clinic where she worked; he in turn was involved in giving lectures on occult theories in a private house in the village of Eversley in northern Hampshire. Moriarty's interests were both Theosophical and metaphysical, encompassing such subject matter as the study of psychology and religion, the so-called 'root races' of lost Atlantis, mystical and Gnostic Christianity, reincarnation, and the occult relationship between mind, matter, and spirit.[3] It is not clear whether Moriarty had any personal connection with the Golden Dawn magicians—many of whom were also Freemasons. But Violet Firth had a close friend, Maiya Tranchell-Hayes (later Mrs. Maiya Curtis-Webb), whom she had known from childhood and who was also an occult devotee, and through her she was introduced to the Golden Dawn Temple of the Alpha and Omega in 1919.[4]

Based in London, this temple was a southern offshoot of the Scottish section of the Golden Dawn headed by Dr. J. W. Brodie-Innes. Maiya Tranchell-Hayes became her teacher at the Alpha and Omega temple, and Firth found the magical ceremonies powerful and evocative.[5] However, she also felt there was a sense of gloom in this particular group. According to Firth: "The glory had departed . . . most of its original members were dead or withdrawn; it had suffered severely during the war, and was manned mainly by widows and grey-bearded ancients."[6] A year later, Firth joined a London temple headed by Mrs. Moina Mathers, who was continuing the esoteric work of her husband following his untimely death from influenza in the epidemic of 1918.

In the Temple of the Alpha and Omega, Violet Firth took the magical name *Deo Non Fortuna*, "by God and not by luck," which was also the Latin motto inscribed upon the Firth family crest. She subsequently became known in esoteric circles as Dion Fortune, a contraction of her magical name, and in 1922 formed her own meditative group. Originally established as the Christian Mystic Lodge of the Theosophical Society, it soon became known as the Fraternity of the Inner Light.

This connection with the Theosophical Society is not as surprising as it may seem, because there was a substantial overlap in membership between the Golden Dawn and the esoteric branch of the Theosophical Society in London at this time, and Dion Fortune herself felt a strong psychic and spiritual connection with the Theosophists. In her mind, the two organizations did not need to compete with each other, but were complementary. The Christian reference in the name of her mystical group is harder to account for. It can in part be explained by the fact that Dion Fortune's teacher, Moriarty, seems to have been a Gnostic Christian who believed strongly that the Christian gospels were esoteric allegories.[7] In her post-humously published book, *Applied Magic*, Dion Fortune also reveals that, like Moriarty, she too held an esoteric view of Jesus Christ, describing him as "a high priest after the Order of Melchizedek," and comparing his spiritual role with that of other "saviors" like Orpheus and Mithra.[8] Dion Fortune even found her own version of the Golden Dawn Secret Chiefs in a cosmic being called Manu Melchizedek, Lord of the Flame and also of Mind, who would become her guiding force on the inner planes.[9] But there would also be a specific, and ongoing, connection with the Golden Dawn. According to Dion Fortune's account in *The Occult Review*, the Fraternity of the Inner Light was established by her "in agreement with Mrs. Mathers, to be an Outer Court to the Golden Dawn system."[10]

Dion Fortune seems to have gotten along reasonably well with Moina Mathers until 1924, when a dispute arose over the publication of Fortune's book *The Esoteric Philosophy of Love and Marriage*—a book which put forward the view that a sexual relationship between two people could be considered as an energy exchange on many levels of being, not just the physical level. While this now seems fairly innocuous, and perhaps even obvious, Moina Mathers charged Dion Fortune with "betraying the inner teaching of the Order." Fortune protested that she hadn't actually received the relevant degree from Mrs. Mathers's temple, and she was then "pardoned." Nevertheless, the dispute with Moina Mathers continued. Soon afterward, Fortune writes, "she suspended me for some months for writing *Sane Occultism*, and finally turned me out because certain symbols had not appeared in my aura—a perfectly unanswerable charge."[11]

Following this significant disagreement with Moina Mathers—Dion Fortune also maintained that Mrs. Mathers had attacked her on the astral plane in the form of a huge cat[12]—Fortune set up a temple of her own in Bayswater. Fortune's temple was loosely affiliated with the Stella Matutina, the splinter group established by R. W. Felkin and other Golden Dawn members following the rift with MacGregor Mathers.

FIGURE 5.1.   Dion Fortune in her later years

Dion Fortune's contribution to Western esoteric thought dates from the formation of the Fraternity of the Inner Light in 1927. Here she increasingly engaged herself in the mythological dimensions of magic, venturing into what she now came to regard as the collective pagan soul of humanity, tapping into the very heart of the Ancient Mysteries. Reversing the male-dominated, solar-oriented tradition that MacGregor Mathers had established in the Golden Dawn, Fortune committed herself completely to the magical potency of the archetypal Feminine, and began exploring Goddess images in the major ancient pantheons. She was also intrigued by the symbolic and sexual polarities in magic, including those of the Black Isis.[13] Isis is best known as the great goddess of magic in ancient Egyptian mythology, as the wife of the sun-god Osiris and the mother of Horus. It was Isis who succeeded in piecing together the fragments of Osiris's body after he had been murdered by Set, and it was she who also tricked Ra into revealing his secret magical name.[14] However, Fortune was apparently interested in a different aspect of Isis, a dimension that the tantric magician Kenneth Grant has called the "primordial essence of Woman (*sakti*) in her dynamic aspect." While Isis was a lunar goddess, and the Moon is traditionally considered "passive," a receptacle or reflector of light, the Black Isis was said to destroy all that was "inessential and obstructive to the soul's development."[15] This in turn led to an exploration of the magic of sexuality. According to Grant, the basis of Fortune's work at this time involved "the bringing into manifestation of this *sakti* by the magically controlled interplay of sexual polarity embodied in the priest (the consecrated male) and the specially chosen female." Together they enacted the immemorial Rite and this formed a vortex on the inner planes "down which the tremendous energies of Black Isis rush(ed) into manifestation."[16] If Grant is correct, and he met Fortune during the 1940s around the same time that he knew Aleister Crowley, this was clearly a type of visionary magic that ventured into new realms, encompassing the use of transcendent sexual energies and the fusion, in ritual, of male and female polarities.[17] It seems to have involved some form of Western magical Tantra, and was a clear departure from the Golden Dawn, which tended to downplay the sexual dimensions of magic.[18]

While the sexual aspects of the most secret Inner Light rituals remain a matter of speculation, it is clear that Fortune's main emphasis was not so much on physical magical activities as on astral encounters with the mythic archetypes of the mind. The Fraternity of the Inner Light continued the experimental work with magical visualization that had first been undertaken in the Golden Dawn during the 1890s, and the Inner Light magicians developed a practical approach to magical "pathworkings," visualizations involving guided imagery, as a direct means of exploring the subconscious mind.[19] An important essay titled "The Old Religion," written by a senior member of Fortune's group, Charles R. F. Seymour, confirms that the Inner Light members believed that inner-plane ventures of this kind could arouse "ancient cult memories" from previous incarnations.[20] Fortune believed that the key to understanding human life and achievement lay in understanding the nature of reincarnation.[21] The archetype of the Great Mother, in particular, could be thought of as a symbolic embodiment of the World Memory, a concept that has a parallel in the Theosophical concept of the Akashic Records.[22] According to Fortune, it was possible to access details of earlier incarnations through contact with the Great Mother, and in this way the nature of one's sacred purpose could be determined. In "The Old Religion," Seymour explains that it was this shared belief in the spiritual authenticity of "ancient cult memories" that united the members of their esoteric group:

> Most of the members of these groups have, in the past, served at the
> altars of Pagan Religions and have met, face to face, the Shining Ones of
> the forests and the mountains, of the lakes and seas. . . . In the course of
> these experiments it was discovered that if anyone of the members of a
> group had in the past a strong contact with a particular cult at a certain
> period, that individual could communicate these memories to others,
> and could link them with cult memories that still lie within the Earth
> memories of Isis as the Lady of Nature.[23]

In many mythic traditions, the magical journey to the ancient gods and goddesses begins on a path that leads through a gateway to the Underworld. The Golden Dawn magicians conceived of Malkuth, the tenth emanation upon the Kabbalistic Tree of Life, as the doorway to the subconscious mind—for them this was like entering the Underworld of the human psyche. Utilizing classical Roman mythology, members of the Inner Light similarly drew on the imagery of the Cumaean Gates which, according to legend, were located near Naples and were guarded by the Sibyl attending the Temple of Apollo. It was through these gates that Aeneas was said to have passed, after deciphering the labyrinth symbol inscribed upon them. Aeneas sought safe passage in the mythic world by first obtaining the golden bough, which would be given as a gift to Proserpine. He also encountered evil spirits, supernatural monsters, and former colleagues, numbered among the dead. Then, having been reunited with his father Anchises, he perceived the "great vision"—a panorama of past and future Roman history—and was granted access to mysterious secrets of the universe.

The Inner Light members had a special interest in visionary journeys of this sort and incorporated them into their guided imagery meditations, although under Dion Fortune's leadership they tended to focus primarily on the feminine aspects of the underworld encounter. Reflecting Dion Fortune's early interest in the psychological concepts of Carl Jung, there is more than a hint here of Jung's concept of the *animus* and *anima*: "It is the woman that holds the keys of the inner planes for a man. If you want to pass the Cumaean Gates you must become as a little child and a woman must lead you. . . . It was Deiphobe, daughter of Glaucus, priestess of Phoebus, and of the Goddess Three-wayed who, for King Aeneas, opened the keyless door and drew the veil that hides life from death and death from life."[24]

The Inner Light guided meditations helped heighten personal awareness of specific mythic imagery and facilitated a switch of consciousness away from one's waking perception to the symbolic inner locale concerned. The author of "The Old Religion" describes a series of inner journeys—"The By-Road to the Cave in the Mountain," "At the Ford of the Moon," "The High Place of the Moon," and "The Hosting of the Sidhe"—the culminating experience being a merging of one's awareness with the ethereal Isis in her "green" aspect as Queen of Nature.

The following account is given from the viewpoint of a male occultist who is initiated by the feminine archetype:

> As he watched, the green of the beech-leaves and the faint silver colour of the bole seemed to merge in a form that was not the tree, and yet it was the tree. He was no longer seeing the tree with his eyes—he was feeling it. He was once again in his inner, subtler, moon-body, and with it he saw and felt the moon-body of the tree. There appeared the tree spirit, the deva, the shining one who lives through the trunk and branches and leaves of the beech tree as a man lives through his torso, limbs and hair. That beech was very friendly and moon-body to moon-body they met, and as his moon-body merged into that of the lady of the beech tree, the sensation of the nature of the season of the caress of the sunlight, of the stimulation of the bright increase of the waxing moon, and of the sleep-time that comes with the decrease of the waning moon, were his.
>
> "You can merge thus into all life," he was told; and then he saw, as the fairy sees, the flowers, the waterfalls, the rivers, and the brightly coloured holy mountain of Derrybawn, which means the home of the Shining Ones. He merged himself into the roaring life that was at the summit of that great and sacred mountain and in so doing he took the initiation of the lady of Nature—the Green Isis—in her temple on the heather-clad hill-top that is above the deep ravine.[25]

Dion Fortune died in 1946, but the approach and techniques of the Fraternity of the Inner Light have continued through the auspices of a contemporary magical order known as Servants of the Light (SOL), whose headquarters are currently located in St. Helier on the island of Jersey. The SOL conducts international correspondence courses on Western magic and has members in many countries. Dion Fortune trained the influential occultist W. E. Butler who, like his teacher, assimilated a vast knowledge of the Kabbalah, mythology, and esoteric symbolism into a practical system of magic.[26] In his later years, Butler passed the leadership of the SOL to the present director of the Order, Dolores Ashcroft-Nowicki, who has herself produced several important works on the Western magical tradition, including *Highways of the Mind: The Art and History of Pathworking* and *The Shining Paths: An Experiential Journey through the Tree of Life.*[27] The international reach of the SOL and the writings of W. E. Butler and Dolores Ashcroft-Nowicki have ensured that the magical ideas of Dion Fortune continue to have a major impact among devotees of the Western esoteric tradition.

Austin Osman Spare

Austin Osman Spare (1886–1956) provides us with a fascinating example of an artist who was both a magician and a trance-visionary. While the formal structures of the Hermetic Order of the Golden Dawn were fragmenting amid schisms and dissent just prior to the onset of World War I, Spare was developing a unique system of practical magic through his exploration of ecstatic trance states. Spare was probably the first occultist in modern times to evolve a self-contained working hypothesis about the nature of psychic energy that could be applied without all the paraphernalia of traditional rituals and magical implements. His system of magical sigils showed how an effort of will, when focused on the subconscious mind, could unleash the most extraordinary psychic material.

One of five children, Austin Osman Spare was born at home in Snowhill, near Smithfield, London, on 30 December 1886. The son of a policeman, Spare had two elder brothers and two sisters—one of whom, Ellen, was younger than him.[28] The family later moved to south London, and Spare attended St. Agnes School in Kennington Park. In 1902 Spare left school and began working for a company named Powells, a manufacturer of stained glass, where he distinguished himself by producing five stained-glass panel designs for one of his senior work colleagues. However, Spare was also taking formal art training at Lambeth Evening Art School, where his precocious artistic talent was noticed. At the age of sixteen, while he was still working for Powells, Spare won a £40 scholarship and a silver medal from the prestigious art journal *The Studio*, which enabled him to study at the Royal College of Art, South Kensington, and in 1904, one of his black-and-white bookplate designs was displayed at the Royal Academy.[29] This particular work had been produced when he was fourteen, making him the youngest exhibited artist in the history of that institution.[30] The president of the Academy, John Singer Sargent, proclaimed Spare to be a genius.[31] Spare also attracted the attention of art connoisseur Pickford Waller, from whom he would receive several commissions for bookplates. He was later commissioned to illustrate Ethel Wheeler's *Behind the Veil* (1906) and a book of aphorisms by J. Bertram and F. Russell titled *The Starlit Mire*, published by the distinguished arts patron John Lane (1911). Around the same time, an article on Spare by Ralph Straus also appeared in *The Book Lovers Magazine*.[32]

In 1916 Spare founded the quarterly magazine *Form*, joined later by Frederick Carter, who became co-editor. The magazine was sponsored by John Lane, who hoped it would emulate the earlier success of *The Yellow Book*, an avant-garde literary publication renowned for its erotic and provocative illustrations by Aubrey Beardsley, with whom Spare was sometimes compared.[33] In May 1917, however, Spare was enlisted, against his will, to join the Royal Army Medical Corps, and no further editions of *Form* were issued under the patronage of John Lane.[34] In 1919, Spare visited France as a special war artist documenting the aftermath of the Great War; several works based on sketches from this period are included in the collection of the Imperial War Museum. After his sojourn in Europe, Spare returned to the genre of journal publishing. Between October 1922 and April 1924 he co-edited an illustrated literary magazine, *The Golden Hind*, which included the work of such notable writers as Aldous Huxley, Alec Waugh, and Havelock Ellis.[35]

Since 1905 Spare had also been involved in creating and publishing his own distinctive and highly unconventional books, however, and it was these self-published limited-edition works that would identify his unique contribution to the Western esoteric tradition while simultaneously consigning him to the periphery of mainstream artistic circles. Although he had been praised by John Singer Sargent, and also by the renowned portrait painter Augustus John, who regarded Spare as one of the great graphic artists of his time, others found Spare's magical compositions deeply confronting.[36] According to Kenneth Grant, Spare's esoteric imagery prompted the noted playwright and critic George Bernard Shaw to remark: "Spare's medicine is too strong for the average man."[37]

Spare's self-published works, which he illustrated, designed, and financed himself, include *Earth: Inferno* (1905); *A Book of Satyrs* (1907); *The Book of Pleasure (Self-Love): The Psychology of Ecstasy* (1913); *The Focus of Life: The Mutterings of Aaos* (1921); and *Anathema of Zos: The Sermon to the Hypocrites* (1927).[38]

Spare's distinctive and unconventional publications placed him clearly within the context of the Western magical tradition through their references to sigil magic and esoteric symbolism. Although Spare had earlier been considered a possible successor to Aubrey Beardsley and was sometimes compared to other notable graphic artists like Charles Ricketts (illustrator of Oscar Wilde's *The Sphinx*) and Harry Clarke (illustrator of Goethe's *Faust* and Poe's *Tales of Mystery and Imagination*), his own publications were polemical in style, graphically complex, and unorthodox in presentation. His two major esoteric works, *The Book of Pleasure*

FIGURE 5.2.   Austin Osman Spare—a self-portrait from 1923. Courtesy Fulgur Ltd., London.

(Self-Love): The Psychology of Ecstasy and *The Focus of Life: The Mutterings of Aaos*, explored sigil magic and the images of the subconscious, and were written in an abstruse and inaccessible style that made few concessions to any mainstream readership, despite the spectacular graphic images that accompanied both texts. *Earth: Inferno, A Book of Satyrs*, and *Anathema of Zos: The Sermon to the Hypocrites*, meanwhile, were satirical works that drew attention to the misery of the human condition and the emptiness and shallow hypocrisy of the privileged classes in contemporary society. *Anathema of Zos* is a vitriolic and bitter invective directed

specifically at the Mayfair artistic elite that had initially supported Spare when his artworks were exhibited in prominent West End galleries.[39]

Spare's *The Book of Pleasure (Self-Love): The Psychology of Ecstasy* is widely regarded as his major work. It develops his concept of Kia, which is central to his magical philosophy, and also contains practical instructions for creating magical sigils and automatic drawings. In addition, it places Spare's magical explorations within the context of modern psychological approaches to the subconscious mind.

Zos and Kia

Spare first makes reference to the term "Zos" in *Earth: Inferno* in a black-and-white line illustration titled *Chaos*.[40] Here a naked man draws aside a curtain revealing a cluster of tangled human forms representing what Spare calls the "inferno of the Normal." The accompanying text reads "Oh! come with me, the Kia and the Zos, to witness this extravagance." Although Spare does not develop his idea of the polarity between Zos and Kia in *Earth: Inferno*, he nevertheless provides tantalizing clues. On page 22 he writes: "Alas! we are children of Earth," indicating that the term Zos refers to human manifestation, the incarnate, the physical. Alongside the preceding image, *Despair*, which shows four forlorn human beings, one of them a prostrate naked woman, Spare writes: "Revere the Kia and your mind will become tranquil."[41] In *The Book of Pleasure (Self-Love): The Psychology of Ecstasy*, Spare explains for the first time what he means by Zos. A small, but nevertheless definitive, text-reference is inserted graphically into an illustration teeming with magical sigils, and the text reads: "The body considered as a whole, I call Zos."[42] Spare's definition of Kia, meanwhile, is included in the introductory section of the book: "Kia," writes Spare, is "the absolute freedom which being free is mighty enough to be 'reality' and free at any time."[43] Later in the book, Spare also refers to Kia in sexual terms: as "the ancestral sex principle" and the "unmodified sexuality."[44]

As Gavin W. Semple notes in his recently published essay on the art and magic of Austin Spare, there is a clear distinction between Zos, representing "all that which is embodied or manifest," and Kia, representing the Absolute.[45] Spare had been reading an English-language translation of the Kabbalistic text *The Zohar* prior to working on *Earth: Inferno*.[46] It has thus been suggested that Spare's reference to Kia may have a Kabbalistic origin. Semple believes that Kia may be an inversion of the Kabbalistic term *AiqBekar*, a reference to "the Kabbalah of Nine Chambers" and the secret Kabbalistic code system of Temurah.[47] An alternative suggestion from William Wallace seems more plausible, however. Wallace believes that Kia probably derives from the Kabbalistic Hebrew word *Chiah*, which denotes the highest form of the world of *Atziluth*, the Absolute.[48] This would certainly appear closer to Spare's own meaning of the word. In the Kabbalah, *Chiah* or *Chi-yah* is an aspect of *Neshamah*, the soul, one of the three principal spiritual agencies mentioned in the *Zohar*, the others being *Nefesh* (life) and *Ruah* (spirit).[49] Even though he was coining his own special term, Kia, Spare nevertheless aligned it conceptually with the mystical idea of the Absolute, or Void—the supreme reality in the Kabbalah—and, as discussed below, Spare's notion of the "void moment" is central to his magical process.

In *The Book of Pleasure (Self-Love): The Psychology of Ecstasy*, Spare uses his concept of Kia to refer to the primal, cosmic life-force which can be channeled into the human organism, Zos. In one of his later esoteric texts, Spare refers to the life-force as "a potency," and his magical technique for arousing the elemental energies latent within this life-potency—a technique he termed "atavistic resurgence"—involved focusing on magical sigils which he employed as vehicles of his magical will.[50] When the mind was in what Spare called a "void" or open state—achieved, for example, through meditation, exhaustion, or at the peak of sexual ecstasy—magical sigils could be used to send "commands" to the subconscious mind. Later these magical commands would be intentionally forgotten in order to remove them from conscious awareness, but in the meantime, according to Spare, they would "grow" within the seedbed of the subconscious mind until they became "ripe" and manifested once again in the familiar world of conscious reality, thereby achieving the magician's initial intent. Spare summarizes this magical process in his esoteric text, *The Witches' Sabbath*: "The ecstatic moment is used as the fecund instant of wish endowment; for at that period of reality, the will, desire and belief are aligned in unison."[51]

Background to Spare's Magical Philosophy

Spare's approach to magical states of consciousness draws on a variety of sources, encompassing archetypal mythic imagery from ancient Egypt, a fascination with the sexual energies of the subconscious mind, and techniques learned through his close personal relationship with an unusual psychic mentor whom he always referred to simply as Mrs. Paterson.[52] Spare's magical approach was also shaped by his fascination with death, by his interest in Taoism, which places great emphasis on the flow of positive and negative life-energy, and by his personal conviction that the psychic energies, or "karmas" of previous incarnations, remained as latent potentials within the mind of every human being.[53] "Ability," writes Spare in his esoteric tract, *Axiomata*, "is an endowment from our past selves."[54] Spare believed that these karmic energies could be activated by the magical will.[55]

Spare also maintained that the ancient Egyptians understood the complex mythology of the subconscious mind: their animal-headed deities provided proof that they understood the process of spiritual evolution:

> They symbolised this knowledge in one great symbol, the Sphinx, which is pictorially man evolving from animal existence. Their numerous Gods, all partly Animal, Bird, Fish . . . prove the completeness of that knowledge. . . . The cosmogony of their Gods is proof of their knowledge of the order of evolution, its complex processes from the one simple organism. . . . They knew they still possessed the rudimentary faculties of all existences, and were partly under their control. Thus their past Karmas became Gods, good and evil forces, and had to be appeased: from this all moral doctrine etc. is determined. So all Gods have lived (being ourselves) on earth, and when dead, their experience or Karma governs our actions in degree: to that extent we are subject to the will of these Gods. . . . This is the key to the mystery of the Sphinx.[56]

Frank Letchford, who was a close friend of Austin Spare from 1937 until the artist's death in 1956, confirms in his biography, *From the Inferno to Zos* (1995), that ancient Egyptian culture and mythology impacted strongly on Spare's art and magical philosophy throughout his life:

> The influence upon Austin of Egyptian art writing and practice were strong. The incidence of Egyptian deities like Isis, Osiris, Horus, Nuit and of amulets, talismans, sigils and magical symbols is varied in his work. . . . According to the Egyptian religion the human "being" is composed of four parts: the body itself, the astral double, the soul and the spark of life from the Godhead. In all Austin's writings, aphorisms, drawings and sketches are found charms, symbols and symbolic figures, namely, the sun, the moon, cats and gods, part-human, part-animal.[57]

The gods and goddesses of ancient Egypt had a profound impact on Austin Spare because they seemed to embody the principle of spiritual evolution through animal and human karma.[58] However, Egyptian cosmology was not his first point of reference: Spare first learned about the transformative potentials of the subconscious mind from an elderly woman called Mrs. Paterson, who was a friend of his parents and used to tell his fortune when he was young. Spare's relationship with his own mother was not close, and he soon came to regard Mrs. Paterson as his "second mother."[59] She was illiterate but generous in spirit, and would often help neighbors and friends in distress. Mrs. Paterson appeared to have an extrasensory ability to project thought-forms. According to Spare she was able to "reify" ideas and thoughts to visible, sometimes even tangible, appearance: "If in her occult prognostications she discovered an event or incident which she could not describe verbally, she would reify the scene."[60] Spare describes her technique in the following way: "She used to tell my fortune when I was quite young. . . . She was a natural hypnotist. She would say, 'Look in that dark corner,' and, if you obeyed, she could make you visualise what she was telling you about your future."[61]

The Thelemic magician and occult writer Kenneth Grant, referred to earlier, first met Spare in 1949 and had extensive contact with him during the last eight years of his life.[62] Grant believes that it was because of his close relationship with Mrs. Paterson that Spare became attracted to older women, and that this was due, in part, to the fact that as a child he had watched her transform herself visually from an old crone into a young woman through the magical process of "reification": "The wrinkled crone had appeared to change into a large-limbed voluptuous girl. So deep was the impression—whether actual or imagined—that for the rest of his life Spare was fascinated by the idea of sexual potency in ageing women. . . . He used this theme in his witch drawings where he frequently combined the hag and the girl in one picture, if not in one image."[63]

The archetypal image of the Universal Woman, or Goddess, in all her various aspects—from sensual maiden through to aged crone—became a central feature in Spare's personal mythology. Spare first refers to her in *Earth: Inferno* where, in an illustration titled *Earth*, she is shown and captioned "lying barren on the Parapet of the Subconsciousness" while humanity itself is depicted "sinking into the pit of conventionality."[64] Spare uses this graphic image to call for what he termed the "resurrection of the Primitive Woman."[65] Grant writes that, for Spare, the "Goddess, the Witch Queen, the Primitive or Universal Woman . . . is the cypher of all 'inbetweenness'" and she is experienced in the unity of Self-love, that is to say, in the ecstatic union of Zos and Kia. "Nor," adds Grant, "is she to be limited as any particular 'goddess' such as Astarte, Isis, Cybele, Kali, Nuit, for to limit her is to turn away from the path and to idealize a concept which, as such, is false because incomplete, unreal because temporal."[66]

One of Spare's most significant compositions, *The Ascension of the Ego from Ecstasy to Ecstasy*, shows the Goddess as a beautiful naked maiden welcoming Spare to higher realms of awareness.[67] Spare is depicted, appropriately, with wings extending from his head, symbolic of ecstatic flight. Spare's "ego," or persona, is shown merging with an earlier animal incarnation, and the two shapes transcend each other in the form of a primal skull, a motif representing the "death" of the ego. Spare believed he could retrace his earlier animal incarnations or karmas back to the very source of life itself, the universal "Oneness of Creation" he called Kia, and that these residual animal energies could in turn become a source of magic power.

Spare's *The Ascension of the Ego from Ecstasy to Ecstasy* provides us with an important insight into this magical process. Although sexual union with a female

FIGURE 5.3. Austin Osman Spare and his atavisms—a self-portrait from *The Book of Pleasure (Self-Love): The Psychology of Ecstasy* (1913)

FIGURE 5.4A.   Austin Osman Spare: *The Ascension of the Ego from Ecstasy to Ecstasy*, from *The Book of Pleasure (Self-Love): The Psychology of Ecstasy*, 1913.

partner was not his only method for attaining an ecstatic state, Spare frequently combined his magical will with the climax of sexual orgasm in his quest for creative inspiration.[68] According to Spare, at the peak of sexual ecstasy, the personal ego (Zos) and the universal life-force (Kia) are united in a state of blissful and transcendent openness: inspiration flows forth from Kia and is transmitted through the primordial Goddess herself.[69] "Inspiration," writes Spare in *The Book of Pleasure*, "is always at a *void* moment."[70]

In Spare's system of trance-magic, two processes are associated with ecstatic states. The first of these employs a technique that Spare termed the Death Posture: by its very nature an ecstatic peak-moment is characterized by the surrender, or "death," of the ego, and the process could therefore be regarded as a simulation of death itself.[71] "Because every other sense is brought to nullity by sex intoxication," writes Spare, "it is called the Death Posture."[72] As Gavin Semple notes: "The Death Posture involves a total negation of conceptual thought and perceptual awareness, and the assumption of the Void, Kia, by its practitioner; its aim is ecstasy, the bliss of union with the Absolute in Self-Love."[73]

The second of Spare's magical processes involved the creation and use of "sentient" magical sigils that could act as vehicles or "messengers" to the subconscious mind. This method embodied both Will and Desire, the magical sigils being used to implant the "Great Wish" within the subconscious mind at the peak-moment of ecstasy. The ecstatic peak itself could be attained through sexual union, but there were other methods of attaining it as well, which are referred to below. Considered together, the two processes became a central feature of Spare's unique approach to trance-magic and his quest for union with Kia, the bliss of the Absolute.

The Death Posture

Spare's intent in utilizing the Death Posture was to "incarnate" the dynamic and inspirational life-force of Kia, the source of artistic genius and sexual freedom.[74] Gavin Semple writes that the Death Posture "employs the flesh itself as the effigy or sigil of Belief, and through its 'death' and resurrection . . . [initiates] the Great Work. The work is the ecstatic fusion of the Zos and the Kia (Ego and Self), the Self-Love which gives the title of Spare's book."[75] Here the attainment of ecstasy is primarily an end in itself. However, because Kia is also the "ancestral sex principle" and the source of "unmodified sexuality," the union of Zos and Kia inevitably leads to expressions of what Spare terms the "new sexuality."[76] In *The Book of Pleasure*, Spare writes: "Know the Death Posture and its reality in the ascension from duality. . . . The Death Posture is the reduction of all conception to the Neither-Neither [Spare's term for the Absolute or true Self] till the desire is contentment by pleasing yourself . . . the restoration of the new sexuality and the ever original self-love in freedom are attained."[77]

Spare describes the actual method as follows:

Lying on your back lazily, the body expressing the emotion of yawning, suspiring while conceiving by smiling, that is the idea of the posture. Forgetting time with those things which were essential reflecting their meaninglessness, the moment is beyond time and its virtue has happened.

Standing on tip-toe, with the arms rigid, bound behind by the hands, clasped and straining to the utmost, the neck stretched— breathing deeply and spasmodically, till giddy and sensation comes in gusts, gives exhaustion and capacity for the former.

Gazing at your reflection till it is blurred and you know not the gazer, close your eyes (this usually happens involuntarily) and visualize. The light (always an X in curious evolutions) that is seen should be held onto, never letting go, till the effort is forgotten; this gives a feeling of immensity (which sees a small form ꝏ) whose limit you cannot reach. This should be practised before experiencing the foregoing. The emotion that is felt is the knowledge which tells you why.[78]

Spare describes the mystical impact of the Death Posture: "The Ego is swept up as a leaf in a fierce gale—in the fleetness of the indeterminable, that which is always about to happen, becomes its truth. Things that are self-evident are no longer obscure, as by his own will he pleases; know this as the negation of all faith by living it, the end of duality of consciousness."[79]

According to Frank Letchford, the essential purpose of the Death Posture—a practice Spare believed should be performed daily—was to "incarnate" a transformative magical process: "the body is allowed to manifest spontaneously. . . . His idea was to form a new body, it was a time for re-birth, incarnating and reincarnating. He *wills* his own death. He awaits the transfiguration, an inversion and reversion, a continuation of evolution; that which he desires will come to pass."[80]

In addition to utilizing the Death Posture, however, Spare also wished to develop a method for focusing his magical desires. This led him to formulate his own unique system of atavistic magical sigils.

Magical Sigils

Spare's use of magical sigils, which he began to develop into a workable system from 1906 onward, was based on the understanding that the dynamics of the subconscious mind depend entirely on symbols and images, that the "language"

of the subconscious is pictorial rather than verbal.[81] As Spare observes in his essay
Mind to Mind and How: "There is a Grimorium of graphic symbology and vague
phonic nuances that conjoin all thought and is the language of the psychic world.
Mind is a continuant [sic] and all concepts are relatable to perceptions and
contact, therefore real; the continuum of all aspects of memory and learning is
consciousness—the past again becoming explicit."[82]

Spare believed that the human psyche contained all the residual karmas of previous incarnations. Kia, as the Absolute, and as the source of all being, encompassed
all evolutionary phases of life that had so far existed on the planet. As Spare notes in
The Book of Pleasure: "By sigils and the acquirement of vacuity, any past incarnation,
experience, can be summoned into consciousness."[83] Spare's sorcery—he himself
labeled it as such—utilized the process of atavistic resurgence in order to summon
"elementals," or karmic "automata," from the subconscious mind for magical purposes.[84] Even when he lived alone in a small run-down flat in South London, Spare
maintained that he was always surrounded by elemental forces and that these
"spirits" were his allies or "familiars."[85]

As mentioned earlier, Spare was fascinated by medieval magical grimoires like
the *Goetia* and *The Greater Key of Solomon* and was intrigued by the magical seals
ascribed to various elemental spirits. It has been suggested that these magical seals
may have been a source of inspiration for the "cryptic letter-forms and devices"
found in *The Book of Pleasure* and that Spare was almost certainly influenced by
the magical scripts found in Cornelius Agrippa's *Three Books of Occult Philosophy
or Magic*, a work first published in 1533.[86] Spare appears to paraphrase the Renaissance magician's writings on sigils and also transcribed two of his signs in a page
of sketches for the *Book of Pleasure* vignettes.[87] However, whereas the magical seals
in the grimoires were linked either to specific demons like those identified in the
Goetia, or to planetary spirits (Saturn, Jupiter, Mars, etc.) like those referred to in
Cornelius Agrippa's *Three Books of Occult Philosophy or Magic*, Spare's great innovation was in realizing that magical seals or sigils could be personalized.[88] As
Gavin Semple has noted:

> While the grimoires dictate the use of specific magical seals for the
> binding and control of spirits and demand a high degree of faith (i.e.,
> consciously formulated belief) in their efficacy, and in the theurgic
> system of which they form a part, Spare realized that *any* symbols must
> be effective provided they are congruent with the patterns of the
> operator's innate beliefs and personal aesthetic. This is certain to be the
> case if they are drawn from his or her own subconsciousness.[89]

Recognizing that they would have to reflect his own magical credo, Spare created his own individualized sigils. In *The Book of Pleasure* he provides a summary

This my wish

To obtain

The strength of a Tiger

Combined as one Sigil   or   .

FIGURE 5.4B. Spare sigils

of his method: "Sigils are made by combining the letters of the alphabet simplified . . . the idea being to obtain a simple form which can easily be visualized at will,
and has not too much pictorial relation to the desire. . . . Verily, what a person
believes by Sigils, is the truth, and is always fulfilled."[90] In effect, Spare was seeking
to focus his magical will on a single graphic symbol so that his intent or purpose
could more readily be grasped as a totality. He did this by first expressing his will
(or desire) in sentence form and then by combining the basic letters, without
repetition, into a unified glyph or sigil. In *The Book of Pleasure*, Spare provides an
example of how a sigil can be created from the sentence: "This is my wish, to obtain
the strength of a tiger" (see figure 5.4b).

Spare then describes the personal conditions required for success in projecting
the sigil into the subconscious mind:

> Now by virtue of this Sigil you are able to send your desire into the
> subconsciousness (which contains all strength); that having happened, it
> is the desire's realization by the manifestation of the knowledge or power
> necessary.
>
>   First, all consciousness of the Sigil has to be annulled; do not
> confuse this with concentration—you simply conceive the Sigil any
> moment you begin to think. Vacuity is obtained by exhausting the mind
> and body . . . the time of exhaustion is the time of fulfilment.[91] At the
> time of exhaustion or vacuity, retain only and visualize the Sigil form—
> eventually it becomes vague, then vanished and success is assured . . . the
> desire for identification carries it [i.e., the Sigil] to the corresponding
> subconscious stratum, its destination. . . . Hence the mind, by Sigils,
> depending upon the intensity of desire, is illuminated or obsessed

(knowledge or power) from that particular Karma (the subconscious stratum, a particular existence and knowledge gained by it) relative to the desire. . . . Knowledge is obtained by the sensation, resulting from the unity of the desire and Karma. Power, by its "actual" vitalization and resurrection.[92]

As mentioned earlier, Spare believed that it was crucially important that once the sigil was dispatched into the subconscious at the moment of "vacuity" (the "void moment"), the instruction then had to be forgotten so that the process of manifesting desire could become "organic." As Spare explains:

Belief to be true must be organic and subconscious. The desire to be great can only become organic at the time of vacuity and by giving it (Sigil) form. When conscious of the Sigil form (any time but the magical) it should be repressed, a deliberate striving to forget it; by this it is active and dominates at the unconscious period; its form nourishes and allows it to become attached to the subconscious and become organic; that accomplished is its reality and realization.[93]

It is reasonable to ask whether Spare's concept of magical sigils actually worked, and the anecdotal evidence is certainly intriguing, if not persuasive. The occultist Kenneth Grant who, as mentioned earlier, had extensive contact with Spare toward the end of his life, describes a situation where Spare needed to move a heavy load of timber without assistance. A sigil was required that could generate great personal strength, and Spare employed the tiger sigil, referred to above, in order to access reserves of strength he did not consciously realize he possessed. According to Grant's account:

Spare closed his eyes for a while and visualised a picture which symbolised a wish for the strength of tigers [i.e., the sigil above]. Almost immediately he sensed an inner response. He then felt a tremendous upsurge of energy sweep through his body. For a moment he felt like a sapling bent by the onslaught of a mighty wind. With a great effort of will, he steadied himself and directed the force to its proper object. A great calm descended and he found himself able to carry the load easily.[94]

Automatic Art

In addition to developing his concept of the Death Posture and the Zos/Kia cosmology, Spare also explored the spontaneous creative process of automatic drawing. It has been argued that Spare can legitimately claim to be the first Surrealist artist, because his earliest atavistic artworks preceded the 1924 Paris Surrealist Manifesto by at least a decade.[95]

Throughout his life, Spare was interested in spiritualism and Theosophy, and his attraction to automatic drawing is directly linked to the psychic automata, or elementals, which he believed surrounded him at all times.[96] *The Book of Pleasure* includes an illustration titled *The Dwellers at the Gates of Silent Memory* that shows a reflective naked woman sitting in a state of repose. What appears to be a tree, but is actually an extended skull with antlers, extends upward from her head, and perched upon the "branches" are several birds, or more specifically, "bird karmas." Nearby, a disembodied winged head floats in space. Spare's accompanying text, titled "The Sub-Consciousness," contains a reference to what he calls the "Storehouse of Memories with an Ever-Open Door," and he goes on to write:

> Know the sub-consciousness to be an epitome of all experience and wisdom, past incarnations as men, animals, birds, vegetable life, etc. etc. everything that exists, has and ever will exist. Each being a stratum in the order of evolution. Naturally then, the lower we probe into these strata, the earlier will be the forms of life we arrive at; the last is the Almighty Simplicity. And if we succeed in awakening them, we shall gain their properties, and our accomplishment will correspond.[97]

The karmic entities referred to in *The Book of Pleasure* as the "Dwellers at the Gates of Silent Memory" provide a key to Spare's automatic art. Spare thought of them as "the nascent selves swarming at our periphery, always *behind* our attention. It is through interaction with these desire-bodies, and their integration into our subjective continua, that we interact directly with Self, through the infinite permutation of its expression."[98] It was these psychic entities that Spare evoked in producing his automatic drawings; he maintained that they could be perceived in a darkened room: "Darken your room, shut the door, empty your mind. Yet you are still in great company—the Numen and your Genius with all their media, and your host of elementals and ghosts of your dead loves—are there! They need no light by which to see, no words to speak, no motive to enact except through your own purely formed desire."[99]

According to his friend, journalist Hannen Swaffer (1879–1962), Spare used self-hypnosis to facilitate the "automatic" process. Frank Letchford refers to Swaffer's account in his biographical study, *From the Inferno to Zos*:

> In [1929] Hannen Swaffer published a little book entitled *Adventures with Inspiration* in which there is a paragraph describing Austin's method of work on automatic drawings. Staring into a mirror to induce

self-hypnotism, he sets to work, sometimes for hours, awakening to find that he has covered hundreds of pages with most beautiful drawings. Try as he would, he could not stop, but if he wished to draw he could not. In this way he filled a drawing book of fifty sheets.[100]

Spare denied that he was acting like a psychic medium on such occasions, always maintaining that his contact with elementals and karmic automata was subject to his magical will.[101] However, Letchford's account suggests that, at least on some occasions, these entities operated spontaneously and were beyond Spare's artistic control.

An article titled "Automatic Drawing," co-authored by Austin Spare and Frederick Carter, and published in *Form* in 1916, throws further light on the process:

Automatic drawing, one of the simplest of psychic phenomena, is a means of characteristic expression and, if used with courage and honesty, of recording subconscious activities in the mind. The mental mechanisms used are those common in dreams, which create quick perceptions of relations in the unexpected, as wit, and psycho-neurotic symptoms. Hence it appears that single or non-consciousness is an essential condition and as in all inspiration, the product of involution not invention. Automatism being the manifestation of latent desires (or wishes) the significance of the forms (the ideas) obtained represent the previously unrecorded obsessions. Art becomes, by this illuminism or ecstatic power, a functional activity expressing in a symbolical language the desire towards joy unmodified—the sense of the Mother of all things. . . .

In the ecstatic condition of revelation from the subconscious, the mind elevates the sexual or inherited power . . . and depresses the intellectual qualities. So a new atavistic responsibility is attained by daring to believe—to possess one's own beliefs—without attempting to rationalize spurious ideas from prejudiced and tainted intellectual sources.

Automatic drawings can be obtained by such methods as concentrating on a Sigil—by any means of exhausting mind and body pleasantly in order to obtain a condition of non-consciousness—by wishing in opposition to the real desire after acquiring an organic impulse toward drawing.

The hand must be trained to work freely and without control, by practice in making simple forms with a continuous involved line without afterthought, i.e., its intention should just escape consciousness. Drawings should be made by allowing the hand to run freely with the least possible deliberation. In time shapes will be found to evolve, suggesting conceptions, forms and ultimately having personal or individual style. The mind in a state of oblivion, without desire towards reflection or pursuit of materialistic intellectual suggestions, is in a condition to produce successful drawings of one's *personal* ideas, symbolic in meaning and wisdom. By this means sensation may be visualized.[102]

The *Form* article clearly indicates that Spare's approach to automatic drawing is linked to his concept of atavistic resurgence. Spare's artistic intention is to create a spontaneous and unimpeded flow of imagery that proceeds directly from his karmic atavisms, from the "Dwellers at the Gates of Silent Memory" that are actually residual metaphysical personifications of his own inner being.

Two limited-edition collections of Spare's automatic art have been published since the artist's death in 1956. The first of these, *A Book of Automatic Drawings*, was published by Catalpa Press, London, in 1972 in a hardcover quarto format, in an edition of 1,000 copies. The drawings themselves were from a sketch-book dated 1925, designed as a complete work. As Ian Law indicates in his introduction to the 1972 edition, the compositions featured in *A Book of Automatic Drawings* were reproduced "in the exact size, style and sequence that Spare indicated."[103] The edition contains twelve full-size visionary images, executed in the meticulous and highly accomplished linear style that had led some critics to compare his work with that of Dürer and Holbein. Many of the images seem perverse and excessively ugly: the limbs of most of his humanoid figures are hideously distorted, many have horns or demonic shapes extending from their limbs, and several are surreal bird— or animal—fusions. However, Spare believed that the act of transfiguring the grotesque could be liberating.[104] In his posthumously published text, *The Witches' Sabbath*, Spare refers to the traditional image of the "ugly witch" and argues, in keeping with the transformative powers he associated with Mrs. Paterson, that this sort of ugliness could produce a new aesthetic of its own:

> The witch . . . is usually old, usually grotesque, libidinously learned and
> is as sexually attractive as a corpse; yet she becomes the entire vehicle of
> consummation. This is necessary for transmutation; the personal
> aesthetic culture is destroyed; perversion is also used to overcome the
> same kind of moral prejudice or conformity. . . . He who transmutes
> the traditionally ugly into another aesthetic value, has new pleasures
> beyond fear.[105]

A second collection of Spare's automatic art, *The Book of Ugly Ecstasy*, was published in London in 1996, in both general and limited-edition hardcover formats. Once again the illustrations were taken directly from one of Spare's sketch-books. The original hand-drawn volume had been purchased from the artist in October 1924 and contained fifty-eight automatic drawings, of which only twenty-three could be considered complete.[106]

The 1996 edition contains only the twenty-three finished artworks, all of them meticulously reproduced. In style, subject matter, and quality, the automatic drawings in *The Book of Ugly Ecstasy* resemble those in *A Book of Automatic Drawings* but are, perhaps, even more grotesque. Distorted human shapes transform into clawed, bestial phantasms with multiple eyes or drooping bulbous breasts; horned devils emerge, one from the other, in a nightmarish sequence of bestial emanations; other creatures have truncated limbs or are simply malformed. However, as Robert Ansell writes in his introduction: "the mystery of their creation may be illumined by a single candle flame. In this light the viewer will find these aberrations slowly become familiar and induce a process of subtle sublimation."[107]

The key to understanding both the source and nature of Spare's unique fantasy images can be found in his concept of the "void moment." Spare utilized magical trance states in order to open his consciousness to an influx of atavistic automata— residual psychic energies he believed were karmas from his own earlier bird, animal, and human incarnations. Spare's occult practice sought to embody these automata through an act of magical obsession, a term Spare actually uses to describe his process.[108] While Spare always denied that he was acting like a passive psychic medium, his technique of seeking the "void moment" and then "opening the door to the Dwellers on the Threshold" allowed his psyche to be overrun with psychic impressions from his subconscious mind.[109] Spare's "ugly ecstasies," produced as automatic drawings, were, to use his own phraseology, his own karmic atavisms— *they were ultimately aspects of himself*. Spare focused both his cosmology and his magic on the potentials of the human organism.

In his *Logomachy of Zos*, he makes such pronouncements as "Man is a potentiality of *anything* becoming actuality," and "The only attribute of God is man," and "God is absolutely my own Idea; otherwise God cannot exist."[110] As Gavin Semple has noted, Spare sought through the Death Posture to make a magical sigil out of his own body, to "flesh" his desires through an act of magical will.[111] As Spare succinctly states: *All ways to Heaven lead to flesh.*[112]

Spare's method is also essentially retrogressive—his ecstatic journey takes him into his previous incarnations and progressively back to the source of all manifestation: Kia.[113] However, as he was an artist affiliated inspirationally with the Left-Hand Path, it is also important to note the chthonic nature of his artistic process. As Marcus M. Jungkurth points out in a recent essay, Spare's artistic oeuvre derives, essentially, from the mythological Underworld. Spare's magical name was *Zos vel Thanatos*—"Death is all"—and during his career as a visionary artist and trance

FIGURE 5.5.   Detail of an atavistic image from Spare's posthumously published work, *The Book of Ugly Ecstasy*. Courtesy Fulgur Ltd., London.

magician, Spare identified himself with Thanatos, Death, which was one of the bynames of the Greek god of the Underworld, Hades.[114] Spare's images arise from the Underworld of his densely populated psyche. His artistic atavisms are incarnations of his personal karmas that lie just beneath the surface of awareness; through acts of metaphysical ecstasy he induces them to swarm into his art.

Spare once wrote: "Out of the flesh of our Mothers come dreams and memories of the Gods."[115] Spare's visionary oeuvre, teeming with atavistic forms and spirit-creatures from the nether-regions, embodies its own sense of magical authenticity. It is the unique vision of an artist who was also a sorcerer, and who was highly aware of the permutations of human form and expression.

Rosaleen Norton

Rosaleen Norton (1917–1979) has been described as Australia's best-known witch, although by now her fame has extended well beyond her native shores. Avant-garde American filmmaker Kenneth Anger, who has had an ongoing fascination with occult mythology and visited Aleister Crowley's sex-magick Abbey in Cefalu, once proposed making a film about her, and she has also inspired contemporary novels and a play. Rosaleen Norton is certainly one of the most interesting painters of supernatural themes to have emerged in modern times.

During the 1950s and 1960s, Norton was a controversial and colorful character in Sydney's Kings Cross district and was known to the public as an eccentric, bohemian witch-lady and visionary artist. She wore flamboyant, brightly colored blouses and vivid bandanas, puffed on an exotic engraved cigarette holder, and plucked her eyebrows so that they arched in a somewhat sinister curve. Norton also claimed certain distinctive body markings that she possessed were a sign that she was "born a witch."

Slight in build, with curly black hair and a smile that revealed irregular teeth, Norton always had something of a magnetic presence that made her stand out in the crowd. The publication of her limited edition art book *The Art of Rosaleen Norton* in Sydney in 1952—which also contained poems by her lover Gavin Greenlees—aroused considerable media controversy. Norton's publisher and sponsor, Walter Glover, was charged in Sydney with releasing an obscene publication, and copies sent to New York were confiscated and burned by U.S. Customs.

During this period of extensive media publicity, Rosaleen Norton became known in the public mind as an artist whose provocative paintings of half-human, half-animal forms were even more controversial than Norman Lindsay's risqué nude figures. Norton depicted naked women wrestling with reptilean elementals or flying on the backs of winged griffins, gods who were both male and female, and demonic forms with menacing claw-tipped wings. During the 1950s, Norton's controversial paintings and drawings seemed to embody a deep-seated pagan impulse and ran counter to orthodox religious sensibilities.

Rosaleen Miriam Norton was born in Dunedin, New Zealand, in 1917, the third of three sisters. Her father, Albert, was a captain in the merchant navy and

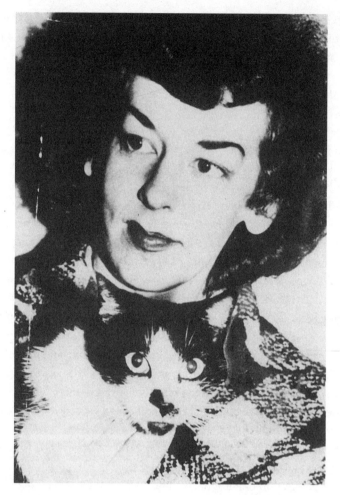

FIGURE 5.6.   Rosaleen Norton in the mid-1950s. Courtesy the estate of Wally Glover.

a cousin of composer Vaughan Williams. The Nortons migrated to Australia from New Zealand in 1925 and settled in the Sydney suburb of Lindfield. As a teenager, Norton was expelled from high school because of her allegedly "depraved nature," which her headmistress claimed "would corrupt the innocence of the other girls." She then studied for two years at East Sydney Technical College under the noted sculptor Rayner Hoff. During this time, she became interested in studying everything she could find about witchcraft, sorcery, and magic, and she was soon well versed in the occult writings of notable magical practitioners like Dion Fortune, Aleister Crowley, and Eliphas Lévi. In 1940, at the age of twenty-three, she began to experiment with self-hypnosis as a means of inducing automatic drawing.

Norton was already familiar with the trance methods of the Surrealists and especially admired the work of Salvador Dali and Yves Tanguy who, like the other artists in their movement, had explored techniques of encouraging the subconscious mind to manifest its visionary contents. Sometimes the Surrealists drew rapidly so that forms came through unimpeded by the intellect. Others experimented with drugs or documented their dream experiences with great detail in order to develop a greater knowledge of the "alternative reality" of the subconscious mind. Norton adopted a different approach, finding that she could shut off her normal consciousness using self-hypnosis, thereby transferring her attention to an inner plane of awareness. As she noted in a lengthy interview conducted with psychologist L. J. Murphy at the University of Melbourne in 1949: "These experiments [with self-hypnosis] produced a number of peculiar and unexpected results . . . and culminated in a period of extra-sensory perception, together with a prolonged series of symbolic visions." Norton spent several years after this studying various systems of occult and mystical thought, including Buddhist and other examples of Eastern literature as well as standard works on Kabbalah, Theosophy, and Western magic.

During this period, Norton also began to focus more specifically on the magical forces associated with the Great God Pan, whose spirit she felt pervaded the entire earth. Her studies had taught her that the ancient Greeks regarded Pan as lord of all things—symbolizing the totality of the elements and all forms of manifest being. He was therefore, in a very real sense, the true god of the world. Pan was a maintainer of the balance of Nature and also had at his command an invisible hierarchy of lesser spirits who could help him in his work of ruling and sustaining the earth.

Norton painted a large-scale interpretation of Pan, complete with horns, pointed ears, cloven hooves, and musical pipes, and mounted it on the wall of her Kings Cross flat, where it effectively became the focal point of her magical altar. She also conducted magical ceremonies dressed in a tiger-skin robe to honor his presence, and would often experience him as a living reality when she entered a trance state.

Meanwhile, her art continued to reflect the entities she encountered in her visions, including a variety of devilish creatures, half animal–half human pagan deities, and various supernatural motifs. Norton lived in a world populated by magical and astral entities whose presence pervaded her paintings and drawings in varying degrees. For her, the ancient gods and goddesses were a living presence in the world, and one could deny their call only at great personal cost. Like Dion Fortune and Austin Spare before her, Rosaleen Norton was a visionary ahead of her time—and also a significant bridging figure in the contemporary occult revival.

FIGURE 5.7.   Rosaleen Norton and the poet Gavin Greenlees in their Kings Cross apartment. Norton's mural of Pan served as a backdrop to her magical altar. Courtesy the estate of Wally Glover.

Norton's Persona as a Witch

When Rosaleen Norton reflected on her youth and discussed her magical background in several interviews with a Sydney journalist in the mid-1950s, she maintained that she had been born a witch and was essentially self-taught: "If you are a witch nobody has to teach you," she explained to her interviewer. "In my case, it came naturally, and nobody had to teach me." Asked if she had a "Devil's mark" on her body, Norton confirmed that she had some atypical physical attributes that she associated with her persona as a witch: "My bodily peculiarities include a pair of freak muscles (extending from armpit to pelvic bone on either side) not normally found in the human body" [and] "a rare, atavistic formation of the upper ears known as 'Darwin's Peak.'" Norton also alluded to two small blue dots on her left knee, which she had always assumed were a sign that she was a traditional witch.[116]

A defining moment in Norton's life came when, as an adolescent, she first discovered the figure of Pan in books on ancient Greek mythology. She was intrigued to learn that Pan was part man, part goat, and was represented with the horns, tail, hind legs, and hoofs of a goat. Pan also had a flat snub nose and beard.[117] Fond of music and dancing, Pan was also associated with shepherds and the woods, and possessed prophetic powers. Because the woods were considered a place of fear at night, and because he often frightened unwary travelers in the countryside, Pan himself was considered unpredictable, lascivious, and lecherous.[118] Norton also discovered that Pan's name literally meant "all," and she would later learn that the philosophical and religious concept of pantheism (which derives from the Greek *pan* = all, and *theos* = God) conveyed the idea that the universe as a whole is divine and that Nature is innately sacred. This was a concept that would shape Norton's perception of the magical universe.[119]

According to an interview conducted in 1965, Norton's attraction to the ancient Greek god Pan coincided with her rejection of her family's Christian beliefs and specifically with her parents' wish that she should be confirmed into the Anglican faith at the age of twelve.[120] Norton's interest in Pan led instead to improvised magical rituals using robes, Chinese joss sticks, and wine taken from secret stock hidden by her parents: "My first act of ceremonial magic was in honour of the horned god, whose pipes are symbol of magic and mystery, and whose horns and hooves stand for natural energies and fleet-footed freedom: And this rite was also my oath of allegiance and my confirmation as a witch. I remember my feelings on that occasion well, and they are valid today."[121]

Even at this early stage, Norton accepted Pan as the true ruler of the world, although she would later acknowledge the magical significance of other deities as well—among them Hecate, Lilith, and Lucifer.

Norton's cosmology was based on an understanding that Nature and the Cosmos are innately sacred. For her, divinity could be "divided" into a number of gods and goddesses, and these ruling deities—headed by Pan—were able to exist and function in more than one dimension of reality. Even as an adolescent, Norton was well aware that Pan would be regarded by the more orthodox Christian members of her family and community as a manifestation of the Devil himself, and yet she felt a distinct sense of excitement embarking on this magical adventure. Already in her teenage years, there were clear signs of the rebellious, antinomian spirit that would align her with the Left-Hand Path later in her magical career.[122]

Hecate, Lilith, and Lucifer

Throughout her life, Pan remained the supreme deity in Norton's magical pantheon—she would later refer to herself as the "High Priestess at the Altar of Pan."[123] However, other ancient deities and supernatural entities also provided inspiration and guidance. Prominent among them were Hecate, Lilith, and Lucifer—the latter in his role as the Adversary.

In classical Greek mythology, Hecate, or Hekate, was goddess of the night and darkness, and ruler of the hidden aspects of Nature. As a goddess of transitions, Hecate was associated with birth and death, and from the fifth century BCE onward, she is also specifically associated with ghosts; Hecate could also cause nightmares.[124] Accompanied by barking dogs and hordes of spirits of the "restless dead"—those people unable to find their way to Hades—Hecate was sometimes called *kleidophoros* ("key-bearer"), and as a gatekeeper of Hades she was able to let spirits in and out of the Underworld.[125] Hecate was only worshiped at night; dogs and black lambs were offered to her as sacrifices.[126] Often shown entwined in coils of snakes, which in ancient Greece were associated with the dead, Hecate was a goddess also associated with the crossroads, especially three-way intersections—such crossroads being in turn considered supernatural places and associated with magic and spirits.[127]

In an interview I conducted with Norton in Sydney in 1977, two years before her death, she told me that she regarded Hecate as an even more imposing deity than Pan. Norton acknowledged that Hecate was often very frightening because she was a shadowy goddess flanked by cohorts of ghouls and night-forms—as well as a dealer in death and curses. However, Hecate could also be a protector. If ever Norton sought to curse people with her "witch current" in order to redress what she believed to be an unfair "balance of events," Norton called on Hecate's hexing powers and believed this was a legitimate use of the magical art.[128]

Although Norton invariably linked Hecate and Lilith in her pantheon of ancient female magical deities, Lilith's mythic and cultural origins are quite different from Hecate's. Lilith is an exotic she-devil who first appears in Sumerian mythology in the middle of the third millennium BCE before entering the Jewish tradition during the Talmudic period (second-fifth centuries CE) and then finally emerging as a queenly consort at God's side during the Kabbalistic era.[129] In the Sumerian tradition, Lilith was acknowledged as a "beautiful maiden." but she was also regarded as a harlot and vampire who would never willingly let her lover depart.[130] During the Talmudic period, Lilith was known as Adam's first wife, but their relationship was deeply troubled, and when Lilith came to believe that Adam intended to overpower her, she uttered the magical name of God, rose into the air, and flew off to the Red Sea, a place believed to be full of lascivious demons. There she indulged herself in unbridled promiscuity, giving rise to more than a hundred demonic offspring each day.[131]

Norton discovered references to Lilith in Carl Jung's *Psychology of the Unconscious* (1919) and quoted from Jung's text in the unpublished notes that accompanied her illustrations in *The Art of Rosaleen Norton*—a controversial collection of drawings and poems, co-authored with her lover and partner in magic, Gavin Greenlees: "Adam, before Eve, already possessed a demon wife, by name Lilith, with whom he quarrelled for mastership. But Lilith raised herself into the air through the magic of the name of God and hid herself in the sea. Adam forced her back with the help of three angels. Lilith became a nightmare, a Lamia, who threatened those with child and who kidnapped the newborn child."[132]

Greenlees, whose poem on Lilith accompanied Norton's drawing in the publication, referred to Lilith as "the Queen of Night and Sympathy," describing her as an "image of the Unconscious with its power to align images and draw together those spirits who have the true affinity—holding man by the soul image."[133] For Norton, however, Lilith was "Queen of Air and Darkness—symbol of Night" and mirrored Hecate's chthonic role as Goddess of the Underworld and the secret forces of Nature.[134]

Lucifer/ The Adversary

The figure of Lucifer/The Adversary completes the triad in Norton's magical cosmology. For Norton, Lucifer was closely associated with the spirit of rebellion and the quest for secret knowledge. In her illuminating essay, *A Vision* (c.1940s, published in *The Supplement to the Art of Rosaleen Norton*, 1984) Norton reminds her readers that "we seek knowledge and truth and . . . 'Lucifer' means 'Light Bringer' . . . our greatest reward is in the eternal adventure of the search itself."[135]

At least two major artworks relating to Lucifer form part of Norton's oeuvre—a painting titled *Lucifer*, which was exhibited in 1949 in Melbourne, and a drawing titled *The Adversary*, reproduced in *The Art of Rosaleen Norton* in 1952.[136] In the Judaeo-Christian tradition Lucifer (Latin: "light-bearer") is another name for Satan. In Isaiah 14.12, the reference to Lucifer relates to the king of Babylon, but was misunderstood to refer to a fallen angel and subsequently passed into Judaeo-Christian theology as a name for the Devil.[137] In heaven, Lucifer had sought to be sufficient unto himself, refusing to admit that he was dependent on God. His sin was therefore one of pride, his ensuing punishment being cast headlong from Heaven for all eternity. As a consequence of his fall from grace, Lucifer was filled with hatred for God.

FIGURE 5.8.   *Lilith*—"Queen of Air and Darkness," from *The Art of Rosaleen Norton*, Walter Glover, Sydney 1952. Courtesy the estate of Wally Glover.

In my 1977 interview with the artist, referred to earlier, Norton told me that although she considered Lucifer's role to be that of an adversary, this did not necessarily make him "evil." As Norton noted at the time: "He binds and limits man when it appears that he is growing too big for his boots. He tries to trick man, not with malicious intent, so much as exposing the limitations of the ego and man's pride in his own existence."[138]

Other Magical Entities In Norton's Cosmology

In addition to Pan, Hecate, Lilith, and Lucifer, who collectively represent the major figures in Norton's pantheon, a range of other magical and mythic entities are referred to in her writings and in her art. Because Norton claimed an existential reality for several of these entities, they should also be considered significant, contributing to both her artistic oeuvre and also to her personal magical cosmology.

In the glossary included in *The Art of Rosaleen Norton*, there are references to a number of magical beings from different cultural traditions, a reflection of Norton's eclectic and idiosyncratic occult interests. They include Bucentauro, whom Norton describes as a "type of eidolon" or phantasm; Eloi, the "phantasy spirit of Jupiter";[139] Makalath, the Laugher, described as "an archangel who expresses himself cosmically through the power that manifests itself in this world as humour"; Fohat, "the dynamic energy of cosmic ideation"–an entity referred to in Theosophical literature;[140] Erzulie, a "voodoo Priestess of Mamaloi";[141] and the Dubouros, whom Norton identifies as "a being representing Mind . . . similar to the Egyptian god Thoth as the detached, enigmatic Recorder."[142] Norton also lists Val, Kephena, Borzorygmus, and Mwystingel as "imaginary beings of Twizzari," the latter her name for the "Dreamworld . . . an aspect of the Astral Plane," and she makes reference also to Trudgepig, whom she describes as "another imaginary creature . . . [a] symbol of hypocritical gravity and gloom."[143]

In addition to this eclectic assortment of mythical entities, there is also an important magical figure whom Norton refers to as her "Familiar Spirit-in-Chief"—a being she knew by many different names, including the Monk, Frater Asmodeus, and Brother Hilarian. This particular magical servitor, however, was more generally known as Janicot—Norton gives his name as Jannicot—and he in turn has fascinating occult connections, for his origins derive from Basque cosmology and witchcraft.

The Powers of Janicot

Norton's magical journals indicate that she regarded Janicot as the guardian of all portals leading to magical awareness. In the text accompanying her drawing *At Home*, reproduced in *The Art of Rosaleen Norton*, Norton says that Janicot "manages most of my occult activities, supervises trances, escorts me into other planes of

FIGURE 5.9.   Norton's "Familiar Spirit-in-Chief," Janicot; a detail from *At Home*, reproduced in *The Art of Rosaleen Norton*, Walter Glover, Sydney 1952. Courtesy the estate of Wally Glover.

Being, and sometimes assists the Sphynx in selecting visions for me." In traditional Basque witchcraft, Janicot, or Jaincoa, was depicted as the Horned God—*Basajaun*, the "Goat-man"–otherwise known as the Lord of the Woods. Janicot was the Basque god of the oak and also god of doorways and the Wheel of the Year. Janicot was a satyr-like being with a human torso and the legs and feet of a goat. There is an immediate affinity here with the figure of Pan, but the mythic connection is more specifically with Dianus or Janus, the Roman two-headed God of the Oak Tree. Janus has been described as "the Door God, the God of the Hidden Portals into the Netherworld, and the 'portal' or gate between one time and the next," and this would seem to be how Norton regarded him as well. The Basque witches of France and northern Spain traditionally paid homage to Janicot in graveyards or forests, dancing around an altar of rock on which a goat's skull had been placed with a glowing candle positioned between the horns. Contemporary Wiccan author

Timothy Roderick describes Janicot's powers in terms that resonate with the way in which Norton may well have viewed him—as a servitor and guardian of the gateways opening to magical awareness: "When you tap into the ancient archetypal energies of Janicot," writes Roderick, "you evoke your ability to see the big picture, to understand the true nature of things. . . . [Janicot] also evokes your ability to see the true nature of your spirit . . . to see each moment in time as a doorway."[144]

The Kabbalistic Tree and the Qliphoth

Both in her writings and in her art, Rosaleen Norton makes frequent reference to the Jewish Kabbalah as one of her principal maps of magical consciousness, and in her glossary listings she reveals her detailed knowledge of the ten spheres of consciousness, or *sephiroth*, associated with the Kabbalistic Tree of Life. Drawing on Dion Fortune's classic text, *The Mystical Qabalah* (1935), a work that heads the list of esoteric publications in her bibliography, Norton refers to Binah, representing the sphere of the "Supernal Mother," and Geburah, the sphere of "Rightful Destruction" on the Kabbalistic Tree.[145]

Norton also makes frequent allusions—both in her captions and in her journal entries and imagery—to the "dark" or negative aspects of the Tree. As noted earlier, these realms are known as the *Qliphoth*: Norton seems to have had several experiences involving these "dark" energies and draws on excerpts from her personal diary to provide a commentary in *The Art of Rosaleen Norton*.[146] The Thelemic magician Kenneth Grant describes the *Qliphoth*—the plural form of the Hebrew *Qlipha*, meaning "harlot" or "strange woman"—as "shells" and "shades" of the dead.[147] According to Grant, the *Qliphoth* signify "otherness" and refer to "the shadowy world of shells or reflections . . . power zones [that] form the Tree of Death."[148]

It is within the magical domain of the *Qliphoth* that Norton claims to have encountered the threatening magical entity she calls the Werplon, a hostile humanoid insect-creature illustrated in *The Art of Rosaleen Norton*.[149] The Werplon is by far the most hostile and confronting creature in Norton's magical cosmology.[150] An entry from her magical journal describes her encounter with this terrifying entity:

> I realised that my consciousness was united with that of a totally
> different Order of Being. Temporarily I was experiencing the sensations
> of one of those great—and to this world terrible—entities called
> Werplons. . . . Sensation was intense; swift vibrant power and precision,
> and awareness below the surface, of some constant danger. . . .
> Deep purple predominated with overtones of black, lit by splashes of

FIGURE 5.10. *Qlipha*, from *The Art of Rosaleen Norton*, Walter Glover, Sydney 1952—the artist's depiction of the terrifying Werplon. Courtesy the estate of Wally Glover.

vari-coloured [sic] light at certain of the power points. . . . Suddenly a
shock of apprehension electrified the Werplon. That needle-keen
precision of operation seemed to waver, to become slightly clumsy. A
wave of fright and disgust swept me as one of the Werplon's senses
registered the loathsome human vibration. . . . I knew terror. . . . Waves
of pain invaded my aetheric body. My mind screamed.[151]

As several art works in *The Art of Rosaleen Norton* clearly indicate, Norton was
fascinated by these "dark" polarities of magical consciousness.[152] What is especially
significant about Norton's magical encounter with the Werplon is that she claimed
it occurred while she was utilizing her "aetheric body," a reference to her out-
of-the-body exploration of the astral planes accessed through trance and self-
hypnosis.

Self-Hypnosis and Trance

Norton's interest in "multiple consciousness" and "other planes or dimensions of
being" led her to experiment with self-hypnosis in 1940, when she was twenty-three
years old.[153] As noted earlier, Norton had already begun reading widely in the field
of witchcraft, occultism, and demonology, and she was convinced that hypnotic
trance states offered practical experiential access to a vast realm of heightened inner
awareness that she wanted to explore first hand.[154]

Norton began her experiments by meditating in a darkened room, restricting
her normal consciousness in an effort to induce automatic drawing and allowing
an "abnormal mode of consciousness" to take over.[155] This produced "a number of
peculiar and unexpected results and some drawings that were later exhibited."
Norton's experiments in states of consciousness culminated in what she referred
to as "a period of extra-sensory perception, together with a prolonged series of
symbolic visions."[156]

Norton records her trance method in quite explicit terms, combining ritual
elements and meditative techniques in order to facilitate an altered state of consciousness:

I decided to experiment in self-induced trance; the idea being to induce
an abnormal state of consciousness and manifest the results, if any, in
drawing. My aim was to delve down into the subconscious and, if
possible, through and beyond it.

I had a feeling (intuitional rather than intellectual) that somewhere
in the depths of the unconscious, the individual would contain, in
essence, the accumulated knowledge of mankind: just as his physical

body manifests the aggregate of racial experience in the form of instinct or automatic reaction to stimulus.

In order to contact this hypothetical source, I decided to apply psychic stimulus to the subconscious: stimulus that the conscious reasoning mind might reject, yet which would appeal to the buried instincts as old as man, and would (I hoped) cause psychic "automatic reflexes" (Religious cults use ritual, incense etc. for the same reason). Consequently, I collected together a variety of things such as aromatic leaves, wine, a lighted fire, a mummified hoof, etc. . . . . all potent stimuli to the part of the subconscious that I wished to invoke. I darkened the room, and focusing my eyes upon the hoof, I crushed the pungent leaves, drank some wine, and tried to clear my mind of all conscious thought. This was the beginning (and I made many other experiments which were progressively successful).[157]

During a period of around five months spent exploring self-hypnosis, Norton's consciousness became "extremely exalted," and her dissociative states of mind gave rise to increased perceptual acuity and feelings of enhanced personal power: "I seemed, while experiencing a great intensification of intellectual, creative and intuitional faculties, to have become detached in a curiously timeless fashion from the world around me, and yet to be seeing things with a greater clarity and awareness than normally. I was working day and night, having very little sleep or rest, yet a supply of inexhaustible power seemed to flow through me."[158]

Norton experienced a sense of detachment accompanied by a feeling of clarity and potency. She now began to combine magical techniques of invocation with her trance method of self-hypnosis, resulting in the spontaneous creation of a magical symbol, or *sigil*, which she associated with the ancient Egyptian figure of Thoth.[159]

One night I felt impelled, quite apart from conscious volition, to perform a kind of ritual of invocation; after which I executed a peculiar waking "automatic" drawing, the composition of which assumed the form of the symbol ☽.

The upper figure is the sign of Thoth—impersonality and balanced force—while the lunar crescent can represent several things, but chiefly (as applied to the individual) receptivity to occult powers; the personality; and, according to the Kabbalists, an emblem of the sphere of magic. I once read of magic defined as "The science and art of causing supernormal change to occur in conformity with will," which seems a fairly comprehensive description.[160]

Norton's Conception of the Magical Universe

One of Norton's earliest findings in relation to what she referred to as "the other Realm of Being" was that the contents of this domain seemed to be directed by thought itself, almost as if one were consciously entering a dream-world. According to Norton, in the magical realm thoughts become tangible and visible and often assume an anthropomorphic form. Visual images and metaphysical "entities" also morph from one form into another, subject to conscious or "willed" intent:

> "Thought" in those realms is very different from that which is normally
> understood by the word. There, "thought"—or rather the energy
> generated by such—is felt as a tangible thing, a current of living force
> which assumes palpable and visual form. I had been told, earlier, that
> "entities in the Plane assumed form at will." This is literally true; one
> actually changes shape very frequently, since the new "sense" referred to
> is that which could be described as "being." Just as one can see, feel, hear
> a thing, state or person; and when this occurs one realises and is the very
> essence of its nature. This sense, if one can call it that, covers a vastly
> wider field than anything comparable to human life; for in addition to
> becoming the essence of male, female, or neither, and beings of other
> orders of Existence, one can "become" a living embodiment of abstract
> Ideas of all descriptions.[161]

According to Norton, many of the familiar god-forms and mythic images from the world's various mythological and religious traditions could be regarded as projections of human consciousness. However, this did not make them any less "real" when experienced in an altered state of consciousness; these powerful mythic images would still have a tangible presence on the magical plane when an individual encountered them in trance. Norton maintained that the actual gods or "intelligences" themselves could not be constrained by the cultural forms imposed by mythological or religious traditions, because these were only human constructs; that is to say, the gods were "greater" than the god-forms through which they manifested. In this regard, Norton emphasized that many metaphysical entities perceived in the trance realm were projections from intelligences whose origins lay far beyond the sphere of human awareness:

> In the other Realm, the structure of phenomena is based on other lines.
> Intelligences are not confined to one form as here; also the consciousness
> pertaining to each type of form bears a far closer relationship to its
> material vehicle. The latter, as I have said, being fluid plasmic matter,

FIGURE 5.11. *Astral Scene*, pencil drawing from the early 1940s that shows Rosaleen Norton in trance, projecting a magical sigil. Courtesy the estate of Wally Glover.

can and does alter its form to any image appropriate to circumstances. Since, however, the form assumed is a direct reflection of the content or state of consciousness, it is an automatic result of the latter. So, in this Realm also "form follows function," but in an utterly different way; as function in this sense is synonymous with "being" or content. . . .

I have spoken of individual mind working upon and moulding plasmic material. Consider the power, then, of this unconscious mass-concentration of human beings, throughout the ages, upon certain idealisations of forms—the God-forms (a generic name for all such forms, including Demons, Faery creatures, "angels" etc.). This unconscious creative thought concentration has built up images in the aether, moulding raw plasmic matter to the form of these images, and providing vehicles for other intelligences to manifest through, relative to humanity. I do not mean that these intelligences are either confined to any or all of these forms, or that they are the product of human thought, conscious or otherwise. The vehicles, or God-forms, yes, or largely so, but not the intelligences themselves. These vehicles, however, form a useful medium of communication, but naturally their visual form is, to a certain extent, anthropomorphic."[162]

According to Norton, the fluid, "plasmic" nature of the astral realm ensured that metaphysical entities and intelligences from higher planes of existence could manifest themselves, or "incarnate," at lower levels of the astral plane, and at this time they would appear in anthropomorphic god-forms culturally appropriate to the consciousness of the beholder. Norton believed that the god-forms themselves provided a mediating link between different levels of reality—the metaphysical and the human—and that human beings could approach the gods by rising through the astral planes toward the manifested god-forms while in a state of trance.[163] Conversely, the gods could "incarnate" or "descend" into the astral realms by manifesting in an appropriate form.

Norton came to regard the astral plane—the altered state of consciousness accessed through trance—as a type of mediating domain between the gods and goddesses on the one hand, and human consciousness (functioning through the vehicle of the plasmic body) on the other. She also formed the view—on the basis of her trance experiences in the plasmic body—that a number of inner-plane "intelligences" pervaded all aspects of the known universe. These intelligences in turn confirmed the nature of their existence through a range of anthropomorphic images—manifesting as gods and goddesses, demons and archangels, as portrayed in the world's various religions and mythologies.

Norton's Relationship with the Gods and Goddesses

Norton's exploration of magical trance states was completely unfamiliar territory to most of her contemporaries in 1940s and 1950s Australia. Her "astral" ventures were essentially solitary affairs where her privacy was safeguarded by close family members like her husband, Beresford, and her elder sister, Cecily.[164] Norton noted in various interviews that her trance journeys often took place during a period of three to five days. This situation suggests that a substantial part of Norton's magical practice was private in nature, and that it was based on a series of personal trance encounters with the god-forms of Pan, Hecate, Lilith, and Lucifer, and with other metaphysical entities, whose images then found their way into her paintings and drawings.

A key discovery made by Norton herself, which distinguishes her from many other occultists operating within the Western esoteric tradition—especially those espousing the philosophy that magic is based, essentially, on directing the

FIGURE 5.12. *Rites of Baron Samedi*, from *The Art of Rosaleen Norton*, Walter Glover, Sydney 1952—a work that reflects Norton's keen interest in Voodoo. The figures in the lower right-hand corner are probably based on Norton and Greenlees. Courtesy the estate of Wally Glover.

will—was that Norton did not believe she was fully in control of the magical energies she was encountering. When I interviewed Norton in 1977, she emphasized that the archetypal gods and cosmic beings she had contacted in trance existed in their own right. In their own particular magical realms they held the upper hand—not she.[165] To this extent Norton differed from thinkers like Carl Jung, who regarded the sacred archetypes as universal forces deep within the collective human psyche, and not as entities with their own separate existence beyond the mind. Although Norton admitted to being influenced by Jung and refers to Jungian archetypes in the 1949 L. J. Murphy interview, for Jung, the archetypes—the ancient gods and goddesses of religion and mythology—were ultimately sacred personifications of the self.[166] On the basis of what she experienced during her trance explorations, Norton did not share this view. For her, magical deities such as Pan, Hecate, Lilith, and Lucifer, as well as other magical entities like the Werplon, were not projections or extensions of her own spiritual consciousness but powerful (and occasionally terrifying) entities who would grace her with their presence only if it pleased them, and not as a consequence of her own personal will or intent. Norton believed she could only depict in her paintings and drawings those qualities and attributes that the god or goddess in question chose to reveal, and that those energies would then filter through her "like a funnel." Norton maintained that she did nothing other than transmit the magical current. If the gods and goddesses were alive *in her* and *through her*, their presence would manifest in her art and through her ceremonial magical practice.[167]

Pan and the Environment

From the late 1970s onward, influential American feminist witches began to speak of the Earth as the "body" of the Goddess. In her book *Rebirth of the Goddess*, Carol P. Christ writes that "the Goddess as earth is the firm foundation of changing life."[168] She also observes that "when the earth is the body of Goddess . . . the female body and the earth, which have been devalued and dominated together, are re-sacralized. Our understanding of divine power is transformed as it is clearly recognized as present within the finite and changing world."[169] The influential Goddess worshiper Starhawk similarly states in *The Spiral Dance*—a sourcebook which has since become a neopagan bible for many feminist witches—that "the model of the Goddess, who is immanent in Nature, fosters respect for the sacredness of all living things. Witchcraft can be seen as a religion of ecology."[170]

During the prefeminist 1950s, Norton similarly drew attention to the sacred qualities of Nature, but ascribed them instead to Pan, whom she regarded as an embodiment of the divine essence of Nature, as noted above. When I interviewed

Norton, she emphasized that Pan was very much a deity for the present day, and not simply an archetypal figure from antiquity. For her, Pan was the creative force in the universe that protected the natural beauty of the planet and conserved the resources of the environment. Like Starhawk, who for many years has combined Goddess spirituality with political activism, Norton believed that magic had political consequences. For her, Pan was alive and well in the anti-pollution lobbies, and among the Friends of the Earth.[171]

That being so, it is reasonable to argue that in addition to being a trance-magician and visionary explorer, Norton was also a significant precursor of those feminist witches and practitioners of Goddess spirituality who would later proclaim, from the late 1970s onward, that the Earth was innately sacred and should be honored as a manifestation of deity. Vivianne Crowley, a well-known advocate of Wicca in Britain, maintains that the Earth should not be symbolized by the Goddess alone, pointing out that witchcraft "worships the Great Mother Goddess and Horned God as representations of all Goddesses and Gods that the human heart has worshipped." Crowley adds the further observation that "many people are attracted to the Earth Traditions because the Divine is found in the form of Goddess as well as God."[172] These are sentiments that Norton would surely have shared.

Norton's Later Years

During the mid-to-late 1970s, Rosaleen Norton lived in a shadowy basement apartment in an ageing block of flats close to the El Alamein fountain in Sydney's Kings Cross district. She was now already withdrawing into obscurity and restricting her day-to-day contacts to just a few close friends and her older sister Cecily, who lived down the corridor in the same block of flats. It was an increasingly private existence, and that was the way she liked it. As Cecily later told me, Rosaleen was quite happy living by herself. Accompanied by her two pet cats, she lived among a litter of easels, paintings, and books, and liked to watch the fish swimming gracefully in her aquarium. She also spent a lot of time listening to classical music—Mozart, Stravinsky, Beethoven, Bach, and Sibelius were among her favorites. And although her flat had a dark and somewhat gloomy sitting room, it did open out onto a courtyard and a profusion of greenery—a secluded corner of Nature. During the summer months she loved sitting in the sun near her French windows, beside a red pot containing an umbrella plant, reading her books on magic and mysticism. She had also retained her youthful habit of spending long hours in the bath in the evenings. Ever a "night" person, she loved lying in the soap suds sucking oranges, drinking endless cups of tea, or alternatively sipping Italian Strega liqueur. These, for her, were the true luxuries of life.

Nevertheless, in recent years she had suffered from intermittent bouts of sickness. This had not alarmed her unduly, even though she sometimes felt down on her energy. But toward the end of 1978 she suddenly became sick, and required hospital tests. Her doctor subsequently told her that she had cancerous growths in her colon and there would have to be an operation. At first it was thought that the surgery was totally successful, but this proved not to be so, and the cancer quickly recurred.

Late in November 1979 Norton was taken to the Roman Catholic Sacred Heart Hospice for the Dying at Sydney's St. Vincents Hospital, the end clearly in sight. Shortly before she died she told her friend Victor Wain: "I came into this world bravely; I'll go out bravely." Unrepentant in her worship of Pan, unfazed by all the crucifixes surrounding her in the hospice, and a pagan to the end, she departed this life on 5 December 1979.

6

The Rebirth of the Goddess

Much of the current interest in Western occultism, and contemporary paganism in particular, is directly related to the rise and importance of feminism as a contemporary social movement. Contemporary witchcraft—often referred to as Wicca—and its more eclectic variant, Goddess worship, both focus on the veneration of the sacred Feminine—the Universal Goddess—in her myriad manifestations. There is, however, no single spiritual pathway within contemporary paganism. Some neopagans are highly structured in their ceremonial practices, while others are much more spontaneous. Some emphasize lineage and authority within their respective covens, others are more egalitarian. Nevertheless, there are many shared perspectives across the broad spectrum of pagan beliefs and ritual practices, and our focus here is on core elements in modern Wicca and Goddess worship.

In this context, it is easy to see why Dion Fortune and Rosaleen Norton are bridging figures who link different generations of esoteric practitioners—especially those attracted to feminine mythic imagery. Of course, the feminist movement per se did not exist in their day. Dion Fortune has acknowledged MacGregor Mathers and the Golden Dawn as her main source of occult information, and Rosaleen Norton, coming a little later, was indebted in turn to the writings of Aleister Crowley, Dion Fortune, A. E. Waite, and Margaret Murray—author of the controversial *Witchcraft in Western Europe*—as well as Theosophical writers like Madame H. P. Blavatsky and Alice Bailey.

Defining Wicca

The term Wicca itself derives from the Old English words *wicca* (masculine) and *wicce* (feminine) meaning "a practitioner of witchcraft." The word *wiccan*, meaning "witches," occurs in the Laws of King Alfred (c. 890 CE), and the verb *wiccian*, "to bewitch," was also used in this context.[1] Some witches believe the words connote a wise person; Wicca is often referred to by practitioners as the Craft of the Wise.[2]

Modern witchcraft is a Nature-based religion with the Great Goddess as its principal deity. In Wicca, the Great Goddess can take many different forms, associated with a range of mythological pantheons: these include Artemis, Astarte, Athene, Dione, Melusine, Aphrodite, Cerridwen, Dana, Arianrhod, and Isis, among many others.[3] Alternatively, reference may be made in general terms to the Great Mother or Mother Nature. The high priestess, who is the ritual leader of an individual group of witchcraft practitioners, or coven, incarnates the spirit of the Goddess in a ceremonial context when her senior male partner, the high priest, "draws down the Moon" into her body. In modern witchcraft, the high priestess is regarded as the receptacle of wisdom and intuition and is symbolized by the sacred ritual cup, whereas her consort is represented symbolically by a short ritual sword or dagger known as an *athame*. Witchcraft rituals associated with the so-called Third Initiation (see below) feature the act of uniting dagger and cup in a symbol of sexual union, and there is also a comparable relationship in Celtic mythology between the sacred oak tree and Mother Earth. Accordingly, the high priest, or consort, is sometimes known as the Oak King, a reference to the sacred Oak of the Celts, and at other times as Cernunnos, the Horned One.[4]

Wiccan covens vary in size, although traditionally the membership number is thirteen, consisting of six men, six women, and the high priestess.[5] When the group exceeds this number, some members leave to form a new coven. Following their initiation into a coven, Wiccans are given magical names that are used in a ritual context and among coven members. Wiccan ceremonies are held at specific times of the year. The coven meetings held through the year at full moon are called *esbats*: there are usually thirteen of these meetings in a calendar year. The major gatherings in the witches' calendar, the so-called Greater Sabbats, are related to the cycle of the seasons and the traditional times for sowing and harvesting crops. In the Northern Hemisphere, the four Greater Sabbats are held on the following dates each year:

Candlemas, known by the Celts as *Imbolc*: 2 February
May Eve, or *Beltane*: 30 April
Lammas, or *Lughnassadh*: 1 August
Halloween, or *Samhain*: 31 October[6]

In addition, there are four minor Sabbats: the two solstices at midsummer and midwinter, and the two equinoxes in spring and autumn.[7]

In pre-Christian times, Imbolc was traditionally identified with the first signs of spring; Beltane was a fertility celebration when the sacred oak was burned, mistletoe cut, and sacrifices made to the gods, and Lughnassadh was related to autumn and the harvesting of crops, and celebrated both the gathering in of produce and the continuing fertility of the earth. Samhain represented the transition from autumn to winter and was associated with bonfires to keep away the winter winds. Samhain was also a time when the spirits of the dead could return to earth once again to contact loved ones. Among contemporary witches, Sabbats are a time for fellowship, ceremonial, and initiation, and ritual performances are followed by feasting, drinking, and merriment.[8]

Wiccan ceremonies take place in a magic circle, which can either be inscribed upon the floor of a special room set aside in a suburban house and designated as the "temple," or marked on the earth in a suitable meeting place: for example, in a grove of trees or on the top of a sacred hill. The earth is swept with a ritual broomstick for purification, and the four elements are ascribed to the four directions: Earth in the north, Air in the East, Fire in the south, and Water in the west. The ritual altar is traditionally placed in the north. Beings known as the Lords of the Watchtowers are believed to govern the four quarters and are invoked in rituals for blessings and protection.[9]

Within the circle and present on the altar are a bowl of water, a dish of salt, candles, a symbolic scourge (representing will and determination), a cord to bind candidates in initiation, and consecrated symbols of the elements: a pentacle or disc (Earth / feminine), a cup (Water / feminine), a censer (Fire / masculine), and a wand (Air / masculine). The high priestess has her personal *athame*, or ritual dagger, and the sword of the high priest rests on the ground before the altar.

Contemporary Wicca recognizes three initiations. The first confers witch status upon the neophyte, the second promotes a first-degree witch to the position of high priestess or high priest, and the third celebrates the bonding of the high priestess and high priest in the Great Rite, which involves either real or symbolic sexual union and is perceived as a mystical marriage. There is also a usual practice in Wicca that a man must be initiated by a woman and a woman by a man, although a parent may initiate a child of the same sex.[10] Most covens do not admit anyone under the age of twenty-one.[11]

Wiccans recognize the threefold aspect of the Great Goddess in her role as Maid (youth, enchantment), Mother (maturity, fulfilment), and Crone (old age, wisdom). This symbolic personification of the three phases of womanhood is represented, for example, by the Celtic triad Brigid–Dana–Morrigan, the Greek goddess in her three aspects Persephone–Demeter–Hecate, or by the three Furies,

FIGURE 6.1. Wiccan group ritual. Courtesy Cinetel Productions, Sydney.

Alecto (goddess of beginnings)–Tisiphone (goddess of continuation)–Megaera (goddess of death and rebirth). The universal presence and threefold nature of the Great Goddess is particularly emphasised by feminist Wicca groups in their development of "women's mysteries." As American neopagan Zsuzsanna Budapest writes in her *Holy Book of Women's Mysteries*: "Images abound of the Mother Goddess, Female Principle of the Universe and source of all life . . . the Goddess of Ten Thousand Names."[12]

In Wicca, magic is usually classified as "black" or "white," a distinction related to personal intent. Black magic is pursued in order to cause harm to another person through injury, illness, or misfortune and may also be practiced in order to enhance personal power as a consequence. By definition, white magic is practiced with a positive intent, seeks a beneficial outcome, and is often associated with rites of healing, with eliminating evil or disease, or with the expansion of spiritual awareness.

The so-called Wiccan Rede, or code of ethics, specifically prohibits Wiccans from causing harm. The Rede is a statement of principle that all Wiccans are asked to adhere to: *Eight words the Wiccan Rede fulfil: An it harm none, do what ye will.*[13] The Pagan Federation in London has expanded upon the Wiccan Rede, issuing a statement that all neopagans are asked to accept as a basic philosophy of life:

Love for and Kinship with Nature: rather than the more customary attitude
   of aggression and domination over Nature; reverence for the life force and
   the ever-renewing cycles of life and death.

The Pagan Ethic: "Do what thou wilt, but harm none." This is a positive
   morality, not a list of thou-shalt-nots. Each individual is responsible for
   discovering his or her own true nature and developing it fully, in harmony
   with the outer world.

The Concept of Goddess and God as expressions of the Divine reality; an
   active participation in the cosmic dance of Goddess and God, female
   and male, rather than the suppression of either the female or the male
   principle.[14]

Gerald Gardner and the Twentieth-Century British Witchcraft Revival

Although the roots of modern witchcraft date from the 1930s, the British Witchcraft Act (1604), which prohibited the practice of witchcraft, was not finally
repealed in the United Kingdom until 1951. Prior to this date, books advocating the
practice of witchcraft were legally restricted from publication in that country. One
of the principal figures associated with the revival of British witchcraft, Gerald
Brosseau Gardner (1884–1964), published a semi-autobiographical title, *High
Magic's Aid*, in 1949 under the nom de plume Scire but was legally required to
portray it as a work of fiction.[15] Gardner's first nonfiction title on Wicca, *Witchcraft Today*, was published in London in 1954, followed by *The Meaning of Witchcraft* in 1959.[16]

   Gardner was born at Blundellsands, a few miles north of Liverpool. He was of
Scottish descent and came from a wealthy family: his father was a partner in the
family firm Joseph Gardner and Sons, founded in 1748, one of the largest hardwood
importers in the world.[17] Gardner received his share of the family inheritance when
his father died in 1935, and was financially independent from that time onward.

   For many years Gardner lived in the East, in such countries as Ceylon, Borneo,
and Malaya.[18] In 1936, he returned to England with his wife Donna and began
planning his retirement. Interested in exotic folk traditions, Gardner joined the
Folk-Lore Society in March 1939 and became interested in witchcraft around this
time.[19] When he was returning to England, Gardner brought with him a large and
valuable collection of swords and daggers.[20] Fearing that this collection could easily
be destroyed during war evacuation plans then current in London, Gardner and his
wife decided to move to the country, purchasing a large brick house in Highcliffe,
near the New Forest in Hampshire. Shortly after moving to Highcliffe, Gardner

FIGURE 6.2.   Gerald Brosseau Gardner

made contact with a group of local occultists that included Mrs. Mabel Besant-Scott, daughter of the well known Theosophist Annie Besant.[21] Known as the Rosicrucian Order Crotona Fellowship (founded in 1920 by George Sullivan, other-wise known as Brother Aureolis), its members held theatrical performances at the Rosicrucian Theatre in nearby Christchurch. Some members of the Crotona Fel-lowship, specifically various members of the Mason family, claimed to be members of an existing hereditary witchcraft coven.[22] It was through contact with this fringe group within the Crotona Fellowship that Gardner was subsequently introduced to witchcraft.

Gardner's Initiation

According to Jack Bracelin's biography of Gardner, *Gerald Gardner: Witch*, a few days after the outbreak of World War II in September 1939, Gardner was taken to a "big house" owned by a wealthy lady known as Old Dorothy.[23] We now know that he was initiated there by a witch named Dafo. Bracelin's account of the initiation reads as follows:

> Gardner felt delighted that he was to be let into their secret. Thus it was that, a few days after the war had started, he was taken to a big house in the neighbourhood. This belonged to "Old Dorothy"—a lady of note in the district, and very well-to-do. She invariably wore a pearl necklace, worth some £5000 at the time.
>
> It was in this house that he was initiated into witchcraft . . . he was stripped naked and brought into a place "properly prepared" to undergo his initiation. . . . It was halfway through when the word Wica [*sic*] was first mentioned.[24]

Additional details are also provided in Gardner's book *Witchcraft Today* (1954):

> I soon found myself in the circle and took the usual oaths of secrecy which bound me not to reveal any secrets of the cult. . . . I was half-initiated before the word "Wica" which they used hit me like a thunderbolt, and I knew where I was, and that the Old Religion still existed. And so I found myself in the Circle, and there took the usual oath of secrecy, which bound me not to reveal certain things.[25]

Bracelin's biography records how Gardner felt after the ceremony was over. Gardner is reported to have said: "It was, I think, the most wonderful night of my life. In true witch fashion we had a dance afterwards and kept it up until dawn."[26]

Gardner accepted the view of his initiators that the hereditary witches of the New Forest region were a surviving remnant of an organized pagan religion that had existed and operated in England up until the seventeenth century, a view expressed by Dr. Margaret Murray (1862–1963) in her controversial book *The Witch-cult in Western Europe* (1921).[27] Murray specialized in near-Eastern archaeology and had undertaken excavations in Egypt, Petra, and southern Palestine. She believed that, as a broad-based fertility religion, the roots of pagan medieval witchcraft could be dated back to Paleolithic times. In a later book, *The God of the Witches* (1933), Murray focused specifically on the figure of the Horned God, whom she believed to be the oldest male deity known to humanity.[28] Murray maintained that the origins of the Horned God could be traced back to the Old Stone Age, and that his pagan worship had extended across Europe to the Near East up until the seventeenth century. According to Murray, the Horned God provided a prototype for the Christian Devil; his principal form in northwestern Europe was the Gallic deity Cernunnos.[29] Gardner would have been familiar with Murray's writings through his membership of the London Folk-Lore Society and probably met her there in person.[30] She later provided an introduction for Gardner's *Witchcraft Today* (1954).

Gardner moved back to London in late 1944 or early 1945 and spent the following ten years consolidating his views on witchcraft and how it should be practiced. According to Philip Heselton, author of a recent history of Wicca, the years from 1944 to 1954 "were an important period in Gardner's life, in the development of his ideas and in the development of what is now known as 'Wicca' or 'Gardnerian Witchcraft.'"[31] One of Gardner's formative influences was the ceremonial magician Aleister Crowley, who was now well known as an advocate of Thelemic sex magic. Crowley had retired to a boardinghouse named Netherwood on the Ridge in Hastings.[32]

Gardner first visited Crowley in Hastings with his friend and fellow witch, Arnold Crowther, in 1946.[33] Crowther (1909–1974) had met Crowley during his wartime travels, and it was he who arranged for the two occultists to meet. The encounter is significant because it has been suggested that Crowley may have composed a set of witchcraft rites for Gardner known as the *Book of Shadows*. Gardner maintained that the rituals in his *Book of Shadows* had been passed to him by members his coven, but it is clear that Gardner also borrowed heavily from Crowley's writings, especially *Magick in Theory and Practice* (1929).[34] The respected Wicca historian Aidan Kelly maintains that Gardner "borrowed wholesale from Crowley."[35]

Doreen Valiente, who was initiated into Gardner's coven in 1953 and later became his high priestess, felt that some of the Crowleyan material which Gardner had incorporated into Wiccan practice was either too "modern," or inappropriate. Much of this material would be written out of the ceremonial procedures between 1954 and 1957, as Gardner and Valiente worked together developing the rituals that would form the basis of the so-called Gardnerian tradition in contemporary witchcraft.[36] Making specific reference to the contributions by Crowley, Valiente confirmed in 1989 that she had to rewrite Gardner's *Book of Shadows*, "cutting out the Crowleyanity as much as I could."[37] Nevertheless, Gardner and Crowley apparently had several meetings during the intervening months before Crowley died in December 1947. As a result of these meetings, during which the two men discussed their respective magical paths, Gardner became a member of Crowley's sex-magic order, the Ordo Templi Orientis; Crowley is known to have charged Gardner £300 for dues and fees. This theoretically authorized Gardner to establish a charter of the O.T.O., although he never did so.[38] Gardner's magical name in the O.T.O. was Scire (meaning "to know").[39]

It is likely that in addition to the ritual input from Crowley and subsequent modifications by Valiente, several aspects of what is now referred to as Gardnerian witchcraft were probably Gardner's own invention. Aidan Kelly believes that Gardner may have introduced the "duotheistic" idea of the God and Goddess into modern witchcraft, and that he initially proposed that the Horned God and the Goddess should be considered equals in Wiccan rituals, even though the Goddess has since become dominant.[40] Another innovation that may have originated with Gardner himself was the modern tendency for witches to work naked, or "sky-clad," in their rituals.[41] Gardner was an enthusiastic naturist and, as Valiente has noted, he had "a deep-rooted belief in the value of going naked when circumstances favoured it." For him, according to Valiente, "communal nakedness, sunshine and fresh air were natural and beneficial, both physically and psychologically."[42] However, it is also possible that Gardner may have derived the concept of ritual nudity from the book *Aradia: Gospel of the Witches*, written by American folklorist Charles G. Leland and published in 1889. Leland first learned about *Aradia* from a hereditary Etruscan witch called Maddalena, while he was visiting Italy. Aradia was the daughter of the Roman Moon goddess Diana, and Leland's text includes details of Diana's role as Queen of the Witches. *Aradia: Gospel of the Witches* mentions that devotees of Diana were instructed to be naked in their rituals as a sign of personal freedom.[43]

Although Gardner's approach to ritual nudity appears well-intentioned, according to occult historian Francis King, other, less appealing, sexual tendencies also found their way into Gardner's witchcraft practices. According to King, "Gardner was a sado-masochist with both a taste for flagellation and marked voyeuristic tendencies. Heavy scourging was therefore incorporated into most of his rituals and what Gardner called the 'Great Rite' was sexual intercourse between the High Priest and the High Priestess while surrounded by the rest of the coven."[44]

In 1951, Gardner moved to Castletown on the Isle of Man, where a Museum of Magic and Witchcraft had already been established in a four-hundred-year-old farmhouse by an occult enthusiast, Cecil Williamson.[45] Gardner bought the museum from Williamson, became the "resident witch," and added his own collection of ritual tools and artifacts. Gardner's Museum of Magic and Witchcraft attracted considerable media attention, as did the publication of Gardner's later books.[46] The release of *Witchcraft Today* in 1954 placed Gardner in the media spotlight, and the ensuing publicity led to the rise of new covens across England.

The media coverage even reached Australia, where Gardner received publicity in the tabloid press and was dubbed "the boss of Britain's witches."[47] It was during this period that the Australian witch Rosaleen Norton made contact with both Gardner and Doreen Valiente, sending them a copy of her book *The Art of Rosaleen Norton*, initiating correspondence, and exchanging personal contacts.[48]

In 1964, Gardner met Raymond Buckland (1934–) a London-born Englishman of gypsy descent who had moved to America two years earlier.[49] Prior to meeting each other, Buckland had developed a "mail and telephone relationship" with Gardner while he was living on the Isle of Man, and Buckland subsequently became Gardner's spokesperson in the United States, responding to American correspondents on Gardner's behalf. In 1964, Gardner's high priestess, Monique Wilson (Lady Olwen) initiated Buckland into the Craft in Perth, Scotland. It was Buckland who subsequently introduced Gardnerian witchcraft to the United States.[50]

Gardnerian witchcraft is now the dominant form of international Wicca, with covens operating in a range of English-speaking countries, including Britain, the United States, Australia, and New Zealand. In 1992, Aidan Kelly estimated that there were between two and four thousand active Wiccan covens in the United States, while data from 1994 suggests that at that time Australian covens would number in the low hundreds.[51] Gardner himself did not live long enough to experience the international impact of the witchcraft movement he had helped create and, based on his own published opinions regarding the future of witchcraft, would probably have been surprised by the ongoing contemporary interest in Wicca.[52] Gardner died at sea on 12 February 1964, returning to England from a trip to Lebanon, and was buried the following day in Tunis.[53] Considered within a historical context, Gardner's major contribution to the twentieth-century magical revival was in working with Doreen Valiente to create a series of magical practices that would help define the nature of contemporary Wicca, both in Britain and internationally.

Esbats and Sabbats

In their ceremonies, Wiccans honor both the lunar and the solar cycles of Nature. Esbats are monthly meetings of the coven held at the time of full moon. Because there are thirteen months in the lunar calendar, there are usually thirteen esbats each year. The solar cycle in Wicca is marked by the eight sabbats mentioned earlier (referred to collectively as the Wheel of the Year; these are the solstices, equinoxes, and the four points between).[54] Wiccan high priestess Margot Adler believes that these Wiccan festivals "renew a sense of living communion with natural cycles, with the changes of the season and the land."[55]

Each of the esbats has its own name, which in turn is linked symbolically to the time of the year in which it occurs.[56] Wiccans believe that esbats are marked by a sense of heightened psychic awareness resulting from the lunar energy of full moon; according to the leading British witch Alex Sanders (1916–1988), it is during the esbat that "the Goddess has her greatest power."[57] For this reason, Wiccans often perform specific magical workings at this time, followed by feasting and drinking. The word "esbat" itself is thought to derive from the Old French word *s'esbattre*, meaning "to frolic and amuse oneself."[58]

Esbats are sometimes referred to as "lesser" Wiccan celebrations. As Doreen Valiente has noted, "the esbat is a smaller and less solemn occasion than the sabbat."[59] The Sabbats, on the other hand, are celebrations which link contemporary Wicca directly with festivals honored by the Celts and Druids, although as religious scholar James W. Baker has observed, some aspects of the Wheel of the Year are not Celtic in origin, and are part of an "invented tradition."[60]

As noted above, the four so-called Greater Sabbats are those of Candlemas (2 February), May Eve (30 April), Lammas (1 August), and Halloween (31 October); the traditional Druidic names for these celebrations are Imbolc (or Oimelc), Beltane (or Beltain), Lughnassadh, and Samhain, respectively.[61] The Lesser Sabbats are those marked by the midsummer and midwinter solstices and the equinoxes in spring and autumn. Considered as a whole, the Wheel of the Year represents not only the cycle of the seasons but more specifically the cycle of Nature's fertility. This is also reflected in the major Wiccan initiations, which culminate in the sacred marriage of the God and Goddess, whose union, according to Wiccan belief, brings forth new life.

The symbolic associations of the Greater Sabbats are as follows, commencing with Halloween, or Samhain, the traditional beginning of the pagan year:

Halloween / Samhain

This is a celebration to honor the dead.[62] As the dying sun passes into the nether world, Samhain is said to be the time of the year when the thin veil between the everyday world and the afterlife is most transparent, allowing Wiccans to communicate more readily with the spirits of the departed. In mythic terms, Samhain is the season during which the dying God sleeps in the underworld, awaiting rebirth. At the same time, the seed of new life gestates within the womb of the Great Mother, who in this cycle is regarded as the Queen of Darkness. The Farrars write that Samhain "was on the one hand a time of propitiation, divination and communion with the dead, and on the other, an uninhibited feast of eating, drinking and the defiant affirmation of life and fertility in the very face of the closing dark."[63]

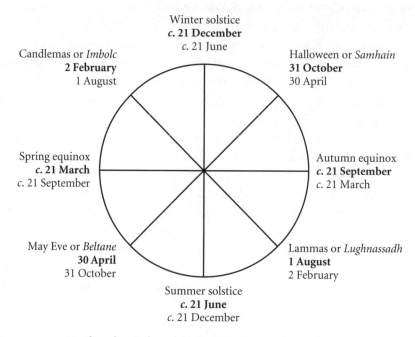

The Wheel of the Year

Winter solstice
c. 21 December
c. 21 June

Candlemas or *Imbolc*
2 February
1 August

Halloween or *Samhain*
31 October
30 April

Spring equinox
c. 21 March
c. 21 September

Autumn equinox
c. 21 September
c. 21 March

May Eve or *Beltane*
30 April
31 October

Lammas or *Lughnassadh*
1 August
2 February

Summer solstice
c. 21 June
c. 21 December

Northern hemisphere dates are in **bold type** with southern
hemisphere corresponding dates given beneath

FIGURE 6.3.   The Wiccan Wheel of the Year indicating the annual cycle of Sabbats

Candlemas / Imbolc

Imbolc has been described as "the quickening of the year, the first stirrings of
Spring within the womb of Mother Earth."[64] The Irish name *Imbolc* means "lacta-
tion," and this Sabbat is related to the beginning of the lambing season, which
commences at this time.[65] Imbolc is very much a fertility celebration. The focus is
on light and new life, "the strengthening spark of light beginning to pierce the
gloom of Winter." For this reason, Imbolc is sometimes referred to by Wiccans
as the Feast of Lights.[66] In mythic terms, Imbolc is associated with the youthful
Goddess, or Virgin.[67]

May Eve / Beltane (Beltain)

Beltane marks the beginning of Summer and is also a fertility celebration. The
name of this Sabbat may derive from the Celtic deity Bel or Balor, god of light and
fire: in ancient times "bel-fires" were lit on the hilltops to celebrate the return of
life and fertility to the world.[68] Wiccans often celebrate Beltane by dancing the

Maypole, offering garlands of May blossom to their partners, and celebrating the love and passion between men and women.[69] Beltane is also a popular time for "handfastings," or Wiccan weddings. In mythic terms, Beltane honors the mating of the Sun God with the fertile Earth Goddess.

Lammas / Lughnassadh

The Old English word *hlaf-maesse*, from which the Anglo-Saxon celebration of Lammas derives its name, means "loaf feast."[70] Lammas is the time of year when the first corn is harvested. Known to the Druids as *Lughnassadh*, this Sabbat marks the season of Autumn and was traditionally a celebration to Lugh, the Celtic sun god. *Lughnassadh* is associated with the waning power of the sun, but is also regarded by Wiccans as a suitable time to reflect upon the fruits of the earth. Wiccans gather at Lammas to celebrate the gifts of abundance that have come forth from the womb of the Goddess. *Lughnassadh* represents fulfillment: the act of reaping "all that has been sown."[71]

Although Wicca is primarily regarded as a religion of the Goddess, the mythic cycle of the Greater Sabbats provides clear evidence that the role of the Sun God is also significant. The Celts acknowledged that just as the Goddess waxed and waned through her lunar cycles as Maiden, Mother, and Crone, so too did the Sun God pass through cycles of death and rebirth. In Wicca, the God of fertility has two personas, representing the God of the Waxing Year and the God of the Waning Year. The Oak King represents the initial phase of expansion and growth and is associated with the time of year when the days grow longer. The Holly King represents withdrawal and rest, and is associated with the time when the days grow shorter. Janet and Stuart Farrar note that the Oak King and Holly King "are the light and dark twins, each the other's 'other self.'. . . . They compete eternally for the for the favour of the Great Mother; and each, at the peak of his half-yearly reign, is sacrificially mated with her, dies in her embrace and is resurrected to complete his reign."[72]

Drawing down the Moon

The invocation known as "Drawing down the Moon" is central to Wiccan practice. Here the high priest invokes the Goddess into the high priestess as part of the opening ceremony: "I invoke Thee and beseech Thee, O Mighty Mother of all life and fertility. By seed and root, by stem and bud, by leaf and flower and fruit, by life and Love do I invoke Thee to descend into the body of this thy servant and High Priestess."[73] This may be preceded by what Wiccans refer to as the "fivefold kiss," an act of psycho-spiritual arousal performed by the high priest:

First he ceremonially kisses her from the feet up to the crown of her head by way of the knees, womb, breasts and lips. Next he visualises links between the chakras (energy centres) of his own body with those of the priestess—beginning at the base of her spine and working up. When the two are connected, linked like electrical circuits, and the energy is flowing between them, he envisages the form of the Goddess behind the priestess. Then the Goddess is asked to "descend into the body" of the priestess. It is not unknown for other participants in the ceremony to see changes in the priestess as she becomes inspired, filled with the Goddess."[74]

Wiccan high priestess and writer Vivianne Crowley has described the experience of having the Goddess drawn down into her by her initiating high priest:

Andy, as High Priest, knelt before me and began the invocation to the Goddess. There was a stillness and silence within me. Then the flow of the power came, down through my crown chakra, down to my feet and out into the circle. She had come. . . .

I was far away, deep into samadhi; that state of consciousness whereby there is no longer any "I and other," "this and that," "far and near," only a sense of oneness with the universe. As though from a long way off, I heard Andy's voice stop. The power of the Goddess flowed through me once more and I made ready to respond.[75]

Once the high priestess has incarnated the Goddess, she then utters what is known in Wicca as the Charge. Here, in effect, the Goddess herself is speaking directly to her followers. First the high priest addresses the coven: "Listen to the words of the Great Mother; she who of old was called among men Artemis, Astarte, Athene, Dione, Melusine, Aphrodite, Cerridwen, Dana, Arianrhod, Isis, Bride, and by many other names." The high priestess now speaks to the group as the Goddess incarnate:

Whenever ye have need of anything, once in the month, and better it be when the moon is full, then shall ye assemble in some secret place and adore the spirit of me, who am Queen of all witches. There shall ye assemble, ye who are fain to learn all sorcery, yet who have not won its deepest secrets; to these will I teach things that are yet unknown. And ye shall be free from slavery; and as sign that ye be really free, ye shall be naked in your rites; and ye shall dance, sing, feast, make music and love, all in my praise. For mine is the ecstasy of the spirit, and mine is also joy on earth; for my law is love unto all beings. Keep pure your highest ideal; strive ever towards it; let naught stop you or turn you aside. For mine is the secret door which opens up the Land of Youth, and mine is the cup of the wine of life, and the Cauldron of Cerridwen, which is the Holy Grail of immortality. I am the gracious Goddess, who gives the gift of joy unto the heart of man. Upon earth, I give the knowledge of the spirit eternal; and beyond death, I give peace, and freedom, and reunion with those who have gone before. Nor do I demand sacrifice; for behold, I am the mother of all living, and my love is poured out upon the earth.

The high priest now briefly intercedes: "Hear ye the words of the Star Goddess; she in the dust of whose feet are the hosts of heaven, and whose body encircles the universe." And then, once again, the Goddess addresses the coven through the high priestess:

I who am the beauty of the green earth, and the white Moon among the stars, and the mystery of the waters, and the desire of the heart of man, call unto thy soul. Arise and come unto me. For I am the soul of Nature, who gives life to the universe. From me all things proceed, and unto me all things must return; and before my face, beloved of Gods and men, let thine innermost divine self be enfolded in the rapture of the infinite. Let my worship be within the heart that rejoiceth; for behold all acts of love and pleasure are my rituals. And therefore let there be beauty and strength, power and compassion, honour and humility, mirth and reverence within you. And thou who thinkest to seek for me, know that seeking and yearning shall avail thee not unless thou knowest the mystery; that if that which thou seekest thou findest not within thee, thou wilt never find it without thee. For behold, I have been with thee from the beginning; and I am that which is attained at the end of desire.[76]

The Three Initiations of Wicca

Esbats and Sabbats are collective celebrations that involve the entire Wiccan coven. However, the three Wiccan initiations, or degrees, relate primarily to the spiritual development of the individual. Wiccan initiations are essentially rites of passage intended to bring about a transformation of consciousness in the person involved. Anthropologist Lynne Hume writes that, with regard to Wicca: "The intention of initiation is to allow the candidate to enter a new dimension of reality; to die as her previous self and be reborn as her witch self. It is not so much an acquisition of knowledge but rather the experience of the process that is crucial. . . . The process of initiation relies primarily upon the will of the person to make the journey towards the Mystery."[77]

The First Initiation

Covens often request that candidates for this initiation fast for several days before the ceremony. Candidates may also be advised to spend time meditating on Nature. Immediately before the first initiation takes place, the candidate is asked to bathe and is then brought naked ("sky-clad") and blindfolded to the sacred circle: usually the candidate's hands are bound with ritual cords.[78] The state of nakedness represents a casting aside of the old persona.

While the new initiate-to-be waits outside the circle, the Great Goddess and Horned God are invoked into the high priestess and high priest for the duration of the rite. At the outer rim of the circle, the candidate is challenged at the point of a sword, an act intended to heighten the candidate's sense of vulnerability and exposure. However, once the new candidate has been accepted within the circle, he or she is welcomed by the initiator, who kneels and bestows kisses upon the new candidate:

> Blessed Be thy feet that have brought thee in these ways
> Blessed Be thy knees that shall kneel at the sacred altar
> Blessed Be thy phallus/womb without which we would not be
> Blessed Be thy breasts formed in beauty and in strength
> Blessed Be thy lips that shall utter the sacred names.[79]

Vivianne Crowley notes that in this ritual process, "the body is honoured and reverenced": the essential message of the First Initiation is one of acceptance.[80] First degree witches are introduced during the ritual to the practical tools of witchcraft. They are also shown how to cast a magical circle and how to call the watchtowers of the four elements from North, East, South, and West. Following their initiation, they will also be expected to develop an increasing familiarity with the principles and philosophy of witchcraft.[81] Initiates usually take a new magical name and will be known by this name among other coven members.

The Second Initiation

In passing through the Second Initiation, Wiccans attain the rank of high priestess or high priest. Some Wiccan covens require three years of ritual work before they grant the second degree to one of their members.[82] In the second degree, a stronger connection is made between the initiator and the initiated, and candidates will need to find an opposite sex partner with whom they can work compatibly in partnership.[83] Vivianne Crowley has described the Second Initiation in Wicca as a journey into the depths of the unconscious mind.[84]

An important feature of the second degree rite includes a mystery play called the *Legend of the Goddess*, in which the initiate and other coven members enact the descent of the Goddess into the Underworld. In the *Legend*, the Goddess goes forth into the underworld to seek an answer to the question: Why dost thou cause all things that I love and take delight in to fade and die? Here the Goddess encounters the God in his role as the Dark Lord of Death.[85] Within the coven, male and female participants are expected to respond differently to the *Legend of the Goddess* because issues related to the "polar opposites" of the psyche are likely to arise.[86] According to Crowley, for a man to find his true self he must encounter the divine feminine.[87] For a woman, the process involves overcoming passivity: "She is challenged to go forth and to seek experience."[88] Crowley also notes that whereas the First Initiation involved confronting vulnerability and exposure, the aim of the Second Initiation is "the transformation of the inner world."[89] At the end of the *Legend of the Goddess*, writes Crowley, "the seeker is given a new message: that from the dark world of the unconscious and the Land of Death may come rebirth."[90] Janet and Stewart Farrar have transcribed this section of the ritual text as follows:

> There are three great events in the life of man: Love, Death and
> Resurrection in the new body; and Magic controls them all. For to fulfil
> love you must return again at the same time and place as the loved one,
> and you must remember and love them again. But to be reborn you
> must die and be ready for a new body; and to die you must be born; and
> without love you may not be born.[91]

The *Legend* closes with the God and Goddess instructing each other in these mysteries: "She teaches him the mystery of the sacred cup which is the cauldron of rebirth, and in return he gives her the necklace which is the circle of rebirth."[92] The rite concludes with the initiator announcing to the four quarters that the initiate has been consecrated as a high priest or high priestess.[93]

The Third Initiation

The third degree in Wicca is referred to as the Great Rite and is bestowed upon two individuals who are already a couple, that is to say, "husband and wife or established lovers."[94] The Great Rite is perceived by Wiccans as a sacred marriage: the ritual union of the Goddess and the God. From a mystical perspective, the ritual itself also points toward transcendence for, in the sacred marriage between Goddess and God, the duality of sexual polarity referred to in the Second Initiation ceases altogether: "The Goddess and the God are united as One."[95] During the first part of the ritual, the Goddess and the God are invoked into the high priestess and high priest by their initiators.[96] In the second part of the ritual, however, they inter-act as incarnate deities themselves: "they themselves have the Divine forces invoked into them so that the Sacred Marriage may be performed between the Goddess and the God."[97]

Wiccans undertaking the Third Initiation do not necessarily consummate their ritual union physically. When the union is enacted symbolically—for example, by ritually plunging the athame into the chalice—it is said to be performed *in token*.[98] However, when two partners taking the role of God and Goddess wish to physically enact their sacred sexual union, the high priest offers the third degree to his partner *in token*, and the high priestess returns it to him *in true*.[99] The final part of the Great Rite, involving either the real or symbolic act of sexual union, is performed in private after other coven members have left the circle.[100]

The Great Sabbats and the three initiations of Wicca focus on concepts of fertility, the cycles of the seasons, and the sacred union of the Goddess and the God. Through their celebrations, Wiccan practitioners emphasize a process of renewal that in turn is reflected psychologically and spiritually within their own inner being. As Lynne Hume observes: "In spite of its seemingly theatrical mode, its tools and paraphernalia, ritual is only a means to an end. Ritual is the *outer form* whose purpose is to act as catalyst to the *inner process*. . . .. Neither ritual nor magic are intended to convert the sceptical or astound the novice, but are used as tools to transform the individual."[101]

The Influence of Alex Sanders

Alongside Gerald Gardner, Alex Sanders (1916–1988) is regarded as one of the most influential figures in the early phase of the contemporary witchcraft revival. He even has an entire Wiccan tradition named after him, for so-called Alexandrian witches—by virtue of a play on the words of his name—are those descended from his initiatory covens in the late 1960s and early 1970s. This period was undoubtedly his heyday, for he was then very much a public figure and, accompanied by his former wife Maxine, provided witchcraft with a certain ceremonial glamor.

By his own account, Sanders was born in Manchester in 1916.[102] And, just as he would later help revive the worship of the lunar Goddess in modern times, it is clear that women rather than men played a formative role in his upbringing. Sanders claimed that his mother, sister, and grandmother were the most significant forces in his early life, his often drunken and wayward father very much a lesser figure. Throughout his magical career, however, Sanders was prone to bouts of exaggeration and deception, and it is often difficult to distinguish between fact and fiction. According to his biographer, June Johns, Sanders was raised on bread and dripping as a youth, and the family had to struggle to make ends meet. Sanders's mother Hannah was a cleaning lady, his father an itinerant musician. But it was his Welsh grandmother, Grandma Bibby, who would determine his future occult career.

According to Sanders, one day when he was seven he paid her an unannounced visit and came upon her naked, "with wrinkled belly and match-stick thighs," engaged in a witchcraft ritual in her kitchen. Sanders recalls that "a number of curious objects surrounded her. These were swords, a black-handled knife, a sickle-shaped knife and various bowls lying around on the floor: other odd objects lay on a large Welsh dresser."[103]

Frightened at first by this unexpected encounter, Sanders claimed he was sworn to secrecy by his grandmother and told he would be duly initiated. Grandma Bibby now ordered him to remove his clothes, step forward into the magical circle, and bend over with his head between his thighs. Taking the sickle-knife in her hands she nicked Sanders' scrotum with it, drawing blood. "You're one of us now," she is alleged to have told him, and Sanders now realized that he was destined to be a witch. Later Grandma Bibby explained to her grandson that she was descended from a line of witches dating back to the fourteenth-century Welsh chieftain Owain Glyn Dwr (Owen Glendower), who had worshiped the Great Goddess and kept the ancient Celtic traditions alive. Over the next few years a strong bond developed between Sanders and his grandmother, as she instructed him in making love potions and good luck charms, and also showed him to the ceremony of Drawing down the Moon—the ritual in which the high priestess is transformed ceremonially into the living Goddess, as just described. Sanders also learned how to prepare and write his own *Book of Shadows*—a private handwritten document including details of ceremonies, invocations, and charms.

According to Wiccan tradition, the *Book of Shadows* is burned when the dying witch "passes over." Sanders maintained that when Grandma Bibby died in 1942, he destroyed her *Book of Shadows* but retained her black-handled knife, her ceremonial sword, and other items of ritual equipment. Sanders also claimed that prior to her death she had initiated him into the third degree, which included token sexual intercourse with her—an act symbolizing the union of the fertility goddess and her consort.

Sanders now had an exotic occult pedigree to offer the world. However, his initial forays into occult covens were characterized by materialistic self-advancement. By his own admission, Sanders engaged in ritual magic with the aim of attracting prosperity and sexual success—and in his case it appeared to work. Sanders was taken up by a wealthy couple who for several years treated him as their son, bestowing gifts and riches upon him, and he also found himself attracted to a frivolous, fun-loving group of promiscuous party goers. This phase passed, however, and Sanders realized that he had more serious esoteric matters to attend to. He resolved to develop several witchcraft covens in the Manchester area and continue the work passed on to him by his grandmother.

It was during this time that Sanders met Maxine Morris, an attractive young woman who had been raised by as a devout Roman Catholic and educated at the local convent. Her mother was a committed Christian, but Maxine herself had had childhood visions of merging with the earth and sky, and Sanders was convinced she was a natural witch. They married in 1967, and Maxine became known in some English neopagan circles as the Witch Queen.

That same year, Sanders and his wife moved to Notting Hill Gate and established the witchcraft coven that in due course would attract Stewart and Janet Farrar—who in turn would later become influential figures in the international neopagan movement. By now Sanders had established himself as a media celebrity and the leading public witch in Britain—the tabloid press had already been referring to him as the King of the Witches. There were numerous television appearances, late-night talks on the BBC, the forthcoming biography by June Johns, record albums of his rituals, and even a film, *The Legend of the Witches*, based loosely on his pagan activities.

Sanders was also emphasizing an apparent point of superiority over Gerald Gardner—for Sanders claimed to have gained a third degree initiation from his grandmother, whereas Gardner had only received a first degree from his initiator. It is a point of distinction that still rankles in some occult circles today when witchcraft pedigrees are discussed, because questions of "authenticity," "tradition," and "lineage," as always, tend to create factionalism and rivalry.

Sanders and his wife separated in 1973. Maxine Morris continued running her coven in London with a new consort and a much more low-key public presence. Sanders, meanwhile, drifted toward semi-retirement and moved to Bexhill in Sussex, where he lived until his death in 1988.

Issues of lineage and authenticity resurfaced once again, however, with the departure of Alex Sanders from the scene, and several highly respected witches in Britain let it be known that they did not promote the public witchcraft endorsed by Alex Sanders and his group. The influential English witch Patricia Crowther—whose husband had introduced Gerald Gardner to Aleister Crowley in 1946—was one of those who objected to Sanders's public style. Patricia Crowther had been initiated by Gardner on the Isle of Man in June 1960 and later established a coven with her husband in Sheffield. She took the initiation of high priestess in October 1961, and had been considered by many to be Gardner's natural successor. When I discussed the issue of occult secrecy with her in the mid-1980s, she told me that she was strongly opposed to witches who "break

FIGURE 6.4.   Alex Sanders initiating Janet Farrar (left) while other members of the Wiccan coven look on. Courtesy of the estate of Stewart Farrar.

their oaths" and release too much information to the public. For her, the "old school" of witches—including Doreen Valiente, Lois Bourne, and Eleanor Bone—were authentic, whereas many of the more public witches had not been properly initiated.[104]

Janet and Stewart Farrar

The issue of how much authentic Wiccan information could be presented to the public also dogged the magical careers of Janet and Stewart Farrar, both of whom had been initiated in Alex Sanders's coven.[105] By the late 1970s, the Farrars had assumed a leading role in London's occult community, and they wrote several major works on neopaganism, including *Eight Sabbats for Witches* (1981), *The Witches' Way* (1984), *The Witches' Goddess* (1987), and *The Witches' God* (1989)—all published in the United States as well as in Britain. As a result, the

FIGURE 6.5.   Alex Sanders in later years. Courtesy Cinetel Productions, Sydney.

Farrars strongly influenced neopagan thought and practice on both sides of the Atlantic. The rituals, spellcraft, and conjurations described in their books, which cumulatively present a working guide to practical witchcraft, provide the sort of information Patricia Crowther believes should remain restricted to the inner circle.

Janet Farrar (née Owen), born in 1950, was raised in East London in a strictly Anglican family. She began to drift away from Christianity in adolescence, and was later briefly involved in Transcendental Meditation.

After working as a model, she became a secretary in the Beatles' London office. Around this time, she visited Alex and Maxine Sanders's coven in Notting Hill Gate, was impressed by Wicca as a spiritual path, and decided to join the circle—it was here that she later met Stewart.

Stewart had a very different background. Born in Essex in 1916, he had been raised as a Christian Scientist, but later became an agnostic. He studied journalism at University College, London, during the 1930s, served as an anti-aircraft gunnery instructor in the Second World War, and later worked for several years as an editor for Reuters. He also produced several radio drama scripts for BBC Radio before becoming a feature writer for the weekly magazine *Reveille* in 1969.

It was in his capacity as a journalist that Stewart Farrar was invited to the Sanders's coven—his task was to write about a Wiccan initiation. Instead, he became a convert to neopaganism.

Despite the thirty-four years' difference in age, Janet Owen and Stewart Farrar became magical partners, and in December 1970, a few months after their initiations, they left Sanders's group to form a coven of their own. They married five years later in a traditional Wiccan "handfasting" ceremony, and in 1976 moved to Ireland, where they established a new coven. Stewart Farrar died on 7 February 2000, but Janet Farrar continues in her role as a strong advocate of practical Wicca. She married fellow Wiccan practitioner Gavin Bone in May 2001, and continues to tour and lecture internationally.

FIGURE 6.6. Janet and Stewart Farrar, photographed in 1984. Courtesy Cinetel Productions, Sydney.

Janet Farrar maintains that the essential aim of witchcraft is a spiritual fusion of male and female polarities, and the restoration of the sacred bond with Nature:

> Once a woman realizes her own psychic potential she becomes fully mature and can reunite man with herself in a way that mankind hasn't seen for aeons. We don't want to replace a male-dominated culture with a female-dominated one. We want to make the two work in perfect harmony. The world needs an injection of the pagan outlook, relating to the earth, relating to the environment, relating to our fellow creatures. We are in danger of losing that contact and the balance needs restoring. Culture, religion and society have been male-dominated for over two thousand years, and life is out of balance. We need to recover the feminine aspect—the Goddess.[106]

Feminism and Goddess Spirituality

In the United States, the late-1960s psychedelic counterculture, associated especially with the Bay Area around San Francisco, fueled a fascination with diverse wisdom traditions and various forms of "alternative spirituality" and esoteric teachings from around the world.[107] The psychedelic revolution itself was short-lived,   but in its aftermath, during the early 1970s, the eclectic fusion of Eastern mysticism, Western esoterica, indigenous spirituality, metaphysics, and popular self-help psychology gave rise in turn to what is now known as the New Age movement.[108] This was a socio-religious movement with identifiable characteristics, and its international influence is still felt today.[109]

Within the context of this burgeoning "alternative spirituality," variations on imported Gardnerian witchcraft began to emerge in the United States during the 1970s. In particular, the blending of feminism and modern witchcraft gave rise to a more broad-based spiritual movement known as Goddess worship or Goddess spirituality.[110] As theologian Mary Farrell Bednarowski has noted, this was a movement that rejected traditional Christianity and Judaism, seeking "truth in the depths of the female psyche and [finding] its energy in the worship of the 'the goddess.'"[111] According to Bednarowski, the primary task of feminist spirituality involved "the resacralization of the cosmos and the reimaging of the sacred." Resacralization in turn required the "reinfusion of the sacred into the universe," and for this to occur there had to be a "redefining of the very nature of the sacred." . . . It could not be "contained solely within the transcendent being of the God of the Bible."[112]

In her book *Changing of the Gods: Feminism and the End of Traditional Religions* (1979), Naomi Goldenberg proposed that feminist witchcraft could create a "powerful new religion" focused on the worship of the Goddess, and that this new religion would encourage feminist witches to reject "a civilization in which males in high places imitate a male god in heaven."[113] Influential thinker Mary Daly similarly claimed that the new feminist witchcraft was an appropriate alternative to a model of the universe in which a male God ruled the cosmos and thereby controlled social institutions to the detriment of women: "The symbol of the Father God, spawned in the human imagination and sustained as plausible by patriarchy, has in turn rendered service to this type of society by making its mechanisms for the oppression of women appear right and fitting."[114]

Jewish writer Judith Plaskow, co-editor of the feminist anthology *Womanspirit Rising* (1979), was equally emphatic, raising issues of male dominance articulated by many women involved with the rise of Goddess spirituality at the time:

> The Bible was written by men. The myths from which the Bible
> borrowed and which it used and transformed were written by men. The
> liturgy was written by men. Jewish philosophy is the work of men.
> Modern Jewish theology is the work of men. . . . The problems we as
> women face in relation to our tradition are deep and complex, involving
> almost every aspect of tradition. Where then are we going to find the
> new words, our words, which need to be spoken?[115]

In the United States, Goddess worship expanded the structure of Gardnerian coven-based witchcraft, adopting rituals that were broader in scope, more diverse, and less bound by the traditional Wiccan concept of a threefold initiation. Although some Goddess worshipers continued to refer to themselves as witches, others abandoned the term altogether, preferring to regard their neopagan practice as a universal feminist religion, drawing on mythologies from many different ancient cultures.[116]

As the Goddess spirituality movement developed in the United States during the 1970s, it would come to include such influential figures as Merlin Stone, Carol P. Christ, Margot Adler, Marija Gimbutas, Judith Plaskow, Naomi Goldenberg, Mary Daly, and the Christian feminist theologians Rosemary Radford Ruether and Carter Heyward.[117] However, the pioneering figures in the rise of Goddess spirituality and feminist witchcraft were unquestionably Zsuzsanna Budapest and Starhawk who, between them, would redefine the very nature of feminist neopaganism in the United States.

Zsuzsanna Budapest (otherwise known as Z., or Zee, Budapest) was born in Hungary in 1940, the daughter of a psychic medium. Budapest's mother, Masika Szilagyi, who claimed shamanic ancestry, composed poems and invocations while in trance and was also a sculptress of note, often featuring pagan and goddess themes in her motifs.[118] At the age of nineteen, Z. Budapest left Vienna, where she had been studying languages, and traveled to Illinois in order to study German literature at the University of Chicago. Later she worked in theater in New York, exploring techniques of improvisation, before moving to Los Angeles in 1970. Soon after arriving in Los Angeles, Budapest opened an occult shop, the Feminist Wicca, on Lincoln Boulevard in Santa Monica. The store served as a "matriarchal spiritual center," dispensing candles, oil, incense, herbs, jewelry, Tarot cards, and other occult paraphernalia. It also developed as a meeting place for women wishing to perform rituals together. Soon there were groups of neopagan women meeting for ceremonies on the equinoxes and solstices and, in Budapest's words, "feminist spirituality had been born again."[119]

In a lengthy interview with journalist Cheri Lesh, published in 1975, Budapest expressed her belief that Wicca was not an inverted form of Christianity but represented the remnants of a much older, matriarchal system of worship that recognized the feminine as the creative force in Nature.[120] Budapest spoke of the bloody transition from a matriarchal society to a patriarchal form, in which roaming

FIGURE 6.7. Zsuzsanna Budapest performing a Goddess ritual in the mid-1980s. Courtesy Cinetel Productions, Sydney.

bands of warriors ravaged the great Queendoms of Anatolia, Sumer, and Thrace and fragmented the "Great Goddess" into a number of minor deities. This led to a much diminished status for the goddesses, who then had confined and restricted roles as a consequence. In Greek mythology, Aphrodite became simply a goddess of love and sexuality, while Artemis represented hunting, and Athena wisdom. Hera, Amphitrite, and Persephone, meanwhile, became adjuncts to Zeus, Poseidon, and Hades. According to Budapest, this transition was a major cultural disaster:

> Mythology is the mother of religions, and grandmother of history. Mythology is human-made, by the artists, storytellers and entertainers of the times. In short, culture-makers are the soldiers of history, more effective than guns and bombers. Revolutions are really won on the cultural battlefields. . . . Women understand this very well, since we became aware of how women's culture had been ripped off by the ruling class. This resulted in a stunted self-image of women which resulted in insecurities, internalizing the cultural expectations of us created by male culture-makers. Most of the women in the world still suffer from this spiritual poverty.[121]

In order to eliminate any male influence, Budapest's practice of Dianic witch-craft has excluded men altogether. According to Budapest, women's mysteries must be kept pure and strong, and men have no place in them: "We have *women's* circles. You don't put men in women's circles—they wouldn't be women's circles any more. Our Goddess is Life, and women should be free to worship from their ovaries."[122]

Budapest's most influential publication, *The Holy Book of Women's Mysteries* (1989), includes a "Self-Blessing Ritual" which she describes as a way of "exorcising that patriarchal 'policeman,' cleansing the deep mind, and filling it with positive images of the strength and beauty of women. This is what the Goddess symbol-izes—the Divine within women and all that is Female in the universe."[123] Budapest favors an equal mix of lesbian and heterosexual women in her circles to "balance the polarities" in her rituals. Her emphasis on women's mysteries allows the different phases of womanhood to be honored in their own right, and group ceremonies are performed for each of these phases of life.[124]

It was through the Feminist Wicca that Budapest first made contact with Miriam Simos.[125] Simos is best known as the acclaimed neopagan author Star-hawk, a Jewish woman who had rejected Judaism, Buddhism, and other "male-dominated" religious traditions.[126] Budapest became one of Starhawk's teachers, although Starhawk claims that her spiritual knowledge also derives from dream and trance experiences.[127] Starhawk formed her first coven, Compost, from a group of men and women who attended a class in Witchcraft that she taught in the

Bay Area Center for Alternative Education, and she was later confirmed as high priestess of this coven.[128] Starhawk became a founding member of Reclaiming, a feminist network of women and men working in the Goddess tradition to unify spirituality and politics through progressive activism.[129] During the mid-1980s she also served on the teaching faculty of theologian Matthew Fox's postgraduate Institute at Holy Names College in Oakland, exploring the common ground between neopaganism and Fox's renegade Roman Catholic-based Creation-centered spirituality.[130]

Since the late 1970s, Starhawk has published several highly influential books, including *The Spiral Dance, Dreaming the Dark,* and *The Pagan Book of Living and Dying,* all widely regarded as key works in the revival of Goddess worship and neo-paganism. During an interview with Toronto-based writer Alexander Blair-Ewart in the mid-1990s, Starhawk explained that her Goddess perspective involved a process of resacralizing the world:

> What's important about witchcraft and about the pagan movement is, essentially, that it's not so much a way of seeing reality, as it's a different way of valuing the reality around us. We say that what is sacred, in the sense of what we are most committed to, what determines all our other values, is this living Earth, this world, the life systems of the earth, the cycles of birth and growth and death and regeneration; the air, the fire, the water, the land.[131]

In her writings, Starhawk also refers specifically to the nurturing and revitalizing power of the Goddess-energy:

> The symbolism of the Goddess has taken on an electrifying power for modern women. The rediscovery of the ancient matrifocal civilizations has given us a deep sense of pride in woman's ability to create and sustain culture. It has exposed the falsehoods of patriarchal history, and given us models of female strength and authority. The Goddess—ancient and primeval; the first of deities; patroness of the Stone Age hunt and of the first sowers of seeds; under whose guidance the herds were tamed, the healing herbs first discovered; in whose image the first works of art were created; for whom the standing stones were raised; who was the inspiration of song and poetry—is recognized once again in today's world. She is the bridge, on which we can cross the chasms within ourselves, which were created by our social conditioning, and reconnect with our lost potentials. She is the ship, on which we sail the waters of the deep self, exploring the uncharted seas within. She is the door, through which we pass to the future. She is the cauldron, in which

we who have been wrenched apart simmer until we again become whole. She is the vaginal passage, through which we are reborn.[132]

Starhawk's seminal work *The Spiral Dance* and Z. Budapest's *Holy Book of Women's Mysteries* have influenced the rise of American Goddess spirituality in the same way that Gerald Gardner and Doreen Valiente's writings helped to establish the foundations of British Wicca. According to Starhawk, the sacred presence of the Goddess remains at the very heart of all forms of feminist witchcraft: "The Goddess is around us and within us. She is immanent and transcendent . . . the Goddess represents the divine embodied in Nature, in human beings, in the flesh."[133] Starhawk also maintains that the encounter with the Goddess should be based on personal experience, and not on religious doctrine or belief: "In the Craft, we do not *believe* in the Goddess—we connect with Her; through the moon, the stars, the ocean, the earth, through trees, animals, through other human beings, through ourselves. She is here. She is within us all. She is the full circle: earth, air, fire, water and essence—body, mind, spirit, emotions, change."[134]

Starhawk's concept of deity is essentially monotheistic, for she regards the Goddess as the source of all life, the ground of all being: "The Goddess is first of all earth, the dark, nurturing mother who brings forth all life. She is the power of fertility and generation; the womb, and also the receptive tomb, the power of death. All proceeds from Her, all returns to Her."[135] Feminist writer Carol P. Christ offers a similarly all-encompassing view of the Goddess: "The earth is the body of the Goddess. All beings are interdependent in the web of life. Nature is intelligent, alive and aware. As part of nature, human beings are relational, embodied, and interdependent. . . . The symbols and rituals of Goddess religion bring these values to consciousness and help us build communities in which we can create a more just, peaceful, and harmonious world."[136]

However, as Margot Adler has noted in *Drawing down the Moon* (1981), many neopagans regard themselves as polytheists or pantheists, rather than monotheists, and there is no general agreement on the nature of sacred reality.[137] Adler also notes that some Wiccans distinguish between the Goddess of the moon, earth, and sea, and the God of the woods, hunt, and animal realm, in what amounts to a type of "duotheism."[138] British Wiccan writer Vivianne Crowley seeks to resolve this issue in a different way when she says: "All Gods are different aspects of the one God and all Goddesses are different aspects of the one Goddess . . . ultimately these two are reconciled in the one divine essence."[139]

7

Dark Forces

Contemporary Satanism and Black Magic

In the popular imagination, witchcraft and Satanism have often meant much the same thing. They have been branded by both cynics and hostile religious fundamentalists alike as forms of "Devil worship." As it happens, this evaluation is one which both contemporary witches *and* modern-day Satanists reject. If the response from key members of the satanic Temple of Set in San Francisco is any guide, contemporary Satanists are inclined to look askance at any form of worship that involves "protective transcendental deities"—whether this worship is addressed to a God *or* a Goddess. And contemporary witches have also been outspoken on this issue of confused image and identity. As Z. Budapest has put it, in her characteristically colorful language:

> Witchcraft is a universal, joy-oriented, artistic kind of religious practice that celebrates the earth and its journey around the sun. Now, we got a bad rap from the Christians about this. We have been told that we worship Satan, the Devil. Well, the Devil is a Christian god. We have never heard of the Devil. Many of us got burned [in the Middle Ages] because we didn't know who they were talking about . . . so many died. Many were going to their death still wondering who the Devil was.[1]

If we are to understand contemporary Satanism, it is vital to consider the occult philosophy of the Church of Satan and its successor, the Temple of Set—for together they occupy a central position in the world of contemporary black magic. However, despite their historical connections, the Church of Satan and the Temple of Set present quite different magical perspectives—the first based primarily on hedonistic indulgences and "sins of the flesh," the second on metaphysical revelations from the ancient Egyptian entity Set. Now greatly diminished in both influence and membership, the Church of Satan that attracted widespread notoriety during the late 1960s was always, in one sense, an offshoot of Californian show business—a form of institutionalized party revelry. The Temple of Set, on the other hand, continues to chart broad esoteric horizons and is based on carefully considered philosophical responses to the magical universe. And yet, despite their ideological differences, these two organizations are central to resolving the issue of satanic intent. As Jean La Fontaine has observed in a recent scholarly overview of twentieth-century magic and witchcraft:

> There are only two long-standing, well-established groups of Satanists and each is largely the creation of one man. . . . The founder of the Church of Satan died only in October 1997 and the founder of the Temple of Set is still its leader. . . . Both organizations have an international membership but it is not clear whether all the groups outside the USA are affiliated to the original organizations, have been founded with their agreement as independent off-shoots, or are simply imitations.[2]

The Church of Satan

The Church of Satan was founded in San Francisco in 1966 by Anton LaVey (1930–1997), who remains a controversial figure not only because of his role in the rise of contemporary Satanism but also because of the substantially fictitious persona that he helped create with the help of two sympathetic co-authors.[3] As religious scholar James R. Lewis points out, LaVey has two categories of biography, "one historical and one legendary . . . [and] his real life was far more prosaic than the story he fabricated for the benefit of the media."[4]

LaVey's main "authorized" biography, written by his former partner and current Church of Satan high priestess, Blanche Barton, and published in 1990,

FIGURE 7.1.   Anton LaVey, founder of the Church of Satan, photographed in 1970 with one of his followers. © Bettmann/CORBIS.

claims that LaVey was born in Chicago and was of French, Alsatian, German, Russian, and Romanian descent.[5] According to this "legendary" account, LaVey learned about vampires from his maternal grandmother Luba Kolton, and immersed himself in reading occult and fantasy literature like Bram Stoker's *Dracula* and the popular magazine *Weird Tales*.[6] After a period spent working as a carnival entertainer in the Clyde Beatty Circus, LaVey studied criminology at San Francisco City College and then became a photographer with the San Francisco Police Department. It was in the latter capacity that LaVey observed the gruesome side of urban life—"people shot by nuts, knifed by friends, kids splattered in the gutter by hit-and-run drivers. It was disgusting and depressing."[7] These grim events had a strong impact on LaVey's spiritual perspectives: he concluded that violence was part of the divine plan and turned away from God as a source of inspiration and benevolence.[8] The "legendary" LaVey also played oboe in the San Francisco Ballet Orchestra, had a cameo role as the Devil in the movie *Rosemary's Baby*, and had an affair with Marilyn Monroe before she became famous. LaVey claimed to be a multimillionaire and maintained that the Church of Satan had "hundreds of thousands" of fully paid-up members.

LaVey's "legendary" biography was not challenged until 1991, when journalist Lawrence Wright, a contributor to *Rolling Stone*, published the results of an investigation into some of LaVey's claims.[9] Wright established that the San Francisco Ballet Orchestra did not actually exist, that LaVey had not worked as a musician or trainer for the Beatty Circus, and that he had never been employed by the San Francisco Police Department. Wright concluded: "As I began to take apart the literary creation he had made of his life, I would realize that 'Anton LaVey' was itself his supreme creation, his ultimate satanic object, a sort of android composed of all the elements his mysterious creator had chosen from the universe of dark possibilities."[10]

Nevertheless, as James Lewis points out, LaVey *was* born in Chicago, his family *did* move to San Francisco, he *did* work as a musician (though not in a ballet orchestra), and he *did* establish the Church of Satan in 1966.[11] In 1998, LaVey's estranged daughter, Zeena, and her husband, Nikolas Schreck, published a more detailed summary of the "legendary" claims and the actual historical reality of events in LaVey's life, thereby extending Wright's earlier findings. They confirmed that LaVey's grandmother was Ukrainian rather than Transylvanian, that he had never met Marilyn Monroe, that he had played no acting role in *Rosemary's Baby*, that he lived in near-poverty for most of the 1970s, and that his Church of Satan had fewer than three hundred members.[12]

The core facts associated with the birth of the Church of Satan are as follows: prior to establishing the Church itself, LaVey had begun holding weekly classes, known as Magic Circle meetings, in order to explore various esoteric topics. These meetings were attended by a diverse range of people, including avant-garde film producer Kenneth Anger, and were held in LaVey's tightly shuttered house at 6114 California Street, San Francisco.[13] They included lectures on vampires, werewolves, haunted houses, extrasensory perception, and zombies—and other related subjects. LaVey also lampooned the Roman Catholic Church with a "Black Mass" that involved desecrating the Host, using an inverted cross and black candles, and reciting Christian prayers backwards.

Fascinated by the concept of Sir Francis Dashwood's eighteenth-century Hellfire Club, where establishment figures would meet for evenings of revelry and debauchery, LaVey believed that the Magic Circle could provide the basis for a modern-day counterpart.[14] With this idea in mind, LaVey shaved his head and announced the formation of the Church of Satan on Walpurgisnacht, 30 April 1966, a night traditionally associated with the ascendancy of the Powers of Darkness. LaVey declared 1966 to be Year One, *Anno Satanas*—the first year of the reign of Satan.[15]

LaVey's Church of Satan celebrated sensual indulgence and personal empowerment; its ceremonies were conceived as a means for channeling magical power into an expression of intense carnal desire. LaVey's ritual altar room was completely black with an inverted pentagram mounted on the wall above the fireplace.[16] LaVey believed that this particular pentagram represented the Sigil of Baphomet, a symbol allegedly adapted from the Knights Templar in the fourteenth century.[17] Services began and ended with satanic hymns and a ritual invocation to Satan. A naked woman—a human symbol of lust and self-indulgence—was used as an "altar." The following contemporary account describes a typical service in the Church of Satan:

> A bell is rung nine times to signal the beginning of the service, the priest turning in the circle counter clockwise, ringing the bell to the four cardinal points. The leopard-skin cover is removed from the mantelpiece, revealing the nude body of the female volunteer altar for the evening. The purification is performed by one of the assistant priests, who sprinkles the congregation with a mixture of semen and water, symbolic of creative force. LaVey then takes a sword from its sheath, held by Diane, his wife and high priestess, and invokes Satan in his cardinal manifestations. Satan, in the South, represents Fire; Lucifer in the East, is symbolic of Air; Belial, in the North, represents Earth; and Leviathan, in the West, is his watery aspect. The officiating priest then drinks from the chalice, which is filled with any liquid he may desire, from lemonade to 100-proof vodka, making a symbolic offering to Satan. The chalice is then placed on the pubic area of the girl-altar, where it stays for the remainder of the evening.[18]

LaVey believed in celebrating Christian "sins" as virtues and formulated the following satanic statements for his key work, *The Satanic Bible* (1969), as an expression of his occult approach:

> Satan represents indulgence instead of abstinence.
> Satan represents vital existence instead of spiritual pipe dreams.

Satan represents undefiled wisdom instead of hypocritical self-deceit.

Satan represents kindness to those who deserve it instead of love wasted on ingrates.

Satan represents vengeance instead of turning the other cheek.

Satan represents responsibility to the responsible instead or concern for psychic vampires.

Satan represents man as just another animal . . . who, because of his "divine spiritual and intellectual development" has become the most vicious animal of all.

Satan represents all of the so-called sins as they all lead to physical, mental or emotional gratification.

Satan has been the best friend the Church has ever had, as he has kept it in business all these years.[19]

LaVey believed that the Church of Satan presented a clear and uncompromising challenge to the conventional Christian mores of Middle America—there was no place in his magical credo for humility, weakness, or "turning the other cheek."[20] LaVey did not regard his Church as anti-Christian, however, arguing instead that Christianity was irrelevant because it failed to address humanity's basic emotional needs, denied man's carnal nature, and placed its devotees in a position of dependence on "an unmerciful God who cares not whether we live or die."[21] LaVey similarly had no illusions about vows of poverty as a means of gaining spiritual redemption, maintaining instead that magic was essentially about power, and that wealth was a type of power.[22] LaVey reserved the right to divert funds otherwise intended for the Church of Satan to his own personal use, and it was this issue that would result in a split in the Church leadership in 1975. At this point, contemporary American Satanism would divide into two opposing camps: those remaining loyal to LaVey and those who would depart, establishing the Temple of Set.

The Temple of Set

By 1975, it had become evident that there were significant rifts within the Church of Satan. According to LaVey's former colleague Dr. Michael Aquino—editor of the Church's newsletter, *The Cloven Hoof*—the Church of Satan was attracting far too many "fad-followers, egomaniacs, and assorted oddballs whose primary interest in becoming Satanists was to flash their membership cards for cocktail-party notoriety."[23] At the same time, LaVey was also complaining that the ten dollar annual fee levied for Church membership was not yielding him sufficient personal income.[24]

In early 1975, LaVey sent out a notice in the Church newsletter advising that, forthwith, all higher degrees of initiation would be available for contributions in cash, real estate, or valuable objects of art. According to Aquino, the effect on many Church members was shattering: "If there had been a single unifying factor that had brought us to Satanism, it was the Church's stand against hypocrisy. So when we learned of this policy, our reaction to it was that Anton LaVey was betraying his office, betraying everything that he had worked for, for so many years."[25]

In June 1975, an act of desertion took place: a number of key members of the priesthood resigned from the Church of Satan, at the same time making it clear that they were not leaving the priesthood itself. "In fact," Aquino has stated, "we had a sacred responsibility to take it with us."[26]

A doctoral graduate from the University of California at Santa Barbara, with a strong interest in comparative religion and philosophy, Aquino had joined the Church of Satan in 1969.[27] At the time of the split within the Church of Satan, he was a priest of the fourth degree and the senior member of the splinter group. Nevertheless, in a manner somewhat comparable to Crowley's revelatory communication from Aiwass in 1904, Aquino now sought new instructions from Satan. On the evening of 21 June 1975, in a ritual magic ceremony, Aquino summoned the

FIGURE 7.2. Dr. Michael Aquino, High Priest of the Temple of Set. Courtesy Cinetel Productions, Sydney.

Prince of Darkness, "to tell us what we may do to continue our Quest."[28] The result, according to Aquino, was an act of automatic writing: "a communication from a god to a human being."[29]

In a document titled *The Book of Coming Forth by Night*, Satan revealed himself as the ancient Egyptian god Set, and named Michael Aquino as LaVey's replacement.[30] Aquino was described in the script as the successor to Aleister Crowley, and Magus, fifth degree, of the new Aeon of Set. *The Book of Coming Forth by Night* also identified a new name for both Church and deity: "Reconsecrate my Temple and my Order in the true name of Set. No longer will I accept the bastard title of a Hebrew Fiend."[31] There were also other instructions for the new magical epoch:

> When I came first to this world, I gave to you my great pentagram, timeless measure of beauty through proportion. And it was shown inverse, that creation and change be exalted above rest and preservation.
>
> With the years my pentagram was corrupted, yet time has not the power to destroy it. Its position was restored by the Church of Satan, but its essence was dimmed with a Moorish name, and the perverse letters of the Hebrews, and the goat of decadent Khar. During the Age of Satan I allowed this curious corruption, for it was meant to do me honor as I was then perceived.
>
> But this is now my Aeon, and my pentagram is again to be pure in its splendor. Cast aside the corruptions, that the pentagram of Set may shine forth. Let all who seek me be never without it, openly and with pride, for by it shall I know them.
>
> Let the one who aspires to my knowledge be called by the name Setian.[32]

Set also announced a sacred magical word for the new era: "The Word of the Aeon of Set is *xeper*—'become.'"

The Implications of Xeper

Aquino claims that the revelation from Set led the priesthood of the former Church of Satan into new areas of enquiry:

> The founders of the Temple of Set knew very little about Egyptology and we had to go and find out who Set was, and why something like this should be happening. We found out some very interesting things. The usual understanding of Set is that he was an evil god in the old Egyptian

system—the benevolent father-god being Osiris and his evil antagonist, Set, who murdered him.

In our research we discovered that this was in fact a much later corruption, and that the initial identity of Set had been that of the god of night, of the darkness, as opposed to the god of the day, the sun. Set symbolized the *isolated psyche*, the spark of life within the self, a creative force in the universe rather than an enemy figure, an inspiration for the individual consciousness.[33]

The magical word *xeper* also became central to the philosophy of the Temple of Set. Pronounced *khefer* and translated as "I have come into being," its associated symbols were the scarab beetle and the dawning sun. In a recent statement exploring the significance of *xeper*, senior Temple of Set member Don Webb has written that this word "generates the Aeon of Set, and is the current form of the Eternal Word of the Prince of Darkness. To know this word is to know that the ultimate responsibility for the evolution of your psyche is in your hands. It is the Word of freedom, ecstasy, fearful responsibility, and the root of all magic."[34]

Webb describes *xeper* as "the experience of an individual psyche becoming aware of its own existence and deciding to expand and evolve that existence through its own actions."[35] Because the Temple of Set emphasizes the magical potential of the individual, the focus of the entire organization reflects this orientation: all Setians are on an individual, self-determined magical journey, and the consequences are entirely up to them. According to Webb: "Xeper is the experience of an individual psyche becoming aware of its own existence through its own actions. Xeper has been experienced by anyone who has decided to seek after his or her own development."[36]

Although the Temple of Set recognizes a system of initiatory degrees, there are no prescribed rituals or dogmas and no specific vows. According to Lilith Sinclair, Aquino's wife and fellow priestess in the Temple of Set, the rituals in the Church of Satan used to be presented "on a very self-indulgent, materialistic level," and Satan himself was "more a symbol than an actual reality."[37] However, Sinclair maintains that her relationship with Satan within the context of the Temple of Set has evolved to a new level. Her ongoing personal contact with the Prince of Darkness is now both tangible and powerful—"a very quiet, serene, beautiful touching of minds." According to Sinclair, there is no pact signed in blood but instead a type of private vow: "It's done on an individual basis, and it's something that I myself wanted to do."[38]

While most forms of mysticism advocate the surrender of the ego in a state of transcendent union with the infinite Godhead—an act described earlier by members of the Dragon Rouge as "melting into God"—according to the Setian

FIGURE 7.3.   Temple of Set member Lilith Sinclair—communicating with the Prince of Darkness involves "a very quiet, serene, beautiful touching of minds." Courtesy Cinetel Productions, Sydney.

perspective an awareness of the personal self should be maintained at all times. According to Sinclair, when a Temple member is communicating with Set, "you retain your individuality . . . but at the same time you are linked with the essence of the Prince of Darkness. It's a natural exchange and flow of energy, of mind awareness."[39]

The Structure of the Temple of Set

During the latter years of the Church of Satan, Anton LaVey and his wife Diane tired of holding meetings solely in their own home and decided to sponsor other branches of the Church—both within San Francisco and also in other cities across the nation. Known as Grottos, these branches were established as far afield as Louisville, Kentucky, as well as Santa Cruz, San Jose, Los Angeles, Denver, Dayton, Detroit, Washington D.C., and New York, and were mostly centered around charsmatic individuals intent on spreading the word. LaVey had titled himself High Priest of Satan, and there were five initiatory degrees: Apprentice Satanist I °; Witch or Warlock II °;

Priest of Priestess of Mendes III °; Magister IV °; and Magus V °. Even within these grades, however, the satanic quest was considered something *personal*—a developing relationship between the individual and the Prince of Darkness.

The Temple of Set adopted a comparable structure of initiatory degrees, although now the Grottos were replaced by "Pylons." A key to the thinking behind this terminology is contained in Michael Aquino's privately published volume on the Church of Satan: "Humanity is like a tall building. It needs stage after stage of scaffolding. Religion after religion, philosophy after philosophy; one cannot build the twentieth floor from the scaffolding of the first."[40] A statement from the Temple of Set makes it clear that the reference to Pylons derives from the massive fortified gateways of the temples of ancient Egypt.[41] The concept of Pylons also implied something much more substantial than LaVey's Grottos and changed the focus of the Temple away from an organization based primarily on self-indulgence to one based more specifically on the evolving Setian philosophy.

The Temple of Set has since authorized the establishment of Pylons in a number of towns and cities across the United States, as well as in such countries as Australia, Britain, Germany, and Finland—although the extent of its membership is not publicly revealed.[42] Just as Grottos could only be established by second degree members of the Church of Satan, Pylons are similarly sponsored by a senior Setian—in this case a third degree member known as a Sentinel. Pylon meetings are generally held in individual members' homes and their purpose is to "provide a focus for the initiate, a place to internalize knowledge."[43] However, Setians clearly regard the Pylon as not just a meeting place but as a type of sacred metaphor. Webb refers to the Temple of Amen-Ra at Luxor by way of illustration: "The gateway presents a passage to the outside world, a narrow gateway within, and serves as a secure wall to the persons within. This is good metaphor for what a Pylon should be. . . . The gateway to Pylons is narrow; it is easily guarded by one man or woman. The role of the Sentinel is a guardianship role."[44]

The Setian commitment itself remains essentially a private and internal process, however: "The gateway to your own initiation is in your heart, but often hidden there by circumstance and habit. External gateways are symbols you can use in making your rites of passage. Most of the rites of passage you need in your life, you will have to create yourself. Pylons are one such gateway. Real initiation doesn't come from texts, it passes from mouth to ear."[45]

The Setian Perspective

As both the first and current high priest of the Temple of Set, Michael Aquino remains its leading advocate: the Temple reflects both his intellectual background and his emphasis on rational thought.[46] The activities of the Temple are also far removed from LaVey's earlier focus on carnality and sensual indulgence. As Aquino observes in *The Crystal Tablet of Set*, "The Church [of Satan] had been arrogantly sensationalistic; the Temple [of Set] was cautiously philosophical."[47]

Aquino's principal text on the nature of magical consciousness is a lengthy essay titled "The Black Magical Theory of the Universe," which is included in a collection of writings assembled in *The Crystal Tablet of Set* (1983, revised 1986).[48] Here Aquino distinguishes between what he calls "Lesser Black Magic" and "Greater Black Magic." In the first of these two approaches, the magician "applies his knowledge to entities and events in the objective universe . . . in accordance with his Will." Greater Black Magic, however, involves what Aquino refers to as "the theory and practice of non-natural interaction with the subjective universe" and is based on the concept of the Magical Link between the objective and subjective universes. Aquino defines Greater Black Magic as "the causing of change to occur in the subjective universe in accordance with the Will. This change in the subjective universe will cause a similar and proportionate change in the objective universe."[49] Aquino also draws on the philosophical writings of Johann Fichte, an eighteenth-century metaphysician, who postulated the existence of a "mental essence" encompassing the objective world: "[Fichte] postulated the original existence of a mental essence [that] divided into the ego (the sensation of the self) and the non-ego (sensations of things not perceived as the self). This mental essence is . . . a sort of 'supermind' which transcends all particular ego and non-ego manifestations."[50]

Applying Fichte's concept to a magical context, Aquino maintains that the "concentrated energies" of the ego can be used to bring about changes in the "non-ego" part of the "mental essence . . . which defines and binds together the laws of consistency in the objective universe." According to Aquino, every individual is essentially *separate* from the universe and it therefore follows that "any conscious act relative to that universe . . . is an exercise in that separateness. Hence to be aware of one's disconnection from that universe is to remain disconnected from it."[51]

Aquino rejects Christianity on philosophical grounds because he believes its doctrines are essentially irrational and are not based on an authentic understanding of the nature of the soul:

> Jesus Christ is reputed to have said that, to enter Heaven, one must be "as a little child." To put it another way, such a person would have to radiate an innocent, selfless passion for the harmony of the Universe; *he would be unable to conceive himself as apart from it* [my italics]. The irony of Christ's admonition, however, is that neither innocence nor selflessness are products of the rational intellect. . . . One can conduct one's life as

though one were innocent and selfless [but] beneath all appearances, all affectations, the actual state of the soul remains as it is: either animal/natural or human/enlightened, either asleep and ignorant or awake and all too aware.[52]

Aquino's magical conception is clearly based on a form of gnosis—on the idea of "being awake and all too aware"—but it is a type of gnosis grounded also in a notion of human existential separateness that sets it apart, for example, from the Gnostic transcendentalism of the Kabbalah, where all aspects of creative manifestation merge eventually into *Ain Soph Aur*, the Limitless Light. Aquino rejects the mystical concept of "melting into God," which he associates with the Right-Hand Path, defining this type of occult approach as a form of "white magic."[53] According to Aquino, white magic "embraces not only all conventional religions, but all pagan and nature-worship ideologies as well. To the Temple, the only distinction between them is one of style and imagery, not of underlying substance."[54] Aquino maintains that Satanism provides a unique approach to the objective and subjective universes because it advocates personal behavior that is entirely self-determined:

All conventional religions, including the pagan ones, are simply a variation on the theme of reunion and submergence of the self within the natural universe. So from our point of view, it really makes no difference whether you pray to a Father god or to a Mother goddess—or to an entire gaggle of gods and goddesses! You are still wishing for their acceptance. You are waiting for them to put their arms around you and say: "You belong. You are part of us. You can relax. We will take care of you. We approve of you. We endorse you . . ." The Satanist, or Black Magician, does not seek that kind of submergence of the self. We do not seek to have our decisions and our morality approved or validated by any higher god or being. We take responsibility unto ourselves.[55]

According to Aquino,

it is in the process of making the preliminary exploration of the subjective and objective universes that the Black Magician begins to discover and ultimately to know how things really work. He exists wholly in neither the subjective universe (like a mystic) nor the objective universe (like a materialist) . . . He moves back and forth between the two with increasing ease and expertise, influencing the Magical Links between them and thus causing changes in accordance with his Will [capitals in the original].[56]

Aquino's wife and Temple priestess Lilith Sinclair claims that the unique magical quest undertaken by members of the Temple of Set justifies the elitist attitude that sets them apart from other occult practitioners: "We regard ourselves very highly because we feel we are superior beings. We feel that we are gaining the knowledge of a deeper universe."[57] Don Webb similarly supports Sinclair's elitist perspective, maintaining that the Setian approach allows its initiated members to think and act like gods:

> If we want to participate in the cultural revolution / evolution of the New Cycle, the best method is to transform ourselves. To actively seek, every day, those experiences and perform those deeds that lead to wisdom. If the magician transforms himself or herself, the actions of the magician lead to a transformation of the world around them. If one becomes as a god, one's words and deeds will have the effect of gods.[58]

Webb also argues that practitioners of the Left-Hand Path have a unique approach to sacred awareness that sets them apart from more conventional religious devotees: "Magic is the way that the follower of the Left Hand Path can have the *lived experience* of being a god, rather than praying to an image of a god created by his or her imagination."[59]

The Nazi Connection

In its most benign aspects one could consider the Temple of Set simply as a magical organization dedicated to exploring the full potential of the individual—a type of magical self-help institution. However, it is certainly much more than this, for its approach to self-deification is reminiscent of the concept of the *spiritual illuminati*—a doctrine of the elect that some have associated with mystical fascism. It therefore comes as no real surprise that Michael Aquino has acknowledged a strong attraction to certain aspects of the former Nazi regime.

The specific links between the Setian philosophy and the magical practices of the esoteric Nazi group led by Heinrich Himmler are hard to identify but are nevertheless present. Although Aquino states very clearly that there are many aspects of the Nazi era that are repugnant to him, he is also convinced that the Nazis were able to summon an extraordinary psychic force which was misdirected—but need not have been. Associated with the Setian quest for the *super* man, or *initiated* man, is the implication that, as a god, the magical adept would gain the means to live forever, becoming a bright star in the firmament.

In an article in his Temple newsletter, *Runes*, Aquino makes the comment that "the successful magician must develop and ultimately master the ability to make himself the *constant*, and everything else *variable*, subject to his Will" (italics added).[60] According to Aquino, this means that the Setian magician "moves gradually towards an existence in which time becomes your servant and not your master." It will also, says Aquino, "enable you to conquer death."

Aquino quotes from the well-known classic by Isha S. de Lubicz, *Her-Bak*, which includes an Egyptian sage's answer to the young priest Her-Bak's inquiry about life and death:

> What is life? It is a form of the divine presence. It is the power, immanent
> in created things, to change themselves by successive destructions of
> form until the spirit or activating force of the original life-stream is freed.
> This power resides in the very nature of things. . . . It is the spiritual aim
> of all human life to attain a state of consciousness that is independent of
> bodily circumstance.[61]

Aquino believes that the Nazis tried to transfer the life-consciousness from the individual to the state, but that members of Himmler's esoteric group understood the process on a deeper level:

> Most Nazis were able to achieve [the transfer of consciousness] only in a
> mundane sense—in a kind of ecstatic selflessness created and sustained
> by propaganda. But the "monk-knights" of the pre-war SS could disdain,
> even willingly embrace, the death of the individual human body because
> the consciousness had been transferred to a larger life-form—that of the
> Hegelian state—and individual sacrifice towards the strengthening of
> that life-form would actually contribute towards one's immortality. All
> of the individual-death references in the SS, such as the *Totenkopf*
> insignia and ritual pledges of "Faithfulness unto death" were in fact
> arrogant affirmations of immortality.[62]

This leads us to a magical ceremony undertaken by Aquino in a chamber in Wewelsburg Castle used by Himmler's magical order, the Ahnenerbe. Himmler established the Ahnenerbe in 1935 with Richard Walther Darré, initially as an independent institute dedicated to researching German prehistory and archaeology. It was subsequently incorporated into to the Nazi SS, with its academic staff having official SS ranks and wearing SS uniforms.[63] Wewelsburg Castle, which is located near Paderborn in Westphalia, was built on the site of ancient Saxon fortifications. The castle in its present form was constructed by Archbishop Theodore von Fuerstenberg in 1604–1607 but was damaged by Swedish artillery during the Thirty Years War. In 1815, the North Tower was struck and nearly destroyed by lightning, and the castle fell into neglect. In 1933, however, the SS acquired Wewelsburg as its inner sanctum, and Himmler began a program of reconstruction. Historian Nicholas Goodrick-Clarke writes that Himmler conceived of Wewelsburg as "an SS order-castle, comparable to the Marienburg of the medieval Teutonic Knights."[64]

One of Himmler's innovations was to build a circular chamber known as the Marmorsaal (Marble Hall) to replace the original chapel of the castle. According to Aquino, it was inspired by the Hall of the Grail created by Alfred Roller, on Hitler's instructions, for the 1934 production of *Parsifal* at Bayreuth. Set in the red Italian marble floor was a dark green marble disc from which extended twelve rune-motifs. The design as a whole, while usually categorized as a "solar symbol," was in fact a magical sigil from an esoteric order, the Westphaelischen Femgerichte, also known as the Vehm. As such, the room was an ideal meeting place for the Ahnenerbe, who believed they belonged to the same magical tradition.

It would seem that Michael Aquino regards his inner group of priests and priestesses in the Temple of Set as the magical successors of the Ahnenerbe and Vehm, for it was beneath the Marble Hall in Wewelsburg, in a secret chamber known as the Walhalla, or Hall of the Dead, that he chose to perform a ritual invocation to the Prince of Darkness on 19 October 1982. The chamber itself had profound esoteric associations. Aquino notes that for Himmler and his twelve highest-ranking SS Obergruppenfuehrers (full generals), the subterranean shrine was considered a holy of holies: "Plinths for the Obergruppenfuehrers' cremation urns encircled a sunken well; on the death of each Knight of the Round Table his escutcheon was burnt on top of a hollowed-out stone pillar, with the smoke—by means of a cunningly-arranged ventilation system—forming a vertical column above the well."[65]

The specific details of Aquino's Wewelsburg invocation remain strictly private. Nevertheless, Aquino has confirmed that during the ceremony he was able to confirm his belief that magically man stands apart from the universe. In his own words: "The Wewelsburg working asserts that Life is conceptually contrary to Nature . . . and 'unnatural' in its very essence."[66]

Xeper and Immortality

As we have seen, for Aquino, the essential task of the magical initiate is to evolve to god-like proportions, subjecting the "natural" universe to his will. Man owes his special status on earth to "the deliberate intervention of a nonnatural intelligence [known as Set] and the respect accorded to the Prince of Darkness is simply an acknowledgment that he inspires man to strive ever higher in his quest for dominance."

Included in this pursuit, as mentioned earlier, is the attempt to conquer death. Whereas most mystics believe they must surrender their individuality to the godhead—*Nirvana, Sunyata, Ain Soph Aur*—Aquino maintains that this is ill-advised: "We would simply say that what they have is a sort of sublimated death-wish of the self and that we, unlike them, do not want to die."[67]

In addition to claiming that the Setian practitioner can journey "back and forth" between the objective and subjective worlds and impose his or her magical Will in both domains, Aquino endorses the classic Gnostic perspective that the psyche is neither dependent on nor imprisoned by the physical body. According to Aquino, the mind of the Setian magician is capable of reaching out "towards the limitlessness of its conscious existence."[68] This, for Aquino, is what *xeper* really implies. For the master Setian, the conscious universe literally has no boundaries. Aquino developed this idea from a statement contained in *The Book of Lucifer* in Anton LaVey's *Satanic Bible*: "If a person has been vital throughout his life and has fought to the end for his earthly existence, it is this ego which will refuse to die, even after the expiration of the flesh which housed it . . . It is this . . . vitality that will allow the Satanist to peek through the curtain of darkness and death, and remain earthbound."[69]

What, then, of the "darkness and death" referred to in this extract from LaVey's *Book of Lucifer*? Paradoxically, the answer emerges in the Setian response to self-determination. Setians regard the image of Set—the Egyptian God of the Night—as a dynamic force for change. Set is the "separator" or "isolator"—the God who slew stasis (represented by Osiris) and overcame chaotic mindlessness (represented by Apep). In this context, Set represents the elimination of obsolete thought patterns and social conditioning—a "dethroning of those internal gods that we have received from society"—and as Don Webb explains in his essay on the sacred word *xeper*, the nature of the Setian quest, as he sees it, is "to become an immortal, potent and powerful Essence."[70] Webb has also stated quite specifically that the mission of the Temple of Set "is to recreate a tradition of *self-deification*."[71] According to Webb, the quest for self-deification and the attainment of immortality are intimately connected:

> We choose as our role model the ancient Egyptian god Set, the archetype of Isolate Intelligence, rather than the somewhat limiting Hebrew Satan, archetype of the Rebel against cosmic injustice. . . . We do not worship Set—only our own potential. Set was and is the patron of the magician who seeks to increase his existence through expansion. . . . Black Magic is to take full responsibility for one's actions, evolution and effectiveness.[72]

In ancient Egyptian mythology, Set was the only god who overcame death, and this is of special significance to Setians because they believe it is possible to transcend physical death through the potency of the magical will. As Michael Aquino explains in his essay "Satanism and the Immortality of the Psyche" (1996):

> The essence of the psyche . . . is such that its existence is neither dependent upon the material not imprisoned in it. . . . Rather, the physical body provides a vehicle in which the psyche can become aware of itself and reach out towards the limitlessness of its consciousness existence. . . . It is all too easy to perceive "life" as only the active functioning of one's material body. Such an attitude fosters a disease of the psyche far worse than any of the body. It numbs you to that immortality which is inherent in the Gift of Set.[73]

Aquino elaborates further on the "Gift of Set" in his privately published *Crystal Tablet of Set*:

> The Temple of Set is . . . an association of the Elect to honor Set, exalt his Gift to ourselves, and exercise it with the greatest possible wisdom. As Set is a metaphysical entity, apart from the objective universe, he may be described as a "god" as conventional society employs the term. In this sense the Temple of Set is a religion—not one which is based upon irrational faith, but one which derives its governing principles from exercise of the evident Gift of its god.[74]

The Symbolism of Black Magic

As we have seen, members of the Temple of Set willingly describe themselves as "black magicians," and yet their idea of black magic is clearly different from that prevailing in the popular imagination. For most people, the idea of black magic involves harmful intent, inflicting serious injury on another person or group of people, or willfully damaging property. Clearly, this is not how Setians themselves regard their magical orientation. Leon Wild, editor of *The Ninth Night*—an Internet journal committed to Setian principles—has drawn a clear distinction between what he calls "the myth of satanic crime" and the core raison d'être of the black magician. In his view, legitimate Satanists do not kill or injure people or animals, do not engage in rape or human sacrifice, do not burn or desecrate the churches of other religions, and do not interfere with burial grounds—even though they are frequently accused of all these things.[75]

There can be little doubt that for the first nine years of its existence, the Church of Satan was an organization dedicated to licentious self-indulgence, advocating uninhibited revelry in "sin" rather than a full-blown engagement in "evil." Nevertheless, its anti-Christian antics are hard to take seriously, offensive though they must have been to many practicing Christians. The Temple of Set presents a more cerebral and philosophical perspective. Aquino's interest in Himmler's esoteric practices provides strong cause for concern, but the appeal seems to be associated with notions of immortality and superhuman aspirations rather than with flagrant evil.

Michael Aquino and his colleagues in the Temple of Set have made no secret of the fact that they believe that man has limitless potential and may even attain conscious immortality, but for them the exploration of this sacred potential is simply a rational goal which requires no further justification. Setian practitioners seek an infinite future, opened to them through the magical will. For these particular magicians, darkness does not represent evil but infinite human potential.

8

Spirit, Myth, and Cosmos

From Shamanism to Chaos Magick

In one respect, the Temple of Set is characteristic of many other contemporary magical groups, in the sense that its members aspire to be like gods. In his *Ritual of the Mark of the Beast*, Aleister Crowley proclaims:

> I am a God . . . very God of very God; I go upon my way to work my will . . . I am Omniscient, for naught exists for me unless I know it. I am Omnipotent, for naught exists save by Necessity my soul's expression through my will to be, to do, to suffer the symbols of itself. I am Omnipresent, for naught exists where I am not, who fashioned space as a condition of my consciousness of myself.[1]

Here Crowley is imagining the cosmos from the perspective of a Creator God, and is doing what many magicians have done in different periods of history—identifying with the God-form. There has always been an assumption in the world of magic that like mirrors like—as above, so below. The magician who imitates the god becomes the god. Margot Adler, a leading spokesperson for American neopaganism, confirms this as well: "The fundamental thing about the magical and pagan religions is that ultimately they say, 'Within yourself you are the god, you are the goddess—you can actualize within yourself and create whatever you need on this earth and beyond.'"[2]

Part of this thinking has to do with the core concept in spiritual humanism that each individual has deep within their being a divine potential, a sacred source of vitality. Nevertheless, there is only a slight shift of emphasis between acknowledging that each human being has a sacred link with the spiritual universe as a whole, and identifying with that divinity from an egoic perspective by asserting: *I have become the god*. The first viewpoint is a statement of connection, the second a statement of dominance and arrogance. Both perspectives, in varying degrees, can be found across the spectrum of beliefs and practices in contemporary Western magic.

The idea that we all have within us a sacred potential is found in Gnosticism and Neoplatonism, and emerged again in the writings of Carl Jung, especially with regard to his concept of the archetypes of the collective unconscious. Jung's mythic perspectives attracted a substantial readership among enthusiasts of the American counterculture in the late 1960s and early 1970s, alongside the mystical novels of Hermann Hesse. Jung's framework of the psyche has also been widely endorsed by practicing occultists—ranging from magicians in the Golden Dawn tradition such as Dion Fortune and Israel Regardie, through to the Chicago-based Gnostic Voodoo magician Michael Bertiaux, whose magical approach is described later in this chapter.[3]

Carl Jung and the Collective Unconscious

Jung believed that deep within the psyche, beyond the biographical and sexual components of the unconscious mind, one could find mythic "archetypes" that provided the core impetus for visionary and religious experience. According to Jung, these archetypes transcended personal and cultural variables and manifested in numerous symbolic forms around the world, invariably having a profound impact on those visionaries fortunate enough to encounter them firsthand in dreams, mystical visions, or acts of creative inspiration.

Jung believed that divinity is not external to humanity but lies within—that it is an aspect of our "humanness" that we all share and can have access to. In parting company with Freud—whose view of the unconscious was essentially biological—Jung would increasingly emphasize that the sacred depths of the psyche provided the origin of all religious and mystical experiences. To this extent he was advocating an essentially Gnostic approach to spiritual knowledge. For Jung, it was not so much a matter of believing in a God who was essentially external to human events as recognizing the sacred potentiality within every human being. Furthermore, the encounter with the archetypes was not simply an act of grace bestowed by God. One could facilitate the process of spiritual awareness oneself—through dream

work and visualization techniques, as well as through other techniques like meditation and yoga.

Jung recognized that the unconscious mind seemed to contain a vast storehouse of imagery that was much greater than the repressions of the individual ego.
It also seemed to him that to a certain extent the unconscious appeared to act independently of the conscious mind. He also discovered that there were certain motifs
within dreams which did not seem to be a part of the individual psyche. It was the
study of these symbols which led him to formulate the concept of the collective
unconscious:

> There are many symbols that are not individual but collective in their
> nature and origin. These are chiefly religious images; their origin is so far
> buried in the mystery of the past that they seem to have no human
> source. But they are, in fact, "collective representations" emanating from
> primeval dreams and creative fantasies. As such, these images are
> involuntary spontaneous manifestations and by no means intentional
> inventions.[4]

According to Jung, at a certain psychic level, motifs common to the whole of
humanity were capable of manifesting in dreams. These motifs were a symbolic
expression of "the constantly repeated experiences of humanity." That is to say,
they were derived from observations about Nature (the sky, changes of the seasons,
and so on) that had become embedded in the psychic patterns of the whole species.
Jung called these primordial images "archetypes" and gave the following example
of how an archetype is formed:

> One of the commonest and at the same time most impressive experience
> is the apparent movement of the sun every day. We certainly cannot
> discover anything of this kind in the unconscious, so far as the known
> physical process is concerned. What we do find, on the other hand, is the
> myth of the sun hero in all its countless modifications. It is this myth and
> *not the physical process* that forms the archetype.[5]

Jung came to regard the archetype as an anthropomorphic rendition of a force
in Nature. Its potency derived from the fact that the observation of the sun's movement constituted one of the universal, fundamental experiences of existence, and
was something that man could not change—a power beyond human manipulation. The sun therefore became an object of mystical veneration—one of a number
of archetypes with which to identify in religious or ritual acts of transcendence.
Naturally, different cultures would conceive of the sun-hero in a different form: for
example, as Apollo-Helios in classical Greece and Rome, or as Ohrmazd in ancient
Persia. Jung regarded all of these variables as patterns on a theme, however—the

core principle common to all of the cultural representations being the archetype itself. And there was another side to the archetype, as well—its awe-inspiring vibrancy and its apparent autonomy, or ability to appear separate. As Jung notes:

> The "primordial images," or archetypes, lead their own independent life . . . as can easily be seen in those philosophical or gnostic systems which rely on an awareness of the unconscious as the source of knowledge. The idea of angels, archangels, "principalities and powers" in St. Paul, the archons of the Gnostics, the heavenly hierarchy of Dionysius the Areopagite, all come from the perception of the relative autonomy of the archetypes.[6]

Furthermore, said Jung, an archetype contains within it a certain type of power or influence—"It seizes hold of the psyche with a kind of primeval force."[7] This perception forced Jung to regard the deepest regions of the psyche as profoundly spiritual, and he gradually embraced the view that the essential aim of personal development was to move toward a state of wholeness by integrating the conflicting contents and archetypal processes of the unconscious. He called this process "individuation."

Jung distinguished different aspects of the personality. These included the persona, the face we present to the world, and the ego, which included all the conscious contents of personal experience. However, Jung also believed that men and women should accommodate opposite gender polarities within their consciousness—he termed these the *anima* for men and the *animus* for women—and he talked of the shadow, an embodiment of memories and experiences repressed from consciousness altogether. The shadow would often appear in dreams and nightmares as a dark, repellent figure. Jung argued, however, that if material from the shadow was acknowledged and allowed back into conscious awareness, much of its dark, frightening nature would disappear. Dealing with the dark side of the psyche remains an important aspect of all Jungian forms of psychotherapy.

Jung regarded the *self* as the totality of the personality, including all the aspects of the psyche mentioned above. He also considered the self to be a central archetype, personified symbolically by a circle or mandala—representations of wholeness. The thrust of all individual self-development was therefore toward wholeness of being. Self-realization, or individuation, simply meant "becoming oneself" in a true and total sense.

Jung described the process of personal growth in his essay "The Relations between the Ego and the Unconscious" (1928):

> The more we become conscious of ourselves through self-knowledge, and act accordingly, the more the layer of the personal unconscious that

is superimposed on the collective unconscious will be diminished. In this way there arises a consciousness which is no longer imprisoned in the petty, oversensitive, personal world of objective interests. This widened consciousness is no longer that touchy, egotistical bundle of personal wishes, fears, hopes and ambitions which always has to be compensated or corrected by unconscious countertendencies; instead, it is a function of relationship to the world of objects, bringing the individual into absolute, binding and indissoluble communion with the world at large.[8]

Jung's impact on contemporary forms of spiritual and esoteric practice has been considerable. His concept of the collective unconscious has encouraged many to look at myths, fables, and legends for insights into the human condition, and also to relate the cycles of symbolic rebirth, found in many of the world's religions, to the process of personal individuation.

Another aspect of Jung's approach is his emphasis on individual transformation. According to Jung, we hold our spiritual destinies in our own hands. This is a profoundly Gnostic attitude—one that is quite different from the spiritual message which emanates from most forms of Western institutionalized religion. However, it is one that resonates strongly with most forms of modern esoteric belief. According to Jung, the archetypes of the collective unconscious provide spiritual milestones along the awe-inspiring pathway that leads to the reintegration of the psyche—and where this journey takes us is really up to each of us as an individual.

Many of Jung's principal ideas correlate with themes found in the Western magical traditions. Here, too, we have the idea of personal spiritual growth through various forms of self-knowledge, initiation, and rites of passage. We find the polarities of the *animus* and the *anima* reflected in the second of the three Wiccan initiations and also in the mythic imagery of alchemy. And the concept of Jungian individuation, too, is mirrored by the magical journey through the various archetypes found on the Kabbalistic Tree of Life, with Tiphareth—symbolic of spiritual rebirth and wholeness—at its very center. Occultists have long sought to explore the visionary potentials of their inner being, and their invocations and visualizations are intended to call the gods forth into consciousness. In a mythic sense, modern magic is essentially about stealing the fire from heaven and then integrating the sacred flame that has been invoked.

The Quest for Mythic Awareness

Following the development of the personal growth movement in the United States from the late 1960s onward—a movement based initially on the self-actualizing ideas of Abraham Maslow and his colleague Anthony Sutich—many people in the spiritual counterculture became increasingly attuned to the idea of an inner mythology of the God or Goddess within.[9] One of the bridging figures who continued the direct legacy of Carl Jung and who also served as a spiritual mentor to many in the personal growth movement was the American writer and teacher Joseph Campbell (1904–1987). Campbell had visited Jung in Zurich in 1953 and was enthusiastic about Jung's interpretation of the universal themes in world mythology. He was also a distinguished scholar in his own right. During his productive life as a teacher and writer, Campbell produced a number of authoritative but accessible studies on oriental, indigenous, and Western mythology, and many insightful essays on metaphor and symbol in comparative religion. This work culminated in a fine series of television interviews on PBS with Bill Moyers, *The Power of Myth*, which explored the universality of myth and brought his wisdom and articulate thought to literally millions of viewers across the world.

Campbell's career reflects a life of solid scholarship. After gaining his Masters degree in cultural history from Columbia University in 1927, Campbell went on to study at the University of Paris from 1927–1928 and then spent a further year at the University of Munich exploring Sanskrit and oriental religion. He later taught at Sarah Lawrence College in Bronxville, New York, for thirty-eight years. It was while he was in Paris that he began to read Freud, Jung, and the works of Thomas Mann, and he also became deeply interested in the universals of the mythic imagination. Like Jung, he came to believe that myths had originated in the collective unconscious:

> Myths originally came out of the individual's own dream consciousness. Within each person there is what Jung called a collective unconscious. We are not only individuals with our unconscious intentions related to a specific social environment. We are also representatives of the species *homo sapiens*. And that universality is in us whether we know it or not. We penetrate to this level by getting in touch with dreams, fantasies, and traditional myths; by using active imagination.[10]

Campbell believed that myths were highly relevant to everyday life. Although on one level they pointed to the mysteries and paradoxes of human existence, myths also validated the social and moral order in specific cultures and marked the various pathways through the different stages of life—from childhood, through to adulthood, old age, and death. "Every culture," said Campbell, "has rites of passage and related myths that serve this need."[11]

Myths were also directly relevant to the life-experience of the individual, a source of inspirational guidance for everyday life. Campbell liked to refer to what he called "the journey of the hero"—the journey that every human makes simply by being purposeful in the world. According to Campbell, each of us, at some point, has to come forth and engage in battle with various obstacles or "powers of darkness." During our lives we may encounter demons, angels, dragons, or helping spirits, but then, after conquering the various obstacles thrown up along the way, we finally emerge victorious and return from our adventures with "the gift of fire," or knowledge.

Campbell's special skill was his ability to relate the themes of mythology to the human condition. In his seminars at Esalen Institute and elsewhere, he would explain that "Mythology helps you identify the mysteries of the energies pouring through you . . . Mythology is an organization of images metaphoric of experience, action, and fulfillment of the human spirit in the field of a given culture at a given time."[12] He rejected fundamentalist concepts of creator gods, regarding them as archetypes of one's inner being. According to Campbell, "Your god is a manifestation of your own level of consciousness. All of the heavens and all of the hells are within you."[13]

Campbell believed that as human beings we all have the same sacred heritage: "We share the same gods, we are informed by the same archetypes. The natural forces that animate us are common and divine."[14] Campbell also proposed that we should explore those myths that touched us most deeply—the archetypal stories and legends that could help enrich our life's journey. As Campbell's biographers, Stephen and Robin Larsen, have observed: "Campbell urged us to *see through* life metaphorically, and to celebrate the myths *as if* they were alive in us—providing windows for deeper insights into ourselves."[15] Indeed, it is in his support for the mythic life that Campbell is best remembered. "Mythology helps you to identify the mysteries of the energies pouring through you," he once remarked, "Therein lies your eternity."[16]

Joseph Campbell remained primarily a scholar and teacher during his long career and probably would not have considered himself part of the personal growth movement or counterculture—even though he knew many of its key figures.[17] And yet one particular saying of Campbell's has had enormous impact and is widely quoted in New Age and esoteric circles: this was his famous expression, "Follow your bliss." Here Campbell was endorsing the idea that we should all follow a "path with heart," a path that defines our place in the cosmos and on this earth. Campbell was not alone in articulating this view, but he helped endorse it, and since his time there has been a substantial resurgence of interest in the role mythology can play in contemporary human life. We can also credit Campbell with directly influencing the emergence of sacred psychology in the United States.

The Rise of Sacred Psychology

Several key figures in the personal growth movement—among them Jean Houston and Jean Shinoda Bolen—have played a prominent role in exploring practical and inspirational ways of introducing archetypal mythic realities into everyday consciousness. Jean Houston, an enthusiastic supporter of the work of Joseph Campbell, first discovered his writings at the age of ten when she read his famous book *The Hero with a Thousand Faces*. For the last thirty years or more she has been one of the leading advocates of sacred psychology.

Houston is a former president for the Association of Humanistic Psychology and a director of the Foundation for Mind Research, now based in Ashland, Oregon. However, her talents also extend into many forms of creative expression. She has developed numerous training programs in spiritual studies, which include the enactment of themes from the ancient Mystery traditions, and her methods include visualization, chanting, storytelling, and rituals. Like Joseph Campbell, Houston believes strongly in the transformative power of myth.

In an interview published in the counterculture magazine *Magical Blend*, she explained her own role in this process: "My task is to evoke people into that place of identifying the god or goddess or archetype that is personal to them and allowing that being to speak for them."[18] She also maintains that not only mythologically but also quite literally our human origins are in the cosmos:

> Earlier peoples saw archetypes in Nature and in the starry Heavens—in the Sun, the Moon, the Earth, the vast oceans—implicitly realizing our descent from these primal entities. . . . Our ancestors storied this deep knowing into tales of the community of Nature: the marriage of Heaven and Earth; the churning of the ocean to create the nectar of life; the action of the wind upon the waters to bring form out of chaos. In these mythic tellings, our forerunners located higher reality and its values in the larger community—in the things of this world, shining reflections of the community of archetypes. They clearly perceived that the pattern connecting both world and archetype was the essential weave that sustains all life.[19]

Houston is interested in a broad range of myths, especially those that describe sacred journeys of transformation, and she is fascinated by archetypal figures like Parsifal, St. Francis of Assisi, Odysseus, Christ, Isis, and Osiris—figures who show us by example how we may undertake the process of spiritual renewal. For Houston, myths and archetypes are of central concern in our daily lives: "Myths serve as source patterns originating in the ground of our being. While they appear to exist solely in the transpersonal realm, they are the keys to our personal and historical existence, the DNA of the human psyche."[20]

Houston believes, like Carl Jung, that although archetypes are universal, they nevertheless manifest in unique ways within each individual. Archetypes bridge spirit with nature, mind with body, and self with universe: "They are always within us, essential structures within the structure of our psyches."[21] According to Houston, one of the key roles of sacred psychology is to assist the individual in transforming his or her life from what she calls the "personal-particular" to the "personal-universal," thereby bringing a new vision and perspective to everyday experience.

It is precisely because myths and archetypes transcend cultural barriers and help define our relationship with the cosmos as a whole that they are of such vital importance today. For Houston, our present era, with its accompanying sense of existential crisis, is characterized not simply by a sense of paradigm shift but by what she calls a "whole system transition, a shift in reality itself." With its profound insights into the nature of personal transformation and renewal, sacred psychology can play a vital role in this important transition. For Houston, the characteristic hallmarks of the age are an increasing sense of planetary ecological awareness, the rebirth of the sacred Feminine, the emergence of new forms of science and the emergence, overall, of a global spiritual sensibility.[22] "In this time of whole system transition," she writes, "the Soul of the World, the *anima mundi*, is emerging. It seems to be with us through all the things and events of the world. Speaking through myths, it enlarges our perception of the deeper story that is unfolding in our time."[23]

Jean Shinoda Bolen is another leading figure in the American personal growth movement who shares a passionate interest in sacred psychology. Bolen's special focus has been on promoting the idea that men and woman alike can become aware of the archetypal processes operating in their everyday lives. Bolen is a professor of psychiatry, a Jungian analyst, and author of such bestselling works as *Goddesses in Everywoman*, *Gods in Everyman*, and *The Tao of Psychology*. Like Jung, Bolen believes that the gods and goddesses of mythology represent different qualities in the human psyche:

> Myth is a form of metaphor. It's the metaphor that's truly empowering
> for people. It allows us to see our ordinary lives from a different
> perspective, to get an intuitive sense of who we are and what is important
> to us. . . . Myths are the bridge to the collective unconscious. They tap
> images, symbols, feelings, possibilities and patterns—inherent, inherited
> human potential that we all hold in common.[24]

Like other practitioners of sacred psychology, Bolen maintains that mythic or archetypal awareness brings a true sense of meaning to everyday life: "If you live from your own depths—that is, if there is an archetypal basis for what you're doing—then there's a meaningful level to it that otherwise might be missing. . . . When people 'follow their bliss' as Joseph Campbell says, their heart is absorbed in what they're doing."[25] In her book *Gods in Everyman*, Bolen describes how this personal experience of "bliss" enables the individual to tap into a universal sense of the sacred: "Bliss and joy come in moments of living our highest truth—moments when what we do is consistent with our archetypal depths. It's when we are most authentic and trusting, and feel that whatever we are doing, which can be quite ordinary, is nonetheless sacred. This is when we sense that we are part of something divine that is in us and is everywhere."[26]

Despite her Japanese ancestry, in her personal life Bolen has identified mostly with the ancient Greek goddesses. She told interviewer Mirka Knaster that, for her, the goddesses who had most reflected in her life were Artemis, Athena, and Hestia, who represented the "independent, self-sufficient qualities in women." Artemis, Goddess of the Hunt, seemed to embody her Japanese family's frequent moves around the United States in the 1940s, to avoid being detained in an American concentration camp; Athena, Goddess of Wisdom, seemed present in her decision to train as a medical doctor; and Hestia, Goddess of the Hearth, epitomized her present love of "comfort in solitude." In her role as a writer and lecturer, however, she has also felt drawn to Hermes as an archetype of communication.

Bolen believes we can all embody both the gods *and* goddesses in our lives, not just the archetypes of our own gender. And, most significant, she sees such mythic attunement as opening out into greater, planetary awareness. Bolen echoes the sentiments of Wiccan practitioners Starhawk and Vivianne Crowley, whose perspectives we discussed earlier:

> The current need is a return to earth as the source of sacred energy. I have a concept that I share with others that we're evolving into looking out for the earth and our connection with everybody on it. Women seem more attuned to it, but increasingly more men are too. I believe that the human psyche changes collectively, when enough individuals change. Basically, the point of life is to survive and evolve. To do both requires that we recognize our planetary community and be aware that we cannot do anything negative to our enemies without harming ourselves.[27]

The "Archaic Revival"—The Rediscovery of Shamanism

One of the characteristic features of the West Coast counterculture was a thirst for "universal wisdom traditions." Shamanism was quickly incorporated into the personal growth movement that arose during the late 1960s, perhaps as a romantic response to the perceived spirituality of indigenous cultures around the world.[28] At a time when there was renewed interest in Native American spirituality in particular, the works of South American author Carlos Castaneda (1925–1998) were an immediate success, eventually selling millions of copies worldwide. Castaneda's first book, *The Teachings of Don Juan*, was published by the University of California Press in 1968, and for many devotees of the new spiritual perspectives surfacing at that time in the popular culture, Castaneda, and his "teacher"—Yaqui sorcerer don Juan Matus—represented the first point of contact with the figure of the shaman.[29] Even after his death in 1998, Castaneda's influence and fame continued to spread, alongside that of his equally controversial female counterpart, Lynn Andrews.[30] And although Casteneda's works are now correctly categorized as fiction, his early writings were unquestionably grounded in solid shamanic research—much of which had been undertaken, as we now know, in the UCLA Library.[31]

Throughout his life, Castaneda remained a highly private person and only sketchy details of his personal history were ever released to the public. He gave few interviews and always refused to have any portrait photographs taken, although he did participate in a weekend seminar at the Esalen Institute in 1970 and consented to a fascinating interview with Sam Keen that was published in *Psychology Today* in December 1972.[32] Between 1959 and 1973, he undertook a series of degree courses in anthropology at the University of California, Los Angeles, and was granted a PhD for his third book, *Journey to Ixtlan* (1972), for what really amounted to an imaginary ethnography.[33]

Castaneda's real name was Carlos Arana, and he was born in Cajamarca, Peru, in 1925.[34] He adopted the name Carlos Castaneda when he acquired United States citizenship in 1959. Castaneda claimed that in 1960, having commenced his studies at UCLA, he traveled to the American Southwest to explore the Indian use of medicinal plants. As the story goes, a friend introduced him to an old Yaqui Indian in a small town called Nogales on the Mexico-Arizona border. The Indian, don Juan Matus, was said to be an expert on the hallucinogen peyote and claimed to be a *brujo*, a term that connotes a sorcerer, or one who cures by means of magical techniques. Born in Sonora, Mexico, in 1891, don Juan Matus spoke Spanish "remarkably well" but appeared at the first meeting to be unimpressed with Castaneda's self-confidence. He indicated, however, that Castaneda could come to see him subsequently, and an increasingly warm relationship developed as the young academic entered into an "apprenticeship" in shamanic magic.

Carlos Castaneda found many of don Juan's ideas and techniques strange and irrational. The world of the sorcerer contained mysterious, inexplicable forces that he was obliged not to question, but had to accept as a fact of life. The apprentice sorcerer would begin to "see," whereas previously he had merely "looked." Eventually he would become a "man of knowledge."

According to Castaneda's exposition of don Juan's ideas, the familiar world we perceive is only one of a number of worlds. It is in reality a description of the relationship between objects that we have learned to recognize as significant from birth, and which has been reinforced by language and the communication of mutually acceptable concepts. This world is not the same as the world of the sorcerer, for while ours tends to be based on the confidence of perception, the *brujo*'s involves many intangibles. His universe is a vast and continuing mystery which cannot be contained within rational categories and frameworks.

In order to transform one's perception from ordinary to magical reality, an "unlearning" process has to occur. The apprentice must learn how to "not do" what he has previously "done." He must learn how to transcend his previous frameworks and conceptual categories and for a moment freeze himself between the two universes, the "real" and the "magically real." To use don Juan's expression, he had to learn how to *stop the world*. From this point onward, he could begin to *see*, acquiring a knowledge and mastery of the mysterious forces operating in the environment which most people close off from their everyday perception.

"Seeing," said don Juan, was a means of perception that could be brought about often, although not necessarily, by hallucinogenic drugs—among them *mescalito* (peyote), *yerba del diablo* (Jimson weed, or datura), and *humito* (psilocybe mushrooms). Through these, the *brujo* could acquire a magical ally, who could in turn grant further power and the ability to enter more readily into "states of non-ordinary reality." The *brujo* would become able to see the "fibers of light" and energy patterns emanating from people and other living organisms, encounter the magical forces within the wind and sacred water-hole, and isolate as visionary experiences—as if on film—the incidents of one's earlier life and their influence on the development of the personality. Such knowledge would enable the *brujo* to tighten his defenses as a "warrior." He would know himself, and have complete command over his physical vehicle. He would also be able to project his consciousness from his body into images of birds and animals, thereby transforming into a myriad of magical forms and shapes while traveling in the spirit-vision.

Although Castaneda's books were strongly attacked by critics like Weston La Barre and Richard de Mille for containing fanciful and concocted elements, it is also true that the early volumes in particular were based substantially on shamanic tradition—even if much of the material had been borrowed from elsewhere.[35] For example, there were strong parallels between the shamanic figure don Genaro, a friend of don Juan, and the famous Huichol shaman Ramon Medina.

One of Castaneda's friends, anthropologist Barbara Myerhoff, was studying the Huichol Indians at the same time that Castaneda was claiming to be studying Yaqui sorcery, and Myerhoff introduced Ramon Medina to Castaneda. It now appears that Castaneda borrowed an incident in his second book, *A Separate Reality*—where don Genaro leaps across a precipitous waterfall clinging to it by magical "tentacles of power"—from an actual Huichol occurrence.

Myerhoff and another noted anthropologist, Peter Furst, watched Ramon Medina leaping like a bird across a waterfall that cascaded three hundred meters below over slippery rocks. Medina was exhibiting the balance of the shaman in "crossing the narrow bridge to the other world." Myerhoff told Richard de Mille how pleased she felt, in terms of validation, when Castaneda related to her how the sorcerer don Genaro could also do similar things. It now seems, she feels, that Castaneda was like a mirror—his own accounts reflecting borrowed data from all sorts of sources, including her own. The rapid mystical running known as "the gait of power," for example, is thought to have come from accounts of Tibetan mysticism, and there were definite parallels between don Juan's abilities and statements in other anthropological, psychedelic, and occult sources.[36]

Even in death, Castaneda remains controversial. However, while Castaneda's brand of shamanic sorcery was always intentionally elusive, a more accessible approach to practical shamanism was being introduced to the personal growth movement by an American anthropologist who really did have impeccable academic credentials—Dr. Michael Harner.

A former visiting professor at Columbia, Yale, and the University of California, Harner is now director of the Foundation for Shamanic Studies in Mill Valley, California—an organization he established in Connecticut in 1979. Born in Washington, D.C., in 1929, Harner spent the early years of his childhood in South America. In 1956 he returned to do fieldwork among the Jivaro Indians of the Ecuadorian Andes, and between 1960 and 1961 visited the Conibo Indians of the Upper Amazon in Peru. His first period of fieldwork was conducted as "an outside observer of the world of the shaman," but his second endeavor—which included his psychedelic initiation among the Conibo—led him to pursue shamanism firsthand. In 1964, he returned to Ecuador to experience the supernatural world of the Jivaro in a more complete way.

After arriving at the former Spanish settlement of Macas, Harner made contact with his Jivaro guide, Akachu. Two days later he ventured with him northward, crossing the Rio Upano and entering the forest. It was here that he told his Indian friend that he wished to acquire spirit-helpers, known to the Jivaro as *tsentsak*. Harner offered gifts to Akachu and was told that that the first preparatory task was to bathe in the sacred waterfall. Later he was presented with a magical pole to ward off demons. Then, after an arduous journey to the waterfall, Harner was led to into a dark recess behind the wall of spray—a cave known as "the house of the Grandfathers"—and here he had to call out, attracting the attention of the ancestor spirits. He now had his first magical experiences: the wall of falling water became iridescent, a torrent of liquid prisms. "As they went by," says Harner, "I had the continuous sensation of floating upward, as though they were stable and I was the one in motion. . . . (It was like) flying inside a mountain."[37]

Deeper in the jungle, Akachu squeezed the juice of some psychedelic datura plants he had brought with him and asked Harner to drink it that night. Reassuring him, Akachu told him he was not to fear anything he might see, and if anything frightening did appear, he should run up and touch it.

That night was especially dramatic, anyway—with intense rain, thunder, and flashes of lightning—but after a while the effects of the datura became apparent, and it was clear that something quite specific was going to happen.

Suddenly Harner became aware of a luminous, multicolored serpent writhing toward him. Remembering his advice from Akachu, Harner charged at the visionary serpent with a stick. Suddenly the forest was empty and silent, and the monster had gone. Akachu later explained to Harner that this supernatural encounter was an important precursor to acquiring spirit-helpers. And his triumph over the serpent had confirmed that he was now an acceptable candidate for the path of the shaman.

Harner believes, as the Jivaro do, that the energizing force within any human being can be represented by what the Indians call a "power animal." One of the most important tasks of the shaman is to summon the power animal while in trance, and undertake visionary journeys with the animal as an ally. It is in such a way that one is able to explore the "upper" and "lower" worlds of the magical universe. The shaman also learns techniques of healing that usually entail journeys to the spirit world to obtain sources of "magical energy." This energy can then be transferred to sick or dis-spirited people in a ceremonial healing rite.[38]

After living with the Conibo and Jivaro, Harner undertook further fieldwork among the Wintun and Pomo Indians in California, the Lakota Sioux of South Dakota, and the Coast Salish in Washington State. The techniques of "practical applied shamanism" that he now teaches in his workshops, and which are outlined in his important book *The Way of the Shaman*, are a synthesis from many cultures, but they are true to the essence of the native traditions themselves. Harner has gone to great lengths to make his anthropological research accessible to a Western audience interested in exploring trance states and mystical consciousness.

"Shamanism," says Harner, "takes us into the realms of myth and the Dreamtime . . . and in these experiences we are able to contact sources of power and use them in daily life."[39] He usually holds his shamanic workshops in city tenement buildings or in large open lecture rooms on different university campus sites, and has also trained numerous shamanic facilitators to continue this work, both within the United States and internationally. Most of his workshop participants are familiar with the concept of the shamanic visionary journey and the idea of "riding" rhythmic drumming into a state of meditative trance.

Harner's sessions begin as he shakes a gourd rattle to the four quarters in nearly total darkness, summoning the "spirits" to participate in the shamanic

FIGURE 8.1.   The founder of Neoshamanism, American anthropologist
Dr. Michael Harner. Courtesy Cinetel Productions, Sydney.

working. He also encourages his group members to sing native shamanic chants
and to enter into the process of engaging with the mythic world. His techniques
include journeying in the mind's eye down the root system of an archetypal
"cosmic tree" or up imaginal smoke tunnels into the sky. As the group participants delve deeper into a state of trance, assisted all the time by the drumming,
they enter the "mythic dreamtime" of their own unconscious minds, frequently
having visionary encounters with a variety of animal and humanoid beings and
perhaps also exploring unfamiliar locales. They may also make contact with
spirit-allies or "power animals." Harner's approach is to show his participants
that they can discover an authentic mythic universe within the depths of their
own being.

In the core shamanic model that Harner utilizes, humanity is said to dwell on
Middle Earth, and two other magical domains—the upper and lower universes—
may then be accessed through the shamanic trance journey. Often the upper and
lower worlds appear to merge into a single "magical reality" that parallels the
familiar world but that also seems invariably to extend beyond it. The shaman seeks
his "power animals" or spirit allies as a way of obtaining new sources of vitality
and sacred knowledge. The central intent is one of personal growth and healing,
with many individual participants feeling that they have extended the boundaries
of their awareness and their being. One woman who participated in a Harner

workshop that was filmed in New York in 1984 for a television documentary ventured to the upper world and had a remarkable "rebirth" experience:

> I was flying. I went up into black sky—there were so many stars—and then I went into an area that was like a whirlwind. I could still see the stars and I was turning a lot, and my power animals were with me. Then I came up through a layer of clouds and met my teacher—she was a woman I'd seen before. She was dressed in a long, long gown and I wanted to ask her how I could continue with my shamanic work, how to make it more a part of my daily life. Then she took me into her, into her belly. I could feel her get pregnant with me and felt her belly stretching. I felt myself inside her. I also felt her put her hands on top of her belly and how large it was! She told me that I should stop breathing—that I should take my nourishment from her—and I could actually feel myself stop breathing. I felt a lot of warmth in my belly, as if it were coming into me, and then she stretched further and actually broke apart. Her belly broke apart and I came out of her, and I took it to mean that I needed to use less will in my work, and that I needed to trust her more and let that enter into my daily life. That was the end of my journey—the drum stopped and I came back at that point.[40]

Michael Harner believes that mythic experiences of this sort are common during the shamanic journey, and he maintains that they reveal a dimension of consciousness rarely accessed in daily life:

> Simply by using the technique of drumming, people from time immemorial have been able to pass into these realms which are normally reserved for those approaching death, or for saints. These are the realms of the upper and lower world where one can get information to puzzling questions. This is the Dreamtime of the Australian Aboriginal, the "mythic time" of the shaman. In this area, a person can obtain knowledge that rarely comes to other people.[41]

This, of course, begs the question of whether the shaman's journey is just imagination. Is the mythic experience *really* real? Harner's reply is provocative:

> Imagination is a modern Western concept that is outside the realm of shamanism. "Imagination" already prejudges what is happening. I don't think it is imagination as we ordinarily understand it. I think we are entering something which, surprisingly, is universal—regardless of culture. Certainly people are influenced by their own history, their cultural and individual history. But we are beginning to discover a map

of the upper and lower world, regardless of culture. For the shaman, what one sees—that's *real*. What one reads out of a book is secondhand information. But just like the scientist, the shaman depends upon firsthand observation to decide what's real. If you can't trust what you see yourself, then what can you trust?[42]

In addition to conducting experiential workshops, Michael Harner is also engaged in training native tribal peoples in shamanic techniques that have disappeared from their own indigenous cultures. Several groups, including the Sami (formerly known as Lapps) and the Inuit (formerly known as Eskimo) have approached him to help restore sacred knowledge lost as a result of missionary activity or Western colonization. Harner and his colleagues at the Foundation for Shamanic Studies have been able to help them with what he calls "core shamanism"—general methods consistent with those once used by their ancestors. In this way, he believes, members of these tribal societies can elaborate and integrate the practices on their own terms in the context of their traditional cultures.

Michael Harner and his fellow practitioners of "core shamanism" have not been without their critics, many of whom feel that authentic shamanic methods cannot meaningfully be removed from specific cultural contexts and transposed into a modern urban environment.[43] Nevertheless, one person who was strongly influenced by Michael Harner and who has since developed her own, uniquely shamanistic approach to the mythic realm is seeress Diana Paxson, who heads the Hrafnar community in San Francisco. Paxson already had a background in women's spirituality, ceremonial magic, and Kabbalah and became interested in shamanism after reading Harner's *The Way of the Shaman*. She also began using Scandinavian runes as a divination device, and when a graduate student led her to explore the northern European shamanic techniques of *seidr*, she began to combine Nordic mythic traditions with Harner's method of experiential "core" shamanism.

Visionary Seidr Magic

Mircea Eliade, whose scholarly overview of world shamanism was first published in English in 1964, and whose work had also been a source of inspiration to Michael Harner, maintained that the best description of oracular *seidr* (also spelt *seidhr)* could be found in the Norse saga of Erik the Red—*Eiriks Saga Rautha*. This saga, which is around a thousand years old, describes the role of a seeress—variously known as a *völva, seiðkona, or spákona*—in a Greenlandic community. In the saga of Erik the Red, a seeress named Thorbjörg is asked by a farmer called Thorkel if she will prophesy on behalf of his community because the farmers have fallen on hard times and are hoping for an end to their oppression. Eliade gives an evocative description of the seeress and her approach:

> The *spákona* has a highly elaborated ritual costume: a blue cloak, jewels, a head-piece of black lamb with white catskins; she also carries a staff and, during the séance, sits on a rather high platform, on a cushion of chicken feathers. The *seidhkona* (or *volva*, *spákona*) goes from farm to farm to reveal men's futures and predict the weather, the quantity of the harvest, and so on. She travels with fifteen girls and fifteen youths singing in chorus. Music plays an essential role in preparing her ecstasy. During the trance the *seidhkona*'s soul leaves her body and travels through space; she usually assumes the form of an animal.[44]

Eliade did not personally believe that Nordic *seidhr* was a form of shamanism, arguing that the practitioner was more a seer or oracle than a shaman: "The specifically shamanic themes—descent into the underworld to bring back a patient's soul or to escort the deceased—although attested . . . in Nordic magic, are not a primary element in the *seidhr* séance. Instead, the latter seems to concentrate on divination."[45]

Nevertheless, when Paxson reconstructed *Eiríks Saga Rauða* and the Eddic *Voluspá* and began to use them experientially as a form of visionary magic, she found them very effective. In the *Voluspá*, which dates from a similar period to the saga of Erik the Red, Odin travels along a treacherous road to the gates of Hel—the realm of the dead—and summons and questions a seeress. Paxson adapted this myth for *seidr* sessions with her Hrafnar community in San Francisco.

During their magical workings, the Hrafnar practitioners wear appropriate Viking clothing and jewelry based on authentic archaeological sources.

A *seidr* séance involves two main figures—the *völva* or seeress, and a person who serves as both guide and singer, chanting the *völva* and the other group participants into a state of trance. The songs are based on Nordic mythology and guide the participants toward Helheim, where the *völva* communicates with the ancestors. The *völva* enters a deeper state of trance as she goes through the gates of Helheim and then encounters the spirits of the dead. At this stage a dialogue develops between the singer and the *völva*. Initially references are made to various Norse myths, reinforcing the context, but then members of the group are able to put oracular questions to the *völva* relating to more specific, local issues and circumstances. The *völva* typically receives "answers" to these questions in the form of visual images received from the deities and ancestor spirits—and then conveys appropriate responses to the people who asked the questions. Dr. Jenny Blain, who has studied *seidr* for many years and has also been a participant, has described a typical *seidr* session. In her account the oracle may be female or male—gender is not an issue:[46]

> In present-day oracular *seidr*, a room is prepared, with a "high seat" or *seidhjallr*. The *seidr* leader may use ways of "warding" this space, by singing a runerow or calling to the dwarf-guardians of the directions. She or he calls to the deities who themselves do *seidr*, Freyja and Odhinn. A song referring to various spirits or wights, and to Freyja and Odhinn, evokes an atmosphere in which people align their awareness with the cosmology of northern Europe: alternatively one could say that the song summons the spirits, and people become aware of them. Those who will "seid" (the word is a verb as well as a noun, in Old Icelandic) ask their spirit or animal allies to assist them or lead them. After a guided meditation which leads all participants down from an initial "safe place," through a tunnel of trees, to the World Tree Yggdrasill and beneath its roots to the lower world, participants reach the realm of Hela and the ancestors. The "audience" are told that they now sit outside the gates: only the seeress or seer will enter Hela's realm, urged on by further singing and drumming, "journeying" to seek answers to participants' questions. Now the guide invites questioners to step forward, and the seeress speaks to them. Usually she sits still, with a veil over her face. Sometimes she may sway . . . and take the participant's hands. When she tires, or when there are no more questions, the guide "calls" her back from the ancestors' world, and she steps down from the high seat, often moving stiffly, cramped and dazed: another may take her place. Finally the guide narrates the return journey meditation, so that all, seers, guide and audience/participants, return together to "ordinary consciousness."[47]

One of Blain's participants described the oracular experience itself:

> I go through Hela's gate. I always nod respectful(ly) to Queen Hela, I'm in her living room. . . . I see a lake, it's night and torchlight and all that, it lights up and the big torch, the lake, will light up the area enough so I can see the dead people, and I walk down there and say okay, time to gather round, and I'll say would those who need to speak with me, or who need to speak with the people I'm here representing please come forward. They look different . . . I have never seen anything scary . . . sometimes they're just like shadows, some look like living men and women, some are somewhere in between, of course there's many, many, many of them. They'll ask questions, sometimes they'll speak, sometimes I'll be in a

trance where I'm answering the questioner and the voice that's
coming out of my mouth, the intonation's different, the accent's a little
different . . . the words coming out of me is me and it's not me,
sometimes it's the strangest feeling. I remember what I say, fairly well.
I'm never possessed, I'm never off somewhere while somebody else runs
the equipment, but ah, I speak to them like I speak to you. Sometimes I
hear voices, sometimes I see pictures, impressions, feelings, ah, I have my
eyes closed physically, and I'm in trance, and I've got a shawl over my
head, sometimes it's almost like pictures on the back of my eyelids.[48]

According to Diana Paxson, sometimes during the *seidr* séance the *völva* is
actually possessed by one of the deities or a spirit of the dead—at other times it
feels as if the deity is responding directly to the questions that have been asked.
Paxson's *seidr* practice is therefore strongly mediumistic, and she concedes that
Hrafnar-style possession is not a form of shamanism in the strict sense of the word
because her approach is eclectic and not specifically "indigenous." Nevertheless, she
describes her magical workings as basically "shamanistic" in style.[49]

Interestingly, Paxson has also researched Brazilian Umbanda—a form of spir-
itist white magic that includes Yoruba deities, Christian saints, and elements of
Voodoo—and she has compared Odin to the Voodoo deity Baron Samedi: both are
lords of the dead in their respective cosmologies.[50] In this context, it is intriguing
that some of Paxson's *seidr* practitioners work with the dying to ease the transition
through death and also employ "ghosts" as spirit-helpers.[51]

Paxson's work with *seidr* shares some elements in common with another
contemporary magician—Chicago-based Voodoo-Gnostic practitioner, Michael
Bertiaux. Like Paxson, Bertiaux utilizes trance states to contact his personal deities.
He also engages in spirit-possession and, like her, has a strong interest in Voodoo.
But there the comparison ends. The magical realms that Michael Bertiaux explores—
and the occult outcomes he strives for—are both very different.

The Voodoo Magic of Michael Bertiaux

High up, on the thirty-third floor of a residential apartment block on South
Michigan Avenue, Chicago, lives a Voodoo priest. He is a gently spoken man with
intense eyes, heavy-rimmed glasses, and until recent times a full-bodied beard.
His apartment is embellished with numerous photographs, paintings, statues, and
plants, and has been described as "a mixture between an art studio and a well-
arranged temple."[52] Until his retirement in the late 1990s, he worked as a govern-
ment social worker, hearing welfare grievances mainly from the Haitian community

in the city. In his private time, however, he celebrates the mysteries of Guede and Legbha, the Voodoo counterpart of the dead and risen Christ.

Michael Bertiaux is by no means a typical occultist. His highly distinctive and idiosyncratic brand of magic also has esoteric affinities with Crowleyan *Thelema*, the sex magic of Paschal Beverly Randolph, and a branch of Martinism associated with nineteenth-century occultist Papus (Dr. Gerard Encausse). Bertiaux has been connected with an exotic assortment of magical orders during the last four decades. They include the Ordo Templi Orientis Antiqua (O.T.O.A.), which has been described as a "gnostic and ophidian church" with connections to "lyncathropic cabbalah";[53] the Thelemic Fraternitas Saturni; the Voodoo-inspired Monastery of the Seven Rays, and La Couleuvre Noire (The Black Serpent)—founded by Lucien-François Jean-Maine. Bertiaux currently describes himself as a hierophant of the Voudon Gnostic Current.

Michael Paul Bertiaux was born in Seattle in 1935 and grew up in a family that was primarily Theosophical. His father tended toward Zen Buddhism, while his mother was interested in spiritualism and the development of psychic powers. The Bertiaux ancestry was a combination of English, French, and Irish. Like a number of ceremonial magicians, Bertiaux's career began within the ranks of orthodox religion and then departed for the fringe. Educated initially by Jesuit fathers, he later attended an Anglican seminary in order to train for a career in the Church. He graduated with honors, was ordained, and became curate of an Anglican parish in West Seattle. It was shortly after this that his career took an oblique turn toward the occult. An opportunity arose for Michael Bertiaux to teach philosophy in the Anglican Church College in Port-au-Prince, Haiti. He decided to go, and as part of his training in "culture shock" transitions, studied with the distinguished anthropologist Margaret Mead. His first visit to Haiti lasted only three months, but some interesting contacts were made. These included traditional Voodoo practitioners with French esoteric leanings, who were keen to see their system of Haitian magic adapted for an American audience. They introduced Bertiaux to the key concepts and asked him to help them present the more positive side of Voodoo which, so far, had not been available in the West. Bertiaux was intrigued and promised to stay in touch. He returned to Seattle, maintained contact with the *vouduns* from Haiti, and began to see that his spiritual path was changing direction. It was becoming increasingly clear to him that he would have to leave the Anglican Church to join the Haitian mystery tradition.

The French occult connection in Haiti derives from two eighteenth-century mystics, Louis Claude de Saint-Martin and Martinez de Pasqually. The latter was a Rosicrucian disciple of Emanuel Swedenborg, and the founder of an occult group called the Order of the Elect Cohens. De Pasqually was inspired by Gnosticism and the Kabbalah, and believed that one could only gain spiritual salvation by contacting the Divine Source of All Being, and by participating in an initiation ceremony to invoke one's Holy Guardian Angel. Saint-Martin joined de Pasqually's order in 1768, and after the leader's death in 1774 became the dominant figure in the group. Collectively they became known as Martinists. There were Martinist orders in several different regions of France—in Foix, Bordeaux, Paris, and Lyons—and by the end of the eighteenth century, also in Haiti. However, here the tradition tended to blend with Voodoo. After a period in abeyance, Martinism revived in Haiti in the 1890s, and between the two world wars the so-called Neo-Pythagorean Gnostic Church came into being. This church advocates the invocation of angels and planetary spirits, is highly ritual-istic, and regards the Eucharist as the central initiation. Members of the clergy claim to be clairvoyant, often have visions during the Mass, and speak in a mys-tical language which—according to Michael Bertiaux—is a type of "Slavonic Voodoo," resembling Pentacostal speaking-in-tongues.

A formative influence on the development of the Gnostic Church in Haiti, otherwise known as the Ecclesia Spiritualis (Eglise Ophitico-Cabbalistique d'Haiti), was the late Dr. Hector Jean-Maine, son of the founder of La Couleuvre Noire. Born in Haiti in 1924 and educated in France, Jean-Maine was initiated by a Martinist bishop and lived in the mountains near Leogane in Haiti. Bertiaux was formally initiated into the Gnostic-Voodoo mysteries by Jean-Maine and Carlos Adhémar on 15 August 1963, and his assigned role within the Gnostic Church was to be its representative for all Caucasian-American members. Bertiaux came to regard Jeane-Maine as his "spiritus rector," and although the two men drifted apart for a time when Bertiaux immersed himself in Theosophy, they would later renew their close contact in the Chicago region after Jeane-Maine was expelled from Haiti by President Duvalier. This friendship continued until Jeane-Maine's death in 1984.

In 1964, Bertiaux resigned from the Anglican Church and moved to Wheaton, Illinois, where he worked as a researcher for the Theosophical Society. This brought him into contact with several prominent Liberal Catholics, including Dr. Henry Smith, Bishop Stephan Hoeller, and Bishop Gregory, who was also a key figure in the Russian Orthodox Church. Liberal Catholicism maintains a high degree of cer-emonial, and appeals to many mystically inclined Theosophists. Its influence has left its mark on Bertiaux to the extent that before he shaved off his beard he could easily be mistaken for an Eastern Orthodox priest. It becomes apparent, however, that the forces he is invoking lie well outside the range of mainstream Christian beliefs.

By the late 1960s, Michael Bertiaux had begun to swing back more heavily into the Voodoo tradition. Several Haitian *vouduns* had moved to suburban Evanston—there was a sizeable Haitian community in Chicago at that time—and

Bertiaux was consecrated as an adept within an organization known as the Monastery of the Seven Rays. Bertiaux considers this occult order to be the "magical
offshoot of Roman Catholicism," although it is rather less likely that the Vatican
would consider it so.

Certainly, the role of the dead and risen Christ remains central to the cosmology, but the spiritual atmosphere is totally different from that in mainstream
Christianity. There is a strong input from Voodoo—a central technique is transforming one's consciousness into that of an "astral tarantula"—and the initiate's
inspirational occult powers are obtained from Voodoo spirits of possession known
as *loas*. A far cry, indeed, from the orthodox scriptures.

The Monastery's cosmology—or map of higher consciousness—resembles the
Kabbalistic Tree of Life except that the Hebrew god-names are replaced by their
Voodoo counterparts. In Bertiaux's magical ceremonies—which feature mono-
tone chanting, specific ritual gestures made with the fingers, and the extensive use
of implements like the censer, bell, and magic crystal—most of the real work is
done on the inner planes. The key to working magic, says Bertiaux, is the development of powers of visualization.

On the walls of Bertiaux's Chicago apartment hang numerous oil paintings of
Voodoo gods, and these are used as an aid to stimulate the imagination, to summon
the Spirit from what he calls the "ocean of the unconscious." Among these works,
many of which Bertiaux painted himself in a primitive, atavistic Haitian style, are
representations of the Voodoo witch-goddess Maconda, "a powerful and stabi-
lizing influence in ritual"; the Voodoo god of lakes and rivers, who confers telep-
athy on his devotees; and the crucified Guede, god of the dead. The latter, says
Bertiaux, is associated with Christ as the resurrected savior, but also demonstrates
that "while the body may die, the spirit comes back many times, taking on a physical embodiment and resurrecting itself continuously through a cycle of reincarna-
tions." But it is Bertiaux's concept of the astral tarantula and the idea of the temple
as a magical space ship that are perhaps most extraordinary of all.

One of the techniques advocated in the Monastery of the Seven Rays is to visualize oneself surrounded by creatures so horrible that they ward off magical attacks
from the hostile possessing entities of inner space. As the magician energizes himself in ritual, or during his meditations at night, he begins to attract what Bertiaux
calls "negative vampires"—the spirits of the dead. It is vital, he says, that one should
appear strong and impregnable on the astral planes, and it is for this reason that he
has to transform the magical circle in his temple into a strong psychic sphere,
guarded at the eight points by different Voodoo *loas*. He then transforms in the
astral imagination into a were-tarantula and prepares to direct his space ship to
different regions of the inner cosmic terrain. As a "spider-sorcerer" or "spider-
magician," writes Bertiaux in one of his order papers, "you have woven your web

FIGURE 8.2. Michael Bertiaux's painting of Guede, Voodoo god of the dead.
Courtesy Michael Bertiaux and Cinetel Productions, Sydney.

by meeting with your own magical force each of the eight sources of cosmic energy.
Thus, cosmic energy is met by god-energy." Bertiaux explains this further within
the broad context of Voodoo ritual:

> Every time we do a ceremony we participate somehow in the god
> consciousness, or the energy behind the ceremony. I think it is a form of
> possession without a doubt, and represents the way in which the gods
> manifest themselves in human experience. . . . Voodoo and Gnosticism
> both work with the number eight because it is a significant power zone.
> In Voodoo it is represented by the mystical symbolism of the spider of
> space, the space deity. It represents the way in which the mind of the
> priest makes contact with all the possibilities of the world of space and
> time. For the magician to achieve a certain state of power he becomes
> that being in order to mediumistically receive the powers from the god
> behind the animal form.[54]

During my meeting with Bertiaux I asked him how the temple could actually transform into a "space ship," thereby enabling the spider-magician to function within it. His response was intriguing:

> The Temple is a space ship because it is a way of moving through the different spaces of consciousness. In fact the gestures of the ritual are designed to build a spherical vehicle for the priest's activities in other worlds. The priest is a spider because what he is doing is actually bringing into his own life the experience of other worlds, and then he's joining himself through the web of his consciousness to all the different parts of the spiritual experience. Every time he does something—a gesture, a word, a movement with some object—he is, in a sense, making contact between his web and something outside it. What he is doing is connecting himself to those worlds and dimensions.[55]

However, in the particular forms of Voodoo practiced by members of the Monastery, there is also something of a magical trade-off. As Bertiaux's order papers make clear, some spirit-entities are allowed to penetrate the protective web and draw on the magician's life-force in return for providing the specific occult powers that are desired. Summoned as the magician arouses himself erotically, the spirits "come down upon his body," draining the vitality of the mind and replacing it with psychic power. It is a method fraught with dangers, for it is a form of spirit-possession and leaves the occultist—at the moment of mental surrender—open to all manner of occult forces. According to Bertiaux it is crucial to retain a spiritual perspective during the act of possession:

> In Voodoo there is so much passive petitioning of the gods. It's a very pious religion. In fact, it is in many ways a religion of fear of the spirits, but once you admit the factor of possession you actually have the individual being possessed by a god, which is an infinite personal experience—of cosmic cause—for they're sharing the same consciousness. Then you overcome this feeling of petitioning and move towards a kind of pure identity where you understand the mind of the god, as if you were the god, or possessing the mind of the god for a moment. I think much of esoteric Voodoo has to do with understanding the mind of the gods, from within. I concur that possessions are facts and an accomplishment. I think that in terms of their mystical way of living—they see Voodoo not as much as a religion, but rather as an environment; a psychic occult environment in which they live. Everything about it is sanctioned by gods. It is a religious universe of mysteries possessing humans or initiates.[56]

Bertiaux invariably asks his students: "Does this occult exchange provide suffi-cient compensation for the man who must sacrifice himself to nocturnal appetites of the most perverse type?" After all, the range of invoked spirits is quite extensive. According to an interview Bertiaux conducted with journalist John Fleming, the master *voudon* claims direct astral communication with "space adepts, sothyrii, genii, and Voodoo Bon-Pa spirits."[57]

Presumably, in his own case, the risks have proven worthwhile. Bertiaux is now one of the chief adepts of the Monastery of the Seven Rays—an organization that has been aligned with Aleister Crowley's sex magick cult of *Thelema* since 1973—and has been largely responsible for disseminating its mysteries by mail to correspondents around the world. He has also published several books aimed at a more general esoteric audience—including *Lucky Hoodoo: A Short Course in Voudoo Power Secrets* (1977), written using the pseudonym Docteur Bacalou Baca; the recently reissued *Voudon Gnostic Workbook* (2007); and a work titled *Cosmic Meditation* (2009).

Although Voodoo Gnostic magic clearly has its dark elements, Bertiaux believes that a substantial part of what he does ritually has a positive side, as well. He claims many of his invocations are intended to distribute healing force to the planet—"a healing intended generally for the whole face of the earth, for all humanity, and for all those beings in need of some kind of spiritual strength." And there is no doubt that in his regal red and gold robe Michael Bertiaux presents an imposing form. Seated on a chair beside his paintings of Voodoo spirits, he has a dignified air—a high priest serving exotic gods before an even stranger altar. Yet it is precisely this sense of ceremonial grandeur that makes one pause and reflect on the paradoxical nature of the moment. Many stories below, in the streets of Chicago, frantic taxi drivers and frenzied commuters bustle about on their daily routines, totally unaware that strange spirits move among them.

Chaos Magick and Occult Anarchy in Britain

While American counterculture spirituality was strongly influenced by sacred psy-chology, goddess worship, and new approaches to shamanism, in Britain something entirely different was taking shape. Chaos Magick—generally spelled with a "k" to acknowledge its connection to Thelemic magick—burst onto the scene in the late 1970s with a radical outlook and a reformist agenda. Chaos Magick was like the punk rock of modern occultism. It was irreverent, iconoclastic, and totally dismis-sive of conventional tradition and belief. Fluid, revolutionary, and self-empowering, Chaos Magick combined Austin Osman Spare's system of sigil magic with Crowleyan individualism, and also added a strong dose of Taoism, anarchic humor, and chaos theory into the mix. It was characterized by small, transient, loosely connected groups of enthusiasts that formed and splintered through the late 1970s and 1980s. Fortunately sufficient traces of these esoteric groups remain so we are able to get a sense of this dynamic phase in recent esoteric history.

There is general agreement that the two early figureheads of the British Chaos Magick movement were Peter J. Carroll and his friend Ray Sherwin, who were members of a loose collective of occultists in London known as the Stoke Newington Sorcerers. Carroll had been contributing to an occult magazine titled *New Equinox*, edited by Ray Sherwin, and both men had become disillusioned with "traditional" approaches to practical magic.[58] Accordingly, in 1978 they decided to branch out in a new direction, establishing a nonhierarchical order called the Pact of the Illuminates of Thanateros—often simply known as The Pact, or the IOT. The IOT marked the historical beginnings of Chaos Magick in Britain. Ray Sherwin recalls that "our aim at that time was to inspire rather than lead magicians interested in the Chaos concept by publishing ideas of a practical nature."[59] The single most important influence on the two men at the time was Austin Osman Spare, whose magical system has been described in an earlier chapter:

> Chaos Magick has its roots in every occult tradition and in the work of many individuals. If any one person can be said to have been responsible, albeit unintentionally, for the present climate of opinion that person would be Austin Osman Spare, whose magical system was based entirely on his image of himself and an egocentric model of the universe. He did not intend that the system he devised for his own use should be used by others since it was clear to him that no two individuals could benefit from the same system. Nor did he fall into the trap of presuming that the information revealed to or by him was pertinent to all mankind as all the messiahs did. Aleister Crowley came to look upon him as a "black brother" purely because he refused to accept Crowley's Law of Thelema, preferring instead to work beyond dogmas and rules, relying on intuition and information uprooted from the depths of self.[60]

As soon as Sherwin and Carroll had established the IOT, however, they were faced with an immediate dilemma. "Both Pete and I held guruship and hierarchy as anathema," writes Sherwin, "yet now we were being expected not only to teach but also to lead."[61] Nevertheless, key principles quickly emerged. Chaos Magick would come to reflect the randomness of the universe and the individual's dynamic relationship with it. Nothing could be conceived as permanent. There were no absolute claims to truth, and all fixed beliefs and doctrines were essentially illusory. There were no gods or demons other than those that an individual had been conditioned to accept, and one could feel free to accept or reject beliefs according to the nature of their individual usefulness and relevance. The guiding paradigm of Chaos Magick soon emerged as a motto: "Nothing is true, everything is permitted—provided it interferes with no-one."[62]

American religious scholar Hugh B. Urban has called Chaos Magick "the first truly "postmodern" and "deconstructionist" form of spirituality."[63] He also notes that the word "Thanateros" is a blend of Eros and Thanatos—the primal forces of love and death.[64] Peter J. Carroll alludes to this theme in his book *Liber Kaos* (1992):

> When Eros moves in us
> We are most intensely ourselves
> But as Eros finally takes us
> The self is eclipsed, destroyed in orgasm the self is lost
> Chaos reminds us with a joke that we are nothing.[65]

However Carroll was also referring here to the Void Moment, articulated by Austin Osman Spare in the *Book of Pleasure* (1913). It is in the infinite creative Void of the Universe—referred to as *Kia* by Spare—that the Chaos magician seeks to implant his magical desire, and this state of consciousness is reached when awareness of self is lost or transcended at a peak moment of sexual or spiritual ecstasy. Carroll and Sherwin agreed that Spare's magical concepts blended in well with scientific Chaos theory and quantum mechanics as key elements in the reigning model of the operative universe. Also, as Hugh Urban has noted, because Chaos Magick rejected belief, it had to become, by its very nature, radically pragmatic, experimental, and experiential. What mattered most was not what one believed but what worked for a given individual in a given situation.[66] The appeal of Austin Spare's sigil magic was that it appeared to achieve tangible and specific outcomes. British magician Phil Hine—a close associate of Carroll and Sherwin—has similarly emphasized the use of magical sigils to achieve positive and effective magical results.[67]

In addition to the formation of the Illuminates of Thanateros in London in 1978, Chaos Magick was also attracting considerable interest in other parts of the country. Chaoists were gathering in strength, especially in the area around Leeds, where the Sorcerers Apprentice occult bookshop was based—the shop and its clientele were early supporters of Chaos Magick—and there was even a strong contingent of support for Chaos Magick in Germany at this time.[68] Following on from the Illuminates of Thanateros, the Circle of Chaos was formed in 1984 by Dave Lee, and during the same period Genesis P. Orridge established Thee Temple Ov Psychick Youth as a fusion of experimental performance art, punk music, and Crowleyan magic in conjunction with Psychic TV; Orridge's Temple also used magical sigils derived from the system of Austin Osman Spare. Carroll then emerged from temporary seclusion to run the Cabal Heraclitus, or Bristol C.H.A.O.S. Temple, from 1982 till 1991, before "retiring" to write two more books, *Liber Kaos* (1992) and *PsyberMagick* (1995).

Meanwhile, a collective known as the Lincoln Order of Neuromancers (L.O.O.N.) also emerged briefly during the 1980s. The Lincoln Order of Neuromancers had derived their name from science-fiction novelist William Gibson's book of the same name—*Neuromancer*—published in London in 1984. According to occult historian Dr. Dave Evans, this group sought to distinguish itself from more conventional forms of magic by concentrating "all occult ability and potential within the human brain rather than investing it in external entities, deities or spirits."[69] L.O.O.N. members reacted strongly against the Age of Aquarius where "truth, justice [and] peaceful pagan frolicking [were said to be] just around the corner," proposing instead that "the possibility of the New Aeon being ruled by cannibal radioactive zombies [could not] be entirely ruled out either."[70] L.O.O.N. was a characteristically short-lived Chaos Magick group and is now defunct.

Meanwhile Phil Hine has acknowledged the natural affinities between British Chaos Magick and the American Discordian Society, founded in a Californian bowling alley in 1958 by Malaclypse the Younger and Omar Khayyam Ravenhurst (Greg Hill and Kerry Thornley, respectively). The Discordian Society set out to break down the barriers between religion, humor, spirituality, and satire—at the same time rejecting the idea of a single Truth or "correct" interpretation of "Reality." According to Malaclypse the Younger, as outlined in the *Principia Discordia*, "reality is fundamentally chaos, confusion and disorder, which we thinly veil with an illusion of stability. . . . The central deity for the Discordian is thus Eris, the Greek Goddess of confusion."[71] Hine has praised the Discordian Movement for promoting the idea of a religion "based on the celebration of confusion and madness" and included a chapter titled "All Hail Discordia!" in his 1997 publication, *Oven-Ready Chaos*.[72]

Chaos Theory—Magickal Style

It may come as a surprise to some readers that Peter Carroll believes that Chaos Magick is compatible with modern science; Carroll argues in his essay "The Magic of Chaos" that "the higher reaches of scientific theory and empiricism actually demand that magic exist."[73] Although at first this appears problematic, it is clear that Carroll is responding to Chaos Magick as a technology of consciousness—a technology of *altered states of consciousness* in particular—for he goes on to say:

> Chaos Magick concentrates on technique . . . practical technique [that
> depends] on visualization, the creation of thought entities and altered
> states of consciousness achieved by either quiescent or ecstatic
> meditations. . . . All notions of absolute truth only exist if we choose to
> believe them at any time. The obverse side of the principle that "nothing
> is true" is that "everything is permitted," and Chaos magicians may often
> create unusual hyperscience and sorcery maps of reality as a theoretical
> framework for their magic. . . . The previously unsuspected parts of our
> brains can be even more creative than the conscious parts, and no
> message from the gods, no matter how extraordinary and overwhelming,
> should be taken as proof of anything beyond our own extraordinary
> powers.[74]

Here Carroll once again reveals his indebtedness to Austin Osman Spare's
approach to visionary magic—Spare's cosmology is similarly based on appreci-
ating the difference between conscious and unconscious human potentials and is
grounded in what can be achieved by the individual in direct response to a
dynamic and ever-changing universe. Interestingly, Carroll appears to share elements of Joseph Campbell's individualistic perspective, referred to earlier—namely,
the latter's credo that "Your god is a manifestation of your own level of consciousness. All of the heavens and all of the hells are within you."[75] As with Campbell,
Carroll and his fellow practitioners of Chaos Magick embrace the "journey of the
hero," but in their magical confrontations with Kia, the Tao, and the forces of
Chaos the heroes are themselves. So ironically, although Chaos Magick appears at
first to be simply confrontational, irreverent, and bombastic—as I said earlier, the
magic of "punk"—its methods and techniques are all about cutting through to the
chase: exploring practical techniques that are effective and actually work. Chaos
magicians maintain that their approach differs from conventional science only to
the extent that the territory under review is different. Scientists propose paradigms and test for results in the physical, observable world, whereas Chaos magicians claim that they propose paradigms and test for results in the metaphysical,
observable world. Their magical territory may be observed, experienced, and
tested in altered states of consciousness but this approach, for them, is no less real.
As Carroll explains:

> To the magician, spirit and matter are both part of the same thing, and
> he exalts neither above the other. He rejects no part of his experience.
> The magician lives in a continuum beginning with the sublime and
> ineffable Tao/God/Chaos through the mysterious and subtle Aethers to
> the awesome and strange material world. To the magician, any piece of
> knowledge, any new power, any opportunity for enlightenment is worth

having for its own sake. The only thing abhorred in this incredible existence is failure to come to grips with some part of it. . . . For [the Chaos magician] life is its own answer, and the way he lives it is his spirituality.[76]

In the end, Chaos Magick is all about "stealing fire from heaven"—about obtaining the vision and clarity for a broader understanding of the awesome, dynamic universe into which we have all been plunged. "Magic," says Carroll provocatively, "is where science is actually heading."[77]

9

Archetypes and Cyberspace

Magic in the Twenty-First Century

Now, in the twenty-first century, it may well be that new paradigms
are required—new paradigms for research into altered states of
consciousness and new paradigms for the study of magic, as well. And
maybe further surprises await us in these fields of enquiry. For example,
who would have expected that ancient spiritual traditions like native
shamanism could prove to be compatible with new developments in
computer technology and cyberspace research? Until recent times
such prospects would have seemed all but impossible. And yet for
cyber-explorers like the late Terence McKenna (1946–2000), fusions of
this sort presented no problems at all. Until his recent death, McKenna
was both a shamanic adventurer and an internationally recognized
spokesperson for the metaphysics of the new technology. For him, the
shamanic tradition was essentially about "externalizing the soul"—about
making both the human spirit and what he called "the Logos of the
planet"—tangible. McKenna also believed that computer networks like
the World Wide Web could take us into a type of global collective
consciousness.

McKenna's original interest was specifically in central Asian
shamanism. During the late 1960s, he went to Nepal to learn the Tibetan
language and also to study indigenous Bon-Po shamanism. He then lived
for a time in both India and the Seychelles before deciding to visit those
regions of the world where shamanism was still being practiced as a
living tradition. This took him to several islands in Indonesia—including

Sumatra, Sumba, Flores, the Moluccas, and Ceram—and later to South America, where he observed native shamanic practices firsthand.

In the upper Amazon basin of Colombia, Peru, and Ecuador shamans make extensive use of *ayahuasca*, a psychedelic beverage made from the tree-climbing forest vine known botanically as *Banisteriopsis caapi*. Taking this beverage allows the shaman to enter the supernatural realm, to have initiatory visions, and to make contact with ancestors and helper-spirits. McKenna was interested in the fact that from a biochemical view, *ayahuasca* appeared to resemble psilocybin, the active principle in the sacred psilocybe mushrooms used by shamans in the highlands of central Mexico. He also believed—and this is where he entered the realm of anthropological controversy—that the intake of psilocybin by primates living in the African grasslands prior to the last Ice Age may have led to the origins of human language itself.[1]

Psilocybe mushrooms produce a mystical state of consciousness where, for some, the soul seems to "speak" to the mind. These mushrooms also grow prolifically in cattle dung, and McKenna argued that the entry of psilocybin into the food chain in Africa between fifteen and twenty thousand years ago, and the subsequent domestication of cattle, may have led to the establishment of the first paleolithic religion—that of the Great Horned Goddess.[2] More specifically still, McKenna maintained that psilocybin itself has a unique role to play in human culture because of its role as an inspirational guiding agent. For him it was quite literally the Logos of the planet:

> Under the influence of psilocybin there is an experience of contacting a
> speaking entity—an interiorised voice that I call the *Logos*. If we don't go
> back to Hellenistic Greek terminology then we are left with only the
> vocabulary of psychopathology. In modern times to hear "voices" is to
> be seriously deviant: there is no other way to deal with this. And yet if we
> go back to the Classical literature the whole goal of Hellenistic
> esotericism was to gain access to this thing called the *Logos*. The Logos
> spoke the Truth—an incontrovertible Truth. Socrates had what he called
> his *daimon*—his informing "Other." And the ease with which psilocybin
> induces this phenomenon makes it, from the viewpoint of a materialist
> or reductionist rooted in the scientific tradition, almost miraculous.[3]

For Terence McKenna, the psilocybin experience was central to understanding the origins of spiritual awareness on our planet, and was also linked to the development of ancient religious structures:

> What I think happened is that in the world of prehistory all religion was
> experiential and it was based on the pursuit of ecstasy through plants.

And at some time, very early, a group interposed itself between people and the direct experience of the "Other." This created hierarchies, priesthoods, theological systems, castes, rituals, taboos. Shamanism, on the other hand, is an experiential science which deals with an area where we know nothing. . . . So the important part of the Human Potential Movement and the New Age, I believe, is the re-empowerment of ritual, the rediscovery of shamanism, the recognition of psychedelics and the importance of the Goddess.[4]

Extending this still further, McKenna maintained that, as with those South American and Mexican shamans who use visionary sacraments respectfully, psychedelics like psilocybin put the individual literally in touch with the "mind" of the planet:

This is the Oversoul of all life on Earth. It's the real thing. . . . I take very seriously the idea that the Logos is real, that there is a guiding Mind—an Oversoul—that inhabits the biome of the planet, and that human balance, dignity and religiosity depend on having direct contact with this realm. That's what shamanism is providing. It was available in the West until the fall of Eleusis and the Mystery traditions—to some people—but then was stamped out by barbarians who didn't realise what they had destroyed.[5]

Shifting now to the contemporary era—and this does involve a very substantial leap in time—McKenna believed there was a parallel between the Oversoul of the planet, which has presented itself in shamanism and the ancient Mystery traditions, and the emerging consciousness now permeating cyberspace via the medium of the Internet. According to McKenna, cyberculture has now forced us to redefine our notions of linear thinking and our relationship to the cosmos-at-large. In an interview with cultural critic Mark Dery, McKenna explained that in his view the future of humanity rests in its capacity to embrace a perspective which is really a type of technological, or scientific, shamanism:

I expect to see the coming decades transform the planet into an art form; the new man, linked in a cosmic harmony that transcends time and space. . . . I believe in what I call a forward escape, meaning that you can't go back and you can't stand still, so you've got to go forward, and technology is the way to do this. Technology is an extension of the human mental world, and it's certainly where our salvation is going to come from; we cannot return to the hunter-gatherer pastoralism of 15,000 years ago.[6]

Nevertheless, according to McKenna, these new techno-shamanic directions in society would be essentially metaphysical, because they would take us beyond notions of linear progress and development: "My position is that all of history involves making the Logos more and more concrete. In the same way that McLuhan saw print culture as replacing an earlier eye-oriented manuscript culture, my hope is that the cyberdelic culture is going to overcome the linear, uniform bias of print and carry us into the realm of the visible Logos . . . what these new technologies are doing is dissolving boundaries."[7]

Techno-Visionary "Realities"

So how do shamanic perspectives relate to the world of cyberspace and how does the world of cyberculture challenge our notions of rational and linear thinking? It is useful in this context to reflect on the increasing cultural impact of the Internet itself.

In her book *The Pearly Gates of Cyberspace*, science writer Margaret Wertheim argues that the Internet is providing us with a new concept of space that did not exist before—the interconnected "space" of the global computer network.[8] And, as she points out, this is a very recent phenomenon indeed. During the early 1980s few people outside the military and academic field of computer science had network access, but this "space" has since sprung into being from nothing, making it surely the "fastest-growing territory in history." However, it is the actual nature of the cyberspace experience that Wertheim finds so fascinating. When one person communicates with another online, there is no sense of physicality, for cyber-journeys cannot be measured in a literal sense. "Unleashed into the Internet," she writes, "my 'location' can no longer be fixed purely in physical space. Just 'where' I am when I enter cyberspace is a question yet to be answered, but clearly my position cannot be pinned down to a mathematical location."[9] All we can really confirm about the nature of cyberspace itself is that it involves a form of digital communication where information is relayed back and forth from one computer site to another, and where people share the outpourings of each other's minds.

This is not simply a communication of *literal* information, however. As many Internet enthusiasts have discovered, the world of cyberspace is also a realm where fantasy personas can be created in *virtual* reality—where human beings can interact with each other in ways limited only by their imagination. Individuals can pose as members of the opposite sex, as fantasy beings—even as dark and evil gods— and this has become a central feature of the development of role-playing on the Internet. So in a very specific way the Internet has become an extension of the human psyche, a forum for both its realities and its fantasies. From an esoteric or mystical perspective, though, what we are really exploring here is a form of inter-play between technology and the human imagination that can be expressed as simple equation—*As I imagine, so I become*—and this is the very essence of magic. It comes as no surprise that neopagans and occultists of all descriptions have been quick to embrace the Internet as a new means of communication and fantasy role-play. For many, the World Wide Web provides a pathway into the mythic conjur-ings of the world-at-large—an enticing and increasingly seductive means of engaging with the global imagination.

Techno-Pagans and Digital Magic

The relationship between neopagans and technology appears to have its roots in American 1960s counterculture, for it is now widely acknowledged that the pres-ent-day computer ethos owes a substantial debt to the psychedelic consciousness movement. The conservative *Wall Street Journal* even ran a front-page article in January 1990 asking whether virtual reality was equivalent to "electronic LSD."[10]

It would seem that the somewhat unlikely fusion between pagans and cyber-space arose simply because techno-pagans are capable of being both technological and mystical at the same time. As cyber-punk novelist Bruce Sterling has written: "Today, for a surprising number of people all over America, the supposed dividing line between bohemian and technician simply no longer exists. People of this sort may have a set of wind chimes and a dog with a knotted kerchief round its neck, but they're also quite likely to own a multi-megabyte Macintosh running MIDI synthe-sizer software and trippy fractal simulations."[11]

The American psychedelic culture of the late 1960s and early 1970s was essen-tially about experiencing the psyche through mind-altering drugs—the word *psychedelic*, coined by Canadian psychiatrist Dr. Humphry Osmond, literally means "mind revealing"—and this type of consciousness exploration in turn appears to have had a direct impact on the rise of the new technology. According to Mark Dery, Timothy Leary regarded the rise of the personal computer phenomenon as a clear vindication of the counterculture, for he believed that without the psychedelic revolution the personal computer would not have burst onto the world scene so soon. "It's well known," he told Dery, "that most of the creative impulse in the software industry, and indeed much of the hardware, particularly at Apple Macin-tosh, derived directly from the '60s consciousness movement. [Apple co-founder] Steve Jobs went to India, took a lot of acid, studied Buddhism, and came back and said that Edison did more to influence the human race than the Buddha. And [Microsoft founder Bill] Gates was a big psychedelic person at Harvard. It makes perfect sense to me that if you activate your brain with psychedelic drugs, the only way you can describe it is electronically."[12]

What Mark Dery calls the "cyberdelic" wing of the computer movement clearly has its roots in the 1960s counterculture, and Wiccan computer buff Sara Reeder remembers the early years well: "Silicon Valley and the modern Wiccan revival literally took root and grew up alongside each other in the rich black clay surrounding San Francisco Bay . . . both blossomed in the 1960s—the Valley through the miracle of the space program, the Pagan community by way of Haight Street's prominence as the worldwide Counterculture HQ."[13]

At this time, Timothy Leary, as patron saint of the hippie movement, was urging his followers to "turn on, tune in, and drop out" on LSD, a psychedelic synthesized from ergot in a Swiss laboratory. A generation later, he would switch his allegiance to the computer generation, announcing a few years before his death in 1996 that "the PC is the LSD of the 1990s." For Leary, there was a clear relationship between the consciousness movement and the new technology:

> What is so intriguing about our own era in history is that the human
> quest for knowledge and understanding in the last 25 years has seen
> an amazing blend of shamanic techniques, psychedelic drugs and
> the international global boom in resurrecting the pre-Christian,
> pagan, totemic and Hindu traditions. At the same time, with these
> computers . . . you have a situation where you can walk around in
> realities of your own construction. So we are very much on a threshold.
> I don't want to put any limits on what I'm saying, but here we have
> ancient techniques merging with the most modern. Computers give us
> the ways to communicate with the basic language of the universe—
> which is *quanta-electronic*. Matter and bodies are just electrons that have
> decided to come together, buzzing around with information.[14]

Meanwhile, Stewart Brand, former Merry Prankster and creator of the *Whole Earth Catalogue*, also reinvented himself as an icon of the cyberdelic movement. Brand has been credited with creating the computer hacker subculture as the direct result of an article he published in *Rolling Stone* magazine in 1972.[15] According to Dery, the psychedelic roots put in place by figures like Leary and Brand have left their mark, and the cyberdelic phenomenon as he understands it subsequently developed clearly identifiable characteristics, encompassing a cluster of subcultures—among them Deadhead computer hackers, "ravers" (habitués of all-night electronic dance parties known as "raves"), techno-pagans, and New Age technophiles. "Cyberdelia," says Dery, "reconciles the transcendentalist impulses of sixties counterculture with . . . [contemporary] infomania. . . . As well, it nods in passing to the seventies, from which it borrows the millenarian mysticism of the New Age and the apolitical self-absorption of the human potential movement."[16]

Cyberculture enthusiast Erik Davis has a similar perception, describing techno-pagans as "a small but vital subculture of digital savants who keep one foot in the emerging technosphere and one foot in the wild and woolly world of Paganism."[17] Meanwhile, for Douglas Rushkoff, author of *Cyberia: Life in the Trenches of Hyperspace*, "the neopagan revival incorporates ancient and modern skills in free-for-all sampling of whatever works, making no distinction between occult magic and high technology. In the words of one neopagan, "The magic of today is the technology of tomorrow. It's all magic. It's all technology."[18]

Neopagans generally regard technology and magic as interchangeable. Ever pragmatic, like the Chaos magicians referred to in the previous chapter, they seem to be primarily concerned with what works. If technology is effective in producing something physically useful, and if rituals and magical incantations can produce a specific spiritual or psychological outcome, for many neopagans this means they are compatible. According to Erik Davis, "it is this pragmatic hands-on instrumentality that allows some Pagans to powerfully re-imagine 'technology' as both a metaphor and a tool for spiritual work."[19]

Many Wiccans openly affirm the relationship between magic and the computer culture. An urban neopagan witch named Green Fire told Douglas Rushkoff:

High technology and high magic are the same thing. They both use tools from inner resources and outer resources. Magic from the ancient past and technology from the future are really both one. That is how we are creating the present; we're speeding up things, we are quickening our energies; time and space are not as rigid as they used to be. . . . Those of us who know how to work through time and space are using our abilities to *bend* time and space into a reality that will benefit people the most. . . . We humans are all shape-shifters. We just learn to access our DNA codes. It's very computer-oriented. We are computers; our minds are computers, our little cells are computers. We are bio-organic computers.[20]

Other neopagans regard the new technology as a type of freedom. For Californian neopagan writer Tom Williams:

Far from being seen as the tool of the oppressor, technology harnessed with the proper spiritual motivation can be a blast of liberation. . . . Take up the athame, the wand and the light-sound machine, the cup and the pentacle and the oscilloscope and the computer. Dedicate them to the service of the Life Force, to the Unio Mystica and to the praise of the

Great Mother and weave their power together into ritual, song and the sacred accomplishment of the Great Work![21]

Meanwhile, Michael Hutchison—author of the New Age bestseller *Mega Brain Power: Transform Your Life with Mind Machines and Brain Nutrients*—feels much the same way. For him, what he calls "consciousness technology" is coming to the aid of humanity in an unexpected way: "To some it may seem odd and paradoxical that machines—the synthetic, hard, material devices of this electronic temporal reality—may serve as gateways to the spirit, tools of transcendence. But in fact this fusion of spirituality, or the 'inner quest,' and science, 'the external quest,' is the central force of the emerging new paradigm.[22]

Many neopagan groups use computer technology and the Internet to advise their friends and members about seasonal rites, celebrations, workshops, and conferences, and they also provide information on pagan rites of passage, including handfastings (Wiccan weddings), child-blessings, and funerals. For example, the London-based Pagan Federation, established in 1971, uses the Internet to promote neopaganism, Druid, Wiccan, Odinic, Northern, Celtic, Eco-magic, and women's spirituality groups; and its American counterparts, like the Church of All Worlds, Circle Sanctuary, and the Church of Wicca, do much the same thing for their equivalent memberships. Contemporary pagans communicate with each other through discussion forums where they can chat in real time about various topics like magical ceremonies, spells, and the occult powers of herbs. Jem Dowse also makes the point that new pagans who happen to live in the American Bible Belt make use of this new technology to access like-minded people without fear of repercussions.[23]

Some techno-pagans have sought to extend the scope of their digital magic still further, conducting whole rituals over the Internet, and even establishing virtual shrines in cyberspace or staging magical encounters in the virtual world of Second Life.[24] Wiccan practitioner Sara Reeder explains that "while Christians and other mainstream religions ignored the Net for years—their members had an established network of churches and clergy to turn to—we became the first religious movement to depend heavily on it for growth and cohesion. And cyberspace, in turn, became the first mass Pagan gathering place since ancient times." For her, computer technology does not eliminate the essential poetry of the ritual experience:

> Our rituals have always taken place in the realm of the imagination, so
> we can make effective ritual anywhere we can exercise our love for poetry
> and storytelling. I've led online rituals for thirty in chat rooms that
> allowed us to talk to each other two lines at a time; some of them were as
> memorable and powerful as any I've attended in person . . . As VRML

and other technologies open the sensual bandwidth, allowing us to share
songs, images, and even virtual bodies to the mix, cyberspace ritual will
allow us to open up our private dreamscapes, and share our internal
visions with each other in much more intimate ways. The traditional
Neo-Pagan focus on individual creativity, combined with our emphasis
on poetry and fluid ritual forms, may well make us the first to pioneer
online altars and sacred sites, once more setting the example for other
religions to follow.[25]

Magical Role-Play

As neopagan rituals begin to extend their reach into cyberspace it is also useful to
consider the origins of magical role-play—for role-playing can also involve the use
of mythic archetypes and computer technology.

Fantasy and magical role-play practices developed initially from games like
Dungeons and Dragons, which were popular in the late-1970s and early 1980s. Here
participants explored underground vaults, tunnels, and mazes, and encountered
various monsters and alien entities—orcs, dwarfs, skeleton men, and the wandering souls of the dead—en route to discovering fabulous gold and jewels. Games
of this sort would usually be located in a fantasy world based either in medieval
Europe, on another planet, or on an "alternate Earth" where history had taken a
different turn of events and magic now ruled the laws of the land. The overall
pattern of the game would be determined by a Gaming Master, and each of the
principal characters would be "designed" or created by the players themselves.

For some players, though, many of these games soon proved unconvincing
and unsatisfying, and some enthusiasts began creating more innovative games by
drawing instead on the imagery of fantasy worlds described by writers like Michael
Moorcock, Marion Zimmer Bradley, André Norton, and H. P. Lovecraft. However,
as Bruce Galloway has observed, it soon became "much more challenging and a
great deal more fun, to design your own world."[26]

In the more developed forms of role-play, the Gaming Master—sometimes
known as the Keeper of Arcane Lore—has to set the rules for the adventure, build
up its legends and history, and establish the main characters and magical weapons.
Avnd there are hierarchies of power. For example, in some forms of magical role-
play a "cunning man" or "wise woman" can develop with time into a Witch or
Wizard or even into a High Runic Sorcerer, and the characters themselves may
acquire a variety of occult skills—including the ability to shape-shift, communicate
with animals, levitate, or achieve invisibility. During these games, participants also
learn magical spells of "absolute command." Spells, according to Galloway, "are

the building blocks of active magic" and can be used for either protection or assault.[27]

Ars Magica: The Storytelling Game of Mythic Magic was one of the pioneering role-playing systems in this genre and offered a variety of enticing magical roles to its participants.[28] *Ars Magica* identified three different types of characters—Magi, Companions, and Grogs—the latter being "lower class characters" like servants, stable-hands, guards, and messengers. There were many individual characters within this threefold hierarchy, and players had to conceptualize the character they wished to play—adding specific details of their own to create a figure they could readily identify with. Nevertheless, all of the characters had acknowledged "virtues" and "flaws," and in this particular game they were accorded point scores for different attributes—intelligence, perception, strength, stamina, presence, communication, dexterity, and quickness.

The key challenge with magical role-play, however, was always to move fantasy worlds of this type online so they could be accessed on the Internet. This was eventually done through the establishment of "multiuser domains" or MUDs. Participants with a personal computer simply had to use a modem and network passwords to log on to a computer containing a MUD. Some MUDs were public, while others were restricted to a select group of role-players controlled by a "wizard" or "tinker" who was essentially in charge of its mythic content and terrain. Nowadays the range of MUDs is extensive, and there are MUDs based on *Star Trek* and Frank Herbert's science-fiction *Dune* series, among many others. As Margaret Wertheim notes:

> Today's MUDs have morphed into a huge range of virtual worlds. . . .
> MUDers are involved in an ongoing process of world-making. To
> name is to create, and in MUD worlds, the simple act of naming and
> describing is all it takes to generate a new alter ego or "cyber self." . . .
> The interlocking imaginative and social mesh of a MUD means that
> actions taken by one player may affect the virtual lives of hundreds of
> others. The very vitality and robustness of a MUD emerges from the
> collective will of the group. As in the physical world, relationships are
> built, trusts are established, bonds are created, and responsibilities
> ensue.[29]

However, there is often a blurring between the worlds of "everyday" reality and "fantasy" reality. One MUDer told online researcher Mizuko Ito: "To me there is no real body. On-line, it is how you describe yourself and how you act that makes up the real you." This may well be a characteristic response from many of the new cyberspace explorers. According to Douglas Rushkoff, for some game-players "all of life is seen as a fantasy role-playing game in which the stakes are physically real but the lessons go beyond physical reality." One of the role-players

Rushkoff interviewed for his book *Cyberia*—Nick Walker, a gamemaster and aikido instructor from New Jersey—believed he could pick and choose the traits of various role-play characters and incorporate them into his own personality: "The object in role-playing games is playing with characters whose traits you want to bring into your own life. You can pick up their most useful traits, and discard their unuseful ones." As Rushkoff notes, this is very much like consciously choosing one's own character traits in order to become a "designer being."[30]

Clearly, for many online role-players the appeal of activities like this can be explained simply by the fact that fantasy is so much more enticing and seductive than the routines of the everyday world. According to Dr. Brenda Laurel, a specialist in the field of interactive computer systems, "Reality has always been too small for the human imagination. The impulse to create an 'interactive fantasy machine' is only the most recent manifestation of the age-old desire to make our fantasies palpable—our insatiable need to exercise our imagination, judgment, and spirit in worlds, situations, and personae that are different from those in the our everyday lives."[31]

However, there is also the possibility that for many participants fantasy role-play will lead to some form of increased spiritual self-awareness, and Brenda Laurel hopes for this too. "Imagination," she says, "is the laboratory of the spirit."

Dark Archetypes

Nevertheless, while many neopagan responses to cyberspace are innovative and essentially positive, there is also an occult underbelly—a darker realm that feeds on fear and powerlessness in a rapidly changing world. And perhaps the archetype that most powerfully embodies these feelings is that of the Alien—the space-entity created by Swiss fantasy artist H. R. Giger that was featured in the Oscar-winning film of the same name and that has since become a cyberculture icon. Giger now has an impressive Web site on the Internet and an increasing sphere of influence.[32] At least one PC game, *Cyberdream's Darkseed*, is based on Giger's artwork, and as Mark Dery has noted, "cyberpunk bands such as Cyberaktif and Front Line Assembly routinely cite him as an inspiration. The highest tribute is paid by modern primitives who emblazon themselves with Giger's slavering, mace-tailed Alien—a cyberpunk rite of passage."[33]

Selections of Giger's work are now on permanent display at his museum in Castle St. Germain in Gruyeres, Switzerland, which opened in June 1998. The Limelight nightclub in Manhattan also has a dedicated H. R. Giger room, featuring exhibits of several of his most surreal and visionary artworks. The paintings themselves draw strongly on the magic of the Left-Hand Path as well as on fantasy and horror fictions like *The Necronomicon*. There is an unquestionable potency—even a macabre beauty—in his biomechanoid creations, but his nightmare fusions of the human and the mechanical also evoke a sense of *no escape*—a sense that we are all trapped in a virtual hell of our own making. Perhaps this is a portent of our times.

A few years ago I met with Giger at his home in Zurich, for I was interested to learn from him, firsthand, about his own creative process—and how he regarded the haunting, nightmarish images now inhabiting his dark, visionary art. Visiting Giger's house, and seeing the large surreal panels that adorn its walls, was like experiencing an exorcism. Giger told me that he did not understand the processes that underlie his paintings, but that he makes use, essentially, of the mediumistic, or "automatic" style adopted by several surrealists, including Max Ernst, Oscar Dominguez, and Wolfgang Paalen. Giger maintains that he opens the door to his unconscious mind by confronting a blank canvas and suspending conscious thought. Then, as the spontaneous images start to build before his eyes, he adds details and texture with his airbrush. Giger likes the airbrush because of its tremendous directness: "It enables me to project my visions directly onto the pictorial surface, freezing them immediately."

There is no doubt that in terms of his art, Giger is very much a magician—conjuring dramatic visionary creations from the darker recesses of his imagination. And his paintings have an evil authenticity about them. They have been praised by distinguished visionary artists like Ernst Fuchs and Salvador Dali, and display a magical caliber rarely seen in modern art. One can also link him in spirit with earlier tortured masters of the visionary perspective, like Hieronymus Bosch and Lucas Cranach.

Giger lives in an unobtrusive double-story terrace house, a few minutes' drive from Zurich's busy international airport. His living room downstairs is dominated by the remarkable paintings that first earned him international recognition—works that feature Medusa-like women with ghostly pale skin and snakes in their hair, and strange shapes and forms writhing all around. Claws, needles, machine-guns, and barbs also feature strongly in these paintings. For most people, the works themselves are both disturbing and fascinating at the same time—they also have an extraordinary three-dimensional quality that lifts them beyond the plane of the wall so that they become part of the living ambience of the room.

In the center of the long table that occupies Giger's living room is an engraved pentagram, and also candlesticks whose flames cast an eerie light on the paintings nearby. A tall row of shelves in one corner of the room reveals a row of skulls and authentic shrunken heads from a cannibal tribe. It is here that Giger has placed the Oscar he received for "special effects" in *Alien*—a tribute to his bizarre imagination.

FIGURE 9.1A AND B. Swiss fantasy artist H. R. Giger photographed in his studio.
Courtesy Cinetel Productions, Sydney.

Upstairs Giger has his studio. At one end it is total chaos—a litter of splattered paint, brushes, and discarded works of art. Here he experiments with his airbrush techniques, spraying patterns through metal grids and exploring different textures of light and shade. At the other end of the long, open room is a large black table with bulbous legs and an extraordinary mirror sheen on its pristine surface. Fashioned substantially from heavy molded plastic, it is accompanied by several tall chairs surmounted with skulls and shaped to give the impression of distorted vertebrae. An ashen-grey version of these chairs—seemingly fashioned from bone itself—has pride of place at the head of the table. And gracing the long wall above is another large panel—this time depicting a horned devil, a silver pentagram and dark, hostile serpents.

Giger has little real explanation for these exotic images. "I try to come close to my imagination," he says in his broken English. "I have something in my head and I try to work it out—like a kind of exorcism." Giger recognizes the adverse effect his work has on many of the people who see it, but he is keen to point out that if his work seems dark, this is not necessarily the way he is himself. "My childhood was very happy," he says, almost apologetically, "and my parents have been very nice to me." He ponders a while and then adds: "I think that most of the images in my paintings are evil, but you can't say that I'm evil. It's just that evil is much, much more interesting than paradise."

Hans Ruedi Giger was born in 1940 in the small Swiss town of Chur, which he describes as an "unbearable" place of "high mountains and petty bourgeois attitudes." Growing up there, he had nightmares in his parents' house and would imagine "gigantic bottomless shafts bathing in pale yellow light." In his master-work, *Necronomicon*—a tribute to H. P. Lovecraft's fictitious creation of the same name—Giger writes that, "on the walls, steep and treacherous wooden stairways without banisters led down into the yawning abyss" and the cellar in the house gave rise to the image of "a monstrous labyrinth, where all kinds of dangers lay in wait for me."[34] This feeling is certainly conveyed in his paintings for, time and again, the figures seem trapped and tormented in gruesome, tortuous tunnels and there is no apparent path of escape.

As a child, Giger built skeletons of cardboard, wire, and plaster, and he recalls that he also had an "overwhelming disgust of worms and snakes"—a loathing that still manifests itself in his paintings today. He also had a fascination for pistols and guns of all sorts, and during his military service was nearly shot on more than one occasion.

If Giger is haunted by images from his past, this is quite understandable, for there have been many crises in his life. Probably the most traumatic involved the beautiful actress, Li Tobler. Giger met Li in 1966 when she was eighteen and living with another man. Giger moved into her attic apartment, however, and they became lovers. Giger recalls that Li had "enormous vitality and a great appetite for life." She also wanted her life to be "short but intense." Li is the prototype for the many ethereal women in Giger's paintings who peer forth from the torment of snakes, needles, and stifling bone prisons—to a world beyond that is forever out of reach. Giger painted Li's body several times with an airbrush, and there are several photographs of her posing naked—like a woman of mystery struggling to emerge from a nightmare that has possessed her soul. Around the time the photographs of Li were taken, Giger inherited his present house as a legacy from his uncle, and Li moved in. But the idyll, says Giger, "was all too short." Li had a hectic schedule for her theatrical performances around the country, was irresistibly drawn to numerous other lovers, and was beginning to wilt under the pressures of life in the fast lane. On Whit Monday 1975, she shot herself with a revolver. It may be too simplistic to say that Li haunts Giger still, for his life is full of beautiful and exotic women who are fascinated by his art and by his glamorous and bohemian lifestyle. But there is no doubting that the simultaneous agony and joy of life with Li Tobler established the dynamic of fear and elusive transcendence that is present in many of his paintings.

Giger maintains that although he has studied the works of Aleister Crowley—like many other cyberspace enthusiasts—he is not a magician in the conventional sense. He says he does not perform rituals, engage in invocations, or summon spirits. But one could hardly find more powerful images to adorn a temple of the black arts than Giger's pantheon of demons. Giger, in a very real way, makes magic spontaneously. When the thin veil across his psyche is drawn aside just a little, tempestuous visions of evil and alienation come forth. It is as if the dark gods are emerging once again from the nightmares of the past.

The Future of Western Magic

So what are the implications of this strange new world of magical cyberspace, and where are the magical undercurrents in contemporary Western culture heading? Will new mythologies emerge to help us define our future?

It seems to me that a distinct polarity is now emerging and that devotees of the various magical traditions in the West may find themselves gravitating in two quite different directions. The first of these options focuses primarily on the sacred dimensions of Nature, and engages us in a magic of the Earth and Cosmos. This is, of course, the option chosen by devotees of Wicca and Goddess worship, who venerate the gods and goddesses associated with the cycles of the Moon and Sun in the natural environment. However there is also another option—which takes us still further into the archetypal realms of cyberspace and virtual reality.

And although techno-paganism seeks to embrace both of these dimensions, it seems to me that the main pathways within Western magic will begin increasingly to diverge. Increasingly, I believe, a choice will be made between Nature and the new technology.

As we have seen, during the last hundred years, Western magic has focused on the quest for personal transformation. Occultists of all persuasions invoke their gods and goddesses as archetypes of the divine potential they seek within themselves, and as Austin Spare observed, this is the magical act of *stealing fire from heaven*. As the information superhighway embraces ever-increasing levels of intensity, it seems to me that many magical devotees will feel powerfully drawn toward embracing the new technology in all its diversity. Sacred shrines and archetypal symbols will find a richer and more convincing graphic expression on the Internet, so that they really do become magical doorways in their own right—the cyberspace equivalent of the Magic Theater in Hermann Hesse's novel *Steppenwolf*. The magical explorers entering these doorways will then engage ever more completely in virtual worlds, blending technological motifs with mythic archetypes to produce fusions we can only begin to envisage at the present time. Perhaps this magic will produce the Gigers of the future—where elements of the mechanistic world merge with what is human, yielding ever more bizarre permutations of cyber-magical mythology.

Other contemporary magical practitioners will, I believe, turn more completely toward the esoteric traditions of former cultures and will choose instead to identify only with the mythic archetypes of the past—but those which have a sense of resonance and meaning for the present. Already this has begun to happen. The contemporary magical revival has not only seen a return to medieval esotericism and the mythic traditions of the Celts, as well as a revival of interest in the gods and goddesses of ancient Greece, Rome, Egypt, and Mesopotamia, but there has also been a very specific resurgence, in certain quarters, of traditions like Odinism and Druidry, and the magic of the various shamanic cultures around the world. In many cases, this return to an archaic past also brings with it a thirst for authentic simplicity—for rituals that embrace the earth, sun, moon, and sky as they are found in the real world, and not in the virtual realms of cyberspace.

For this reason I believe that many magical devotees, in time, will take the decision to withdraw from the new technology, at least in part—using it peripherally perhaps as a means of information exchange, but channeling the quest for personal transformation into an engagement with completely natural processes. Andrew Siliar, a neopagan from Arizona, makes this point very effectively in a letter published in the Wiccan journal *Green Egg*:

> Paganism is a Nature religion, rooted deep in the Earth, honoring the
> Gods and Goddesses, feeling the heartbeat of the Mother Earth, loving

and honoring all of Her creatures. And now we have this wonderful new technology, along with computer graphics. We can link up with other people on-line, and now we can be techno-witches, and cyber wizards. . . . I'm sorry, but that doesn't sound like much of a Nature Religion to me anymore. . . . I need no on-line link to let me feel the power of the Goddess, I just touch the Earth and connect.[35]

Contemporary British shaman Gordon MacLellan sees it much the same way. For him, magic is essentially a dynamic, spiritual response to Nature: "The spirit world . . . is not separate from the earth we walk upon. . . . The spirit world is here beside us, always; and unseen, often unguessed, it touches and changes the world of physical forms that we live in. Our actions, in turn, change the spirit world, and we can work to heighten our awareness of it so that we . . . learn to operate in all worlds at once."[36] MacLellan goes on to positively affirm: "Shamanism is ecstatic. My magic moves most strongly in dance and with the wild, whirling dances of the animal spirits; with others it takes other forms, but for us all the power, the strength to act, lies in an ecstasy of life—that living is such a delight!"[37]

So we may well find ourselves engaging in the future with two quite different traditions—natural shamanistic magic and cutting-edge techno-cybermagic—along with all the assorted mythologies they will bring in their wake. Nevertheless, in spite of the gathering pace of the new technologies, I am personally convinced that many people drawn to the various paths in contemporary Western magic will opt finally for a type of "authentic simplicity" in choosing what is most meaningful for them. For these people the magical quest will remain an eclectic journey of self-knowledge, enabling each individual to find a sense of sacred meaning in his or her own way—honoring the cycles of the seasons, the Gods and Goddesses of Creation, and their own sacred connection with the Universe as a whole. As Gordon MacLellan has expressed it, "The Otherworld is this world—there are no barriers. . . . The life of the Earth is sacred and is part of the Infinite. To be alive is to move in celebration."[38]

Notes

1. Hugh Urban's *Magia Sexualis* (2006) is the only notable exception, but even here the coverage is relatively brief.

INTRODUCTION

1. In his classic work, *The Book of Pleasure (Self Love): The Psychology of Ecstasy* (self-published, London, 1913) Spare writes: "Now let him imagine an union takes place between himself (the mystic union of the Ego and Absolute). The nectar emitted, let him drink slowly, again and again. After this astonishing experience his passion is incomparable. . . . The ecstasy in its emotion is omnigenous. Know it as the nectar of life, the Syllubub of Sun and Moon. Verily he steals the fire from Heaven: the greatest act of bravery in the world." Reprinted by 93 Publishing, Montreal 1975: 38.

2. For an overview of the development of the human potential movement, or New Age movement as it is now known, readers are referred to my recent publication, *The New Age: The History of a Movement* (Thames & Hudson, New York 2004).

3. Regardie made several important observations on the nature of the modern magical process. Here is a selection of key statements: "In the system propounded by Dr C. G. Jung . . . the Unconscious itself is . . . conceived to have a dual aspect. That part of it which is personal and individual, and that great stream of power, archetype and image of which the former is only a part—the Collective Unconscious. It is a universal and uniform substratum common to the whole of mankind. We may consider it to be the historical background from which every psyche and every consciousness has proceeded or evolved. . . . It is

this that the medieval alchemists called Anima Mundi." (I. Regardie, *The Middle Pillar*, Aries Press, Chicago 1945: 46–47). "As a practical system, Magic is concerned not so much with analysis as with bringing into operation the creative and intuitive parts of man. . . . Magic may be said to be a technique for realizing the deeper levels of the Unconscious" (Regardie, *The Middle Pillar*: 19). "The magician conceives of someone he calls God, upon whom attend a series of angelic beings, variously called archangels, elementals, demons etc. By simply calling upon this God with a great deal of ado, and commemorating the efforts of previous magicians and saints who accomplished their wonders or attained to the realization of their desires through the invocation of the several names of that God, the magician too realizes the fulfilment of his will" (Regardie, *Ceremonial Magic: A Guide to the Mechanisms of Ritual*, Aquarian Press, Wellingborough, UK 1980: 93). "The union or identification with the God is accomplished through suggestion, sympathy and the exaltation of consciousness. . . . The magician imagines himself in the ceremony to be the deity who has undergone similar experiences. The rituals serve but to suggest and to render more complete the process of identification, so that sight and hearing and intelligence may serve to that end. In the commemoration, or rehearsal of this history, the magician is uplifted on high, and is whirled into the secret domain of the spirit" (Regardie, *Ceremonial Magic*: 93–94). "The higher Magic . . . has as one of its objectives a communion both here and hereafter with the divine, a union not to be achieved by mere doctrine and sterile intellectual speculations, but by the exercise of other more spiritual faculties and powers in rites and ceremonies. By the 'divine' the Theurgists recognized an eternal spiritually dynamic principle and its refracted manifestation in Beings whose consciousness, individually and severally, are of so lofty and sublime a degree of spirituality as actually to merit the term Gods" (Regardie, *The Tree of Life: A Study in Magic*, Rider, London 1932: 85). "Magical ritual is a mnemonic process so arranged as to result in the deliberate exhilaration of the Will and the exaltation of the Imagination, the end being the purification of the personality and the attainment of a spiritual state of consciousness, in which the ego enters into a union with either its own Higher Self or a God" (Regardie, *The Tree of Life*: 106). "All the characteristics of the higher worlds are successively assumed by the Magician, and transcended, until in the end of his magical journey, he is merged into the being of the Lord of every Life. The final goal of his spiritual pilgrimage is that peaceful ecstasy in which the finite personality, thought and self-consciousness, even the high consciousness of the highest Gods, drops utterly away, and the Magician melts to a oneness with the Ain Soph wherein no shade of difference enters" (Regardie, *The Tree of Life*: 246–247).

4. In my view, the Hermetic Order of the Golden Dawn assumes much greater historic significance than the Theosophical Society, established in New York in 1875. The latter was concerned primarily with introducing Eastern spiritual teachings to the West, and its cosmological concepts are, for the most part, theoretical. The Golden Dawn, on the other hand, provided its initiates with an extensive range of practical occult methods and techniques that laid the basis for the twentieth-century magical revival. For a consideration of the scope of these magical approaches—which included magical invocation and the exploration of trance states, as well as various forms of meditation and visualization—interested readers are referred to Israel Regardie's definitive four-volume compilation *The Golden Dawn* (Aries Press, Chicago, 1937–1940), since reissued in many different editions and formats.

5. The Kabbalistic Tree of Life is referred to in the Jewish mystical tradition by its Hebrew name *Otz Chiim* and represents a process of sacred emanation from the Godhead. The Tree is a composite symbol consisting of ten spheres, or *sephiroth*, through which the creation of the world—indeed, all aspects of creation—have come about. The ten *sephiroth* are aligned in three columns headed by the first three emanations, Kether (The Crown), Chokhmah (The Great Father/Wisdom) and Binah (The Great Mother/Understanding). Collectively, the ten *sephiroth* on the Tree of Life symbolize the process by which the Infinite Light and Formlessness of the Godhead (*Ain Soph Aur*) becomes manifest in the universe. The seven emanations beneath the supernal triad of Kether, Chokhmah and Binah (i.e., the remaining *sephiroth* Chesed, Geburah, Tiphareth, Netzach, Hod, Yesod, and Netzach) represent the "seven days of Creation."

CHAPTER 1

1. See G. G. Scholem, *Jewish Gnosticism, Merkabah Mysticism, and Talmudic Tradition* (Jewish Theological Seminary of America, New York 1960): 1–3. Gnosticism focuses on the quest for *gnosis* (ancient Greek: "spiritual knowledge"). The origins of Gnosticism remain a matter of debate, but there is broad consensus that Gnosticism as a historical movement parallels the rise of early Christianity. Some scholars, like Hans Jonas (author of *The Gnostic Religion*, Boston 1958), have seen in Gnosticism residues of pre-Christian Iranian dualism, while others believe that it developed in response to the failure of Jewish apocalyptic expectations and have dated its origins to around 70 CE, coinciding with the fall of the Jerusalem Temple. Others regard Gnosticism as a response to the failure of Christian messianic expectations—where some early Christian devotees, feeling that the Messiah had not returned as soon as had been hoped, turned away from religious faith toward spiritual inner knowledge. Gnostic thought was certainly well established by the second century of the Christian era. The unearthing of a major Gnostic library near the town of Nag Hammadi in upper Egypt in 1945 provided a rich body of source material on the Gnostic philosophies. Until this time, much of the existing Gnostic scholarship had been based on other surviving Gnostic commentaries written by Church Fathers such as Irenaeus, Clement, and Hippolytus, who were hostile to Gnostic tenets. The Nag Hammadi codices, a collection of texts written in Coptic, revealed the syncretistic nature of Gnosticism, demonstrating that as a movement Gnosticism incorporated elements from Christianity, Judaism, Neoplatonism, and the Greek mystery religions, as well as material from Egypt and Persia. Essentially Gnosticism was a call for transcendence, a movement seeking a return to the Spirit and a movement away from the constrictions of the material world, which was regarded as a source of pervasive evil. James M. Robinson, editor of the English translation of the Nag Hammadi Library, has explained the Gnostic philosophy in the following terms: "In principle, though not in practice, the world is good. The evil that pervades history is a blight, ultimately alien to the world as such. But increasingly for some the outlook on life darkened; the very origin of the world was attributed to a terrible fault, and evil was given status as the ultimate ruler of the world, not just a usurpation of authority. Hence the only hope seemed to reside in escape. . . . And for some a mystical inwardness undistracted by external factors came to be the only way to

attain the repose, the overview, the merger into the All which is the destiny of one's spark of the divine." See J. M. Robinson, Introduction to *The Nag Hammadi Library in English* (Harper & Row, San Francisco 1977): 4. In the Gnostic conception, there is a clear divide between the spiritual world which is good, and the physical world which is evil, that is to say, a clear demarcation between the cosmic and the divine on the one hand, and the physical, or material, on the other. The Gnostic texts portray humanity as being increasingly separated from the sustaining realm of divinity and spirit, and this in turn provides a rationale for spiritual transcendence, for in the Gnostic conception there is a vital need to liberate the "divine spark" entombed in the physical world.

2. Admittedly, not all scholars agree on this point. The late Ioan P. Couliano believed that Scholem overstated the connection between Kabbalah and Gnosticism; see Couliano's *The Tree of Gnosis* (HarperCollins, San Francisco 1992): 42 et seq. However, Scholem states quite emphatically that the Kabbalistic text *Bahir*—which predates the *Zohar*—makes it clear that the "thirteenth century Kabbalists became the heirs of Gnostical symbolism." See *Major Trends in Jewish Mysticism* (Schocken, New York 1961): 214.

3. Scholem, *Major Trends in Jewish Mysticism*: 14.

4. G. G. Scholem, *Origins of the Kabbalah* (Princeton University Press, Princeton 1990): 363–364, 389–390.

5. See D. C. Matt, *The Essential Kabbalah* (HarperCollins, New York 1995): 7

6. Ibid.: 3.

7. For En-Sof, see Scholem, *Major Trends in Jewish Mysticism*: 12, and for Ein-Sof, see Matt, *The Essential Kabbalah*: 40.

8. See Scholem, *Major Trends in Jewish Mysticism*: 209.

9. See M. Idel, *Kabbalah: New Perspectives* (Yale University Press, New Haven 1988): 119, and also G. G. Scholem, *On the Mystical Shape of the Godhead* (Schocken, New York 1991): 43.

10. Scholem, *Major Trends in Jewish Mysticism*: 215–216.

11. Ibid.: 218–219.

12. Ibid.

13. C. Ginsburg, *The Kabbalah: Its Doctrines, Development and Literature* (Routledge & Kegan Paul, London 1956): 102.

14. See Matt, *The Essential Kabbalah*: 7.

15. Ibid.: 41.

16. A. E. Waite, *The Holy Kabbalah* (University Books, New York 1960): 201.

17. See V. Crowley, *A Woman's Kabbalah* (Thorsons, London 2000): 189; and R. Patai, *The Hebrew Goddess*, third edition (Wayne State University Press, Detroit 1990): 116.

18. J. Bonner, *Qabalah* (Skoob Publishing, London 1995): 23.

19. S. A. Fisdel, *The Practice of Kabbalah: Meditation in Judaism* (Jason Aronson, Northvale, New Jersey 1996): 100.

20. Bonner, *Qabalah*: 25.

21. See Crowley, *A Woman's Kabbalah*: 189; and Patai, *The Hebrew Goddess*: 32.

22. J. Ferguson, *An Illustrated Encyclopaedia of Mysticism and the Mystery Religions* (Thames & Hudson, London 1976): 99.

23. Hermetic scholar Dan Merkur has emphasized in a recent article that Gnosticism and Hermeticism are frequently, and wrongly, confused with each other—they present completely different concepts of God. Merkur writes: "Like the God of Stoicism, the Hermetic God was omnipresent and omniscient through the material cosmos. In Gnosticism, by contrast, God was transcendent, and the physical universe was an evil place created by an evil Demiurge. Hermetic ethics celebrated the divine within the world; Gnostic ethics were abstemious, ascetic efforts to escape from the world." See D. Merkur, "Stages of Ascension in Hermetic Rebirth," *Esoterica* 1 (1999): 81.

24. Ficino's texts are now held in the Medici Library in Florence.

25. See W. Barnstone (ed.), *The Other Bible* (Harper & Row, San Francisco 1984): 567; and the entry on Hermetic books in *The New Columbia Encyclopedia* (Columbia University Press, New York 1975): 1232.

26. In Greek mythology, Hermes was the messenger of the gods, the protector of sacrificial animals and also god of the wind. He conducted the souls of the dead on their passage to the Underworld. In ancient Egyptian mythology, Thoth is a scribe and moon god and is best known as god of wisdom and magic. He also invented numbers and writing, and measured time. Thoth presided with his consort, Maat, in the Judgment Hall, where the hearts of the deceased were weighed against the feather of truth. Thoth recorded all judgments made in relation to the dead. The ancient Greeks identified Thoth with Hermes. See J. E. Zimmerman, *Dictionary of Classical Mythology* (Harper & Row, New York 1964), and P. Turner and C. R. Coulter, *Dictionary of Ancient Deities* (Oxford University Press, Oxford 2000).

27. Zimmerman, *Dictionary of Classical Mythology*; and Turner and Coulter, *Dictionary of Ancient Deities*.

28. Pico also distinguished between "bad" magic, which had to do with demons and devils, and "natural" magic, which was essentially "good" and compatible with God's freedom of will. See D. P. Walker, *Spiritual and Demonic Magic from Ficino to Campanella* (Sutton Publishing, Stroud, UK 2000): 54–55.

29. Quoted in T. Churton, *The Gnostics* (Weidenfeld & Nicolson, London 1987): 113.

30. Ibid.: 114.

31. Ibid.: 112.

32. This in turn became a guiding maxim within the Western esoteric tradition up until the time of the Golden Dawn. However, a polarizing split subsequently occurred within this tradition with the introduction of Crowley's doctrine of Thelema: thereafter an influential chthonic element was introduced to twentieth-century magical practice which led many occult devotees away from the quest for mythical renewal and toward accentuated occult individualism and/or esoteric anarchy.

33. K. Seligmann, *Magic, Supernaturalism, and Religion* ([1948] Pantheon, New York 1971): 82–83.

34. Quoted in H. S. Redgrove, *Alchemy Ancient and Modern* (Rider, London 1922): 10–11.

35. Quoted in M. Berthelot, *La chimie au moyen age*, vol. 2 (Paris 1893): 262.

36. E. J. Holmyard, *Alchemy* (Penguin, Harmondsworth 1957): 22.

37. Redgrove, *Alchemy Ancient and Modern*: 14.

38. See T. Burckhardt, *Alchemy* (Penguin Books, Baltimore 1971): 97.

39. Ibid.: 73–75.

40. R. Cavendish, *The Tarot* (Michael Joseph, London 1975): 11.

41. Ibid.

42. R. Decker, T. Depaulis, and M. Dummett, *A Wicked Pack of Cards: The Origins of the Occult Tarot* (St. Martin's Press, New York 1996): 27.

43. Tarot decks that reflect this cultural tendency include the Tarocchi of Mantegna deck, the Tarocchi of Venice deck, the Tarocchino of Bologna decks. and the Michiate of Florence decks. See S. R. Kaplan, *Tarot Classic* (Grossett & Dunlap, New York 1972): 18–22.

44. One of the earliest known Tarot decks is the fifteenth-century Visconti-Sforza deck associated with the fourth Duke of Milan, Francesco Sforza. This deck consisted of seventy-eight cards and featured the four suits of *spade* (spades), *bastoni* (diamonds), *coppe* (hearts), and *denari* (clubs). It also featured twenty-two Major Arcana cards, including *Il Matto*, The Fool. See ibid.: 24.

45. The Rider-Waite deck was created by Arthur Edward Waite (1857–1942) and Pamela Colman Smith (1878–1951), both of whom were members of the Hermetic Order of the Golden Dawn. For Waite's biography, see R. A. Gilbert, *A. E. Waite: Magician of Many Parts* (Crucible, Wellingborough, UK 1987); for Colman Smith's biography, see M. K. Greer, *Women of the Golden Dawn* (Park Street Press, Rochester, Vermont 1985): 406–409.

46. See, for example, *Ishbel's Temple of Isis Egyptian Tarot* (Llewellyn Publications, St. Paul, Minnesota 1989).

47. See Decker, Depaulis, and Dummett, *A Wicked Pack of Cards*: 57.

48. Ibid.: 58.

49. Ibid.: 59–60.

50. Ibid.: 61.

51. Kaplan, *Tarot Classic*: 35.

52. Published in Amsterdam and Paris in 1783.

53. Kaplan, *Tarot Classic*: 42.

54. C. McIntosh, *Eliphas Lévi and the French Occult Revival* (Rider, London 1972): 51.

55. Kaplan, *Tarot Classic*: 45.

56. Lévi's personal set of cards was catalogued for sale in 1940 through Dorbon's, a well-known Parisian antique book dealer. See Decker, Depaulis, and Dummett, *A Wicked Pack of Cards*: 91. The deck had been heavily adorned with Hebrew letters, drawings, and personal comments.

57. Kaplan, *Tarot Classic*: 45.

58. *Dogme et rituel de la haute magie* was first published in one volume in Paris by Germer Baillière, 1856. See Kaplan, *Tarot Classic*: 46.

59. Quoted in Kaplan, *Tarot Classic*: 47.

60. *The Tarot of the Bohemians* was translated into English by A. P. Morton and published in London in 1892. A revised edition, edited by A. E. Waite, was published in 1910. The Tarot of Marseilles is an eighteenth-century French adaptation of earlier Italian Tarot decks. According to occult historian Fred Gettings, this deck was first printed by Nicholas Conver in Paris in 1761 but appears to be based on earlier versions produced by such printers as Arnoud (1748) and Dodal, whose designs were executed in the first decade

of the eighteenth century. See F. Gettings, *The Book of Tarot* (Triune/Trewin Copplestone, London 1973): 140.

61. All twenty-two cards of the Major Arcana are reproduced as line drawings in *The Tarot of the Bohemians*. See second revised edition with preface by A. E. Waite (Rider & Son, London 1919).

62. Volume 1 of *The Golden Dawn*, ed. I. Regardie (Aries Press, Chicago 1937) contains Frater S.R.M.D's (i.e., MacGregor Mathers's) "'Notes on the Tarot.'" Here Mathers writes quite explicitly: "In the Tree of Life in the Tarot, each path forms the connecting link between two of the Sephiroth" (see p. 141). Mathers then lists all twenty-two cards in the Major Arcana, together with a brief summation of their symbolism (pp.141–143).

CHAPTER 2

1. J. F. Newton, *The Builders: The Story and Study of Masonry* ([1914] George Allen & Unwin, London 1918): 173.

2. Ibid.: 175–176.

3. W. H. Harris and J. S. Levey (eds.), "Freemasonry" in *The New Columbia Encyclopedia* (Columbia University Press, New York 1975): 1007.

4. C. McIntosh, *The Rosicrucians: The History, Mythology, and Rituals of an Esoteric Order* (Weiser, York Beach, Maine 1997): 64.

5. According to Dr. Anderson's account, this first meeting in Covent Garden took place in 1716. J. Anderson, *The New Book of Constitutions* (London 1738); text of the meetings quoted in full in Newton, *The Builders*: 135–136.

6. Newton, *The Builders*: 136.

7. Harris and Levey (eds.), "Freemasonry."

8. Newton, *The Builders*: 72–73.

9. McIntosh, *The Rosicrucians*: 64.

10. Ibid.

11. Christopher McIntosh believes this particular theory may have originated with Abbé Barruel, an expatriate priest who took refuge in England to escape the ravages of the French Revolution. See C. McIntosh, *Eliphas Lévi and the French Occult Revival* (Rider, London 1972): 36–39, 62.

12. McIntosh, *The Rosicrucians*: 65.

13. Ibid.: 66.

14. Harris and Levey (eds.), "Freemasonry."

15. Newton, *The Builders*: 162 n.

16. Newton, *The Builders*: 17–18. Occult historian James Webb writes, somewhat cynically, with regard to Freemasonry: "a practical craft, that of stone-working, was made to bear a symbolic significance and all matter of weighty concepts about the destiny of the soul were allied to the Mason's tools." See J. Webb, *The Flight from Reason* (Macdonald, London 1971): 139.

17. This first edition did not contain an account of the 1716 and 1717 lodge gatherings which led to the formation of the Grand Lodge of England. Dr. Anderson rectified that omission in *The New Book of Constitutions* (London 1738).

18. C. W. Heckethorn, *The Secret Societies of All Ages and Countries*, vol. 2 ([1897] University Books, New York 1965): 16–17.

19. Ibid.: 3–7.

20. These pillars feature on the Major Arcana Tarot card of *The High Priestess*, where they are inscribed B (dark pillar) and J (light pillar).

21. Heckethorn, *The Secret Societies of All Ages and Countries*, vol.1 (University Books, New York 1965): 64–65. See Newton, *The Builders*: 40–43 for a Masonic interpretation of the Osiris/Isis myth.

22. Quoted in F. A. Yates, *The Rosicrucian Enlightenment* (Routledge & Kegan Paul, London 1972): 213.

23. Newton, *The Builders*: 192.

24. Quoted ibid.: 130.

25. The *Fama* had been circulating in manuscript form for some time, possibly as early as 1610. See McIntosh, *The Rosicrucians*: xviii.

26. See chapter 7.

27. See *The Fame and Confession of the Fraternity of R: C:, Commonly, of the Rosie Cross* [1652] by Eugenius Philalethes, in P. Allen (ed.), *A Christian Rosenkreutz Anthology* (Rudolf Steiner Publications, Blauvelt, New York 1968): 163–190.

The text of Eugenius Philalethes's translation begins as follows: "We, the Brethren of the Fraternity of the R.C., bestow our Greeting, Love and Prayers upon each and everyone who reads this our Fama of Christian intent. Seeing the only Wise and Merciful God in these latter days hath poured out so richly his mercy and goodness to Mankind, whereby we do attain more and more to the perfect knowledge of his Son Jesus Christ and *Nature*, that justly we may boast of the happy time, wherein there is not only discovered unto us the half part of the World, which was heretofore unknown & hidden, that he hath also made manifest unto us many wonderful, and never-heretofore seen, Works and Creatures of *Nature*, and more over hath raised men, imbued with great Wisdom, which might partly renew and reduce all Arts (in thus our Age spotted and imperfect) to perfection; so that finally Man might thereby understand his own Nobleness and Worth, and why he is called *Microcosmus*, and how far his knowledge extendeth in Nature."

28. Ibid.: 164, 166, 167, 168–169. The four members are three brothers and himself, the others being Brothers G. V., J. A., and J. O.

29. Ibid.: 169, 173.

30. Ibid.: 173, 174. Interestingly, Paracelsus is not claimed in the *Fama* as a member of the R. C. Fraternity.

31. Ibid.: 175.

32. Ibid.: 172, 177. See also Yates, *The Rosicrucian Enlightenment*: 44.

33. Fludd defended the Rosicrucians in two texts: *Apologia compendiaria fraternitatem de Rosae Cruce*, published by Gottfried Basson, Leiden 1616 and *Tractatus Apologeticus Integritatem Societatis de Rosea Cruce*, Basson, Leiden 1617. See J. Godwin, *Robert Fludd: Hermetic Philosopher and Surveyor of Two Worlds* (Thames & Hudson, London 1979): 10, and Yates, *The Rosicrucian Enlightenment*: 74–77.

34. Text quoted in F. King, *Ritual Magic in England* (Neville Spearman, London 1970): 15–16.

35. Yates, *The Rosicrucian Enlightenment*: 45, 47, 48.

36. Ibid.: 49.

37. Except for Trajano Boccalini. who had authored *Allgemeine und General Reformation, der gantzen weiten Welt.*

38. McIntosh, *The Rosicrucians*: xix.

39. Yates, *The Rosicrucian Enlightenment*: 39.

40. Rosencreutz refers to himself by name during the "Second Day" cycle. See E. Foxcroft, "The Hermetic Romance, The Chymical Wedding," in P. Allen (ed.), *A Rosicrucian Anthology*: 83.

41. McIntosh, *The Rosicrucians*: xix.

42. P. Allen, "The English Translation of the Chymical Wedding," in *A Rosicrucian Anthology*: 61–62. Allen maintains that the original German manuscript existed as early as 1603 (ibid.: 57).

43. F. A. Yates compares this to the Book of Genesis (see *The Rosicrucian Enlightenment*: 60), but it is worth noting that the medieval Kabbalists believed that the Creation account in Genesis is itself an allegory relating to the sacred emanations from the Godhead which manifest as the forms of Creation through the seven lower *sephiroth* on the Tree of Life.

44. The solar disc and lunar crescent are alchemical symbols of King Sol and Queen Luna, the archetypal male and female principles, respectively. See L. Abraham, *A Dictionary of Alchemical Imagery* (Cambridge University Press, Cambridge 1998): 119, 185.

45. Foxcroft, "The Hermetic Romance, The Chymical Wedding": 80.

46. According to the alchemist Paracelsus, salt is one of the three "first principles," the other two being sulphur and mercury. Paracelsus maintained that all metals contained all three principles. Salt represented the "body," sulphur the "soul," and mercury the "spirit." See Abraham, *A Dictionary of Alchemical Imagery*: 176.

47. In alchemy, the phoenix is a symbol of renewal and resurrection, and is closely linked to the attainment of the Philosopher's Stone, the elixir of life (see ibid.: 152). As a resurrection symbol, the phoenix is also associated with Christ.

48. In medieval alchemy, the so-called Great Work (*summum bonum*) is an expression used to describe mastery of the secrets of transmutation, especially the power to transform base metals into gold. See D. W. Hauck, *The Emerald Tablet* (Penguin Putnam, New York 1999): 152–153.

49. Foxcroft, "The Hermetic Romance, The Chymical Wedding": 156.

50. Ibid.: 159.

51. Yates, *The Rosicrucian Enlightenment*: 65.

52. Ibid.: 64–65.

53. McIntosh, *The Rosicrucians*: 51.

54. Both works were published by Luca Jennis in Frankfurt and stressed that the R. C. Brotherhood really existed. In *Symbola Aureae Mensae* in particular, Maier referred to the "all-wisdom of Hermes" and the sacredness of the "Virgin," or "Queen Chemia," concluding with a Hermetic hymn of regeneration. See Yates, *The Rosicrucian Enlightenment*: 84–85.

55. Ibid.: 85.

56. Abraham, *A Dictionary of Alchemical Imagery*: 145.

57. Allen (ed.), *A Christian Rosenkreutz Anthology*.

58. According to the *Hermetica*, the fabled tablet of emerald, *Tabula Smaragdina*, was found clasped in the hands of the corpse of Hermes Trismegistus, the mythic founder of the Hermetic tradition. The table was said to contain the essential wisdom teaching of the Hermetic and alchemical traditions.

59. See Allen (ed.), *A Rosicrucian Anthology*: 244 (image), 246 (text) and also McIntosh, *The Rosicrucians*: 59. Part of the explanatory text in *A Rosicrucian Anthology* reads in translation:

> Three separate shields are to be seen,
> And on them are eagle, lion and free star,
> And painted in their very midst,
> Artfully stands an imperial globe.
> Heaven and Earth in like manner
> Are also placed here intentionally,
> And between the hands outstretched toward each other
> Are to be seen the symbols of metals.
> And in the circle surrounding the picture
> Seven words are to be found inscribed.
> Therefore I shall now tell
> What each meaneth particularly
> And then indicate without hesitation
> How it is called by name.
> Therein is a secret thing of the Wise
> In which is to be found great power.
> And how to prepare it will also
> Be described in the following:
> The three shields together indicate
> *Sal, Sulphur* and *Mercurium* [given elsewhere as *Mercurius*].
> The *Sal* hath been one *Corpus* that
> Is the very last one in the Art.
> The Sulphur henceforth is the soul
> Without which the body can do nothing.
> *Mercurius* is the spirit of power,
> Holding together both body and soul,
> Therefore it is called a medium
> Since whatever is made without it hath no stability,
> For soul and body could not die
> Should spirit also be with them.
> And soul and spirit could not be
> Unless they had a body to dwell in,
> And no power had body or spirit
> If the soul did not accompany them. (246)

60. McIntosh, *The Rosicrucians*: 67.

61. See S. L. MacGregor Mathers (trans.), *The Kabbalah Unveiled* (Redway, London 1887); and, for van Helmont, see H. S. Redgrove, *Alchemy: Ancient and Modern*, second revised edition (Rider, London 1922): 77.

62. McIntosh, *The Rosicrucians*: 67.

63. Ibid.: 82–83.

64. See chapter 7.

65. For the nine grades in the Gold-und Rosenkreuz Order, see McIntosh, *The Rosicrucians*: 70.

66. Ibid.

67. A full and detailed account of this meeting is included in McIntosh, *Eliphas Lévi and the French Occult Revival*: 116–122. It was first published in *The Rosicrucian and Red Cross*, May 1873.

68. King, *Ritual Magic in England*: 28.

69. The ritual grades of the Societas Rosicruciana in Anglia did not derive from the Gold-und Rosenkreuz Order alone. According to Christopher McIntosh, Robert Wentworth Little and Kenneth Mackenzie also incorporated ritual grades from the Societas Rosicruciana in Scotia into their new ritual structure. See McIntosh, *The Rosicrucians*: 98.

70. Dr. W. R. Woodman had succeeded Robert Wentworth Little as Supreme Magus of the Societas Rosicruciana in Anglia, which emphasises the historical connection between the SRIA and the Golden Dawn.

71. Quoted in J. J. Bode, *Starke Erweise* (Göschen, Leipzig 1788): 25. Christopher McIntosh comments on the Gnostic flavor of this particular statement: "This passage confirms . . . the Gnostic character of the Gold-und Rosenkreuz. The reference to light which has been buried in dross as a result of a primal curse, or fall, is very similar to the kind of language used by the Gnostic sects of the early Christian era." See *The Rosicrucians*: 75.

72. See McIntosh, *Eliphas Lévi and the French Occult Revival*, especially chapters 13, 14, and 15.

73. See Appendix G, "The Golden Dawn's Official History Lecture" in King, *Ritual Magic in England*: 212–217.

74. Ibid. Surprisingly, there is no mention of Robert Wentworth Little's Masonic colleague Kenneth Mackenzie in the Golden Dawn History Lecture, despite Mackenzie's meeting with Lévi in Paris in 1861.

75. First published in Paris by Germer Baillière in 1856.

76. First published in Paris by Germer Baillière in 1860.

77. First published in Paris by Alcan in 1861.

78. A. E. Waite's translation of *Dogme et rituel de la haute magie* was published by the London firm Redway in 1896, and his translation of *Histoire de la magie* was published by Rider & Co., London, 1913. A. E. Waite had earlier prepared a digest of Lévi's writings titled *The Mysteries of Magic*, drawing on a variety of sources and covering such subjects as ceremonial magic, the "hierarchy of spirits," the symbolism of the Tarot, the Hermetic tradition, and Mesmerism. This volume was published by Redway in 1886.

79. *The Key of the Mysteries* was first published in book form by Rider & Co. in London in 1959, twelve years after Crowley's death. Crowley had negotiated the contract

with Ralph Shirley of Rider & Co. in the early 1920s but for some reason the book did not appear in volume form until 1959, long after Ralph Shirley had sold the Rider imprint to Hutchinson in 1925.

80. Lawrence Sutin, author of the recent biography, *Do What Thou Wilt: A Life of Aleister Crowley* (St. Martin's Press, New York 2000), writes (p. 56) that "Lévi died in May 1875, some four months before Crowley was born. Crowley would, nonetheless, later claim Lévi as one of his previous incarnations, Lévi's soul having passed into the fetus Crowley *in utero*." Crowley actually refers to his claim in his *Confessions*, where he writes about various events that "led me to the discovery that in my last incarnation I was Eliphas Lévi." See A. Crowley, *The Confessions of Aleister Crowley*, ed. J. Symonds and K. Grant (Hill and Wang, New York 1970): 190.

81. Volume 1 of *The Golden Dawn*, ed. I. Regardie (Aries Press, Chicago 1937), contains Frater S.R.M.D's (i.e., MacGregor Mathers's) "Notes on the Tarot." Here Mathers writes quite explicitly: "In the Tree of Life in the Tarot, each path forms the connecting link between two of the Sephiroth" (see p. 141).

82. *The Mysteries of Magic* was first published by Redway, London 1886. See A. E. Waite, "Biographical and Critical Essay" in *The Mysteries of Magic: A Digest of the Writings of Eliphas Lévi* (University Books, Secaucus, N.J. 1974): 39.

83. Waite, "Biographical and Critical Essay," 39, 40.

84. Ibid.: 41. Azoth is an alchemical term for the Universal Medicine, the "first matter of metals" and the universal agent of transmutation, sometimes referred to as Mercurius. See Abraham, *A Dictionary of Alchemical Imagery*: 15, 124.

85. McIntosh, *Eliphas Lévi and the French Occult Revival*: 170.

86. Webb, *The Flight from Reason*: 107.

87. See ibid., and McIntosh, *The Rosicrucians*: 94.

88. These had the somewhat pedestrian titles "Biology," "Theory," and "Practice," and were overseen by the six senior members of the Order. See Webb, *The Flight from Reason*: 107.

89. McIntosh, *The Rosicrucians*: 94, 95.

90. Quoted in O. Wirth, *Stanislas de Guaita: souvenirs de son secrétaire*, (Edition du Symbolisme, Paris 1935).

CHAPTER 3

1. The Societas Rosicruciana in Anglia (SRIA) had been founded in England on 1 June 1867 by Robert Wentworth Little and W. J. Hughan, drawing on a system of grades employed by an Edinburgh-based group known as the Rosicrucian Society in Scotia. See R. A. Gilbert, *A. E. Waite: Magician of Many Parts* (Crucible, Wellingborough, UK 1987): 105. Other members of the SRIA included Frederick Hockley, Kenneth Mackenzie, and Sir Edward Bulwer-Lytton. See also R. A. Gilbert, *Revelations of the Golden Dawn: The Rise and Fall of a Magical Order* (Quantum/Foulsham, Slough UK 1997): 93.

2. Gilbert, *Revelations of the Golden Dawn*: 21.

3. Traditionally, women have not been admitted to the Order of Freemasons. However, there have been some exceptions to this rule. Count Alessandro di Cagliostro

(1743–1795) admitted women to his so-called Egyptian rite, the Duchess of Bourbon presided as grand mistress in the Grand Orient of France lodge (1775), and the Rite of Mizraim established Masonic lodges for both men and women as early as 1819. In so-called Co-Masonic orders, the rites follow orthodox Freemasonry, and men and women hold corresponding ranks.

4. Gilbert, *Revelations of the Golden Dawn*: 23. Nevertheless, the form of Christianity that was adopted in the Golden Dawn, namely, the spiritual rebirth symbolism of Christian Rosencreutz, was far from the mainstream, and few orthodox Christians would have embraced the concept of assigning Christ to Tiphareth in the center of the Kabbalistic Tree of Life alongside the many other "god-forms" and archetypal mythic images associated by the Golden Dawn members with the different spheres on the Tree of Life.

5. Franz Anton Mesmer (1734–1815) was born in Germany near Lake Constance and studied medicine at the University of Vienna. Here he embraced the then-current scientific view that a magnetic fluid permeated all aspects of life. Mesmer then came to the view that when this natural source of energy was blocked in the body, disease and ill-health would result. After graduating from the University of Vienna, Mesmer worked as a healer, first in Vienna and later in Paris, using magnets to "correct" imbalances in the human organism. He transmitted "healing energy" to his patients by making passes over his patients with his hands, or by using iron rods or wands that he had magnetized. A Royal Commission established in Paris in 1784 to test Mesmer's concept of "animal magnetism" (Mesmer's term for the magnetic life-energy), found that his healing method had no scientific basis but that some patients nevertheless responded positively because their own imagination provided the healing benefit. Mesmer is rightly regarded as one of the pioneers of psycho-somatic medicine and hypnotherapy. During the late-Victorian era of the Golden Dawn, the term "Mesmerist" was used to connote a hypnotist.

Spiritualism is the belief that the spirits of the dead can communicate with the living through a psychic medium. Seances are conducted to summon a particular deceased spirit, and the medium then enters a state of trance. The deceased spirit subsequently "possesses" the trance medium and either addresses the gathering directly or communicates through "automatic" writing, painting, or drawing. Spiritualism was a popular practice in late-Victorian Britain and was widely believed to provide proof of life after death.

On the final restriction, see Gilbert, *Revelations of the Golden Dawn*: 23.

6. See G. M. Harper, *Yeats's Golden Dawn* (Macmillan, London 1974): 9.

7. R. Hutton, *The Triumph of the Moon: A History of Modern Pagan Witchcraft* (Oxford University Press, Oxford 1999): 75. Hockley died in 1885.

8. Gilbert, *A. E. Waite: Magician of Many Parts*: 107.

9. See Gilbert, *Revelations of the Golden Dawn*: 30. Some members of the Golden Dawn itself also had their doubts about the authenticity of Anna Sprengel. In his autobiographical *Shadows of Life and Thought*, A. E. Waite—later a key member of the Golden Dawn—notes that Dr. Robert Felkin (who became a member of the Amen Ra Temple of the Golden Dawn in Edinburgh) was personally acquainted with Fraulein Sprengel's niece (she was one of his patients), and that both Fraulein Sprengel and her niece belonged to the German esoteric organization that had allegedly authorized Westcott to found the Golden Dawn. See A. E. Waite, *Shadows of Life and Thought* (Selwyn and Blount, London 1938): 220.

10. Mme Blavatsky established the so-called Esoteric Section of the Theosophical Society in London in October 1888 in direct response to the earlier formation of the Golden Dawn in February that year. See Gilbert, *Revelations of the Golden Dawn*: 39. Westcott had met Madame Blavatsky on several occasions, and they were on friendly terms, but this does not mean that they were not competitive with one another when it came to establishing their "occult authority" and seeking members for their respective organizations.

11. Quoted in E. Howe, *The Magicians of the Golden Dawn* (Routledge & Kegan Paul, London 1972): 12.

12. See F. King (ed.), *Astral Projection, Ritual Magic and Alchemy* (Neville Spearman, London 1971): 21.

13. See F. King, *Ritual Magic in England* (Neville Spearman, London 1970): 43, and Gilbert, *Revelations of the Golden Dawn*: 44.

14. Samuel Mathers and Moina Bergson married in 1890. Details of the Golden Dawn membership are included in Howe, *The Magicians of the Golden Dawn*; I. Colquhuon, *Sword of Wisdom: MacGregor Mathers and the Golden Dawn* (Neville Spearman, London 1975); Gilbert, *Revelations of the Golden Dawn*; and M. K. Greer, *Women of the Golden Dawn* (Park Street Press, Rochester, Vermont 1995). According to Ellic Howe (*The Magicians of the Golden Dawn*: 49), 170 people had been initiated into the Golden Dawn by 2 September 1893 and 315 by 1896. These figures include the membership of four Golden Dawn temples at that time: Isis-Urania in London; Osiris in Weston-super-Mare; Horus in Bradford, and Amen-Ra in Edinburgh, and after 1894, Mathers's Ahathoor temple in Paris.

15. King, *Ritual Magic in England*: 57–58.

16. Ibid.: 57.

17. According to Golden Dawn historian R. A. Gilbert, the Second Order, the *Rosae Rubeae et Aureae Crucis*, had existed since the earliest days of the Golden Dawn, but had worked no actual rituals. "Members who advanced to become adepti of the Second Order did so by means of passing examinations." See Gilbert, *A. E. Waite: Magician of Many Parts*: 107.

18. The magical names of the leading Golden Dawn members are provided in Harper, *Yeats's Golden Dawn*: 314–316.

19. King, *Ritual Magic in England*: 43.

20. Westcott must have had some interest in developing a Second Order in the Golden Dawn because he referred to a Rosicrucian $5°=6°$ ritual in a Golden Dawn "Flying Roll" document (no. XVI). See See King (ed.), *Astral Projection, Ritual Magic and Alchemy*: 91.

21. King, *Ritual Magic in England*: 43.

22. Moina Mathers was initiated into the Golden Dawn in March 1888. See Greer, *Women of the Golden Dawn*: 74.

23. Colquhoun, *Sword of Wisdom*: 81

24. King, *Ritual Magic in England*: 56.

25. Quoted ibid.: 44. The "Vault of the Adepts" was a ritual crypt representing the burial tomb of Christian Rosencreutz.

26. Gilbert, *A. E. Waite: Magician of Many Parts*: 112.

27. J. Bonner, *Qabalah* (Skoob Publishing, London 1995): 98–99.

28. King, *Ritual Magic in England*: 65.

29. Quoted in Howe, *The Magicians of the Golden Dawn*: 127.

30. Ibid.: 127. Emphasis in the original text.

31. Gilbert, *Revelations of the Golden Dawn*: 79.

32. See Hutton, *The Triumph of the Moon*: 76, and Gilbert, *Revelations of the Golden Dawn*: 48.

33. Publication of this text would later be financed by Frederick Leigh Gardner, a collector of esoterica, the grimoire being issued by John M. Watkins, London, in 1898, but it was not a commercial success in Britain. The Chicago-based De Laurence Company issued a pirated edition in the United States in 1932, and this was more successful. It was reprinted in 1939 and 1948.

34. Although only a clerk and infantryman by profession—he had been a private in the Hampshire Infantry Volunteers—Mathers believed that the Jacobite title of Count of Glen Strae had been bestowed on one of his ancestors by King James II.

35. Annie Horniman was providing Mathers with an allowance of £420 per annum. See Harper, *Yeats's Golden Dawn*: 163, n10.

36. The statement quoted earlier on the Secret Chief is an extract from one of his letters to her. See Howe, *The Magicians of the Golden Dawn*: 127. Ellic Howe confirmed in a letter to the Yeats scholar George Mills Harper in July 1971 that Annie Horniman terminated her financial allowance to Mathers in July 1896 with a final payment of £75. See Harper, *Yeats's Golden Dawn*: 163, n10.

37. According to Ithell Colquhoun, Mathers also derived income by providing "inside information" on the stock market and share prices on commission from would-be investors. See Colquhoun, *Sword of Wisdom*: 88.

38. Howe, *The Magicians of the Golden Dawn*: 127.

39. Quoted in Harper, *Yeats's Golden Dawn*: 15.

40. Letter to Mrs. Emery quoted ibid.: 21.

41. Ibid.: 22.

42. Crowley had been initiated into this degree by Mathers on 16 January 1900. See King, *Ritual Magic in England*: 67.

43. Harper, *Yeats's Golden Dawn*: 23. See also Howe, *The Magicians of the Golden Dawn*: 225.

44. Harper, *Yeats's Golden Dawn*: 23.

45. Five members of Isis-Urania's Second Order remained loyal to Mathers. They were: Dr. Edward Berridge (*Frater Resurgam*); George C. Jones (*Frater Volo Noscere*); Mrs. Alice Simpson (*Soror Perseverantia et Cura Quies*); Miss Elaine Simpson (*Soror Fidelis*), and Col. Webber (*Frater Non Sine Numine*). See King, *Ritual Magic in England*: 69.

46. Greer, *Women of the Golden Dawn*: 257. Greer explains how the Cup of Stolistes had been created as a sacred image based on the specific *sephiroth* from the Kabbalistic Tree of Life: "There were twelve people in the 'Sphere Working,' evenly divided into six women and six men. . . . Every Sunday from noon to 1pm in their own separate homes but working simultaneously, they began by creating an image of the Cup of Stolistes (Holy Grail) containing a burning heart that represented Tiphareth. The *sephiroth* of the 'middle pillar' (Kether, Daath, Tiphareth, Yesod, and Malkuth) were aligned in a central column, with Kether envisaged as a flame arising from the top of the Cup and Malkuth forming its

base. The remaining six *sephiroth* were doubled (to form twelve) and arched toward the four directions, creating a sphere around Tiphareth. Each person took one of the twelve sphere positions. envisioning themselves not only as the corresponding *sephira* but as an entire Tree of Life within that *sephira*. They saw themselves clothed in the color of the planet, bathed in an aura the color of the sephira, and they consciously projected appropriately colored rays of light to the nearest sephiroth on the central column and to the *sephiroth* above and below them." The visualizations focused the energy initially on the Second Order meeting rooms and were then expanded in range to cover the whole of London, the entire planet, and then the Universe itself. The purpose of these visualizations, says Greer, was to "transmute evil into good through the actions of the greater forces on the lesser" (ibid.).

47. Skrying, or scrying, is a form of divination in which the practitioner gazes at a shiny or polished surface to induce a trance-state in which images appear as part of a "psychic" communication. Crystal balls, mirrors, polished metal, and cups of clear liquid have all been used for the purpose of skrying. An essay titled "Of Skrying and Travelling in the Spirit-Vision," written by Soror V.N.R. (Moina Mathers) was included in Israel Regardie's monumental work, *The Golden Dawn*, vol. 4 (Aries Press, Chicago 1940): 29–42.

Color meditation is a practice whereby a practitioner visualizes various colors because of their perceived healing properties. Red, orange, and yellow are stimulants, whereas green, blue, indigo, and violet are relaxants, and each of these colors is believed to have specific healing effects. In the Golden Dawn, each of the different *sephiroth* on the Tree of Life was ascribed a color, for the purpose of visualization and meditation. In his work on Kabbalistic meditation, *The Middle Pillar*, Israel Regardie (who was a member of the Stella Matutina) provides the following correlations between specific colors and the *sephiroth* on the Tree: Kether: white; Chokmah: grey; Binah: black; Daas (Daath): lavender-blue; Chesed: blue; Gevurah (Geburah): red; Tipharas (Tiphareth): gold; Netzach: green; Hod: orange; Yesod: puce; Malkus (Malkuth): "mixed colors" (these are usually interpreted in the Golden Dawn system as citrine, olive, russet, and black). See I. Regardie, *The Middle Pillar* (Aries Press, Chicago 1945): 140. For the "mixed colours of Malkuth," see W. E. Butler, *The Magician: His Training and Work* (Aquarian Press, London 1959): 81.

On spirit communication, see Greer, *Women of the Golden Dawn*: 260.

48. Harper, *Yeats's Golden Dawn*: 28.

49. See Colquhoun, *Sword of* Wisdom: 191–192.

50. Israel Regardie (1907–1985), a one-time secretary to Aleister Crowley, joined the Stella Matutina in 1933, attained a ritual grade of Theoricus Adeptus Minor, and then left in December 1934. Between 1937 and 1940 he published a four-volume treatise, *The Golden Dawn* (Aries Press, Chicago), which included the bulk of the Golden Dawn's rituals and teachings, thereby providing an invaluable source of esoteric material that might otherwise have faded into obscurity. See www.hermeticgoldendawn.org/regardie.htm.

51. King, *Ritual Magic in England*: 97, 127, 128.

52. See Harper, *Yeats's Golden Dawn*: 77.

53. King, *Ritual Magic in England*: 57.

54. See I. Regardie (ed.), *The Golden Dawn*, vol.1 (Aries Press, Chicago 1937): 35–36.

55. Ibid.: 99–109.

56. Ibid.: 119–128.

57. Ibid.: 129–132.

58. Ibid.: 135–151.

59. This correlation did not derive from the Jewish mystical tradition but was proposed by the nineteenth-century French occultist Alphonse Louis Constant (1810–1875), better known as Eliphas Levi.

60. Regardie (ed.), *The Golden Dawn* , vol.1: 153–174.

61. For the last two subject areas, see ibid.: 158–159, 165.

62. Within the Golden Dawn system of ritual grades, this would not actually be achieved until the candidate had attained the Second Order 5°=6°degree associated with Tiphareth, the sphere of "spiritual rebirth."

63. Colquhoun, *Sword of Wisdom*: 104–105.

64. See A. Crowley, *Liber 777*, in *The Qabalah of Aleister Crowley* (Weiser, New York 1973): 1–10.

65. Crowley's *Liber 777* listings included several psychoactive plants: opium poppy, nux vomica, mandrake, peyote (*Anhalonium lewinii*), and damiana, a sure sign that these were his additions and not part of the original Mathers/ Westcott listings. Moly is a mythical plant: it was given by Hermes to Odysseus to protect him from the magic of Circe. See C. Ratsch, *The Dictionary of Sacred and Magical Plants* (Prism Press, Dorset, 1992): 127.

66. According to Jung's colleague, Dr. Jolande Jacobi, Jung at first referred to "primordial images'" and later to the "dominants of the collective unconscious." It was "only later that he called them archetypes." Jacobi notes that Jung took the term "archetype" from the *Corpus Hermeticum* and from *De Divinis nominibus* by Dionysius the pseudo-Areopagite. See J. Jacobi, *The Psychology of C. G. Jung* (Routledge & Kegan Paul, London 1942): 39.

67. A. Crowley, *Magick in Theory and Practice* ([1929], Castle Books, New York, n.d.): 120, 152–153.

68. E. Levi, *The Key of the Mysteries* (Rider, London 1959): 174.

69. The Kabbalistic sphere of Malkuth, for example, was associated with the earth, crops, the immediate environment, and living things. Yesod was linked symbolically to the Moon and was regarded as the sphere of "astral imagery," the dream-world, and the element Water. Yesod was also the seat of the sexual instincts and corresponded to the genital area when "mapped" upon the figure of Adam Kadmon, the archetypal human being. Hod was associated with the planet Mercury, representing intellect and rational thinking, and symbolized the orderly or structured aspects of the manifested universe. Netzach was linked to the planet Venus, and was said to complement the intellectual and orderly functions of Hod. While Hod could be considered clinical and rational, Netzach represented the arts, creativity, subjectivity, and the emotions. See also the mythological listings in *Liber 777* referred to above.

70. See I. Regardie, *The Tree of Life: A Study in Magic* (Rider, London 1932): 106.

71. A. Crowley, "The Initiated Interpretation of Ceremonial Magic" in S. L. Mathers (ed.), *The Goetia: The Lesser Key of Solomon the King* [1889], revised edition (Weiser, Boston 1997): 16.

72. G. G. Scholem mentions the Kabbalist Jehudah the Hasid who spoke of the holy spirit "having no form, but a voice,'" and he also refers to a medieval Kabbalistic document titled the "Book of Life" (c.1200 CE), which defines the divine will or "holy spirit" as the word of God, which is "inherent in all creatures." See G. G. Scholem, *Major Trends in Jewish Mysticism* (Schocken, New York 1961): 112.

73. F. Bardon, *The Practice of Magical Evocation* (Rudolf Pravica, Graz-Puntigam, Austria, 1967): 20; Crowley, *Magick in Theory and Practice*: 43.

74. See E. A. Wallis Budge (ed.), *Lefefa Sedek: The Bandlet of Righteousness* (Luzac, London 1929): 3.

75. Ibid.: 4.

76. Ibid.: 5.

77. A. Crowley, *Book Four* ([1913] Sangreal Foundation, Dallas 1972): 71.

78. D. Fortune, *Applied Magic* (Aquarian Press, London 1962): 56–57.

79. According to the Hermetic dictum, "As above, so below," the sacred nature of the Godhead (or Macrocosm) is mirrored in the individual (Microcosm). Aleister Crowley writes in *Magick in Theory and Practice* that "There is a single main definition of the object of all magical Ritual. It is the uniting of the Microcosm with the Macrocosm. The Supreme and Complete Ritual is therefore the Invocation of the Holy Guardian Angel, or, in the language of Mysticism, Union with God" (p. 11).

80. Crowley, *Book Four*: 57. Crowley also writes in *Magick in Theory and Practice* that "the first task of the Magician in every ceremony is . . . to render his Circle absolutely impregnable. If one littlest thought intrude upon the mind of the Mystic, his concentration is absolutely destroyed" (p. 101).

81. In their influential book *Techniques of High Magic: A Manual of Self-Initiation* (C. W. Daniel, London 1976), Francis King and Stephen Skinner describe invocation as "the process by which the trained magician 'calls down' into himself a particular force from the cosmos personified as a god. The physical manifestation of this process is the intoxication and possession of the magician by the god, so that the magician not only becomes one with the god but acts *as* the god, even with the power of that god" (p. 158).

82. Crowley, *Book Four*: 58.

83. Ibid.: 57, 58.

84. W. E. Butler (1898–1978), a colleague of Dion Fortune in the Fraternity of the Inner Light, offers the following definition of invocation and evocation: "In invocation we act in such a way as to attract the attention of some Being of a superior nature to our own, or some cosmic force of a higher order. In evocation we impose our will upon beings of a lesser order of existence and compel them to execute our wishes." See W. E. Butler, *Magic: Its Ritual Power and Purpose*, second edition (Aquarian Press, London 1958): 41.

85. By way of clarification: the ceremonial magician remains within the magical circle while evoking the spirit contained within the triangle. See King and Skinner, *Techniques of High Magic*: 178.

86. A magical seal is a motif produced by creating the magic number square of a planet in the Zodiac (e.g., Saturn) and then connecting the numbers in the square with a sequence of lines, thereby producing a graphic motif or "sigil." The magic number square itself is a square arranged so that the numbers in each row of the square add to the same

total in all directions. In ritual magic, the number square for each planet is known as its "kamea."

87. Mathers's editions of such grimoires as the *Goetia: the Book of Evil Spirits*, *The Sacred Magic of Abramelin the Mage*, and also *The Grimoire of Armadel* and *The Greater Key of Solomon*, have already been referred to above.

88. Crowley explored magical evocation and the Goetia with Golden Dawn member Allan Bennett (Frater Iehi Aour) in his Chancery Lane, London flat in 1898, and the following year acquired a manor house called Boleskine near Loch Ness in Scotland, so he could carry out the ritual evocations described in *The Book of the Sacred Magic of Abra-Melin the Mage*, the fifteenth-century magical grimoire that had been translated by MacGregor Mathers and published in 1898. See L. Sutin, *Do What Thou Wilt: A Life of Aleister Crowley* (St. Martin's Press, New York 2000): 64–72.

89. See Crowley, *Book Four*: 62–63.

90. Ibid.: 67.

91. Ibid.: 71.

92. Regardie (ed.), *The Golden Dawn*, vol.4: 37–39.

93. The Golden Dawn color for Pisces on the magical wand was crimson and not purple, as one would expect. See ibid.: 39.

94. Ibid.: 40.

95. The magical wand was associated in the Golden Dawn with the element Fire. See ibid.: 66. However, Francis King and Stephen Skinner maintain that the Golden Dawn ascription of the magical wand to the element Fire was a "blind,"' and that the sword, or dagger, should have been ascribed symbolically to Fire. King and Skinner associate the wand with the element Air. See King and Skinner, *Techniques of High Magic*: 60.

96. King and Skinner, *Techniques of High Magic*: 61.

97. Regardie (ed.), *The Golden Dawn*: 68.

98. Crowley, *Book Four*: 89–90.

99. Regardie (ed.), *The Golden Dawn*: 69; King and Skinner, *Techniques of High Magic*: 61; Crowley, *A Woman's Kabbalah*: 202. As the tenth and final emanation on the Kabbalistic Tree of Life, Malkuth represents the first step upon the mystical journey back to the Godhead and is associated with the ritual grade of Zelator ($1° = 10°$).

100. Crowley, *Book Four*: 99.

101. Ibid.: 108.110, 113, 111.

102. Ibid.: 112, 106, 107.

103. Quoted in King (ed.), *Astral Projection, Magic and Alchemy*: 73–74.

104. Details of two Tattva visions by Soror Vestigia (Moina Mathers) are included in Regardie (ed.), *The Golden Dawn*, vol.4: 43–46.

105. King (ed.), *Astral Projection, Magic and Alchemy*: 69.

106. Quoted in Regardie (ed.), *The Golden Dawn*, vol.4: 43n. The god-name HCOMA is not Kabbalistic but derives from an "angelic language" called Enochian, transcribed by the Elizabethan occultists Dr. John Dee (1527–1608) and Edward Kelley (1555–1595), and utilized in some Golden Dawn rituals and visualizations.

107. Quoted in King (ed.), *Astral Projection, Magic and Alchemy*: 66.

108. Ibid.: 67.

109. This is a specific allusion to the Golden Dawn Second Order ritual grade Adeptus Minor, associated with the Kabbalistic sphere of Tiphareth.

110. Quoted in King (ed.), *Astral Projection, Magic and Alchemy*: 58–59.

CHAPTER 4

1. MacGregor Mathers, the influential co-founder of the Golden Dawn, died in 1918.

2. The Witchcraft Act of 1735 was repealed in New South Wales by the Imperial Acts Application Act, 1969. See L. Hume, *Witchcraft and Paganism in Australia* (Melbourne University Press, Melbourne 1997): 224.

3. The movements influenced by Crowleyan *Thelema* and its various derivative include the Ordo Templi Orientis (O.T.O.) in the United States, the Typhonian O.T.O. in Britain, and the Church of Satan and the Temple of Set in the United States. Chaos Magick has also been strongly influenced by Crowley.

4. In the 2001 National Census for England and Wales, out of 79,404 neopagan respondents there were only 1,657 Druids, 508 Celtic pagans, and 93 followers of Asatrú (Odinist practitioners). See D. Evans, *The History of British Magick after Crowley* (Hidden Publishing, London 2007): 74.

5. See N. Drury, *The History of Magic in the Modern Age* (Constable, London 2000): 110.

6. *John Bull* used this headline on 24 March 1923, for an article deploring what it described as "the blasphemous and bestial ceremonies—or orgies" which had taken place in Crowley's Abbey of Thelema in Cefalu, Sicily. Crowley was also described in the same article as a "degenerate poet and occultist, traitor, drug fiend and Master of Black Magic."

7. R. Sutcliffe, "Left-Hand Path Ritual Magick," in G. Harvey and C. Hardman (eds.), *Pagan Pathways: A Guide to the Ancient Earth Traditions* (Thorsons, London 2000): 110.

8. Ibid.

9. See L. Sutin, *Do What Thou Wilt: A Life of Aleister Crowley* (St. Martin's Press, New York 2000): 91. Crowley also acknowledged the considerable Tantric knowledge of the occultist David Curwen, who later became a high-ranking member of the O.T.O. See Evans, *The History of British Magick after Crowley*: 288.

10. Born in the Ukraine, Madame Helena Petrovna Blavatsky (1831–1891) co-founded the Theosophical Society with Colonel Henry Steel Olcott in New York in 1875. After an unsuccessful marriage at the age of seventeen, Blavatsky traveled widely through Europe and the Middle East and claimed that she had been initiated by "Mahatmas," or spiritual Masters, into the secrets of esoteric mysticism. She believed that the Masters helped her write many of her major works, thereby providing the foundation for modern Theosophy. These works include *Isis Unveiled, The Secret Doctrine, The Key to Theosophy,* and *The Voice of Silence*. Madame Blavatsky presented herself to her followers as a powerful psychic medium, but it is likely that many of the psychic powers she claimed she had received from the Masters were clever deceptions. Her main contribution to mystical thought was the manner in which she sought to synthesize Eastern and Western philosophy and religion, thereby providing a framework for understanding universal occult teachings.

11. For the sheep and the goats, see Matthew 25:33.

12. V. Crabtree, "Left Hand Path Practices in the West," 2002, www.dpjs.co.uk/lefthandpath.html.

13. *Apollodorus*, Bibl.iii, 10, 3, 8–9, quoted in Evans, *The History of British Magick after Crowley*: 177.

14. Ibid.: 182–183.

15. A. E. Waite, *The Book of Ceremonial Magic* (Rider, London 1911): 16.

16. Chaos Magick, which dates from the late 1970s, was inspired initially by both Austin Osman Spare and Aleister Crowley. Its anarchistic and chthonic orientation, its pursuit of magical individualism, and its tendency toward antinomianism locate it on the "left-hand path" in contemporary Western magic.

17. Crabtree, "Left Hand Path Practices in the West."

18. Ibid. The LaVey quotation is from his key work, *The Satanic Bible*: "Book of Lucifer," para. 30.

19. Crabtree, "Left Hand Path Practices in the West."

20. Ibid.

21. General information statement from the Dragon Rouge, www.dragonrouge.net.

22. Ibid.

23. See D. Lee, review of Stephen E. Flowers, *Lords of the Left-Hand Path* (Runa-Raven Press, Smithville, Texas 1997), www.philhine.org.uk (including lengthy quotations from the text).

24. Sutin, *Do What Thou Wilt*: 69.

25. While he was at Cambridge University, Crowley changed his name from Edward Alexander Crowley to Aleister Crowley, by adopting a variant Gaelic spelling of his middle name. See ibid.: 48.

26. Ibid.: 65.

27. A. Crowley, *Magick in Theory and Practice* ([1929] Routledge & Kegan Paul, London 1973): xv.

28. Ibid.: xvi.

29. Ibid.: xvii.

30. Ibid.: 4.

31. Ibid.

32. The Secret Chiefs of the Golden Dawn were high-ranking spiritual beings who, it was claimed, provided guidance and inspiration to the leaders of the Inner Order. MacGregor Mathers, in particular, emphasized their importance.

33. Crowley, *Magick in Theory and Practice*: 69.

34. Sutin, *Do What Thou Wilt*: 118.

35. Crowley believed that Aiwass was messenger from the Egyptian deity Horus, the falcon-headed god that had the sun and the moon for his eyes. Crowley came to believe that he was Lord of the Aeon of Horus, which began in 1904, replacing Christianity and the other major religious traditions of both West and East.

36. Although a psychoanalytic perspective on why there should have been an anti-Christian component to Crowley's spiritual revelation is outside the scope of this book, Crowley's new role as the Beast 666 is almost certainly related to his restrictive and oppressive Christian upbringing within a Plymouth Brethren family: Crowley's entire

magical philosophy is grounded in notions of personal freedom and a libertine philosophy.

37. Babalon was Crowley's unique spelling for the Scarlet Woman of the Apocalypse, as revealed in *The Book of the Law*. The spelling "Babalon" has a Kabbalistic numerical value of 156 which, according to Crowley's disciple Kenneth Grant, equates with the number of shrines in the City of Pyramids. Grant maintains that the name Babalon means "Gateway of the Sun, or solar-phallic power"—see Grant, *Nightside of Eden* (Muller, London 1977): 259—thereby revealing its symbolic significance to practitioners of sex-magick.

38. See J. Symonds, *The Great Beast: The Life and Magick of Aleister Crowley* (Mayflower/Granada, London 1973): 81.

39. The Boulak Museum no longer exists; the antiquities housed in this museum were transferred to the National Museum, Cairo; ibid.: 81n.

40. Ibid.: 82.

41. Ibid.

42. The text of *The Book of the Law* is included as an appendix in *The Magical Record of the Beast 666*, ed. J. Symonds and K. Grant (Duckworth, London 1972).

43. See stanzas I: 15 and 16 of *Liber Al vel Legis*, in the appendix to *The Magical Record of the Beast 666*, ibid.: 303.

44. See Crowley, *Magick in Theory and Practice*: 12.

45. See stanza I: 40 of *Liber Al vel Legis*, in the appendix to J. Symonds and K. Grant (eds.), *The Magical Record of the Beast 666*: 304. See also *The Comment* that comes at the conclusion of *Liber Al vel Legis*, ibid.: 315.

46. Crowley, *Magick in Theory and Practice*: xv.

47. Ibid.

48. K. Grant, *The Magical Revival* (Muller, London 1972): 20.

49. See stanza I: 49 of *Liber Al vel Legis*, in the appendix to J. Symonds and K. Grant (eds.), *The Magical Record of the Beast 666*: 305.

50. See J. Symonds and K. Grant (eds.), *The Confessions of Aleister Crowley* (Hill and Wang, New York, 1970): 22.

51. See appendix containing the text of *Liber Al vel Legis* in J. Symonds and K. Grant (eds.), *The Magical Record of the Beast 666*: 314.

52. Ibid.: stanzas III: 44–45.

53. Grant, *The Magical Revival*: 45. Grant elaborates on this point later in the same book: "In sexual congress each coition is a sacrament of peculiar virtue since it effects a transformation of consciousness through annihilation of apparent duality. To be radically effective the transformation must be also an initiation. Because of the sacramental nature of the act, each union must be magically directed . . . the ritual must be directed to the transfinite and non-individualised consciousness represented by Egyptian Nuit. . . . The earthly Nuit is Isis, the Scarlet Woman" (ibid.: 145).

54. Crowley's insatiable search for sexual partners is described in Colin Wilson's *Aleister Crowley: The Nature of the Beast* (Aquarian Press, Wellingborough 1987).

55. See appendix containing the text of *Liber Al vel Legis* in J. Symonds and K. Grant (eds.), *The Magical Record of the Beast 666*: 311–312.

56. Sutin, *Do What Thou Wilt*: 292.

57. King maintains that Crowley joined the O.T.O. in 1911. See King (ed.), *The Secret Rituals of the O.T.O.*: 28. However, according to the O.T.O. *History of the Ordo Templi Orientis* (www. oto-usa.org/history html), Crowley was admitted to the first degrees of the O.T.O in 1910. Reuss made frequent trips to England. The reference to "the germ of life" is on p. 226 of King's book.

58. King (ed.), *The Secret Rituals of the O.T.O.*: 225.

59. John Michael Greer and Carl Hood have suggested (*Gnosis* magazine 43, Spring 1997) that there may have been a secret sexual dimension to the rituals of the Golden Dawn, but in my view their arguments are unconvincing. MacGregor Mathers, arguably the most influential figure in the formation of the Golden Dawn, valued celibacy and virginity, and never consummated his marriage to Moina Bergson (see Colquhoun, *Sword of Wisdom*: 54).

60. J. G. Melton, "The Origins of Modern Sex Magick" (Institute for the Study of American Religion, Evanston, Illinois, June 1985): 3.

61. These writings included such texts as *Liber A'ash* (*Equinox* 1: 6, September 1911: 33–39), *Liber Cheth* (*Equinox* 1: 6, September 1911: 23–27) and *Liber Stellae Rubae* (*Equinox* 1:7, March 1912: 29–38).

62. See Melton, "The Origins of Modern Sex Magick."

63. The Second Order rituals related to the Kabbalistic *sephiroth* Tiphareth, Geburah, and Chesed on the Kabbalistic Tree of Life.

64. F. King, *Ritual Magic in England* (Spearman, London 1970): 117.

65. See stanza 1:15 of *Liber Al vel Legis* in J. Symonds and K. Grant (eds.), *The Magical Record of the Beast 666*: 303.

66. Neuburg's magical diary describes how Crowley on one occasion rebuked him by giving him thirty-two strokes of a gorse switch, drawing blood. "He is apparently a homosexual sadist," wrote Neuburg, "for he performed the ceremony with obvious satisfaction." Quoted in Wilson, *Aleister Crowley: The Nature of the Beast*: 91. See also J. O. Fuller, *The Magical Dilemma of Victor Neuburg* (W. H. Allen, London 1965), where Neuburg's diaries are also discussed in detail.

67. Enochian magic derives historically from the work of Elizabethan occultists Dr. John Dee (1527–1608) and Edward Kelley (1555–1595), who met in 1581. Dee and Kelley made use of wax tablets called almadels, engraved with magical symbols, and also used a large number of forty-nine-inch squares filled with letters of the alphabet. Nearby, on his table, Kelley had a large crystal stone upon which he focused his concentration and entered a state of trance reverie. Kelley maintained that while he was in a state of trance "angels" would appear, and they in turn would point to various letters on the squares. These letters were written down by Dee as Kelley called them out. When these invocations were completely transcribed, Kelley then reversed their order, believing that the angels had communicated them backward to avoid unleashing the magical power which they contained. Dee and Kelley considered that the communications formed the basis of a new language known as Enochian. These magical conjurations were subsequently incorporated into magical practice by the ritual magicians of the Hermetic Order of the Golden Dawn, who used them to induce trance visions on the "astral plane."

68. These magical visions are described in A. Crowley, *The Vision and the Voice* ([1929] Sangreal Foundation, Dallas, Texas 1972).

69. Crowley, *The Confessions of Aleister Crowley*: 621. According to Lawrence Sutin, Crowley was deeply ashamed of his homosexuality because it "conflicted with his status as a manly gentleman coming of age" (*Do What Thou Wilt*: 43). Crowley was also well aware of the famous libel action that led to the imprisonment of Oscar Wilde. This had occurred in 1895, during Crowley's first year at Cambridge University.

70. Spare was briefly a member of the O.T.O. circa 1910, but soon quarreled with Crowley and thereafter sought to avoid him. Even though Spare became friendly with Thelemite Kenneth Grant in the late 1940s, Spare and Crowley were never reconciled. See chapter 5, and also K. Grant and S. Grant, *Zos Speaks!: Encounters with Austin Osman Spare* (Fulgur, London 1998).

71. King (ed.), *The Secret Rituals of the O.T.O.*: 28. See also note 57 above.

72. Crowley writes in *The Confessions*: "I protested that I knew no such secret. He said, 'But you have printed it in the plainest language.' I said that I could not have done so because I did not know it. He went to the bookshelves and, taking out a copy of *The Book of Lies*, pointed to a passage in the despised chapter." See Crowley, *The Confessions of Aleister Crowley*: 710.

73. A. Crowley, *The Book of Lies* ([1912] Hayden Press, Ilfracombe, Devon 1962): 82.

74. Symonds, *The Great Beast: The Life and Magick of Aleister Crowley*: 182n.

75. Crowley later visited Berlin, where he received instructional documents from the German O.T.O. He was also granted the grandiose title "King of Ireland, Iona and all the Britains within the Sanctuary of the Gnosis" and took Baphomet as his new magical name. Later Crowley adapted the Ninth degree of the O.T.O so that it identified the priest and priestess as Osiris and Isis, "seeking Nuit and Hadit through the vagina and the penis." He also developed a series of homosexual magical rituals with Victor Neuburg featuring invocations to Thoth-Hermes. At one point in these rituals, which became known collectively as the *Paris Working*, Crowley scourged Neuburg on the buttocks and cut a cross on his chest. For details, see Fuller, *The Magical Dilemma of Victor Neuburg*: 203–216.

76. See F. King (ed.), *The Secret Rituals of the O.T.O.*: 29. King points out that Crowley was not accepted by a majority of German O.T.O. members until 1925. The Order was suppressed by the Nazis in 1937.

77. P-R. Koenig, "Introduction to the Ordo Templi Orientis,'" www.user.cyberlink. ch/~koenig/intro.htm.

78. Ibid.

79. P-R. Koenig suggests that Kellner may have been one of the twelve co-founders of the Hermetic Brotherhood of Light in Boston/Chicago in 1895. See www.user.cyberlink. ch/~koenig/spermo.htm. See also H. B. Urban, *Magia Sexualis: Sex, Magic and Liberation in Modern Western Esotericism* (University of California Press, Berkeley 2006): 96.

80. Urban, *Magia Sexualis*: 97.

81. Ibid.: 99.

82. T. Reuss, *Lingam-Yoni* (Verlag Willsson, Berlin and London 1906).

83. P-R. Koenig, "Spermo-Gnostics and the Ordo Templi Orientis," www.user. cyberlink.ch/~koenig/spermo.htm.

84. Urban, *Magia Sexualis*: 101.

85. Koenig, "Introduction to the Ordo Templi Orientis."

86. Sabazius X° and AMT IX°, *History of Ordo Templi Orientis* (U.S. Grand Lodge, 2006): 12–13. www.oto-usa.org/history.html.

87. Koenig, "Introduction to the Ordo Templi Orientis,"

88. Sabazius X° and AMT IX°, *History of Ordo Templi Orientis*: 17.

89. Published in *Equinox* 3.1, March 1919—the so called *Blue Equinox.*

90. Sabazius X° and AMT IX°, *History of Ordo Templi Orientis*: 17.

91. H. B. Urban, "*Magia Sexualis*: Sex, Secrecy and Liberation in Modern Western Esotericism," *Journal of the American Academy of Religion* vol. 72 no. 3 (September 2004): 711.

92. P-R. Koenig, "Spermo-Gnostics and the Ordo Templi Orientis."

93. A. Crowley, *De Arte Magica*, ch. 12, www.skepticfiles.org.

94. Ibid., ch. 13.

95. Ibid.

96. Ibid., ch. 16.

97. See King (ed.), *The Secret Rituals of the O.T.O.*: 207.

98. Baphomet was Crowley's magical name after he assumed leadership of the British branch of the O.T.O. in 1912. It is also the name of a demonic deity represented graphically by Eliphas Lévi as a goat-headed god with wings, breasts, and an illuminated torch between his horns. The Knights Templar were accused by King Philip IV of France of worshiping Baphomet, although few members of the Order admitted to this ritual practice. It has been suggested that the name Baphomet may be a corruption of Mohammed.

99. See A. Crowley, "Emblems and Modes of Use," private text intended for the Ninth degree O.T.O., www.aethyria.com.

100. See Frater Osiris, "Analysis of the Mass of the Phoenix," Seattle 2003, www.hermetic.com/osiris, and also A. Rhadon, "Sex, Religion and Magick: A Concise Overview,' 2004, www.baymoon.com.

101. Frater Osiris, "Analysis of the Mass of the Phoenix."

102. See Frater Osiris, "Analysis of Liber XXXVI, *The Star Sapphire*," Seattle 2004, www.hermetic.com/osiris.

103. A .Crowley, chapter 69, "The Way to Succeed—and the Way to Suck Eggs," in *The Book of Lies* ([1912], Haydn Press, Ilfracombe, Devon 1962): 148.

104. Frater Osiris, "Analysis of Liber XXXVI, *The Star Sapphire*."' Frater Osiris is probably referring to Crowley's sex magic text *Emblems and Modes of Use*, where it is suggested that the "elixir" should be consumed in this way.

105. This is Crowley's expression. IAO was one of the sacred names ascribed to the archon Abraxas, a planetary deity associated with Basilides, a Gnostic philosopher who lived and taught in Alexandria c. 125–140 CE. The name Abraxas in Greek letters has a numerical value of 365, thereby linking the deity to the number of days in a year. Abraxas was said to rule over 365 heavens and was depicted on numerous charms, amulets, and talismans in order to attract good luck.

106. A. Crowley, *Energized Enthusiasm: A Note on Theurgy*, www.luckymojo.com/esoteric/occultism/magic/ceremonial/crowley. htm. This text was first published in *Equinox* 1.9 (March 1913), and was republished by Weiser, New York 1976.

107. Ibid.

108. See the section in the present chapter dealing with altered states of consciousness in modern magical practice.

109. See L. Abraham, entry for the "Chemical Wedding" of King Sol and Queen Luna, *A Dictionary of Alchemical Imagery* (Cambridge University Press, Cambridge 1998): 36.

110. A. Crowley, *Gnostic Mass* (*Liber XV, Ecclesiae Gnosticae Catholicae Canon Missae*), composed in Moscow in 1913.

111. A. Crowley, Liber XVIV, *The Mass of the Phoenix* (1912), www.thelemicgoldendawn.org/rituals/phoenix.htm.

112. In *Liber Aleph*, Crowley writes: "Neglect not the daily Miracle of the Mass, either by the Rite of the Gnostic Catholic Church, or that of the Phoenix." Quoted in Frater Osiris, *On the Mass of the Phoenix: An Analysis*, Seattle 2003, www.hermetic.com/osiris.

113. The Mark of the Beast is "the sign of the Sun and Moon or Cross and Circle conjoined." See www.thelemicgoldendawn.org/rituals/phoenix.htm.

114. Frater Osiris, *On the Mass of the Phoenix*.

115. First published in the Thelemite journal *Mezla* vol. 1 no. 111, 1 (Ithaca, New York 1985).

116. Crowley, *Emblems and Modes of Use*. My italics—Crowley generally presents his magickal texts from the viewpoint of the male practitioner, even when a woman is involved.

117. Ibid.

118. Ibid.

119. Ibid.

120. Crowley, *Liber A'Aash vel Capricorni Pneumatici (Liber CCCLXX)*, first published in *Equinox*, vol.1 no.6. See listing of key Crowley texts on sex magic published on line at www.hollyfeld.org. *Liber A'ash-vel Capricorni Pneumatici* heads the list. A "Class A" document in the Argenteum Astrum was one that could not be altered or modified in the slightest way and had to be adhered to by members strictly as presented by Crowley.

121. Melton, "The Origins of Modern Sex Magick."

122. R. North, Introduction to P. B. Randolph, *Sexual Magic*, tr. M. de Naglowska (Magickal Childe, New York 1988); original French-language text: *Magia Sexualis*, Paris 1931; www.supoervirtual.com.br.

123. Urban, *Magia Sexualis*: 63.

124. North, Introduction to P. B. Randolph, *Sexual Magic*.

125. Melton, "The Origins of Modern Sex Magick"; C. Yronwode, *The Reverend Hargrave Jennings and Phallism*, www.luckymojo.com.

126. Yronwode, *The Reverend Hargrave Jennings*.

127. Randolph received this initiation from an Islamic sect usually referred to as the Nusairi, who live mainly in the mountains near the city of Latakia in Syria. These sect members were formerly known as the Namiriya, or Ansariyya—a reference to the mountainous region where they come from. Randolph's reference to "Ansairetic Mysteries" is based on an early variant spelling.

128. Scrying is a form of divination using the trance state to achieve a magical outcome.

129. North, Introduction to P. B. Randolph, *Sexual Magic*.

130. P. B. Randolph, *Eulis!* (Randolph, Toledo, Ohio 1873, republished 1896).

131. Urban, *Magia Sexualis*: 65.

132. P. B. Randolph, *Eulis!*: 48, 218.

133. See Urban, *Magia Sexualis*: 67, and C. Yronwode, "Paschal Beverly Randolph and the Ansairetic Mysteries," www.luckymojo.com. Also see Randolph, *Magia Sexualis*: 76–77; this is a composite work published in an English-language edition (see n. 122 above).

134. B. H. Springett, *Secret Sects of Syria and Lebanon* (Allen & Unwin, London 1922). See also n. 127 above.

135. P. B. Randolph, *Eulis!*, quoted in C. Yronwode, "Paschal Beverly Randolph and the Ansairetic Mysteries." Emphasis in the original text.

136. See P. B. Randolph, *The Ansairetic Mystery: A New Revelation Concerning Sex!* (Toledo, Ohio, c.1973–1774); republished in J. P. Deveney, *Paschal Beverly Randolph: A Nineteenth-Century American Spiritualist, Rosicrucian and Sex Magician* (State University of New York Press, Albany 1997): 319–325.

137. Ibid.

138. Urban, *Magia Sexualis*: 72.

139. This is especially true of Crowley during his visit to the United States around the time of World War I. Crowley arrived in New York in October 1914 and during his first year in America experimented with a range of sexual partners—both male and female—in the IX° and XI° O.T.O. sex magick rituals. This included the use of prostitutes in his magical rituals. See Sutin, *Do What Thou Wilt*: 244.

140. Urban, *Magia Sexualis*: 73.

141. Crowley, *Energized Enthusiasm: A Note on Theurgy*.

142. According to Joscelyn Godwin, the original French-language edition of this book was probably not written by Randolph himself but adapted by M. de Naglowska in Paris, where the book was first published in 1931. See letter dated 13 October 1994 from Godwin to P-R. Koenig quoted in "Correct Gnosticism," www.user.cyberlink.ch/~koenig/correct.htm.

143. M. A. Kazlev, "The Teachings of Max Théon," www.kheper.net/topics/Theon/Theon.htm.

144. J. Godwin, C. Chanel, and J. P. Deveney, *The Hermetic Brotherhood of Luxor* (Weiser, York Beach, Maine 1995): 6, 92–97.

145. S. Scarborough, "The Influence of Egypt on the Modern Western Mystery Tradition: The Hermetic Brotherhood of Luxor," *Journal of the Western Mystery Tradition*, No.1 (Autumn 2001): 2.

146. J. Godwin, letter dated 13 October 1994 to P-R. Koenig quoted in "Correct Gnosticism." See also T. A. Greenfield, "Peter Davidson, Occultist," *Agape*, 2 May 2003.

147. Greenfield, "Peter Davidson, Occultist."

148. P-R. Koenig, "Correct Gnosticism."

149. These Gnostic sects include the Carpocratians, the Ophites, and the Phibionites, and they are of interest because of their libertine tendencies, chthonic snake-imagery, and ritual consumption of blood and semen, respectively. The Phibionites provide arguably the most intriguing parallel to Thelema in relation to Crowley's sacramental sex-magick practices. See also Koenig, "'Spermo-Gnostics and the O.T.O," and Koenig, "'Correct Gnosticism."

150. M. Eliade, *Occultism, Witchcraft, and Cultural Fashions* (University of Chicago Press, Chicago 1976): 109; Koenig, "Spermo-Gnostics and the O.T.O."

151. Eliade, *Occultism, Witchcraft, and Cultural Fashions*: 113.

152. Epiphanius, *Panarion* 26: 9, 3–4.

153. Ibid.: 26: 17, 1 ff., quoted in Eliade, *Occultism, Witchcraft, and Cultural Fashions*: 110.

154. Crowley, *Gnostic Mass*.

155. Koenig, "Spermo-Gnostics and the O.T.O."

156. According to the official historical statement issued by the U.S. Grand Lodge of the O.T.O., the various European branches of the Order were "largely destroyed or driven underground during the War." See Sabazius X° and AMT IX°, *History of Ordo Templi Orientis*: 19.

157. See ibid.: 18, and Sutin, *Do What Thou Wilt*: 286, 334.

158. Sabazius X° and AMT IX°, *History of Ordo Templi Orientis*: 22–23.

159. The American O.T.O. remains vigilant in policing pirated editions of Crowley's voluminous writings on magick and the doctrine of Thelema. However, it has been less successful in preventing various Web sites on the Internet from publishing most of Crowley's significant magickal texts on line. These rival Web sites include www.thelemicgnosticism.org; www.luckymojo.com; www.hermetic.com; www.rahoorkhuit.net; www.bbs.bapho.net; www.skepticfiles.org; www.sacred-texts.com, and www.aethyria.com.

160. The Fraternitas Saturni was established in Germany in 1926 by Eugen Grosche (1888–1964) and was the second magical order to be based on Crowley's doctrine of *Thelema*. The first was Crowley's Argenteum Astrum, which in turn merged into the O.T.O. after 1922.

161. One can sense this rivalry in such articles as Michael Staley's "Typhonian Ordo Templi Orientis: The O.T.O. after Crowley," which seeks to reinterpret various historical events in the O.T.O. as documented by the American branch of the O.T.O. Staley, who is a senior member of the Typhonian O.T.O. in Britain and editor of its publication *Starfire*, is widely regarded as Grant's deputy and heir apparent. See www.freespeech.org/magick/koenig/staley2.htm.

162. H. Bogdan, "Kenneth Grant: Marriage between the West and the East," edited extract taken from "Challenging the Morals of Western Society: The Use of Ritualised Sex in Contemporary Occultism," *Pomegranate*, 8, 2 (Equinox Publishing, London 2006); www.fulgur.co.uk.

163. These works by Grant include *The Magical Revival*, 1972; *Aleister Crowley and the Hidden God*, 1973; *Cults of the Shadow*, 1975; *Nightside of Eden*, 1977, and *Hecate's Fountain*, 1992; see Bibliography.

164. See Introduction to K. Grant and S. Grant, *Zos Speaks!: Encounters with Austin Osman Spare* (Fulgur, London 1998).

165. Grant defines the Draconian Cult as "the cult of the Fire Snake represented celestially by the stellar complex, Draco, the Dragon or Fire-breathing Beast of the Great Deep (of Space)." Grant claims that "Draco is identical with the Goddess Kali of the later Tantric Cults of the Left Hand Path. The Draconian Cult is also alluded to as the Ophidian Current when no specifically Egyptian reference is intended," and he notes further that "It is also known as the Typhonian Tradition, for Typhon was the primal

Goddess and the Mother of Set." See K. Grant, *Cults of the Shadow* (Muller, London 1975): 214.

166. The manifesto is undated, but Grant has confirmed that it was circulated around 1948. See Bogdan, "Kenneth Grant: Marriage between the West and the East": 4 n2.

167. Ibid.: 3.

168. See Frater Zephyros, "The Ophidian Current," n.d., www.groups.msn.com/TheMage/theophidiancurrent.msnw.

169. See M. Eliade, *Yoga, Immortality, and Freedom* (Princeton University Press, Princeton 1970): 5.

170. According to Swami Sivananda Radha, the concept of Kundalini also conveys "the implication . . . of a double spiral moved up into three dimensions." See S. Radha, *Kundalini Yoga for the West* (Shambhala, Boulder, 1981): xviii.

171. O. V. Garrison, *Tantra: The Yoga of Sex* (Julian Press, New York 1964): xxi–xxii.

172. A. Bharati, *The Tantric Tradition* (Rider, London 1965): 293.

173. Quoted in Radha, *Kundalini Yoga for the West*: 25–28.

174. J. Mumford, *Psychosomatic Yoga* (Aquarian Press, Wellingborough, UK 1979): 44.

175. Each of the first six chakras is governed by a particular aspect of Shakti. Muladhara is governed by Kakindi, Svadisthana by Rakini, Manipura by Lakini, Anahata by Kakini, Vishuddha by Shakini, and Ajna by Hakini. See I. Fischer-Schreiber et al. (eds.), *The Encyclopedia of Eastern Philosophy and Religion* (Shambhala, Boston 1994): 313.

176. These are Muladhara, Svadisthana, Manipura, Anahata, and Vishuddha, respectively. See Radha, *Kundalini Yoga for the West*.

177. Samadhi is the state of yogic consciousness which leads to self-realization. It is referred to in the *Bhagavad-Gita* as "seeing the self in all things and all things in the self."

178. The Sahasrara chakra is regarded as the abode of god Shiva, and "corresponds to cosmic consciousness." "If the kundalini is unified with the god Shiva in the Sahasrara chakra, the yogi experiences supreme bliss." Fischer-Schreiber et al. (eds.), *The Encyclopedia of Eastern Philosophy and Religion*: 61.

179. Some Western interpreters of Kundalini Yoga have identified the chakras with specific nerve plexuses, ganglia, and glands in the body. However, yoga authority Haridas Chaudhuri notes in his article "Yoga Psychology," in C. Tart (ed.), *Transpersonal Psychologies* (Harper & Row, New York 1975) : 231–280, that this is misleading and contrary to Tantric teaching. Chaudhuri describes the chakras as "consciousness potentials'" (p. 265) that only assume meaning as the Kundalini is aroused. The chakras themselves lie within the so-called Brahmanadi—the innermost channel within the Sushumna. Although there is a correlation between the chakras and various regions and organs of the body, the chakras do not literally equate with them. Nevertheless, because the chakras are visualized in certain locations it useful to summarize their positions in the body. The following listing also includes the Tattva, or element, associated with each chakra (where applicable) and the associated Hindu deities:

First chakra: *Muladhara*, located at the base of the spine, near the coccyx; Element: Earth; Meditation color: red; Deities: Child Brahma and Dakini
Second chakra: *Svadisthana*, located two inches below the navel in the sacral region; Element: Water; Meditation color: orange or silver; Deities: Vishnu and Rakini

Third chakra: *Manipura*, located three inches above the navel in the lumbar region; Element: Fire; Meditation color: red-gold or yellow-gold; Deities: Rudra and Lakini

Fourth chakra: *Anahata*, located near the heart; Element: Air; Meditation color: green or smoky grey; Deities: Isa (or Isvara) and Kakini

Fifth chakra: *Visuddha*, located in the throat; Element: Spirit; Meditation color: indigo or smoky purple; Deities: Sadashiva and Sakini

Sixth chakra: *Ajna*, located between the eyebrows; Element: all elements in their pure essence; Meditation color: white; Deities: Shambu/Paramashiva or Ardhanarisshvara, and Hakini

Seventh chakra: *Sahasrara*, located above the crown of the head; no Element assigned for this is a transcendent realm of pure consciousness; Meditation color: white; Deity: Brahman (Oneness)

180. See M. P. Pandit, *Kundalini Yoga* (Ganesh, Madras 1968): 54–55.

181. A. Voigt, *The Chakra Workbook* (Thunder Bay Press, San Diego, 2004): 150.

182. Radha, *Kundalini Yoga for the West*: 336.The divine androgyne, which represents the fusion of male and female polarities within one being, is a symbol of mystical unity. It occurs not only in the Hindu tradition but also in Western spiritual alchemy, where King Sol and Queen Luna are joined together in "the conjunction of opposites."

183. C. G. Jung, "Psychological Commentary in Kundalini Yoga," lecture given on 26 October 1932, *Spring* (New York 1976): 17.

184. Sutin, *Do What Thou Wilt*: 91, 92.

185. Fischer-Schreiber et al. (eds.), *The Encyclopedia of Eastern Philosophy and Religion*: 355.

186. Sutin adds the pertinent observation that "There is, in this tradition, no moral judgment attached to the use of 'left' and 'right,' although Western interpreters have frequently interposed a negative connotation to 'left' that is native to their own, but not Hindu, cultures." See Sutin, *Do What Thou Wilt*: 92–93.

187. King, *Tantra: The Way of Action* (Destiny Books, Rochester, Vermont 1990): 89.

188. Ibid.: 89–90.

189. Ibid.: 90.

190. Ibid.: 126–127.

191. Ibid.: 92.

192. Bharati, *The Tantric Tradition*: 179.

193. Melton, "The Origins of Modern Sex Magick." Quote is from Woodroffe, *Śakti and Śakta* (Ganesh, Madras 1975): 87.

194. Melton, "The Origins of Modern Sex Magick."

195. K. Grant, "Cults of the Shadow," in J. White (ed.), *Kundalini: Evolution and Enlightenment* (Paragon House, St. Paul, Minnesota 1990): 400–401.

196. Grant, *The Magical Revival*: 21.

197. See appendix containing the text of *Liber Al vel Legis* in J. Symonds and K. Grant (eds.), *The Magical Record of the Beast 666*.

198. In *Magick in Theory and Practice* (1929) Crowley writes: "Man is capable of being and using anything which he perceives, for everything that he perceives is in a certain sense

a part of his being. He may thus subjugate the whole Universe of which he is conscious to his individual will" (see n. 29 above). This approach is clearly mirrored in the practice of Greater Black Magic, as expounded by Michael Aquino in the Temple of Set.

199. In an interview published in 1998, Zeena Schreck confirmed to Kiki Scar that "the Temple of Set does not have an official curriculum concerning sexual magic and prefers to allow individual initiates to experiment with this method privately, if they wish to." See K. Scar, "Sado-Magic for Satan: An Interview with Zeena Schreck," *Cuir Underground*, 4 (Summer 1998): 4, also at www.black-rose.com. Schreck was briefly High Priestess of the Temple of Set in 2002, and was succeeded by Michael Aquino, the current High Priest and co-founder of the Temple of Set.

200. D. Webb, "The Black beyond Black," 2004, www.xeper.org/australasia.html.

201. See www.hekate.timerift.net/whois.htm; W. Burkert, *Ancient Mystery Cults* (Harvard University Press, Cambridge 1987), and J. Sellers, *Qadosh: The Johannite Tradition* (Manutius Press, Oakhurst, California 2006). Also see Burkert, *Ancient Mystery Cults*, and M. W. Meyer (ed.), *The Ancient Mysteries: A Sourcebook* (Harper & Row, San Francisco 1987).

202. V. Moore, "Chthonic: From Beast to Godhead," *Rose Noire*, 2004, also at www.vadgemoore.com/writings/beast_to_godhead.html. The Gnostic archon Abraxas was said to rule over 365 heavens and was depicted on numerous charms, amulets, and talismans throughout the ancient Middle East in order to attract good fortune.

203. Moore, "Chthonic: from Beast to Godhead."

204. Ibid. Emphasis in the original text.

205. Ibid.

206. For an overview of the nature of these altered states, see C. Tart (ed.), *Altered States of Consciousness* (Wiley, New York 1969) and D. Goleman and R. J. Davidson (eds.), *Consciousness: Brain, States of Awareness, and Mysticism* (Harper & Row, New York 1979).

207. Anthropologists who have studied shamanism in preliterate societies are especially aware of the highly significant relationship between altered states of consciousness and the nature of magical practice in these societies. See I. M. Lewis, *Ecstatic Religion: An Anthropological Study of Spirit Possession and Shamanism* (Penguin, Harmondsworth, UK 1971), and M. D. de Rios and M. Winkelman, "Shamanism and Altered States of Consciousness: An Introduction," in the *Journal of Psychoactive Drugs* 21.1 (San Francisco, January-March 1989): 1–7. Shamanic and visionary elements within the Western esoteric tradition have received somewhat less attention but are addressed in N. Drury, *Sacred Encounters: Shamanism and Magical Journeys of the Spirit* (Watkins, London 2003), and A. S. Cook and G. A. Hawk, *Shamanism and the Esoteric Tradition* (Llewellyn, St. Paul, Minnesota 1992).

208. F. King (ed.), *Astral Projection, Magic and Alchemy* (Spearman, London 1971): 29.

209. Regardie (ed.), *The Golden Dawn*, four volumes (Aries Press, Chicago, 1937–1940). Francis King first published a collection of the Flying Rolls under the title *Astral Projection, Magic and Alchemy* in 1971.

210. See M. Stavish, "The Body of Light in the Western Esoteric Tradition," www.hermetic.com/stavish/essays/bodylight.html.

211. Aquino, *The Crystal Tablet of Set: Selected Extracts* (Temple of Set, San Francisco 1983): 37.

212. Brodie-Innes had a ritual rank of Zelator Adeptus Minor, or 5° = 6°: see chapter 3 for ritual grades based on the Kabbalistic Tree of Life.

213. Brodie-Innes (*Frater Sub Spe*), "Flying Roll No. XXV": 73–74.

214. Dion Fortune was initiated into the London Temple of the Alpha and Omega in 1919. See A. Richardson, *Priestess: The Life and Magic of Dion Fortune* (Aquarian Press, Wellingborough, UK 1987): 111.

215. D. Fortune, *Applied Magic* (Aquarian Press, London 1962): 56–57.

216. Brodie-Innes (*Frater Sub Spe*), "Flying Roll No. XXV": 73.

217. See www.dragonrouge.net/english/general.htm.

218. Anon., *The Book of the Black Serpent*, c.1900, circulated among initiates of the Isis-Urania Temple in London. Included as an appendix in R. A. Gilbert, *The Sorcerer and His Apprentice* (Aquarian Press, Wellingborough, UK 1983).

219. D. Merkur, "Stages of Ascension in Hermetic Rebirth," *Esoterica* 1 (1999): 82, 84.

220. *Corpus Hermeticum XIII: 3*, quoted ibid.: 85.

221. *Corpus Hermeticum XI: 19–20*, quoted ibid.; "god" is spelled without a capital in Merkur's quotation.

222. Merkur, "Stages of Ascension in Hermetic Rebirth," 89, 90.

223. S. L. MacGregor Mathers (*Frater Deo Duce Comite Ferro*), "Flying Roll No. XI: Clairvoyance."

224. Moore, "Chthonic: From Beast to Godhead."

225. Webb, "The Black beyond Black."

226. Grant, *Cults of the Shadow*: 169–170.

227. See www.dragonrouge.net/english/general.htm. The Qliphothic Qabalah is an inverted Kabbalistic Tree featuring ten "demonic" *sephiroth*.

228. See www.dragonrouge.net/english/general.htm.

229. According to the *Book of the Black Serpent*, the Qliphothic planetary rulers associated with the ten spheres on the reverse side of the Tree of Life are Thamiel (Neptune/Kether); Chaigidel (Pluto/Chokmah); Sateriel (Saturn/Binah); Gamehioth (Jupiter/Chesed); Galeb (Mars/Geburah); Tagaririm (Sol/Tiphareth); Harab-Serapel (Venus/Netzach); Samael (Mercury/Hod); Gamaliel (Luna/Yesod), and Nahemoth (Terra/Malkuth). Ten "evil chiefs" are also assigned to these spheres. They are, respectively, Satan, Beelzebub, Lucifuge, Ashtaroth, Asmodai, Belphegor, Baal, Adramalach, Lilith, and Nahemah. See *The Book of the Black Serpent*.

230. Ibid.

CHAPTER 5

1. A. Richardson, *Dancers to the Gods: The Magical Records of Charles Seymour and Christine Hartley 1937–1939* (Aquarian Press, Wellingborough, UK 1985): 16.

2. A. Richardson, *Priestess: The Life and Magic of Dion Fortune* (Aquarian Press, Wellingborough, UK 1987): 52.

3. The concept of "root races" is a nineteenth-century Theosophical teaching which states that humanity has evolved through different phases of spiritual growth and intellectual development, each of these being known as a "root race." The present state of humanity is

said to be the fifth root race. It was preceded by the Atlantean (fourth) and Lemurian (third), both of which were engulfed in cataclysms. According to Madame H. P. Blavatsky, the first root race consisted of "Celestial Men" (see *The Secret Doctrine*, 1888, Vol. 1: 214), whereas the second root race were of asexual origin and were known as "The Fathers of the 'Sweat-born'"; *The Secret Doctrine*, ([vol. 3, 1897] fifth edition, Theosophical Publishing House, Madras, 1962); vol 3: 125.

4. Richardson, *Priestess*: 111.

5. According to Kenneth Grant, Fortune based the character of Vivian le Fay Morgan in her two novels *The Sea-Priestess* (1938) and *Moon Magic* (1956) on Maiya Tranchell-Hayes. See K. Grant, *The Magical Revival* (Muller, London 1972): 177. Tranchell-Hayes was a pupil of J. W. Brodie-Innes, a leading member of the Amen-Ra Temple in Edinburgh.

6. Quoted in Richardson, *Priestess*: 112.

7. Richardson, *Dancers to the Gods*: 34.

8. D. Fortune, *Applied Magic* (Aquarian Press, London 1962): 91.

9. A Gnostic sect, the Melchizedekians, maintained that there was a spiritual power greater than Jesus Christ. This was Melchizedek, "the light gatherer," who was believed to perform a comparable role in the heavens to that of Jesus on Earth. In Gnostic thought the archons, as intermediary cosmic powers and gatekeepers associated with the Earth, were regarded as fundamentally evil. But Melchizedek was believed to gather particles of light in their midst, returning them to the "Treasure House," or Pleroma, in the transcendent realms of the cosmos. For this reason Melchizedek was highly regarded as a "figure of light" in Gnostic tradition.

10. Richardson, *Priestess*: 117.

11. Quoted in R. A. Gilbert, *Revelations of the Golden Dawn* (Quantum/Foulsham, Slough, UK 1997): 124.

12. For details of this remarkable incident, see Dion Fortune's *Psychic Self-Defense* (Weiser, York Beach, Maine 1999): 156.

13. Grant, *The Magical Revival*: 176.

14. See P. Turner and C. R. Coulter, "Isis" in *Dictionary of Ancient Deities* (Oxford University Press, Oxford 2000): 243; and R. A. Armour, "The Adventures of Osiris and Isis" in *Gods and Myths of Ancient Egypt* (American University in Cairo Press, Cairo 1986): 72–88, among many other accounts of this classic ancient Egyptian myth.

15. Isis was identified as a lunar goddess by Plutarch. See Turner and Coulter, "Isis": 243.

16. Grant, *The Magical Revival*: 177.

17. According to his wife Steffi, Kenneth Grant met Crowley in 1945. See Introduction in K. Grant and S. Grant, *Zos Speaks: Encounters with Austin Osman Spare* (Fulgur, London 1998): 16. Dion Fortune died in 1946, Crowley in 1947.

18. Sexual magic was more the domain of occultists like Austin Osman Spare, who was never a member of the Golden Dawn, and Aleister Crowley, who developed his interest in Thelemic sex magic after leaving the Golden Dawn in 1903.

19. Magical "pathworkings" were developed in the Fraternity of the Inner Light and by its more recent offshoot, Servants of the Light (SOL), and employ a guided imagery technique in which one person reads from a written text so that a subject (or subjects) may be led along "inner meditative pathways" in order to experience archetypal visions.

Pathworkings often utilize the symbolism of the Major Arcana, drawing on descriptions of the Tarot images associated with the ten *sephiroth* on the Kabbalistic Tree of Life (a symbolic connection first proposed by the ninetenth-century occultist Eliphas Levi). Pathworkings are intended to trigger personal meditative experiences of the gods and goddesses of the various mythological pantheons.

20. The chapter titled "The Old Religion" in Basil Wilby (ed.), *The New Dimensions Red Book* (Helios, Cheltenham, UK 1968) identified the author only as F.P.D. It is now known that F.P.D. was Colonel Charles R. F. Seymour (1880–1943). See Richardson, *Dancers to the Gods*: 90.

21. Fortune, *Applied Magic*: 4.

22. The concept of the Akashic Records derives from the teachings of Madame Helena Blavatsky (1831–1891) and the Theosophical Society (founded in New York in 1875). According to the Theosophists, the Akashic Records are an astral memory of all events, thoughts, and emotions since the world began. Psychics are said to be able to receive "impressions" from this astral realm, and some Theosophical descriptions of the legendary lost continent of Atlantis are based on this psychic approach. *Akasha* is a Sanskrit word meaning "luminous," and Akasha is one of the five Hindu elements, or Tattvas, whose symbol is the "black egg" of Spirit.

23. See F.P.D, "The Old Religion": 47.

24. Ibid.: 49.

25. Ibid.: 78.

26. Butler's books on the Western esoteric tradition include *Magic: Its Ritual Power and Purpose* (1952), *The Magician: His Training and Work* (1959), *Apprenticed to Magic* (1962), and *Magic and the Qabalah* (1964); see Bibliography.

27. See Bibliography for further details.

28. His parents were Philip Newton Spare and Eliza Ann Adelaide Osman. Philip Spare was a constable in the City of London police force.

29. R. Ansell, *The Bookplate Designs of Austin Osman Spare* (Bookplate Society/ Keridwen Press, London 1988): 1.

30. Ibid.: 2.

31. See I. Law, "Austin Osman Spare" in G. Beskin and J. Bonner (eds.), *Austin Osman Spare 1886–1956: The Divine Draughtsman*, exhibition catalogue (Morley Gallery, London, 1987): 5; and K. Grant, *Images and Oracles of Austin Osman Spare* (Muller, London 1975): 11.

32. It was published by Otto Schutzer & Co., 1909. See W. Wallace, *The Early Work of Austin Osman Spare* (Catalpa Press, Stroud, UK 1987): 20.

33. See Ansell, *The Bookplate Designs of Austin Osman Spare*: 5. *The Yellow Book* was published between 1894 and 1897. Henry Harland was its literary editor and Beardsley its art editor until 1896. Spare himself did not acknowledge any direct influence from Beardsley, although he was very familiar with his graphic work.

34. *Form* was revived in 1921, but issued in a more modest format.

35. *The Golden Hind* was co-edited with Clifford Bax and published by Chapman & Hall, London.

36. For Augustus John's opinion, see K. Grant, introduction to A. O. Spare, *The Book of Pleasure (Self-Love): The Psychology of Ecstasy* ([London 1913] facsimile reprint, 93 Publishing, Montreal 1975).

37. See Grant, *Images and Oracles of Austin Osman Spare*: 16. According to Robert Ansell, this quote is hearsay and no documentary evidence has so far been produced to support it.

38. Grant and Grant, *Zos Speaks!*: 286–288.

39. Ansell, *The Bookplate Designs of Austin Osman Spare*: 6. Ansell writes that Spare was acclaimed as the "darling of Mayfair" between 1907 and 1913. The latter date coincides with the release of Spare's most revolutionary and confronting work, *The Book of Pleasure (Self-Love): The Psychology of Ecstasy*.

40. A. O. Spare, *Earth: Inferno* (London 1905): 21.

41. Ibid.: 18.

42. Spare, *The Book of Pleasure (Self-Love)*: 45.

43. Ibid.: iii.

44. Ibid.: 7.

45. G. W. Semple, *Zos-Kia: An Introductory Essay on the Art and Sorcery of Austin Osman Spare* (Fulgur, London 1995): 11.

46. Specifically, the translation was S. L. MacGregor Mathers's translation of Knorr Von Rosenroth's selection of key texts from the Zohar, *Kabbala Denudata*, published in an English language edition as *The Kabbalah Unveiled* (Redway, London 1887).
F. W. Letchford, *From the Inferno to Zos* (First Impressions, Thame, UK 1995): 79.

47. G. W. Semple, "A Few Leaves from the Devil's Picture Book," in A. O. Spare, *Two Tracts on Cartomancy* (Fulgur, London 1997): 21n.

Temurah, or Temura, is a Kabbalistic coding technique intended to work as a disguise. The first half of the Hebrew alphabet is written in reverse order and located above the remaining section so that the letters form vertical pairs:

k y th ch z v h d g b a
l m n s op tz q r sh t

Here k=l, y=m, th=n, and so on. A given word can be disguised in Temurah by substituting the code letter in each case. See C. Poncé, *Kabbalah* (Garnstone Press, London 1974): 172.

48. Wallace, *The Early Work of Austin Osman Spare*: 13.

49. G. G. Scholem, *Major Trends in Jewish Mysticism* (revised edition, Schocken, New York 1961): 240.

50. A. O. Spare, *Axiomata* (Fulgur, London 1992): 9. According to the publisher, Robert Ansell, this work is based on previously unpublished texts from the early 1950s. Atavistic resurgence has been defined as "the return into the sorcerer's consciousness of latent powers and knowledge, resurrecting the 'dead' from the pre-human strata; typically manifesting through bestial and elemental forms, evoked by intense nostalgia." See Semple, *Zos-Kia*: 48.

51. A. O. Spare, *The Witches' Sabbath* (Fulgur, London 1992): 7. This is a posthumously published text, based on manuscripts dating from the early 1950s and is not one of Spare's self-published works.

52. Spare was familiar with the writings of Freud, Krafft-Ebing, and Havelock Ellis, all specialist authors in the field of the psychology of sexuality.

53. One of Spare's magical names was *Zos vel Thanatos* which, according to Frank Letchford, was derived "from the theory posited by Dr. Sigmund Freud of the eternal conflict between Eros (love) and Thanatos (the so-called Death-wish)." See Letchford,

Inferno to Zos : 137. In ancient Greek mythology, Thanatos was the Greek god of Death, the brother of Sleep and the son of Night.

According to Frank Letchford, a close friend of Spare's, "The Tao was one of *the* most important influences upon Austin" (see Letchford, *Inferno to Zos*: 231) and it is of interest that the colored self-portrait of Spare titled *Prayer* (1906), reproduced opposite the title page in William Wallace's *The Early Work of Austin Osman Spare 1900–1919*, shows the artist wearing a Taoist *yin-yang* pendant around his neck. Spare makes a very Taoist remark in his posthumously published text *The Living Word of Zos*: "I believe in the life; in the flesh of infinite variety. We are eternity, with—as now—a fleeting and fluxing consciousness. Possibilities of being are limitless." See Grant and Grant, *Zos Speaks!*: 273.

For an explanation of karmas, see n. 58 below.

54. Spare, *Axiomata*: 19. This publication is not one of Spare's self-published works but a more recent publication based on previously unpublished manuscripts assembled and edited long after his death in 1956.

55. Spare illustrated these "karmas" in his graphic compositions. Examples may be found in *The Book of Pleasure (Self-Love)* on pages 49 and 57.

56. Spare, *The Book of Pleasure (Self-Love*: 52–53).

57. Letchford, *From the Inferno to Zos*: 161. Letchford provides the dates of his friendship with Spare in his foreword to Wallace, *The Early Work of Austin Osman Spare 1900–1919*.

58. The Hindu concept of karma is based on the principle of cause and effect, and states that for every action there is an equal and opposite reaction. The renowned Indian spiritual teacher Vivekananda (1862–1902) described karma as "the eternal assertion of human freedom . . . our thoughts, our words and deeds are the threads of the net which we throw around ourselves." In Hindu philosophy, the law of karma extends beyond the physical world into the mental, emotional, and spiritual aspects of life and applies not only to physical actions but also to every conscious thought and action that arises in everyday life. According to the karmic philosophy of life, positive thoughts and actions produce a positive outcome and create good karma. Negative thoughts and actions result in negative outcomes and create bad karma. Austin Spare may have developed his interest in karma through reading the Theosophical writings of Madame H. P. Blavatsky and Annie Besant.

59. Grant, *Images and Oracles of Austin Osman Spare*: 9.

60. Ibid.: 10.

61. Quoted in Semple, *Zos-Kia*: 7

62. Grant, *Images and Oracles of Austin Osman Spare*: 21. Grant's close friendship with Spare, and their voluminous correspondence, are documented in Grant and Grant, *Zos Speaks!*

63. Grant, *Images and Oracles of Austin Osman Spare*: 23.

64. Spare, *Earth: Inferno* [1905].

65. Grant, *Images and Oracles of Austin Osman Spare*: 71.

66. Ibid.: 73.

67. Spare, *The Book of Pleasure (Self-Love)*: 6.

68. Steffi Grant claims in her Introduction to *Zos Speaks!* that Spare had numerous lovers. Many of them were local women who also modeled for him. Grant writes that "He said that until he was forty-five he never thought of anything except sex; that he was seriously in love every single week. He must have been very attractive to women, and never found any difficulties in satisfying his desires." See Grant and Grant, *Zos Speaks!*: 18.

To this extent, Spare's approach resembles the Thelemic sex magic of Aleister Crowley, discussed in chapter 4. However, Spare was already developing his Zos/Kia cosmology as early as 1906 (elements of it appear in *Earth: Inferno*), so it would appear that Spare did not derive his sexual practice from Crowley, even though he was briefly a member of Crowley's sex-magic order, the Argenteum Astrum, 1909–1910.

69. Grant, *Images and Oracles of Austin Osman Spare*: 61.

70. Spare, *The Book of Pleasure (Self-Love)*: 48.

71. In *The Focus of Life*, Spare actually defines it in these terms: the Death Posture, he writes is "a simulation of death by the utter negation of thought." See A. O. Spare, *The Focus of Life* ([1921] Askin Publishers, London 1976): 18.

72. A. O. Spare, *Metamorphosis by Death Posture*, quoted in Grant, *Images and Oracles of Austin Osman Spare*: 61.

73. Semple, *Zos-Kia*: 29.

74. In *The Book of Pleasure*, Spare writes: "Magical obsession is that state when the mind is illuminated by sub-conscious activity evoked voluntarily by formulae at our own time, etc. for inspiration. It is the condition of Genius. (p. 41) . . . The chief cause of genius is realization of 'I' by an emotion that allows the lightning assimilation of what is perceived. . . . Its most excellent state is the "Neither-Neither" [Kia], the free or atmospheric 'I.' (p. 43) . . . My formula and Sigils for sub-conscious activity are the means of inspiration, capacity or genius, and the means of accelerating evolution" (p. 48).

75. Semple, *Zos-Kia*: 26.

76. Spare, *The Book of Pleasure (Self-Love)*: 7.

77. Spare says specifically that the Self is the "Neither-Neither." It is the Absolute because it transcends duality. See Spare, *The Book of Pleasure (Self-Love)*: 33, 18.

78. Ibid.

79. Ibid.

80. Letchford, *Inferno to Zos*: 119. In *The Book of Pleasure*, Spare writes with regard to the Death Posture: "Let him practise it daily, accordingly, till he arrives at the centre of desire": 19.

81. As Gavin Semple astutely observes, "A sigillic language enables the sorcerer to think in symbols . . . allowing consciousness to prevade hitherto occluded regions; the sigil acts as a 'courier' in the transference across the threshold." See Semple, *Zos-Kia*: 33.

The first publication of one of Spare's pictographic magical sigils appears in the illustration "Existence," included in *A Book of Satyrs*, 1907. The illustration itself is dated 1906 and also includes the motif of the vulture-head, one of Spare's symbols for Kia. However, as Robert Ansell has pointed out in a personal communication to the author (June 2007), sigils do not appear in Spare's art throughout his career. For the most part they are a feature of his art between 1909 and 1912, and much later, between 1948 and 1956.

82. A. O. Spare, "Mind to Mind and How," in *Two Tracts on Cartomancy* (Fulgur, London 1997): 32.

83. Spare, *The Book of Pleasure (Self-Love)*: 48.

84. Gavin W. Semple's edition of Spare's *Two Tracts on Cartomancy* (Fulgur, London 1997) contains a text written by Spare himself. It is titled "Mind to Mind and How," "by a Sorcerer," and makes reference to the rationale underpinning Spare's magic of Zos/Kia: "The law of sorcery is its own law, using sympathetic symbols" (p. 31).

According to Kenneth Grant, Spare regarded elementals as a "dissociated part of the subconsciousness." See Grant, *Images and Oracles of Austin Spare*: 22. Gavin Semple similarly defines "elemental automata" as "residual fragments of consciousness, independent and motivated within a specific field of activity and influence. Once rendered perceptible these are delegated by the sorcerer to new functions according to intent." See Semple, *Zos-Kia*: 48.

85. In his introduction to the 1975 facsimile reprint of *The Book of Pleasure* (93 Publishing, Quebec), Kenneth Grant writes: "Towards the end of his life, when Spare lived more or less reclusively in a Dickensian South London slum, he was asked whether he regretted his lonely existence. 'Lonely !,' he exclaimed, and with a sweep of his arm he indicated the host of unseen elementals and familiar spirits that were his constant companions; he had but to turn his head to catch a fleeting glimpse of their subtle presences."

86. Semple, "A Few Leaves from the Devil's Picture Book," in Spare, *Two Tracts on Cartomancy*: 21. Cornelius Agrippa (1486–1535) first published his text in 1533 and an English translation appeared in 1651. A revised edition of Book One ("Natural Magic") of *Occult Philosophy or Magic*, edited by Willis F. Whitehead, was published in 1897 and would have been accessible to Spare. This particular edition was subsequently reissued by Aquarian Press, London, in 1971. The so-called *Fourth Book of Occult Philosophy* was issued as a limited-edition facsimile reprint by Askin Publishers, London in 1978.

87. Semple, "A Few Leaves from the Devil's Picture Book": 21.

88. See Agrippa, *Three Books of Occult Philosophy or Magic* [1533], ed. W. F. Whitehead,: 113.

89. Semple, "A Few Leaves from the Devil's Picture Book": 21.

90. Spare, *The Book of Pleasure (Self-Love)*: 50.

91. Exhaustion could be brought about in a variety of ways. Spare cites "Mantras and Posture, Women and Wine, Tennis, and the playing of Patience, or by walking and concentration on the Sigil etc. etc." See A. O. Spare, *The Book of Pleasure (Self-Love)*: 51.

92. Ibid.

93. Ibid.: 45.

94. Kenneth Grant's account of atavistic resurgence, first published in *Man, Myth and Magic*, vol. 6 (Marshall Cavendish, London 1970), is quoted in N. Drury and S. Skinner, *The Search for Abraxas* (Neville Spearman, London 1972): 66.

95. Kenneth Grant writes in his introduction to Spare's *Book of Zos vel Thanatos*: "Spares's relationship to the Surrealist Movement, which he claims to have anticipated by at least a decade, remains to be explained. The Movement was a phenomenon of major occult importance. It not only explored and explicated the creative potential of the

subconscious, it also influenced powerfully the direction of the Arts, bringing to the fore the subjective treatment of external 'reality.' The Movement was, of course, intimately related to the researches of Freud, whose exploration of subconscious mechanisms fired the Surrealists to experiment with the method of 'free association.' Freud's *The Interpretation of Dreams* was first published in English translation in 1913, the year in which *The Book of Pleasure* (1909–1913) appeared. The latter showed that Spare's knowledge of the predominating role of the Subconsciousness in Art and Sorcery had already matured and was well in place by the time his book appeared." See Grant and Grant, *Zos Speaks!*: 158.

96. An observation of Spare's interest in spiritualism and Theosophy was forwarded by Robert Ansell, June 2007.

97. Spare, *The Book of Pleasure (Self-Love)*: 47.

98. Semple, *Zos-Kia*: 31.

99. A. O. Spare, "The Logomachy of Zos," an unpublished manuscript quoted in Semple, *Zos-Kia*: 31.

100. Letchford, *Inferno to Zos*: 161–163.

101. Semple, *Zos-Kia*: 37.

102. The article appeared in issue no.1, volume 1 of *Form*, April 1916, and was republished in a facsmile edition by 93 Publishing, South Stukely, Quebec in 1979, in an edition of 250 copies.

103. I. Law, introduction to A. O. Spare, *A Book of Automatic Drawing* (Catalpa Press, London 1972).

104. See R. Ansell, introduction to A. O. Spare, *The Book of Ugly Ecstasy* (Fulgur, London 1996).

105. A. O. Spare, *The Witches' Sabbath* (Fulgur, London 1992): 5.

106. Ansell, introduction to Spare, *The Book of Ugly Ecstasy*.

107. Ibid.

108. In *The Book of Pleasure*, Spare writes: "Magical obsession is that state when the mind is illuminated by sub-conscious activity evoked voluntarily by formula at our own time, etc. for inspiration. It is the condition of genius." Spare, *The Book of Pleasure (Self-Love)*: 41.

109. Spare appears to admit this in *The Book of Pleasure* when he writes: "Depending on its degree of intensity and resistance shown at some time or another, the Ego has or has not knowledge of the obsession; *always is its expression autonomous, divorced from personal control*" (my emphasis in italics). See Spare, *The Book of Pleasure (Self-Love)*: 41.

110. A. O. Spare, *The Logomachy of Zos*, in Grant and Grant, *Zos Speaks!*: 184.

111. Semple, *Zos-Kia*: 26.

112. Spare, *The Logomachy of Zos*: 172.

113. Spare writes: "I believe in the Eternity of the Ego whether I am carnate, discarnate, reincarnate or whatever metamorphosis I suffer. For I am *change* and forever ultimate, however I may appear." A. O. Spare, *The Living Word of Zos*, in Grant and Grant, *Zos Speaks!*: 172.

114. M. M. Jungkurth, "Neither-Neither: Austin Spare and the Underworld," in *Austin Osman Spare: Artist, Occultist, Sensualist* (Beskin Press, London 1999).

115. R. Norton, "I Was Born a Witch," *Australasian Post*, Sydney, 3 January 1957: 4.

116. Ibid.

117. See Guiley, *The Encyclopedia of Witches and Witchcraft*: 262; and "Pan," in Turner and Coulter, *A Dictionary of Ancient Deities*: 371.

118. See "Pan'" in J. E. Zimmerman, *Dictionary of Classical Mythology*, (Harper and Row, New York, 1964): 190.

119. P. Harrison, *The Elements of Pantheism* (Element, Shaftesbury, Dorset, 1999): 1.

120. Anon. "Inside Rosaleen Norton," *Squire*, Sydney, April 1965: 41, 42.

121. Ibid.

122. For a more detailed exploration of Norton's association with the magic of the Left-Hand Path, interested readers are referred to my recent biography, *Homage to Pan: The Life, Art and Magic of Rosaleen Norton* (Creation Oneiros, London, 2009).

123. *The Bulletin*, Sydney, 27 January 1981.

124. See R. Von Rudloff, *Hekate in Ancient Greek Religion* (Horned Owl Publishing, Victoria, Canada 1999): 95 and 123. Patricia A. Marquardt notes that, prior to the fifth century BCE, Hecate was not especially chthonic in nature, but that her identification with witchcraft and black magic in literature dates from Euripedes' *Medea*. Marquardt also notes that Hecate may have become identified around this time with the Thessalian goddess Einoda, who was similarly associated with witchcraft. See P. A. Marquardt, "A Portrait of Hecate," *American Journal of Philology* 102.3 (Autumn 1981): 252.

125. R. Von Rudloff, *Hekate in Ancient Greek Religion*: 121, 123, 95–96.

126. See "Hecate," in Turner and Coulter, *A Dictionary of Ancient Deities*: 208. According to Rabinowitz, other offerings to Hecate included bread, eels, and mullet. See J. Rabinowitz, *The Rotting Goddess: The Origin of the Witch in Classical Antiquity* (Autonomedia, New York 1998): 62.

127. See Rudloff, *Hekate in Ancient Greek Religion*: 113 and 122.

128. N. Drury, *The History of Magic in the Modern Age* (Constable, London 2000: 138).

129. R. Patai, *The Hebrew Goddess* (third enlarged edition, Wayne State University Press, Detroit 1990): 221.

130. Ibid.: 222.

131. Ibid.: 223.

132. C. G. Jung, *Psychology of the Unconscious* (Kegan Paul, Trench, Trubner, London 1919): 153–154.

133. Ibid.

134. From unpublished notes accompanying Norton's illustration *Lilith*, reproduced in *The Art of Rosaleen Norton*, Sydney 1952.

135. R. Norton, "A Vision," included in the *Supplement to the Art of Rosaleen Norton* (Walter Glover, Sydney 1984).

136. A painting of *The Adversary*, comparable in all major details, had also been exhibited at the Rowden White Gallery in Melbourne in 1949.

137. See "Lucifer" in *The New Columbia Encyclopedia* (Columbia University Press, New York 1975): 1626.

138. See N. Drury, *Inner Visions: Explorations in Magical Consciousness* (Routledge & Kegan Paul, London 1979): 106.

139. Despite its resemblance to a Jewish god-name, Eloi is not strictly Kabbalistic. The god-name of Chesed, the fourth sphere upon the Tree of Life associated with Jupiter in

Dion Fortune's *Mystical Qabalah* (1935: 161), is given as El and not Eloi. It is likely that Norton derived the reference to Eloi from Madame H. P. Blavatsky, who refers to the Eloi of Jupiter in *The Secret Doctrine* ([1897] Theosophical Publishing House, Adyar, Madras 1962): ii: 301 and iv: 108. Blavatsky ascribes this reference to the planetary spirit of Jupiter to the early Christian theologican Origen, who in turn is said to have ascribed it to the Gnostics.

140. See Blavatsky, *The Secret Doctrine* [1897] 1962. Blavatsky refers specifically to Fohat as the "dynamic energy of Cosmic Ideation" and "the guiding power of all manifestation" (I: 81) and later describes him as "the personified electric vital power, the transcendental binding unity of all cosmic energies, on the unseen as on the manifested planes, the action of which resembles—on an immense scale—that of a living Force created by Will. . . . Fohat is not only the living Symbol and Container of that Force, but is looked upon by the Occultists as an Entity; the forces he acts upon being cosmic, human and terrestrial, and exercising their influence on all these planes respectively" (I: 170–171; capital letters in Blavatsky's text).

141. In Haiti, Erzulie is revered as the Voodoo goddess of love, beauty, flowers, and jewelry. She also enjoys dancing and fine clothes. See Maya Deren, *Divine Horsemen: The Voodoo Gods of Haiti* (Thames and Hudson, London 1953): 62 (second edition 1970). During her lifetime, Norton could have had access to this well-known book, a classic study of voodoo, although it was first published a year after *The Art of Rosaleen Norton*. It is likely that Norton drew at least part of her enthusiasm for voodoo from William B. Seabrook's *Magic Island* (New York, 1929), which she lists in the bibliography in *The Art of Rosaleen Norton* (p. 79) as a reference under the heading "witchcraft and demonology." Norton lists its title incorrectly as *The Magic Isle* in her bibliography.

142. For all of these metaphysical beings, see Norton, *The Art of Rosaleen Norton*: 78.

143. Ibid.

144. T. Roderick, *Wicca: 366 Days of Spiritual Practice in the Craft of the Wise* (Llewellyn, St. Paul, Minnesota 2005): 284.

145. See the bibliography in *The Art of Rosaleen Norton*: 79.

146. See Plate XV, *Qlipha*, in *The Art of Rosaleen Norton*: 44—which is accompanied by an extract from Norton's personal journal.

147. K. Grant, *Outside the Circles of Time* (Muller, London 1980): 287.

148. K. Grant, *Nightside of Eden* (Muller, London 1977): 275–276.

149. *The Art of Rosaleen Norton*: 44. "Werplon" appears to be a concocted term combining "were," as in werewolf, with *plon*, the Scandinavian term for a dragon.

150. It is more confronting even than the Djinn, a being which it superficially resembles and which is depicted in the painting *The Djinn*, which is reproduced in *Supplement to The Art of Rosaleen Norton*: 28. Both the Werplon and the Djinn are shown grabbing helpless human beings in their clawed fingers.

151. *The Art of Rosaleen Norton*: 44

152. The most confronting examples from *The Art of Rosaleen Norton* include Plate V, *Panic*; Plate XIV, *Rites of Baron Samedi*; Plate XV, *Qlipha*; Plate XVII, *Black Magic*; Plate XIX, *Fohat*; Plate XXIV, *Symphony in 3 Movements*; Plate XXVIII, *Dinner Time*; and Plate XXXI, *The Master*.

153. The date is confirmed in the Norton article "She Hates Figleaf Morality," *People*, Sydney, 29 March 1950: 30.

154. Ibid.

155. See Norton's personal statement to L. J. Murphy, and Norton, "She Hates Figleaf Morality."

156. Norton, "She Hates Figleaf Morality."

157. Extract from Norton's personal statement to L .J. Murphy.

158. Ibid.

159. It is important to distinguish between magical invocation and evocation. In *Magic: Its Ritual Power and Purpose* (1952: 41) Dion Fortune's colleague W. E. Butler writes: "In invocation we act in such a way as to attract the attention of some Being of a superior nature to our own, or some cosmic force of a higher order. In evocation we impose our will upon beings of a lesser order of existence and compel them to execute our wishes. In both cases the actual contact takes place through our mental channel."

160. Extract from Norton's personal statement to L .J. Murphy.

161. Ibid.

162. Ibid.

163. See references to "rising in the planes" in chapter 3.

164. Norton was married to Beresford Conroy from 1940 to 1951. Cecily Boothman remained Norton's closest family member and friend throughout her life, and ensured Norton's privacy during the trance sessions: personal communication from Boothman to the author, 1982.

165. Interview with Norton at Roslyn Gardens, Kings Cross, Sydney 1977.

166. See Jung, *Psychology of the Unconscious*; *The Archetypes of the Collective Unconscious* (Routledge & Kegan Paul, London 1959); *Symbols of Transformation* (Bollingen Foundation / Princeton University Press, Princeton 1956; and *Man andHis Symbols* (Dell, New York 1968).

167. Interview with Norton at Roslyn Gardens, Kings Cross, Sydney 1977.

168. C. P. Christ, *Rebirth of the Goddess: Finding Meaning in Feminist Spirituality* (Routledge, New York 1997): 90.

169. Ibid.: 91.

170. Starhawk, *The Spiral Dance* (revised edition, HarperCollins, San Francisco 1999): 34–35.

171. N. Drury, *Pan's Daughter: The Strange World of Rosaleen Norton* (Collins, Sydney 1988): 142.

172. V. Crowley, *A Woman's Guide to the Earth Traditions* (Thorsons, London 2001): 1, 2.

CHAPTER 6

1. D. Valiente, *An ABC of Witchcraft, Past and Present* (revised edition, Hale, London 1984): 343.

2. P. Crowther, *Lid off the Cauldron: A Handbook for Witches* (Muller, London 1981): 1.

3. The goddesses named here are all included in the so-called Witches' Charge, a key element in Wiccan ritual.

4. In modern witchcraft the Horned God personifies fertility, the Celtic counterpart of the Great God Pan, the goat-footed god, who in ancient Greece personified the untamed forces of Nature and the universal life-force. There is no connection between the Horned

God of witchcraft and the Christian horned Devil although, since the time of the witchcraft persecutions of the Middle Ages this has been a common error.

5. Valiente, *An ABC of Witchcraft*: 69.

6. The equivalent dates for the Southern Hemisphere are as follows: *Candlemas/Imbolc*: 1 August; *Beltane*: 31 October; *Lammas/Lughnassadh*: 2 February; *Halloween/Samhain*: 30 April.

7. In the Southern Hemisphere, midsummer solstice occurs on 21 December and midwinter solstice on 21 June. Spring equinox is on 21 September and Autumn equinox on 21 March.

8. See J. Farrar and S. Farrar, *Eight Sabbats for Witches* (Hale, London 1981).

9. The Lords of the Watchtowers are the Wiccan equivalent of the four archangels, Raphael, Michael, Gabriel and Uriel, who are invoked as protectors in the Golden Dawn banishing ritual of the Lesser Pentagram.

10. During his initiation in the New Forest in September 1939, Gerald Gardner was told by his initiators: "The law has always been that power must be passed from man to woman or from woman to man, the only exception being when a mother initiates her daughter or a father his son, because they are part of themselves." See G. Gardner, *Witchcraft Today* (Rider, London 1954): 78.

11. See Valiente, *An ABC of Witchcraft*: 203.

12. Z. Budapest, *The Holy Book of Women's Mysteries* (Wingbow Press, Los Angeles 1989): 277–278.

13. This is the version given by Patricia Crowther, high priestess of the Sheffield Coven, in *Lid off the Cauldron* (Muller, London 1981): 6. The Wiccan Rede is regarded by some as a reformulation of Aleister Crowley's magical dictum: "Do what thou wilt shall be the whole of the Law." Crowley influenced Gardner in developing modern witchcraft practices, and Crowley's dictum may have contributed, directly or indirectly, to the Wiccan Rede. However, the crucial element of "harm none" was missing from Crowley's statement of magical purpose. Graham Harvey notes that in the Wiccan Rede the word "will" means "your true self." He also mentions that although the word *an* is Anglo-Saxon for "if," some Wiccans interpret it as a shortened form of "and." See G. Harvey, *Listening People, Speaking Earth: Contemporary Paganism* (Hurst, London 1997): 38.

14. Quoted from *The Pagan Federation Information Pack* (second edition, London 1992): 14.

15. Scire ("to know") was Gerald Gardner's magical name in the Ordo Templi Orientis. Gardner joined the O.T.O. after meeting Aleister Crowley in Hastings in 1946.

16. These three titles were published by Michael Houghton (London 1949), Rider & Co (London 1954) and Aquarian Press (London 1959), respectively.

17. P. Heselton, *Wiccan Roots: Gerald Gardner and the Modern Witchcraft Revival* (Capall Bann Publishing, Milverton, Somerset 2000): 12.

18. Gardner was interested in the history of Malayan civilization and had written a book titled *Keris and Other Malay Weapons*, a pioneering study of the history and folklore of local armaments, published in Singapore in 1936.

19. Heselton, *Wiccan Roots*: 26.

20. Patricia Crowther writes in *Lid off the Cauldron* (p. 28) that Gardner's collection of daggers and swords came "from all parts of the world."

21. Dr. Annie Besant (1847–1933) became president of the Thesophical Society in 1891. She was involved in a number of social movements, including the Fabian Society, the Indian Home Rule League, and the Boy Scouts. Together with Charles Leadbeater, she also sponsored the spiritual cause of Jiddu Krishnamurti, establishing the Order of the Star in the East to promote him as a "world teacher," a role he later rejected. Dr. Besant was a leader in the Co-Masonry movement and also founded the Order of the Temple of the Rose Cross in 1912. The rituals of this Order may have influenced those of the Crotona Fellowship.

22. Heselton, *Wiccan Roots*: 56, 58, 114.

23. The text *Gerald Gardner: Witch* by J. L. Bracelin, published by Octagon Press, London 1960, is now believed to have been written by the well-known scholar of Sufi mysticism, Idries Shah (1924–1996), who met Gardner in the mid-1950s and got to know him well. See R. Hutton, *The Triumph of the Moon: A History of Modern Pagan Witchcraft* (Oxford University Press, Oxford 1999): 205, 445 n.1; and Heselton, *Wiccan Roots*: 8–9.). Shah apparently did not want to put his name to the Gardner biography so Jack Bracelin, another friend of Gardner's, agreed that his name could be substituted. It is of interest that Octagon Press is an imprint best known for its Sufi publications.

The Sheffield-based witch Patricia Crowther, a friend of Gardner's, has suggested that if Gardner was initiated on a night of the new moon (the first after the beginning of World War II on 3 September 1939), he would have been initiated on 13 September 1939. See Heselton, *Wiccan Roots*: 178.

24. Bracelin, *Gerald Gardner: Witch*: 165. It has recently been established by Philip Heselton (see *Wiccan Roots*) that Gardner was initiated by Edith Woodford-Grimes (also known as Dafo), who was a member of the Crotona Fellowship.

25. Gardner, *Witchcraft Today*: 19.

26. Bracelin, *Gerald Gardner: Witch*: 166.

27. M. A. Murray, *The Witch-cult in Western Europe* (Oxford University Press, Oxford, 1921).

28. M. A. Murray, *The God of the Witches* (Sampson Low, London 1931; second edition Oxford University Press, Oxford 1970).

29. See Hutton, *The Triumph of the Moon*: 196.

30. Dr. Murray was also a member of the Folk-Lore Society. Philip Heselton believes that Gardner may have met her in late 1938 or early 1939 and discussed her theories of the origins of pagan witchcraft. See Heselton, *Wiccan Roots*: 27.

31. Ibid.: 273.

32. Crowley had lived in Hastings since January 1945. See J. Symonds, *The Great Beast: The Life and Magick of Aleister Crowley* (Macdonald, London 1971, Mayflower reprint 1973): 450.

33. Arnold Crowther's widow, Patricia Crowther, gives this date in her book *Lid off the Cauldron* (p. 26), although Lawrence Sutin maintains that it was May 1947, "according to Crowley's diary." See L. Sutin, *Do What Thou Wilt: A Life of Aleister Crowley* (St. Martin's Press, New York 2000): 409.

34. Sutin, *Do What Thou Wilt*: 409, 410.

35. A. Kelly, *Crafting the Art of Magic*, vol.1, *A History of Modern Witchcraft 1939–1964* (Llewellyn, St. Paul, Minnesota 1991): 174.

36. J. Farrar and S. Farrar, *The Witches' Way: Principles, Rituals and Beliefs of Modern Witchcraft* (Hale, London 1984): 3.

37. D. Valiente, *The Rebirth of Magic* (Robert Hale, London 1989): 61.

38. Sutin, *Do What Thou Wilt*: 409.

39. I. Colquhoun, *Sword of Wisdom: MacGregor Mathers and the Golden Dawn* (Spearman, London 1975): 207.

40. See Kelly, *Crafting the Art of Magic*: 179–184, and L. Hume, *Witchcraft and Paganism in Australia* (Melbourne University Press, Melbourne 1997): 28.

41. Noted contemporary exponents of witchcraft Janet and (the late) Stewart Farrar write in *The Witches' Way*: "Ritual nudity is a general practice in Gardnerian and Alexandrian witchcraft and is to be found among other Wiccan paths as well." See Farrar and Farrar, *The Witches' Way*: 193.

42. Valiente, *An ABC of Witchcraft*: 156.

43. The pertinent text from *Aradia* reads:

> *Sarete liberi dalla schiavitu!*
> *E cosi diverrete tutti liberi!*
> *Pero uomini e donne*
> *Sarete tutti nudi, per fino.*
> Ye shall be free from slavery!
> And thus shall ye all become free!
> Therefore, men and women,
> Ye too shall be naked.

Quoted in Farrar and Farrar, *The Witches' Way*: 194.

44. Francis King probably overemphasised the scourging. Doreen Valiente is reported as having advised Janet and Stewart Farrar that when the scourge is used in ritual practice, "no pain should be either inflicted or expected; it is always used gently." Quoted ibid.: 194. See F. King, *Ritual Magic in England* (Spearman, London 1970): 180.

45. See R. E. Guiley, *The Encyclopedia of Witches and Witchcraft* (Facts on File, New York 1989): 134.

46. Gardner's quest for publicity angered members of his former coven. According to Michael Howard, "It has . . . been said that Gardner's decision to 'go public,' even in fictional form, upset the Elders of his parent coven and he left them." See M. Howard, "Gerald Gardner: The Man, the Myth & the Magick," Part 2, *The Cauldron* , Beltane/Midsummer 1997: 19.

47. This is how Gardner is described in lengthy magazine feature article published in Sydney in 1958. An earlier article (Sydney 1955) had dubbed Gardner the "Witchmaster." See P. Lucas, "Witches in the Nude," *People*, Sydney, 5 March 1958: 54; and (anon.), "Witchmaster!: The Devil Is on Our Doorstep," *Australasian Post*, Sydney 14 July 1955: 11.

48. Valiente included a lengthy section on Rosaleen Norton in her book *The Rebirth of Witchcraft*. See also N. Drury, *Homage to Pan: The life, Art and Sex Magic of Rosaleen Norton* (Creation Oneiros, London 2009).

49. See Guiley, *The Encyclopedia of Witches and Witchcraft*: 40.

50. See ibid.: 134. Occult historian Aidan Kelly notes that Buckland, with his wife Rosemary acting as High Priestess, subsequently founded a coven of Gardnerian witchcraft

in Bayside, Long Island. "Almost all the 'official' Gardnerians in America," writes Kelly, "are descendants of that coven." See Aidan A. Kelly, "An Update on Neopagan Witchcraft in America," in J. R. Lewis and J. G. Melton (eds.), *Perspectives on the New Age* (State University of New York Press, Albany, New York 1992): 137. More recently it has been suggested by Mike Howard, editor of *The Cauldron* in the United Kingdom, that Gardnerian Wicca may have been introduced to the United States via two separate and independent routes: through Buckland and his wife on the East Coast and through a Gardnerian practitioner named Queen Morrigan on the West Coast. Morrigan allegedly settled in Stockton, California, in 1960–1962 and established what is now known as Central Valley Wicca. See Howard, "Gerald Gardner: The Man, the Myth and the Magick," parts 1–4, *The Cauldron*, 1997.

51. Kelly, "An Update on Neopagan Witchcraft in America": 141. The Pan Pacific Pagan Alliance, which has regional councils in every state of Australia, had a subscription membership of 150 in January 1994, each subscription covering several people. If a single membership extended to an individual coven, the national total would have been between 100 and 200 covens in 1994. See L. Hume, *Witchcraft and Paganism in Australia* (Melbourne University Press, Melbourne 1997): 244–45.

52. Gardner was doubtful whether Wicca would survive in the long term. In *Witchcraft Today* (1954), he wrote: "I think we must say goodbye to the witch. The cult is doomed, I am afraid, partly because of modern conditions, housing shortage, the smallness of modern families, and chiefly by education. The modern child is not interested . . . and so the coven dies out or consists of old and dying people." Quoted in S. Farrar, *What Witches Do* (revised edition, Phoenix Publishing, Custer, Washington 1983): 7.

53. In his will, Gardner bequeathed the Isle of Man museum to his High Priestess, Monique Wilson, and she in turn ran it with her husband for a short time, before selling it to the Ripley organization.

54. See diagram of the Wheel of the Year, with accompanying dates for both Northern and Southern hemispheres (figure 6.3).

55. Quoted in J. R. Lewis (ed.), *Magical Religion and Modern Witchcraft* (State University of New York Press, Albany 1996): 61–62.

56. The first esbat occurs in October just before the festival of Samhain (All Hallows' Eve, or Halloween) and is known as *Blood Moon*. It is traditionally associated with the slaughter of animals for food prior to the onset of winter and is therefore represented by the color red. *Snow Moon* rises in November and is associated with the first falls of snow. *Oak Moon* is the full moon in December. It is linked to the color black and also to the oak, sacred symbol of the Dark Lord aspect of Cernunnos, since it is his wood which is burned at Yule. *Ice Moon*, represented by the color purple, rises in January, followed by *Storm Moon* in Februar, a time when the ice and sleet may turn to rain. This full moon is linked to the element Water, and to the color blue. March brings the *Chaste Moon*, the return of Spring from the depths of winter, and is represented by the color white. In April, *Seed Moon* is a time when the seeds in the earth bring forth new life, and this esbat is represented by the color green. *Hare Moon* rises in May and is dedicated both to the Goddess and to fertility. Its color is pink, symbolic of love. June brings the *Dyad Moon* and, as Gwydion O'Hare notes, this name alludes to "the visible presence of the God and Goddess

reflected in the bright sun and green fields." The associated color is orange, "the color of the summer sun." The *Mead Moon* rises in July and is a time for dancing and revelry. Traditionally this is the time when honey mead was made for the ensuing harvest celebrations, and accordingly its symbolic color is yellow. August brings the *Wort Moon*, a reference to the dark green abundance of harvest time. September is the month of the *Barley Moon*. This is the season when grain is harvested: brown is the symbolic color for this esbat. Finally, *Wine Moon* is the esbat that arises as a consequence of the difference between the solar and lunar calendars. Unlike the twelve-month cycle of the solar calendar, there are usually thirteen full moons in any given year, and this esbat is the thirteenth in the cycle. It honors the sacrament of wine and its symbolic color is burgundy red. *Wine Moon* precedes *Blood Moon*, and so the lunar cycle continues. See G. O'Hara, *Pagan Ways* (Llewellyn, St. Paul, Minnesota 1997): 64–67.

57. A. Sanders, *The Alex Sanders Lectures* (Magickal Childe Publishing, New York 1984): 57.

58. See Valiente, *An ABC of Witchcraft*: 108.

59. Ibid.

60. James W. Baker, in his essay "White Witches: Historic Fact and Romantic Fantasy," points out that the Wiccan Wheel of the Year is by no means purely Celtic. The major Sabbats—Samhain, Imbolc, Beltane, and Lughnassadh—were Celtic festivals, but Yule was an Anglo-Saxon celebration. Midsummer did not feature in Celtic celebrations, and the vernal equinox was not considered important, either. For this reason Baker refers to the eightfold cycle of the Wheel of the Year as a modern invention, an "invented tradition." See Lewis (ed.), *Magical Religion and Modern Witchcraft*: 178, 187.

61. See G. Harvey, *Listening People, Speaking Earth* (Hurst, London 1997): 3–12.

62. Ibid.: 6.

63. Farrar and Farrar, *Eight Sabbats for Witches*: 122.

64. Ibid.: 61.

65. Harvey, *Listening People, Speaking Earth*: 8.

66. Farrar and Farrar, *Eight Sabbats for Witches*: 61.

67. Harvey, *Listening People, Speaking Earth*: 8.

68. Farrar and Farrar, *Eight Sabbats for Witches*: 82.

69. Harvey, *Listening People, Speaking Earth*: 10.

70. Ibid.: 12.

71. Hume, *Witchcraft and Paganism in Australia*: 123.

72. Farrar and Farrar, *Eight Sabbats for Witches*: 24.

73. See Kelly, *Crafting the Art of Magic*: 52; and also Farrar and Farrar, *Eight Sabbats for Witches*.

74. Harvey, *Listening People, Speaking Earth*: 40.

75. V. Crowley, "The Initiation,'" in P. Jones and C. Matthews (eds.), *Voices from the Circle: The Heritage of Western Paganism* (Aquarian Press, London 1990): 77–79.

76. Quoted in Farrar and Farrar, *Eight Sabbats for Witches*: 42–43.

77. Hume, *Witchcraft and Paganism in Australia*: 131, 134.

78. According to the Farrars, the binding is done with three red cords—one nine feet long, the other pair four-and-half feet long: "The wrists are tied together behind the back

with the middle of the long cord, and the two ends are brought forward over the shoulders and tied in front of the neck, the ends left hanging to form a cable-tow by which the Postulant can be led. One short cord is tied round the right ankle, the other above the left knee—each with the ends tucked in so that they will not trip [the Postulant] up." See Farrar and Farrar, *The Witches' Way*: 16.

79. Quoted in V. Crowley, "Wicca as Modern-Day Mystery Religion," in G. Harvey and C. Hardman (eds.), *Pagan Pathways* (Thorsons, London 2000): 88.

80. Ibid.

81. Hume, *Witchcraft and Paganism in Australia*: 132.

82. Ibid.: 133.

83. Single-gender Wiccan groups develop their own rules and responses in relation to this issue.

84. Crowley, "Wicca as Modern-Day Mystery Religion": 89.

85. Ibid.: 90.

86. Vivienne Crowley describes the impact of the *Legend of the Goddess* on male and female initiates as "a meeting with their contra-sexual side. For a woman, this is a meeting with her Animus and for a man a meeting with his Anima." See V. Crowley, *Wicca: The Old Religion in the New Millennium* (Thorsons, London 1996): 205.

87. Ibid. For a man this the archetypal feminine dimension of the male unconscious mind, epitomised as an aspect of the Goddess. See Crowley, *Wicca: The Old Religion in the New Millennium*: 205.

88. Ibid.: 89.

89. Ibid.: 108, 200.

90. Crowley, "Wicca as Modern-Day Mystery Religion": 91.

91. Farrar and Farrar, *The Witches' Way*: 30.

92. Crowley, "Wicca as Modern-Day Mystery Religion": 91.

93. Crowley, *Wicca: The Old Religion in the New Millennium*: 205.

94. Farrar and Farrar, *The Witches' Way*: 32.

95. Crowley, *Wicca: The Old Religion in the New Millennium*: 235.

96. Those conducting the first part of the Third Initiation as initiators must themselves be Third Degree witches. See Farar and Farrar, *The Witches' Way*: 31.

97. Crowley, *Wicca: The Old Religion in the New Millennium*: 227–228.

98. Farrar and Farrar, *The Witches' Way*: 32.

99. That is to say, the sexual act takes place physically, not symbolically. See Crowley, *Wicca: The Old Religion in the New Millennium*: 227.

100. Farrar and Farrar, *The Witches' Way*: 37.

101. Hume, *Witchcraft and Paganism in Australia*: 143.

102. Many writers, including Ronald Hutton, have stated that Sanders was born in 1926. However, when I interviewed Sanders at his home in Bexhill, Sussex, for an Australian television documentary—*The Occult Experience*, screened in 1985—he told me that he had always lied about his age and was actually ten years older than he had acknowledged. Sanders partially disrobed for a trance possession sequence in the documentary—he claimed to be "possessed" from time to time by an Aztec spirit—and his body was very much that of an older man.

103. Quoted in *Man, Myth and Magic*, issue 40 (Marshall Cavendish, London 1970).

104. It must be noted, though, that Patricia and Arnold Crowther were not averse to a certain amount of media publicity themselves. They produced the first radio series in Britain dealing with witchcraft—*A Spell of Witchcraft*—for Radio Sheffield in 1971, and also wrote two books together: *The Witches Speak* (1965) and *The Secrets of Ancient Witchcraft* (1974). After her husband's death in 1974, Patricia Crowther continued her appearances on both radio and television, and has since published several other books, including her autobiography, *Witch Blood!* (1974), and *Lid off the Cauldron* (1981).

105. Janet Owen (Farrar) was initiated by Alex Sanders, and Stewart Farrar by Sanders's wife, Maxine, in 1970.

106. Personal interview with the author, Drogheda, Ireland, December 1984.

107. The Californian psychedelic counterculture was at its peak between November 1965 and January 1967. For coverage of this colorful period, see G. Anthony, *The Summer of Love* (Celestial Arts, Millbrae, California 1980); J. Stevens, *Storming Heaven: LSD and the American Dream* (Atlantic Monthly Press, New York 1987); and T. Leary, *Flashbacks: An Autobiography* (Tarcher, Los Angeles 1983).

This period saw strong popular interest in the *Tibetan Book of the Dead*, which first appeared in the W.Y. Evans-Wentz edition (Oxford University Press, New York 1960) and then provided the basis for a psychedelic experiential manual (T. Leary, R. Metzner, and R. Alpert, *The Psychedelic Experience* (University Books, New York 1964), which became a bestseller in counterculture circles, enjoying seven reprints between 1964 and 1971. The American counterculture also embraced a wide range of other Eastern wisdom traditions, including Zen Buddhism, Taoism, Tai Chi, and Tantric yoga. However, it was also a period of renewed interest in magic, the Tarot, and the Kabbalah, and many occult classics by such authors as A. E. Waite, Lewis Spence, Eliphas Lévi, E. A. Wallis Budge, and Aleister Crowley were reprinted at this time, as well. Following the release of Mircea Eliade's classic work, *Shamanism* (Princeton University Press, Princeton 1964), interest in this subject area was further heightened by the release in 1968 of the first of Carlos Castaneda's many books: *The Teachings of Don Juan: A Yaqui Way of Knowledge* (University of California Press, Berkeley) and this in turn stimulated a developing interest in Native American culture and indigenous spirituality generally. For an overview of the spiritual and metaphysical undercurrents operating in the American counterculture, see T. Roszak, *Unfinished Animal: The Aquarian Frontier and the Evolution of Consciousness* (Harper & Row, New York 1975).

108. Much of the psychedelic counterculture in San Francisco had begun to disperse by 1968. See Anthony, *The Summer of Love*: 175, and N. Drury, *The New Age: The History of a Movement* (Thames & Hudson, New York 2004): 95.

The history of American counterculture spirituality and the rise of the New Age movement are described in such publications as R. S. Ellwood, *The Sixties Spiritual Awakening* (Rutgers University Press, New Brunswick 1994); W. J. Hanegraaff, *New Age Religion and Western Culture* (State University of New York Press, Albany 1998); P. Heelas, *The New Age Movement* (Blackwell, Oxford 1996); and Drury, *The New Age: The History of a Movement*.

109. Robert S. Ellwood, a scholar specializing in alternative and minority religions, believes that four different explanatory models can be advanced to account for the rise of

new spiritual movements in the United States during the 1960s. In the first of these models, "the dominant paradigm moves from mainline to nonconformist religion in various forms," the civil rights and antiwar movements being followed by the "occult/mystical counterculture." A second model focuses on what Ellwood calls "the quest for relevance," while a third explanatory framework contrasts the rediscovery of natural religion with the "revealed'" nature of established religions like Christianity: "Natural religion believes that [the divine] presence may be tapped by a normal quickening of spiritual sensitivity, which can be aided by various techniques or insights but does not require extraordinary grace. Faith in nature and nature's God may affirm hidden ('occult') natural forces that go beyond reason as ordinarily understood, including trust in psychic energies and powers of mind that seem almost magical." Ellwood's fourth model focuses on the quest for freedom: many symbols of religious hierarchy were abandoned by members of the 1960s countercul-ture. All of these models contribute to an understanding of the rise of feminist witchcraft as a post-counterculture phenomenon in the 1970s. See Ellwood, *The Sixties Spiritual Awakening*: 331–334.

110. American feminist Goddess worshipers quickly focused on "sisterhood," on close bonds between women, and for some devotees this has involved taking the Goddess tradition beyond the male domain altogether. As Judy Davis and Juanita Weaver expressed it in the mid-1970s: "Feminist spirituality has taken form in Sisterhood—in our solidarity based on a vision of personal freedom, self-definition, and in our struggle together for social and political change. The contemporary women's movement has created space for women to begin to perceive reality with a clarity that seeks to encompass many complexi-ties. This perception has been trivialized by male dominated cultures that present the world in primarily rational terms. . . . [Feminist spirituality involves] the rejoining of woman to woman." See Carol P. Christ and Judith Plaskow (eds.), *Womanspirit Rising: A Feminist Reader in Religion* (Harper and Row, San Francisco 1979): 272.

111. M. F. Bednarowski, "Women in Occult America," in H. Kerr and C. L. Crow (eds.), *The Occult in America: New Historical Perspectives* (University of Illinois Press, Urbana 1983): 188.

112. See M. F. Bednarowski, "The New Age Movement and Feminist Spirituality: Overlapping Conversations at the End of the Century," in J. R. Lewis and J. G. Melton (eds.), *Perspectives on the New Age* (State University of New York Press, Albany 1992): 169. Feminist writer Carol P. Christ goes even further, arguing that the resacralization of the earth is part of the process of individual transformation: "When the earth is the body of the Goddess, the radical implications of the image are more fully realized. The female body and the earth, which have been devalued and dominated together, are resacralized. Our understanding of divine power is transformed as it is clearly recognized as present within the finite and changing world. The image of earth as the body of the Goddess can inspire us to repair the damage that has been done to the earth, to women, and to other beings in dominator cultures." See C. P. Christ, *Rebirth of the Goddess: Finding Meaning in Feminist Spirituality* (Routledge, New York 1997): 91.

113. N. Goldberg, *Changing of the Gods: Feminism and the End of Traditional Religions* (Beacon Press, Boston 1979): 90.

114. Daly, *Beyond God the Father* (Beacon Press, Boston 1973): 13.

115. See J. Plaskow, "Women's Liberation and the Liberation of God," in R. S. Gottlieb (ed.), *A New Creation: America's Contemporary Spiritual Voices* (Crossroad, New York 1990): 230–232.

116. In her influential book *The Holy Book of Women's Mysteries*, Z. Budapest refers to the Mother Goddess as the "Female Principle of the Universe and source of all life." She is the "Goddess of the Ten Thousand Names" (pp. 277–278).

117. These American advocates of broad-based Goddess spirituality also had notable counterparts in the UK and Ireland, among them Caitlin Matthews, Olivia Durdin-Robertson, Vivienne Crowley, Asphodel P. Long, and Elizabeth Brooke.

118. See Budapest, *The Holy Book of Women's Mysteries*: 308.

119. Personal communication to the author, Berkeley, California, December 1984, during filming of the television documentary *The Occult Experience* (Cinetel Productions for Channel Ten, Sydney, released in the United States on Sony Home Video).

120. C. Lesh, "Goddess Worship: The Subversive Religion," *Twelve Together*, Los Angeles, May 1975.

121. Ibid.

122. Personal communication to the author, Berkeley, California, December 1984, during filming of the television documentary *The Occult Experience*.

123. Budapest, *The Holy Book of Women's Mysteries*: 112.

124. Personal communication to the author, Berkeley, California, December 1984, during filming of the television documentary *The Occult Experience*.

125. According to Z. Budapest, Simos was driving past the Feminist Wicca on Lincoln Boulevard and came in to look. Budapest was staffing on that particular day and invited Simos to attend a forthcoming Spring Equinox Festival. Their friendship and mutual advocacy of Goddess spirituality developed from this point onward. See Budapest, *The Holy Book of Women's Mysteries*: xiv.

126. Starhawk, *The Spiral Dance* (revised edition, HarperCollins, San Francisco 1999): 33, 51. Starhawk's response to male-dominated traditions would appear to be characteristic of the rise of feminist witchcraft in the United States since the late 1970s. Theologian Mary Farrell Bednarowski believes the rise of feminist spirituality was a response to the "alienation from the cosmos" associated with male-dominated religions: "According to New Age thinkers and feminists, Judaism and Christianity espouse a deity who is male, transcendent and 'other.' This is a static deity, omnipotent, omniscient, omnipresent, static, unchanging in his perfection. This God has created the world but does not inhabit it, for the creation, along with humankind, is fallen. At the centre of creation, at the center of human existence, there is brokenness rather than wholeness, sin and estrangement rather than creativity. To be saved means salvation from the world, from the body. . . . The result is alienation from the rest of the cosmos as well as estrangement from the divine." See Bednarowski, "The New Age Movement and Feminist Spirituality: 168–169.

127. Guiley, *The Encyclopedia of Witches and Witchcraft*: 327.

128. Ibid.

129. Starhawk remains strongly committed to political activism. Her recent publication, *Webs of Power: Notes from the Global Uprising* (New Society Publishers, Victoria, Canada 2002), explores the relationship between magical ritual and progressive activism.

130. Following his association with Starhawk, Matthew Fox came to believe that there was a connection between the Nature-spirituality in Wicca and the sense of wholeness-in-Christ expressed in his own Creation Spirituality. However, he was heavily criticized by the Roman Catholic authorities for this perception, Cardinal Joseph Ratzinger (now Pope Benedict) referring to Fox's book *Original Blessing* as "dangerous and deviant." See T. Peters, *The Cosmic Self* (HarperCollins, San Francisco 1991): 126–127.

131. See A. Blair-Ewart, *Mindfire: Dialogues in the Other Future* (Somerville House, Toronto 1995): 128.

132. Starhawk, "The Goddess," in Roger S. Gottlieb (ed.), *A New Creation: America's Contemporary Spiritual Voices* (Crossroad, New York 1990): 213.

133. Starhawk, *Dreaming the Dark* (Beacon Press, Boston 1982): 8–9.

134. Starhawk, "The Goddess": 213–214.

135. Ibid.: 214.

136. Christ, *Rebirth of the Goddess*: xv.

137. Adler, *Drawing down the Moon*: 24–25.

138. Ibid.: 35.

139. Quoted in D. D. Carpenter, "Emergent Nature Spirituality," in J. R. Lewis (ed.), *Magical Religion and Modern Witchcraft* (State University of New York Press, Albany, 1996): 57.

CHAPTER 7

1. Personal communication to the author, Berkeley, December 1984—during filming for the television documentary, *The Occult Experience* (released in the United States on Sony Home Video).

2. J. La Fontaine, "Satanism and Satanic Mythology" in B. Ankarloo and S. Clark (eds.), *Witchcraft and Magic in Europe: The Twentieth Century* (Athlone Press, London 1999): 94.

3. These "co-authors" were Burton Wolfe, in *The Devil's Avenger* (1974), and Blanche Barton, in *The Secret Life of a Satanist* (1990)—see Bibliography.

4. J. R. Lewis, "Diabolical Authority: Anton La Vey, The Satanic Bible and the Satanist 'Tradition,'" *Marburg Journal of Religion* 7. 1 (September 2002): 5.

5. B. Barton, *The Secret Life of a Satanist* (Feral House, Los Angeles 1990).

6. LaVey's daughter, Zeena Schreck, confirmed to me that these elements of LaVey's personal biography are largely fabricated: personal communication to the author, 1999.

7. Quoted in A. Lyons, *The Second Coming: Satanism in America* (Dodd Mead, New York 1970): 173.

8. Ibid.

9. L. Wright, "Sympathy for the Devil," *Rolling Stone*, 5 September 1991.

10. Ibid.

11. Lewis, "Diabolical Authority": 6.

12. Z. Schreck and N. Schreck, "Anton LaVey: Legend and Reality," 2 February 1998, www.churchofsatan.org/aslv.html.

13. Journalist Gavin Baddeley interviewed Anger a few months after LaVey's death in 1997 and confirmed that "the Black Pope" and Anger had been friends for almost forty

years; Anger had been active in the Church of Satan since its earliest days. See G. Baddeley, *Lucifer Rising* (Plexus, London 1999): 78.

14. Sir Francis Dashwood (1708–1781) was a wealthy English aristocrat who combined a life of privilege with a taste for the bizarre. Dashwood worked for Frederick, Prince of Wales, and met many leading figures of the day. His contacts allowed him the opportunity of numerous liaisons with aristocratic mistresses and an outlet for his promiscuous and voracious tendencies. Despite his marriage to the somewhat pious widow of Sir Richard Ellis, Sarah, he continued to gather like-minded friends around him and decided to form a group of "initiates" who would hold sexual orgies to worship the Great Goddess. Dashwood called his brotherhood The Knights of St. Francis—naming it after himself, not the saint—and attracted a membership of thirteen, including the Marquis of Queensberry, the Earl of Sandwich, and the Prince of Wales himself. Meetings were held at Medmenham Abbey near Marlow on the Thames, and employed the services of whores who were transported from London by coach. These sexual practices at the Abbey continued for around fifteen years, and it became known as the Hell-fire Club after acquiring a reputation as a place of devil-worship. Sir Francis Dashwood later moved the premises to a location at West Wycombe, where he had underground tunnels and a central chamber excavated, allowing his group to continue to meet in secret.

15. A. S. LaVey, *The Satanic Bible*, introduction by Burton H. Wolfe, (Avon, New York 1969): 17.

16. Lyons, *The Second Coming*: 183–184.

17. See note 98 in chapter 4.

18. Lyons, *The Second Coming*: 183–184.

19. See LaVey, *The Satanic Bible*: 25. According to Zeena and Nikolas Schreck in "Anton LaVey: Legend and Reality," LaVey was strongly influenced by Galt's speech in Ayn Rand's novel *Atlas Shrugged* in formulating these Satanic precepts.

20. LaVey, *The Satanic Bible*: 18.

21. LaVey quoted in Lyons, *The Second Coming*: 184.

22. Ibid.

23. Interview between the author and Dr. Michael Aquino for the television documentary *The Occult Experience*, San Francisco 1984.

24. Ibid.

25. Ibid.

26. Ibid.

27. Ibid.

28. Ibid.

29. Ibid.

30. See *The Book of Coming Forth by Night*, in M. Aquino (ed.), *The Crystal Tablet of Set: Selected Extracts* (Temple of Set, San Francisco 1983), Appendix 1.

31. Henceforth all reference to Satan was replaced by reference to Set.

32. See *The Book of Coming Forth by Night*.

33. Interview between the author and Dr. Michael Aquino for the television documentary *The Occult Experience*.

34. D. Webb, "Xeper: The Eternal Word of Set" (Temple of Set, San Francisco 1999), www.xeper.org/pub/tos/xeper2.html.

35. Ibid.

36. Ibid.

37. Interview between the author and Lilith Sinclair for the television documentary *The Occult Experience*, San Francisco 1984.

38. Ibid.

39. Ibid.

40. M. Aquino, *The Church of Satan* (Temple of Set, San Francisco 1983): 68.

41. D. Webb, "The Pylon System," Internet statement from the Temple of Set, 25 November 1998, www.xeper.org/pub/tos/pylons.html.

42. Nevertheless, membership of the Temple of Set probably numbers in the low hundreds, rather than thousands. Although there were claims that the Church of Satan had 50,000 card-carrying members, the initial San Francisco membership was only around 50, climbing to a nationwide peak of 300 by 1975—and the Temple of Set began as a splinter group from the Church of Satan.

43. Webb, "The Pylon System."

44. Ibid.: 3.

45. Ibid.: 4.

46. Aquino was the first high priest of the Temple of Set, and this position was later held by other senior figures within the organization, including Don Webb and (briefly) Zeena Schreck. Aquino returned to the post of high priest in 2002.

47. Aquino, "Origins of the Temple of Set," in *The Crystal of Set: Selected Extracts*: 47.

48. M. Aquino, "Black Magic in Theory and Practice," *The Crystal of Set: Selected Extracts*: 1–55.

49. Ibid.: 17, 18, 19, 28.

50. Ibid.: 15.

51. Ibid.: 19, 16.

52. Ibid.: 16.

53. M. Aquino, "The Two Paths," in *The Crystal of Set: Selected Extracts*: 41.

54. M. Aquino, "Black Magic in Theory and Practice": 16.

55. Interview between the author and Dr. Michael Aquino for the television documentary *The Occult Experience*.

56. M. Aquino, "Black Magic in Theory and Practice": 19.

57. Interview between the author and Lilith Sinclair.

58. D. Webb, "Seven of the Many Gateways," in L. D. Wild (ed.), *The Ninth Night*, 1, 2, Sydney, June 1998, www.xeper.org.

59. D. Webb, "The Black beyond Black," 2004, www.xeper.org/australasia.html.

60. M. Aquino, *Runes*, II: 6, San Franscisco 1984.

61. I. S. de Lubicz, *Her-Bak* (Inner Traditions, New York 1954).

62. M. Aquino, *Runes*, II: 6.

63. N. Goodrick-Clarke, *The Occult Roots of Nazism: Secret Aryan Cults and Their Influence on Nazi Ideology* (New York University Press, New York 1992): 178.

64. Ibid.: 186.

65. M. Aquino, *The Church of Satan* (Temple of Set, San Francisco 1983): 382.

66. M. Aquino, *Runes*, I: 2,San Francisco 1983.

67. Interview between the author and Dr. Michael Aquino for the television documentary *The Occult Experience*.

68. M. Aquino, "Satanism and the Immortality of the Psyche," Temple of Set 1996, www.xeper.org/nan_madol/immortal.html.

69. LaVey, *The Satanic Bible*: 94.

70. D. Webb, "Xeper: the Eternal Word of Set," Temple of Set 1999, www.xeper.org/pub/tos/xeper2.html.

71. Webb, "Seven of the Many Gateways."

72. Webb, "The Black beyond Black."

73. M. Aquino, "Satanism and the Immortality of the Psyche," Temple of Set, San Francisco 1996, www.xeper.org/nan_madol/immortal.html.

74. Aquino (ed.), *The Crystal Tablet of Set*: 6.

75. L. D. Wild, "An Introduction to the Left-Hand Path," *The Ninth Night*, 1: 1, Sydney, June 1998.

CHAPTER 8

1. Quoted in *Starfire: A Magazine of the New Aeon* 1 .3. (London 1989): 89.

2. Interview with the author for the television documentary *The Occult Experience*, New York, December 1984 (released in the United States on Sony home video).

3. I have already referred to Dion Fortune's interest in Jung in chapter five, and to Israel Regardie's similar endorsement of Jung in the introduction—see my lengthy n.3 there for examples of such endorsements from Regardie's key texts. Michael Bertiaux told journalist John Fleming: "You need to have read as much Husserl and Jung as I have, which means everything they ever wrote. . . . I lecture on Jung. But I don't look at the Jungian system from the outside. *I live inside it.*" See Fleming, "An Encounter with Chicago's Black Magic Theosophic Neo-Pythagorian Gnostic Master."

4. C. G. Jung, *Man and His Symbols* (Dell, New York 1968) : 41–42.

5. C. G. Jung, *Two Essays in Analytical Psychology* (Routledge & Kegan Paul, London 1953): 68.

6. Ibid.: 65–66.

7. Ibid.: 70.

8. See C. G. Jung, "The Relations between the Ego and the Unconscious" (1928), in *Two Essays on Analytical Psychology*.

9. For a summary of the rise of humanistic and transpersonal psychology and the contribution of Maslow and Sutich, see N. Drury, *The New Age: The History of a Movement* (Thames & Hudson, New York 2004).

10. Interview with Joseph Campbell (1971) included in Sam Keen (ed.), *Voices and Visions* (Harper & Row, New York 1976): 73.

11. Ibid.: 72.

12. Quoted in D. K. Osbon (ed.), *Reflections on the Art of Living: A Joseph Campbell Companion* (HarperCollins, New York 1991): 40.

13. Ibid.: 123.

14. S. Keen (ed.), *Voices and Visions*: 76.

15. S. Larsen and R. Larsen, *A Fire in the Mind: The Life of Joseph Campbell* (Doubleday, New York 1991): xix–xx.

16. Osbon (ed.), *A Joseph Campbell Companion*: 40.

17. Campbell was a close friend of Zen writer and counterculture guru Alan Watts and also encouraged Michael Murphy and Richard Price to establish the Esalen Institute. Watts and Campbell both lectured at Esalen on numerous occasions.

18. R. Daab and S. Smith, "Midwife of the Possible: An Interview with Jean Houston," part 3, *Magical Blend*, Fall 1988: 22.

19. Ibid.: 10.

20. J. Houston, *The Hero and the Goddess* (Ballantine, New York 1992): 7.

21. Ibid.: 13.

22. J. Houston, *The Search for the Beloved: Journeys in Sacred Psychology* (Crucible, Wellingborough, UK 1990): 13.

23. J. Houston, *The Passion of Isis and Osiris: A Union of Two Souls* (Ballantine, New York 1995): 6.

24. See M. Knaster, "The Goddesses in Jean Shinoda Bolen," *East West*, March 1989: 45. An interesting interview with Bolen is also included in Alexander Blair-Ewart, *Mindfire: Dialogues in the Other Future* (Somerville House, Toronto 1995).

25. Knaster, "The Goddesses in Jean Shinoda Bolen": 44.

26. J. S. Bolen, *Gods in Everyman* (HarperCollins, New York 1989): 287.

27. Knaster, "The Goddesses in Jean Shinoda Bolen": 73.

28. Dr. Andrei Znamenski's recent book *The Beauty of the Primitive: Shamanism and the Western Imagination* (Oxford University Press, New York 2007), is a very thorough examination of traditional and contemporary shamanism, and is highly recommended.

29. Mircea Eliade's classic academic overview of world shamanism, *Shamanism: Archaic Techniques of Ecstasy*, originally published in Paris in 1951, had already been published in an English-language edition by Princeton University Press in 1964, but it was Castaneda's work that struck a popular chord in the first instance.

30. For a more detailed discussion of the debate surrounding Carlos Castaneda and Lynn Andrews, readers are referred to Andrei Znamenski's *The Beauty of the Primitive: Shamanism and the Western Imagination* (Oxford University Press, New York 2007), and also to the chapter "Two Controversies" in my book *The Elements of Shamanism* (Element, Shaftesbury, UK 1989).

31. For details of this intriguing situation, see Znamenski, *The Beauty of the Primitive*.

32. Republished in Keen (ed.), *Voices and Visions*.

33. See Znamenski, *The Beauty of the Primitive*, and also Richard de Mille's *Don Juan Papers: Further Castaneda Controversies* (Ross-Erikson, Santa Barbara 1980), for details of what many writers continue to believe was an academic scandal.

34. Znamenski, *The Beauty of the Primitive*: 193.

35. Castaneda's first four books remained his most influential: *The Teachings of Don Juan, A Separate Reality, Journey to Ixtlan,* and *Tales of Power* (see Bibliography).

36. See Richard de Mille's interview with Barbara Myerhoff in his fascinating book *The Don Juan Papers*: 336 et seq.

37. M. Harner, *The Way of the Shaman* (Harper & Row, San Francisco 1980): 14.

38. According to shamanic tradition, when a person is "dis-spirited," their animating force, or spirit, has departed. The role of the shaman is to retrieve it.

39. Personal communication to the author in New York, December 1984, during filming for the television documentary *The Occult Experience*—in which I was involved as interviewer. This documentary, screened in Australia by Channel 10 and released in the United States through Sony Home Video, included a lengthy segment on one of Harner's shamanic workshops.

40. Personal communication from a participant in the Harner workshop which was featured in the Cinetel Productions television documentary *The Occult Experience*, New York, December 1984.

41. Michael Harner quoted in N. Drury, *The Occult Experience* (Robert Hale, London 1987): 145.

42. Ibid.

43. In her article "Speaking Shamanistically: Seidr, Academia and Rationality" (*Diskus*, 6: 2000, http://www.uni-marburg.de/religionswissenschaft/journal/diskus), anthropologist Jenny Blain notes that "Some researchers have described a curious 'double standard'—'native informants,' but not academics, can speak and theorize from within 'irrational' discourses of magic or spirit-helpers. . . . Others mention 'shamanophobia' within academia: a reluctance to consider 'shamanic' constructions for human events or ideas." For some academics—especially those who object strongly to the "universalism" of scholars like Eliade and Harner—neoshamanism removes shamanism from its innate social context, and, in so doing, renders it meaningless. As Blain remarks, "Those who study shamanisms within context point out that the images are not the same in all cultures: not only the meaning, but what is seen or heard, changes. Perception and meaning are embedded within specific cultural and historic community interpretations." Such scholars would also take exception, no doubt, to Harner's neoshamanic technique of summoning "spirits" during his experiential sessions. As Blain observes, narratives involving "spirits" are "problematic for a Western rationalist audience, for whom nonbelief in 'spirits' is axiomatic."

44. M. Eliade, *Shamanism: Archaic Techniques of Ecstasy* (Princeton University Press, Princeton 1964): 386.

45. Ibid.: 387.

46. On the issue of gender, Mircea Eliade refers to Snorri Sturluson, the twelfth-century Icelandic chieftain, historian, and saga teller, who authored the *Prose Edda*—a compendium of Norse mythology: "Odin, Snorri tells us, knew and used the magic called *seidhr*: by it, he could foresee the future and cause death, misfortune, or sickness. But, Snorri adds . . . men did not practise it 'without shame'; *seidhr* remained the concern of the *gydhjur* ('priestess' or 'goddess'). And in the *Lokasenna* Odin is reproached with practising *seidhr*, which is 'unworthy of a man.'" On the face of it, Eliade acknowledges, one could assume that *seidhr* was a feminine speciality, and according to the key texts *seidhr* séances are always conducted by a *seidhkona* or a *spákona*—a clairvoyant or prophetess. But as Eliade also notes, there are references elsewhere to both male and female practitioners—*seidhmenn*—and *seidhkonur*, respectively, and Odin is said to have learned *seidhr* from the

goddess Freyja. Freyja, mistress of *seidhr*, was said to own a magic feather garment that enabled her to fly like a shamaness. See ibid.: 385.

47. Blain, "Speaking Shamanistically."

48. Ibid.

49. R. J. Wallis, *Shamans / Neo-Shamans* (Routledge, London 2003): 106.

50. As R. J. Wallis observes: "Hrafnar's reconstruction of Heathen possession from the Nordic sources obviously borrows heavily from Umbanda . . . (and) the parallels between Heathen and Umbanda mythology and terminology are striking"; *Shamans / Neo-Shamans*: 97.

51. Ibid.: 232.

52. B. S. Pedersen, "Arts and the Occult: An Interview with Michael Bertiaux," www.fulgur.co.uk/authors/bertiaux/articles/pedersen.

53. See P. R. Koenig, "Ordo Templi Orientis—a Gnostic Inflation," http://user.cyberlink.ch/~koenig/sunrise/otoa.htm.

54. Personal communication to the author in December 1984, during filming for the television documentary *The Occult Experience*. Bertiaux was not included in the final cut, but his interview was included in the accompanying book of the same name (first published in Australia in 1985, American edition 1989; see Bibliography).

55. Ibid.

56. Pedersen, "Arts and the Occult."

57. Fleming, "An Encounter with Chicago's Black Magic Theosophic Neo-Pythagorian Gnostic Master."

58. D. Evans, *The History of British Magick after Crowley* (Hidden Publishing, London 2007): 355.

59. R. Sherwin, "Chaos Magick," www.chaosmatrix.org/library/chaos/texts/sher2.html.

60. Ibid.

61. Ibid.

62. Ibid.

63. H. B. Urban, *Magia Sexualis: Sex, Magic and Liberation in Modern Western Esotericism* (University of California Press, Berkeley 2006): 18–19.

64. Ibid.: 238.

65. P. J. Carroll, *Liber Kaos* (Weiser, York Beach, Maine 1992): 144.

66. Urban, *Magia Sexualis*: 242.

67. Hine writes: "Sigilisation is one of the simplest and most effective forms of results magick used by contemporary magicians. . . . The first stage of the process is that you should get your magical intent clear. . . . Vague intentions usually give rise to vague results. . . . sigils are excellent for bringing about precise, short-term results, which makes them excellent for works of Results Magick—healing, habit manipulation, inspiration, dream-control and the like." See P. Hine, *Oven-Ready Chaos* (electronic book) 1997, originally published by Chaos International in a limited edition of 300 copies, 1992: 31–32.

68. D. Evans, *The History of British Magick after Crowley*: 359.

69. Ibid.

70. L.O.O.N., *Apikorsus*, electronic book, published on-line, 1986: 6, quoted in Evans, *The History of British Magick after Crowley*: 359.

71. Urban, *Magia Sexualis*: 234.

72. Hine, *Oven-Ready*: 23 et seq. Hine began to distance himself from Chaos Magick soon after the publication of this book and now practices a form of Tantric magic (email communication to the author, October 2009).

73. P. J. Carroll, "The Magic of Chaos," www.philhine.org.uk/writings/ess_mach.html

74. Ibid.

75. Ibid.: 123.

76. P. J. Carroll, *Liber Null & Psychonaut* (Weiser, York Beach, Maine 1987): 181–182. Elsewhere, Carroll writes: "Magic arises to prominence when the boundary of the self is either expanding or contracting. For example, during times of innovation and discovery, or during times of repression. A profound magical renaissance is now in progress because the boundary of self is both expanding and contracting simultaneously. Science, drugs, psychology, communications networks and all the paraphernalia of late twentieth century life have expanded aspects of awareness to a degree inconceivable a century ago" (see Carroll, *The Magic of Chaos*).

77. Carroll, *Liber Null & Psychonaut*: 111.

CHAPTER 9

1. McKenna explores these issues in his book *Food of the Gods* (Bantam, New York 1992).

2. See "Magic Plants and the Logos: Terence McKenna in Conversation with Alexander Blair-Ewart," in A. Blair-Ewart, *Mindfire: Dialogues in the Other Future* (Somerville House, Toronto 1995): 60 et seq.

3. See "Sacred Plants and Mystic Realities: An Interview with Terence McKenna," in my anthology *Echoes from the Void* (Prism Press, Dorset, UK 1994: 158 et seq.). An edited version of this interview also appeared in Terence McKenna's anthology *The Archaic Revival* (HarperCollins, San Francisco 1991).

4. Ibid.: 159–160, 166.

5. Ibid.: 166.

6. M. Dery, "The Inner Elf," in A. Crawford and R. Edgar (eds.), *Transit Lounge: Wake-up Calls and Travelers' Tales from the Future* (Craftsman House / Interface, Sydney 1997): 94–95.

7. Ibid.: 95.

8. M. Wertheim, *The Pearly Gates of Cyberspace* (Norton, New York 1998): 223.

9. Ibid.: 228

10. H. Rheingold, *Virtual Reality* (Mandarin / Reed International, London 1992): 354.

11. B. Sterling, *The Hacker Crackdown: Law and Disorder on the Electronic Frontier* (Bantam, New York 1992): 235.

12. M. Dery, *Escape Velocity: Cyberspace at the End of the Century* (Hodder & Stoughton, London 1996): 28.

13. S. Reeder, "Children of the Digital Gods," *Green Egg* 29. 129 (August-September 1997): 15.

14. See "Computers, Consciousness and Creativity: An Interview with Dr Timothy Leary" in N. Drury (ed.), *Echoes from the Void*: 172.

15. "Frantic Life and Symbolic Death among the Computer Bums," quoted in M. Dery, *Escape Velocity*: 27.

16. Ibid.: 22.

17. E. Davis, "Technopagans: May the Astral Plane Be Reborn in Cyberspace," *Wired*, July 1995: 128.

18. D. Rushkoff, *Cyberia: Life in the Trenches of Hyperspace* (HarperCollins, San Francisco 1994): 143.

19. Davis, "TechnoPagans": 41.

20. Rushkoff, *Cyberia*: 145–146.

21. T. Williams, "Navigation Systems for the Spirit," *Green Egg* 29. 129 (August-September 1997): 39.

22. M. Hutchison, *Mega Brain Power* (Hyperion, New York 1994): 431.

23. See J. Dowse, "Cyberpagans!" in *Pagan Dawn* 119 (Beltane 1996): 11.

24. In Second Life, practitioners in the virtual world acquire exclusive right to a section of cyber-territory on the Internet and then populate their "space" with personas and settings of their own creation. The sites are interactive and assume their own "reality."

25. Reeder, "Children of the Digital Gods": 16. VRML stands for "virtual reality markup language" and is used to create three-dimensional imagery in cyberspace, whereas text-based Web sites are created with HTML (hypertext markup language).

26. See B. Galloway (ed.), *Fantasy and Wargaming* (Patrick Stephens, Cambridge 1981: 6–7.

27. Ibid.: 7.

28. *Ars Magica* was published by White Wolf, Stone Mountain, Georgia, third edition 1992.

29. Wertheim, *The Pearly Gates of Cyberspace*: 230.

30. Rushkoff, *Cyberia*: 198.

31. B. Laurel, "Toward the Design of a Computer-Based Interactive Fantasy System," doctoral dissertation, Ohio State University, 1986: 1.

32. The H. R. Giger Web site is www.hrgiger.com/bio.htm.

33. Dery, *Escape Velocity*: 280.

34. *The Necronomicon* is a work said to contain blasphemous magical incantations and was attributed to a wizard named Abdul Alhazred. However, it was actually created by American fantasy novelist H. P. Lovecraft (1890–1937). Lovecraft provided a brief history of this imaginary book in an essay titled "History of the *Necronomicon*," written in 1927. Alhazred is said to have wandered from Babylon through Egypt and thence to the southern desert of Arabia, where he learned the metaphysical secrets of the universe. Later in Damascus he composed a work known as *Al Azif, azif* being an Arab word associated with the howling of demons. This book subsequently became known as the *Necronomicon*. Lovecraft's bizarre vision has inspired several other works bearing the same title, each claiming to be authentic.

35. See Andrew Siliar, "Cyber-Space Cadets," *Green Egg* 29. 120 (August-September 1997): 65.

36. G. MacLellan, "Dancing on the Edge: Shamanism in Modern Britain," in C. Hardman and G. Harvey (eds.), *Pagan Pathways: A Complete Guide to the Ancient Earth Traditions* (Thorsons, London 2000): 139.

37. Ibid.: 147.

38. Ibid.

Bibliography

Abraham, L., *A Dictionary of Alchemical Imagery*, Cambridge University Press, Cambridge 1998.

Adler, M., *Drawing Down the Moon*, Beacon Press, Boston 1981.

Agrippa, H. C., *Fourth Book of Occult Philosophy*, Askin Publishers, London 1978.

———, *Three Books of Occult Philosophy or Magic* [1533], ed. W. F. Whitehead, Aquarian Press, London 1971.

Aldrich, M, Ashley, R., and M. Horowitz (eds.), *High Times Encyclopedia of Recreational Drugs*, Stonehill Publishing, New York 1978.

Allen, P. (ed.), *A Christian Rosenkreutz Anthology*, Rudolf Steiner Publications, Blauvelt, New York 1968.

Ankarloo, B., and S. Clark (eds.), *Witchcraft and Magic in Europe: The Twentieth Century*, Athlone Press, London 1999.

Anon., "Inside Rosaleen Norton," *Squire*, Sydney, April 1965.

Anon., *The Book of the Black Serpent* [c.1900], in R. A. Gilbert, *The Sorcerer and His Apprentice*, Aquarian Press, Wellingborough, UK 1983.

Ansell, R., *The Bookplate Designs of Austin Osman Spare*, Bookplate Society/ Keridwen Press, London 1988.

——— (ed.), *Borough Satyr: The Life and Art of Austin Osman Spare*, Fulgur, London 2005.

Aquino, M., *The Church of Satan*, Temple of Set, San Francisco 1983.

———, "Origins of the Temple of Set" in *The Crystal Tablet of Set: Selected Extracts*, Temple of Set, San Francisco 1986.

———, *The Crystal Tablet of Set*, Temple of Set, San Francisco 1983.

———, "Satanism and the Immortality of the Psyche," Temple of Set 1996, www.xeper.org/nan_madol/immortal.html4.

Armour, R. A., *Gods and Myths of Ancient Egypt*, American University in Cairo Press, Cairo 1986.

Ashcroft-Nowicki, D., *The Shining Paths: An Experiential Journey through the Tree of Life*, Aquarian Press, Wellingborough, UK 1983.

————, *Highways of the Mind: The Art and History of Pathworking*, Aquarian Press, Wellingborough, UK 1987,

Baddeley, G., *Lucifer Rising*, Plexus, London 1999.

Bado-Fralick, N., *Coming to the Edge of the Circle: A Wiccan Initiation Ritual*, Oxford University Press, New York 2005.

Bailey, M. D., "The Meanings of Magic," in *Magic, Ritual, and Witchcraft*, vol. 1, University of Pennsylvania Press, Summer 2006: 1–23.

Balakian, A., *Surrealism: The Road to the Absolute*, Allen & Unwin, London 1973.

Bardon, F., *The Practice of Magical Evocation*, Rudolf Pravica, Graz-Puntigam, Austria 1967.

Barnes, D., "Rosaleen Says She Could be a Witch," *Australasian Post*, Sydney, 9 October 1952.

————, "I Am a Witch," *Australasian Post*, Sydney, 20 December 1956.

————, "Confessions of a Witch," *Australasian Post*, 15 June 1967.

Barnstone, W. (ed.), *The Other Bible*, Harper & Row, San Francisco 1984.

Barton, B., *The Secret Life of a Satanist*, Feral House, Los Angeles 1990.

Bednarowski, M. F., "Women in Occult America," in H. Kerr and C. L. Crow (eds.), *The Occult in America: New Historical Perspectives*, University of Illinois Press, Urbana 1983:

177–195.

————, "The New Age Movement and Feminist Spirituality: Overlapping Conversations at the End of the Century," in J. R. Lewis and J. G. Melton (eds.), *Perspectives on the New Age*, State University of New York Press, Albany 1992.

Bertiaux, M., *Lucky Hoodoo: A Short Course in Voudoo Power Secrets*, Absolute Science Institute, Chicago 1977.

————, *Voudon Gnostic Workbook*, Magickal Childe, New York 1988; expanded edition, Red Wheel/Weiser, York Beach, Maine 2007.

————, *Cosmic Meditation*, ed. Robert Ansell, Fulgur, London 2009.

Beskin, G., and J. Bonner (eds.), *Austin Osman Spare 1886–1956: The Divine Draughtsman*, exhibition catalogue, Morley Gallery, London 1987.

Bharati, A., *The Tantric Tradition*, Rider, London 1965.

Blaikie, G., *Remember Smith's Weekly?* Rigby, Adelaide 1966.

Blain, J., "Speaking Shamanistically: Seidr, Academia and Rationality," *Diskus* 6, 2000, http://www.uni-marburg.de/religionswissenschaft/journal/diskus.

————, *Nine Worlds of Seid-Magic: Ecstasy and Neo-Shamanism in Northern European Paganism*, Routledge, London 2001.

Blair-Ewart, A. (ed.), *Mindfire: Dialogues in the Other Future*, Somerville House, Toronto 1995.

Blavatsky, H. P., *The Secret Doctrine*, fifth edition [vols. 1 & 2, 1888; vol. 3, 1897], Theosophical Publishing House, Madras 1962.

Bogdan, H., *Western Esotericism and Rituals of Initiation*, State University of New York Press, Albany 2007.

————, "Kenneth Grant: Marriage between the West and the East," extract from "Challenging the Morals of Western Society: The Use of Ritualised Sex in Contemporary Occultism," *The Pomegranate*, 8, 2, Equinox Publishing, London 2006, www.fulgur.co.uk.

Bolen, J. S., *Gods in Everyman*, HarperCollins, New York 1989.

Bonner, J., *Qabalah*, Skoob Publishing, London 1995.

Bracelin, J. L., *Gerald Gardner: Witch*, Octagon Press, London 1960.

Brodie-Innes, J. W. (Frater Sub Spe), "Flying Roll No. XXV: Essay on Clairvoyance and Travelling in the Spirit Vision," in F. King (ed.), *Astral Projection, Magic and Alchemy*, Spearman, London 1971: 71–75.

Budapest, Z., *The Holy Book of Women's Mysteries*, Wingbow Press, Los Angeles, 1989.

Budge, E. A. Wallis (ed.), *Lefefa Sedek: The Bandlet of Righteousness*, Luzac, London 1929.

Burckhardt, T., *Alchemy*, Penguin Books, Baltimore 1971.

Burkert, W., *Ancient Mystery Cults*, Harvard University Press, Cambridge 1987.

Butler, W. E., *Magic: Its Ritual Power and Purpose*, Aquarian Press, London 1952.

————, *The Magician: His Training and Work*, Aquarian Press, London 1959.

————, *Apprenticed to Magic*, Aquarian Press, London 1962.

————, *Magic and the Qabalah*, Aquarian Press, London 1964.

Campbell, J., *The Hero with a Thousand Faces*, Pantheon, New York 1949.

————, *Myths to Live By*, Viking, New York 1972.

————, *The Inner Realms of Outer Space: Metaphor as Myth and as Religion*, Harper & Row, New York 1988.

Carpenter, D. D., "Emergent Nature Spirituality," in J. R. Lewis (ed.), *Magical Religion and Modern Witchcraft*, State University of New York Press, Albany 1996: 35–72.

Carroll, P. J., "The Magic of Chaos," www.philhine.org.uk/writings/ess_mach.html.

————, *Liber Null & Psychonaut*, Weiser, York Beach, Maine 1987.

————, *Liber Kaos*, Weiser, York Beach, Maine 1992.

Castaneda, C., The Teachings of Don Juan, University of California Press, Berkeley 1968.

————, *A Separate Reality*, Simon & Schuster, New York 1971.

————, *Journey to Ixtlan*, Simon & Schuster, New York 1972.

————, *Tales of Power*, Simon & Schuster, New York 1974.

————, *The Art of Dreaming*, HarperCollins, New York 1993.

Cavendish, R., *The Tarot*, Michael Joseph, London 1975.

————, *The Magical Arts*, Arkana, London 1984.

Chapman, C., *Quest for Dion Fortune*, Weiser, Maine 1993.

Chaudhuri, H., "Yoga Psychology," in C. Tart (ed.), *Transpersonal Psychologies*, Harper & Row, New York 1975: 231–280.

Choucha, N., *Surrealism and the Occult*, Mandrake, Oxford 1991.

Christ, C. P., and J. Plaskow (eds.), *Womanspirit Rising*, Harper & Row, San Francisco 1979.

————, *Rebirth of the Goddess: Finding Meaning in Feminist Spirituality*, Routledge, New York 1997.

Churton, T., *The Gnostics*, Weidenfeld & Nicolson, London 1987.

Colquhoun, I., *Sword of Wisdom: MacGregor Mathers and the Golden Dawn*, Spearman, London 1975.

Cook, A. S., and G. A. Hawk, *Shamanism and the Esoteric Tradition*, Llewellyn, St. Paul, Minnesota 1992.

Couliano, I. P., *The Tree of Gnosis*, HarperCollins, San Francisco 1992.

Crabtree, V., "Left Hand Path Practices in the West," 2002, www.dpjs.co.uk/lefthandpath.html.

Crawford, A., and R. Edgar (eds.), *Transit Lounge: Wake-up Calls and Travelers' Tales from the Future*, Craftsman House /Interface, Sydney 1997.

Crowley, A., "Emblems and Modes of Use," www.aethyria.com, n.d.

————, *De Arte Magica*, www.skepticfiles.org, n.d.

————, *Liber A'ash vel Capricorni Pneumatici, Equinox* 1:6, September 1911.

————, *Liber Cheth, Equinox* 1:6, September 1911.

————, *Liber Stellae Rubae, Equinox* 1:7, March 1912.

————, *Liber XVIV, The Mass of the Phoenix*, 1912, www.thelemicgoldendawn.org/rituals/phoenix.htm.

————, *Energized Enthusiasm: A Note on Theurgy, Equinox* 1:9, March 1913; republished by Weiser, New York 1976.

————, *Magick in Theory and Practice* [1929], Castle Books, New York 1964; Routledge & Kegan Paul, London 1973.

————, *The Book of Lies*, Haydn Press, Ilfracombe, Devon 1962.

————, *The Confessions of Aleister Crowley*, ed. J. Symonds and K. Grant, Hill and Wang, New York 1970.

————, *The Magical Record of the Beast 666*, ed. J. Symonds and K. Grant, Duckworth, London 1972.

————, *Liber Al vel Legis*, in *The Magical Record of the Beast 666* (ed. J. Symonds and K. Grant), Duckworth, London 1972:01–315.

————, *Book Four*, Sangreal Foundation, Dallas 1972.

————, *The Vision and the Voice*, Sangreal Foundation, Dallas 1972.

————, *The Qabalah of Aleister Crowley*, Weiser, New York 1973.

————, "Talismans: The Lamen: The Pantacle," in *Magick without Tears*, New Falcon Publications, Tempe, Arizona 1982: chapter 12.

Crowley, V., *Wicca: the Old Religion in the New Millennium*, Thorsons, London 1996.

————, "Wicca as Modern-Day Mystery Religion," in G. Harvey and C. Hardman (eds.), *Pagan Pathways*, Thorsons, London 2000.

————, *A Woman's Kabbalah*, Thorsons, London 2000.

————, *A Woman's Guide to the Earth Traditions*, Thorsons, London 2001.

Crowther, P., *Lid off the Cauldron: A Handbook for Witches*, Muller, London 1981.

Daab, R., and S. Smith, "Midwife of the Possible: An Interview with Jean Houston," part 3, *Magical Blend*, Fall 1988: 22.

Daly, M., *Beyond God the Father*, Beacon Press, Boston 1973.

————, *Gyn/Ecology*, Beacon Press, Boston 1978.

Davis, E., "Technopagans: May the Astral Plane be Reborn in Cyberspace," *Wired*, July 1995.

———, "TechnoPagans: The Roots of Digital Magick," *Green Egg*, 29, August- September 1997

De Rios, M. D., and M. Winkelman, "Shamanism and Altered States of Consciousness: An Introduction," *Journal of Psychoactive Drugs*, 21,1, San Francisco, January-March 1989: 1–7.

Decker, R., T. Depaulis, and M. Dummett, *A Wicked Pack of Cards: The Origins of the Occult Tarot*, St. Martin's Press, New York 1996.

De Mille, R., *Don Juan Papers: Further Castaneda Controversies*, Ross-Erikson, Santa Barbara, California 1980.

Deren, M., *Divine Horsemen: The Voodoo Gods of Haiti*, Thames and Hudson, London 1953.

Dery, M., *Escape Velocity: Cyberspace at the End of the Century*, Hodder & Stoughton, London 1996.

———, "The Inner Elf," in A. Crawford and R. Edgar (eds.), *Transit Lounge: Wake-up Calls and Travelers' Tales from the Future*, Craftsman House/Interface, Sydney 1997: 94–95.

Deveney, J. P., *Paschal Beverly Randolph: A Nineteenth-Century American Spiritualist, Rosicrucian and Sex Magician*, State University of New York Press, Albany 1997.

Dowse, J., "Cyberpagans!" in *Pagan Dawn*, 119, Beltane 1996.

Drury, N., *Inner Visions: Explorations in Magical Consciousness*, Routledge & Kegan Paul, London 1979.

———, *The Occult Experience*, Robert Hale, London 1987; Avery, New York 1989.

———, *The Elements of Shamanism*, Element, Shaftesbury, UK 1989.

———, *Echoes from the Void: Writings on Magic, Visionary Art and the New Consciousness*, Prism Press, Dorset, UK 1994.

———, *Sacred Encounters: Shamanism and Magical Journeys of the Spirit*, Watkins, London 2003.

———, *Magic and Witchcraft: From Shamanism to the Technopagans*, Thames & Hudson, London 2003.

———, *The New Age: The History of a Movement*, Thames & Hudson, London 2004.

———, "The Modern Magical Revival," in J. R. Lewis and M. Pizza (eds.), *Handbook of Contemporary Paganism*, Brill, Leiden 2009: 13–80.

———, *Homage to Pan: The Life, Art and Sex Magic of Rosaleen Norton*, Creation Oneiros, London 2009.

Eliade, M., *Cosmos and History*, Harper & Row, New York 1959.

———, *The Sacred and the Profane*, Harper & Row, New York 1961.

———, *Birth and Rebirth*, Harper & Row, New York 1964.

———, *Yoga, Immortality, and Freedom*, Princeton University Press, Princeton 1970.

———, *Shamanism, Archaic Techniques of Ecstasy*, Princeton University Press, Princeton 1972.

———, *Occultism, Witchcraft, and Cultural Fashions*, University of Chicago Press, Chicago 1976,

Ellwood, R., *The Sixties Spiritual Revival*, Rutgers University Press, New Brunswick 1996.

Evans, D., *The History of British Magick after Crowley*, Hidden Publishing, London 2007.

Faivre, A., and J. Needleman (eds.), *Modern Esoteric Spirituality*, SCM, London 1992.

Farrar, J., and S. Farrar, *Eight Sabbats for Witches*, Hale, London 1981.

————, *The Witches' Way: Principles, Rituals and Beliefs of Modern Witchcraft*, Hale, London 1984.

————, *The Witches' Bible*, Magickal Childe, New York 1985.

————, *The Witches' Goddess*, Hale, London 1987.

————, *The Witches' God*, Hale, London 1989.

Farrar, S., *What Witches Do*, revised edition, Phoenix Publishing, Custer, Washington 1983.

Feldman, D. H., *Qabalah: The Mystical Heritage of the Children of Abraham*, Work of the Chariot, Santa Cruz, California 2001.

Ferguson, J., *An Illustrated Encyclopaedia of Mysticism and the Mystery Religions*, Thames & Hudson, London 1976.

Fischer-Schreiber, I., et al. (eds.), *The Encyclopedia of Eastern Philosophy and Religion*, Shambhala, Boston 1994.

Fisdel, S. A., *The Practice of Kabbalah: Meditation in Judaism*, Jason Aronson, Northvale, New Jersey 1996.

Fleming, J., "An Encounter with Chicago's Black Magic Theosophic Neo-Pythagorian Gnostic Master," *Neighborhood News*, Chicago 1979, published online at www.fulgur. co.uk/authors/bertiaux/artiles/fleming/.

Flowers, S. E., *Lords of the Left-Hand Path*, Runa-Raven Press, Smithville, Texas 1997.

Fortune, D., *Psychic Self-Defence*, Rider, London 1930; republished by Weiser, York Beach, Maine 1999.

————, *The Goat-Foot God*, Williams and Norgate, London 1936.

————, *The Mystical Qabalah*, Benn, London 1957.

————, *Applied Magic*, Aquarian Press, London 1962.

Foxcroft, E., "The Hermetic Romance, The Chymical Wedding," in P. Allen (ed.), *A Rosicrucian Anthology*: 83: 67–162.

Fuller, J. O., *The Magical Dilemma of Victor Neuburg*, W. H. Allen, London 1965.

Galloway, B. (ed.), *Fantasy and Wargaming*, Patrick Stephens, Cambridge 1981.

Gardner, G. B., *High Magic's Aid*, Michael Houghton, London 1949.

————, *Witchcraft Today*, Rider, London 1954.

————, *The Meaning of Witchcraft*, Aquarian Press, London 1959.

Garrison, O. V., *Tantra: The Yoga of Sex*, Julian Press, New York 1964.

Gettings, F., *The Book of Tarot*, Triune/Trewin Copplestone, London 1973.

Gilbert, R. A., *A. E .Waite: Magician of Many Parts*, Crucible, Wellingborough, UK, 1987.

————, *Revelations of the Golden Dawn: The Rise and Fall of a Magical Order*, Quantum/ Foulsham, Slough, UK 1997.

Ginsburg, C., *The Kabbalah: Its Doctrines, Development and Literature*, Routledge & Kegan Paul, London 1956.

Ginzburg, C., *Ecstasies: Deciphering the Witches' Sabbath*, Hutchinson Radius, London 1990.

Godwin, J., *Robert Fludd: Hermetic Philosopher and Surveyor of Two Worlds*, Thames and Hudson, London 1979.

Godwin, J., C. Chanel, and J. P. Deveney, *The Hermetic Brotherhood of Luxor*, Weiser, York Beach, Maine 1995.

Goldberg, N., *Changing of the Gods: Feminism and the End of Traditional Religions*, Beacon Press, Boston 1979.

Goleman, D., and R. J. Davidson (eds.), *Consciousness: Brain, States of Awareness, and Mysticism*, Harper & Row, New York 1979.

Goodrick-Clarke, N., *The Occult Roots of Nazism: Secret Aryan Cults and Their Influence on Nazi Ideology*, New York University Press, New York 1992.

———, *The Western Esoteric Traditions*, Oxford University Press, New York 2008.

Gottlieb, R. S. (ed.), *A New Creation: America's Contemporary Spiritual Voices*, Crossroad, New York 1990.

Graf, F., *Magic in the Ancient World*, Harvard University Press, Cambridge 1997.

Graf, S. J., *W. B. Yeats: Twentieth Century Magus*, Weiser, York Beach, Maine 2000.

Grant, K., *The Magical Revival*, Muller, London 1972.

———, *Aleister Crowley and the Hidden God*, Muller, London 1973.

———, *Cults of the Shadow*, Muller, London 1975.

———, *Images and Oracles of Austin Osman Spare*, Muller, London 1975.

———, *Nightside of Eden*, Muller, London 1977.

———, *Outside the Circles of Time*, Muller, London 1980.

———, "Cults of the Shadow," in J. White (ed.), *Kundalini: Evolution and Enlightenment*, Paragon House, St. Paul, Minnesota 1990: 399–402.

———, *Hecate's Fountain*, Skoob, London 1992.

Grant, K., and S. Grant, *Zos Speaks!: Encounters with Austin Osman Spare*, Fulgur, London 1998.

Grant, R. (ed.), *Gnosticism—An Anthology*, Collins, London 1961.

Greenfield, T. A., "Peter Davidson, Occultist," *Agape*, 2 May 2003.

Greenwood, S., *Magic, Witchcraft and the Otherworld*, Berg, Oxford 2000.

———, *The Nature of Magic: An Anthropology of Consciousness*, Berg, Oxford 2005.

Greer, M. K., *Women of the Golden Dawn*, Park Street Press, Rochester, Vermont 1985.

Guiley, R. E., *The Encyclopedia of Witches and Witchcraft*, Facts on File, New York, 1989.

Hanegraaff, W. J., *New Age Religion and Western Culture*, State University of New York Press, Albany 1998.

Harner, M. J. (ed.), *Hallucinogens and Shamanism*, Oxford University Press, New York 1973.

———, *The Way of the Shaman*, HarperCollins, San Francisco 1980.

Harper, G. M., *Yeats's Golden Dawn*, Macmillan, London 1974.

Harrison, P., *The Elements of Pantheism*, Element, Shaftesbury, Dorset 1999.

Harvey, G., *Listening People, Speaking Earth: Contemporary Paganism*, Hurst, London 1997.

Harvey, G., and C. Hardman (eds.), *Pagan Pathways*, Thorsons, London 2000.

Hauck, D. W., *The Emerald Tablet*, Penguin Putnam, New York 1999.

Heckethorn, C. W., *The Secret Societies of All Ages and Countries*, [1897] University Books, New York 1965.

Heseltine, N., *Capriol for Mother, a Memoir of Philip Heseltine (Peter Warlock)*, Thames Publishing, London 1992.

Heselton, P., *Wiccan Roots: Gerald Gardner and the Modern Witchcraft Revival*, Capall Bann Publishing, Milverton, Somerset 2000.

Hine, P., *Oven-Ready Chaos* (electronic book) 1997. Originally published by Chaos International in a limited edition of 300 copies, 1992.

Holmyard, E. J., *Alchemy*, Penguin Books, Harmondsworth, 1957.

Houston, J., *The Search for the Beloved: Journeys in Sacred Psychology*, Crucible, Wellingborough, UK 1990.

———, *The Hero and the Goddess*, Ballantine, New York 1992.

———, *The Passion of Isis and Osiris: A Union of Two Souls*, Ballantine, New York 1995.

Howard, M., "Gerald Gardner: The Man, the Myth & the Magick," *The Cauldron*, Beltane/Midsummer 1997.

Howe, E., *The Magicians of the Golden Dawn*, Routledge & Kegan Paul, London 1972.

Hume, L., *Witchcraft and Paganism in Australia*, Melbourne University Press, Melbourne 1997.

Hutchison, M., *Mega Brain Power*, Hyperion, New York 1994.

Hutton, R., *The Triumph of the Moon: A History of Modern Pagan Witchcraft*, Oxford University Press, Oxford 1999.

Idel, M., *Kabbalah: New Perspectives*, Yale University Press, New Haven 1988.

Jacobi, J., *The Psychology of C. G. Jung*, Routledge & Kegan Paul, London 1942.

Johns, J., *King of the Witches: The World of Alex Sanders*, Coward-McCann, New York 1969.

Johnson, M., "The Witch of Kings Cross: Rosaleen Norton and the Australian Media," conference presentation, Symbiosis: Institute for Comparative Studies in Science, Myth, Magic and Folklore, University of Newcastle, 2002.

———, "The Witching Hour: Sex Magic in 1950s Australia," conference presentation, University of Melbourne, 2004.

Jonas, H., *The Gnostic Religion*, Beacon Press, Boston 1958.

Jones, P., and C. Matthews (eds.), *Voices from the Circle: The Heritage of Western Paganism*, Aquarian Press, London 1990.

Jung, C. G., *Psychology of the Unconscious*, Kegan Paul, Trench, Trubner, London 1919.

———, *Symbols of Transformation*, Bollingen Foundation / Princeton University Press, Princeton 1956.

———, *The Archetypes of the Collective Unconscious*, Routledge & Kegan Paul, London 1959.

———, *Memories, Dreams, Reflections*, Collins/Routledge & Kegan Paul, London 1963.

———, *Man and His Symbols*, Dell, New York 1968.

———, "Psychological Commentary on Kundalini Yoga," lecture given 26 October 1932, *Spring*, New York 1976.

———, *Two Essays in Analytical Psychology*, Routledge & Kegan Paul, London 1953.

Jungkurth, M. M. "Neither-Neither: Austin Spare and the Underworld," in *Austin Osman Spare: Artist, Occultist, Sensualist*, Beskin Press, London 1999.

Kaplan, A., *Meditation and Kabbalah*, Weiser, New York 1982.

Kaplan, S. R. *Tarot Classic*, Grossett & Dunlap, New York 1972.

Kazlev, M. A., "The Teachings of Max Théon," www.kheper.net/topics/Theon/Theon.htm.

Keen, S. (ed.), *Voices and Visions*, Harper & Row, New York 1976.

Kelly, A., *Crafting the Art of Magic* (vol.1), *A History of Modern Witchcraft 1939–1964*, Llewellyn, St. Paul, Minnesota 1991.

Kelly, E. F., et al., *Irreducible Mind: Toward a Psychology for the 21st Century*, Rowman & Littlefield, Lanham, Maryland 2006.

Kerr, H., and C. L. Crow (eds.), *The Occult in America: New Historical Perspectives*, University of Illinois Press, Urbana 1983.

Kieckhefer, R., *Magic in the Middle Ages*, Cambridge University Press, Cambridge 2000.

King, F., *Ritual Magic in England*, Spearman, London 1970.

———, (ed.), *Astral Projection, Magic and Alchemy*, Spearman, London 1971.

———, *Sexuality, Magic and Perversion*, New English Library, London 1972.

——— (ed.), *The Secret Rituals of the O.T.O.*, C. W. Daniel, London 1973.

———, *Tantra: The Way of Action*, Destiny Books, Rochester, Vermont 1990.

King, F., and S. Skinner, *Techniques of High Magic: A Manual of Self-Initiation*, C. W. Daniel, London 1976.

King, F., and I. Sutherland, *The Rebirth of Magic*, Corgi, London 1982.

Knaster, M., "The Goddesses in Jean Shinoda Bolen," *East West*, March 1989.

Knight, G., *A Practical Guide to Qabalistic Symbolism* (vols. 1 and 2), Helios, Cheltenham, UK 1968.

———, *A History of White Magic*, Mowbray, London 1978.

Koenig, P.-R., "Introduction to the Ordo Templi Orientis," www.user.cyberlink. ch/~koenig/intro.htm.

———, "Spermo-Gnostics and the Ordo Templi Orientis," www.user.cyberlink. ch/~koenig/spermo.htm.

———, "Ordo Templi Orientis—A Gnostic Inflation," www.user.cyberlink.ch/~koenig/ sunrise/otoa.htm.

La Fontaine, J., "Satanism and Satanic Mythology, in B. Ankarloo and S. Clark (eds.), *Witchcraft and Magic in Europe: The Twentieth Century*, Athlone Press, London 1999: 81–140.

Larsen, S., and R. Larsen, *A Fire in the Mind: The Life of Joseph Campbell*, Doubleday, New York 1991.

LaVey, A. S., *The Satanic Bible* (introduction by Burton H. Wolfe), Avon, New York 1969.

———, *The Satanic Rituals*, Avon, New York 1972.

Law, I., "Austin Osman Spare,"' in G. Beskin and J. Bonner (eds.), *Austin Osman Spare 1886–1956: The Divine Draughtsman*, exhibition catalogue, Morley Gallery, London, 1987.

Lesh, C., "Goddess Worship: The Subversive Religion," *Twelve Together* (videocassette produced by Trudy Gallant), Los Angeles, May 1975.

Letchford, F. W., *From the Inferno to Zos*, First Impressions, Thame, UK 1995.

Levi, E., *The History of Magic*, Rider, London 1913.

———, *The Key of the Mysteries*, Rider, London 1959.

Lewis, I. M., *Ecstatic Religion: An Anthropological Study of Spirit Possession and Shamanism*, Penguin, London 1971.

Lewis, J. R. (ed.), *Magical Religion and Modern Witchcraft*, State University of New York Press, Albany, 1996.

————, "Diabolical Authority: Anton LaVey, The Satanic Bible and the Satanist 'Tradition,'" *Marburg Journal of Religion*: 7, 1 (September 2002): 1–16.

Lewis, J. R., and S. M. Lewis (eds.), *Sacred Schisms: How Religions Divide*, Cambridge University Press, Cambridge 2009.

Lewis, J. R., and J. G. Melton (eds.), *Perspectives on the New Age*, State University of New York Press, Albany 1992.

Lewis, J. R., and Pizza, M. (eds.), *Handbook of Contemporary Paganism*, Brill, Leiden 2009.

Lippard, L. R. (ed.), *Surrealists on Art*, Prentice-Hall, Englewood Cliffs, New Jersey 1970.

Luhrmann, T. M., *Persuasions of the Witch's Craft*, Harvard University Press, Cambridge 1989.

Lyons, A., *The Second Coming: Satanism in America*, Dodd Mead, New York 1970.

MacLellan, G., "Dancing on the Edge: Shamanism in Modern Britain," in C. Hardman and G. Harvey (eds.), *Pagan Pathways: A Complete Guide to the Ancient Earth Traditions*, Thorsons, London 2000: 138–148.

Marquardt, P. A., "A Portrait of Hecate," *American Journal of Philology*, 102, 3 (Autumn 1981): 243–260.

Mathers, S. L. MacGregor (ed.), *The Kabbalah Unveiled*, Redway, London 1887.

———— (ed.), *The Greater Key of Solomon*, De Laurence, Chicago 1914.

———— (ed.), *The Lesser Key of Solomon*, De Laurence, Chicago 1916.

———— (ed.), *The Book of the Sacred Magic of Abramelin the Mage*, De Laurence, Chicago 1932.

————, *Frater Deo Duce Comite Ferro*, "Flying Roll No. XI: Clairvoyance," in F. King (ed.), *Astral Projection, Magic and Alchemy*, Spearman, London 1971: 61–69.

————, *The Grimoire of Armadel*, Routledge & Kegan Paul, London 1980.

———— (ed.), *The Goetia: The Lesser Key of Solomon the King* [1889], revised edition, Weiser, Boston 1997.

Matt, D. C., *The Essential Kabbalah*, HarperCollins, New York 1995.

Matthews, C., and J. Matthews, *The Western Way*, Arkana, London 1994.

McCall, A., *The Medieval Underworld*, Hamish Hamilton, London 1979.

McIntosh, C., *Eliphas Lévi and the French Occult Revival*, Rider, London 1972.

————, *The Rosicrucians: The History, Mythology, and Rituals of an Esoteric Order*, Weiser, York Beach, Maine 1997.

McKenna, T., *The Archaic Revival*, HarperCollins, San Francisco 1991.

————, *Food of the Gods*, Bantam, New York 1992.

Melton, J. G., "The Origins of Modern Sex Magick," Institute for the Study of American Religion, paper prepared for the meeting of the Society for the Scientific Study of Sex, Chicago, Illinois June 7–9, 1985.

Merkur, D., "Stages of Ascension in Hermetic Rebirth," *Esoterica* 1, 1999: 79–96.

Meyer, M. W. (ed.), *The Ancient Mysteries: A Sourcebook*, Harper & Row, San Francisco 1987.

Moore, V., "Chthonic: From Beast to Godhead," *Rose Noire*, 2004, www.vadgemoore.com/writings/beast_to_godhead.html.

Mumford, J., *Ecstasy through Tantra*, Llewellyn, St. Paul, Minnesota 1988.

Murray, M. A., *The Witch-cult in Western Europe*, Oxford University Press, Oxford 1921.

———, *The God of the Witches*, Sampson Low, London 1931; second edition, Oxford University Press, Oxford 1970.

Newton, J. F., *The Builders: The Story and Study of Masonry*, [1914] George Allen & Unwin, London 1918.

North, R., "Introduction" to P. B. Randolph, *Sexual Magic*, Magickal Childe, New York 1988; original French-language text: *Magia Sexualis*, Paris 1931.

Norton, R., *The Art of Rosaleen Norton*, Walter Glover, Sydney 1952; republished 1982.

———, "I Was Born a Witch," *Australasian Post*, Sydney, 3 January 1957.

———, "Inside Rosaleen Norton," interview, *Squire*, Sydney, April 1965.

———, *Supplement to The Art of Rosaleen Norton*, Walter Glover, Sydney 1984.

O'Hare, G., *Pagan Ways*, Llewellyn, St. Paul, Minnesota 1997.

Osbon, D. K. (ed.), *Reflections on the Art of Living: A Joseph Campbell Companion*, HarperCollins, New York 1991.

Osiris, Frater, "Analysis of Liber XXXVI, *The Star Sapphire*," Seattle 2004, www.hermetic.com/osiris.

———, "Analysis of the Mass of the Phoenix," www.hermetic.com/osiris.

Owen, A., *The Place of Enchantment*, University of Chicago Press, Chicago 2004.

Pagels, E., *The Gnostic Gospels*, Weidenfeld & Nicolson, London 1979.

Pandit, M. P., *Kundalini Yoga*, Ganesh, Madras 1968.

Papus, *The Tarot of the Bohemians*, second revised edition with preface by A. E. Waite, Rider, London 1919.

Patai, R., *The Hebrew Goddess*, third edition, Wayne State University Press, Detroit 1990.

Pedersen, B. S., "Arts and the Occult: An Interview with Michael Bertiaux," www.fulgur.co.uk/authors/bertiaux/articles/pedersen.

Petersen, A. P. (ed.), *Contemporary Religious Satanism*, Ashgate, Farnham, UK 2009.

Philalethes, E., *The Fame and Confession of the Fraternity of R: C:, Commonly, of the Rosie Cross* [1652], in P. Allen (ed.), *A Christian Rosenkreutz Anthology*, Rudolf Steiner Publications, Blauvelt, New York 1968: 163–190.

Pinch, G., *Magic in Ancient Egypt*, British Museum Press, London 1994.

Plaskow, J., "Women's Liberation and the Liberation of God,'" in R. S. Gottlieb (ed.), *A New Creation: America's Contemporary Spiritual Voices*, Crossroad, New York 1990: 229–235.

Pollard, J., *Seers, Shrines and Sirens*, Allen & Unwin, London 1965.

Poncé, C., *Kabbalah*, Garnstone Press, London 1974.

Rabinowitz, J., *The Rotting Goddess: The Origin of the Witch in Classical Antiquity*, Autonomedia, New York 1998.

Radha, S., *Kundalini Yoga for the West*, Shambhala, Boulder, Colorado 1981.

Raine, K., *Yeats, the Tarot and the Golden Dawn*, Dolmen Press, Dublin 1976.

Randolph, P. B., *Eulis!*, Toledo, Ohio 1873, republished 1896.

———, *Sexual Magic*, Magickal Childe, New York 1988; original French-language text: *Magia Sexualis*, Paris 1931.

———, *The Ansairetic Mystery: A New Revelation Concerning Sex!*, Toledo, Ohio, c.1973–1974, republished in J. P. Deveney, *Paschal Beverly Randolph: A Nineteenth-Century*

American Spiritualist, Rosicrucian and Sex Magician, State University of New York Press, Albany 1997: 319–325.

Redgrove, H. S., *Alchemy Ancient and Modern*, Rider, London 1922.

Reeder, S., "Children of the Digital Gods," *Green Egg*, 29, August-September 1997.

Regardie, I., *The Tree of Life: A Study in Magic*, Rider, London 1932.

——— (ed.), *The Golden Dawn*, vols. 1–4, Aries Press, Chicago 1937–1940.

———, *The Middle Pillar*, Aries Press, Chicago 1945.

———, *Ceremonial Magic: A Guide to the Mechanisms of Ritual*, Aquarian Press, Wellingborough, UK 1980.

———, *The Eye in the Triangle: An Interpretation of Aleister Crowley*, Falcon Press, Phoenix, Arizona 1982.

Reuss, T., *Lingam-Yoni*, Verlag Willsson, Berlin 1906.

Rheingold, H., *Virtual Reality*, Mandarin/Reed International, London 1992.

Richardson, A., *Dancers to the Gods: The Magical Records of Charles Seymour and Christine Hartley 1937–1939*, Aquarian Press, Wellingborough, UK 1985.

———, *Priestess: The Life and Magic of Dion Fortune*, Aquarian Press, Wellingborough, UK 1987.

Richardson, E., *Seiðr Magic*, in *Chaos International* magazine, issue 20, www.philhine. org.uk.

Robbins, R. H., *The Encyclopedia of Witchcraft and Demonology*, Crown, New York 1959.

Robinson, J. M. (ed.), *The Nag Hammadi Library in English*, Harper & Row, San Francisco 1977.

Rushkoff, D., *Cyberia: Life in the Trenches of Hyperspace*, HarperCollins, San Francisco 1994.

Russell, J. B., *Witchcraft in the Middle Ages*, Cornell University Press, Ithaca 1972.

———, *The Devil: Perceptions of Evil from Antiquity to Primitive Christianity*, Cornell University Press, Ithaca 1977.

———, *A History of Witchcraft: Sorcerers, Heretics and Pagans*, Thames & Hudson, London 1980.

———, *Satan: The Early Christian Tradition*, Cornell University Press, Ithaca 1981.

Sabazius X° and AMT IX°, *History of Ordo Templi Orientis*, U.S. Grand Lodge, New York 2006.

Sarmiala-Berger, K., "Rosaleen Norton—a Painter of Occult and Mystical Pictures," *Overland*, 162, Autumn 2001: 59–63.

Scar, K., "Sado-Magic for Satan: An Interview with Zeena Schreck," *Cuir Underground*, 4, Summer 1998, 4, www.black-rose.com.

Scarborough, S., "The Influence of Egypt on the Modern Western Mystery Tradition: The Hermetic Brotherhood of Luxor," *Journal of the Western Mystery Tradition*, 1, Autumn 2001: 1–16.

Scholem, G., *Jewish Gnosticism, Merkabah Mysticism, and Talmudic Tradition*, Jewish Theological Seminary of America, New York 1960.

———, *Major Trends in Jewish Mysticism*, Schocken, New York 1961.

———, *Kabbalah*, Quadrangle, New York 1974.

———, *Origins of the Kabbalah*, Princeton University Press, Princeton 1990.

————, *On the Mystical Shape of the Godhead*, Schocken, New York 1997.

Schreck, Z., and N. Schreck, "Anton LaVey: Legend and Reality," 2 February 1998, www. churchofsatan.org/aslv.html.

————, *Demons of the Flesh: The Complete Guide to Left Hand Path Sex Magic*, Creation Books, Washington D.C. 2002.

Seabrook, W. B., *Magic Island*, Harcourt, Brace, New York, 1929.

Seligmann, K., *Magic, Supernaturalism, and Religion* [1948], Pantheon, New York 1971.

Semple, G. W., *Zos-Kia: An Introductory Essay on the Art and Sorcery of Austin Osman Spare*, Fulgur, London 1995.

————, "A Few Leaves from the Devil's Picture Book" in A. O. Spare, *Two Tracts on Cartomancy*, Fulgur, London 1997: 9–24.

Shah, I., *The Secret Lore of Magic*, Abacus, London 1972.

Shapiro, M. S., and Hendricks, R. A., *A Dictionary of Mythologies*, Granada, London 1981.

Sherwin, R., "Chaos Magick," www.chaosmatrix.org/library/chaos/texts/sher2.html.

Shumaker, W., *The Occult Sciences in the Renaissance*, University of California Press, Berkeley 1979.

Siliar, A., "Cyber-Space Cadets," *Green Egg*, 29, August-September 1997.

Skinner, S. (ed.), *The Magical Diaries of Aleister Crowley*, Weiser, York Beach, Maine 2003.

Spare, A. O., *Earth: Inferno*, self-published, London 1905.

————, *A Book of Satyrs*, self-published, London 1907.

————, *A Book of Automatic Drawing*, Catalpa Press, London 1972.

————, *Axiomata/The Witches' Sabbath*, Fulgur, London 1992.

————, *The Book of Pleasure (Self-Love): The Psychology of Ecstasy*, self-published, London 1913; facsimile reprint, 93 Publishing, Montreal 1975.

————, *The Book of Ugly Ecstasy*, Fulgur, London 1996.

————, "Mind to Mind and How," in *Two Tracts on Cartomancy*, Fulgur, London 1997: 31–37.

————, *The Logomachy of Zos*, in K. Grant and S. Grant, *Zos Speaks! Encounters with Austin Osman Spare*, Fulgur, London 1998 .

Spare, A. O., and F. Carter, *Automatic Drawing* [1916], 93 Publishing, Montreal 1979.

Sprenger, J., and H. Kramer, tr. M. Summers, *Malleus Maleficarum (The Hammer of the Witches)*, Folio Society, London 1968.

Springett, B. H., *Secret Sects of Syria and Lebanon*, Allen & Unwin, London 1922.

Starhawk, *Dreaming the Dark*, Beacon Press, Boston 1982.

————, "The Goddess," in R. S. Gottlieb (ed.), *A New Creation: America's Contemporary Spiritual Voices*, Crossroad, New York 1990: 212–228.

————, *The Spiral Dance* [1979], revised edition, Harper San Francisco 1999.

————, *Webs of Power: Notes from the Global Uprising*, New Society Publishers, Victoria, Canada 2002.

Stavish, M., "Assumption of the Godform," www.hermetic.com.

————, "The Body of Light in the Western Esoteric Tradition," www.hermetic.com/ stavish/essays/bodylight.html.

Sterling, B., *The Hacker Crackdown: Law and Disorder on the Electronic Frontier*, Bantam, New York 1992.

Stevens, J., *Storming Heaven: LSD and the American Dream*, Atlantic Monthly Press, New York 1987.

Suster, G., *The Legacy of the Beast*, Weiser, York Beach, Maine 1989.

Sutcliffe, R., "Left-Hand Path Ritual Magick," in G. Harvey and C. Hardman (eds.), *Pagan Pathways: A Guide to the Ancient Earth Traditions*, Thorsons, London 2000: 109–137.

Sutin, L., *Do What Thou Wilt: A Life of Aleister Crowley*, St. Martin's Press, New York 2000.

Symonds, J., *The Great Beast*, Rider, London 1951; republished 1993.

———, *The Magic of Aleister Crowley*, Muller, London 1958.

Symonds, J., and K. Grant (eds.), *The Confessions of Aleister Crowley*, Hill and Wang, New York 1969.

——— (ed.), *The Magical Record of the Beast 666*, Duckworth, London 1972.

Tart, C. (ed.), *Altered States of Consciousness*, Wiley, New York 1969.

——— (ed.), *Transpersonal Psychologies*, Harper & Row, New York 1975.

Taylor, F. S., *The Alchemists*, Paladin, London 1976.

Turner, P., and C. R. Coulter, *Dictionary of Ancient Deities*, Oxford University Press, Oxford 2000.

Urban, H. B., *Magia Sexualis: Sex, Magic and Liberation in Modern Western Esotericism*, University of California Press, Berkeley 2006.

Valiente, D., *Witchcraft for Tomorrow*, Hale, London 1978.

———, *An ABC of Witchcraft, Past and Present*, revised edition, Hale, London 1984.

———, "The Search for Old Dorothy," in J. Farrar and S. Farrar, *The Witches' Way: Principles, Rituals and Beliefs of Modern Witchcraft*, Hale, London 1984: 283–293.

———, *The Rebirth of Witchcraft*, Hale, London 1989.

Versluis, A., *The Secret History of Western Sexual Mysticism*, Destiny Books, Rochester, Vermont 2008.

Von Rudloff, R., *Hekate in Ancient Greek Religion*, Horned Owl Publishing, Victoria, British Columbia 1999.

Waite, A. E., *The Book of Ceremonial Magic*, Rider, London 1911.

———, *Shadows of Life and Thought*, Selwyn and Blount, London 1938.

———, *The Holy Kabbalah*, University Books, New York 1960.

——— (ed.), *The Mysteries of Magic: A Digest of the Writings of Eliphas Lévi*, [1886] University Books, Secaucus, New Jersey 1974.

Walker, D. P., *Spiritual and Demonic Magic from Ficino to Campanella*, Sutton Publishing, Stroud, UK 2000.

Wallace, W., *The Early Work of Austin Osman Spare*, Catalpa Press, Stroud, UK 1987.

Wallis, R. J., *Shamans/Neo-Shamans*, Routledge, London 2003.

Webb, D., "Seven of the Many Gateways," in L. D. Wild (ed.), *The Ninth Night*, 1, 2, Sydney, June 1998, www.xeper.org.

———, "The Pylon System," Temple of Set, San Francisco 1998, www.xeper.org/pub/tos/pylons.html.

———, "Xeper: The Eternal Word of Set," Temple of Set, San Francisco 1999, www.xeper.org/pub/tos/xeper2.html.

———, "The Black beyond Black," 2004, www.xeper.org/australasia.html.

Webb, J., *The Flight from Reason*, Macdonald, London 1971.

Wertheim, M., *The Pearly Gates of Cyberspace*, Norton, New York 1998.

White, J. (ed.), *Kundalini: Evolution and Enlightenment*, Paragon House, St. Paul, Minnesota 1990.

Wilby, B. (ed.), *The New Dimensions Red Book*, Helios, Cheltenham, UK 1968.

Williams, T., "Navigation Systems for the Spirit," *Green Egg*, 29, August-September 1997.

Wilson, C., *Aleister Crowley: The Nature of the Beast*, Aquarian Press, Wellingborough, UK 1987.

Wirth, O., *Stanislas de Guaita: souvenirs de son secrétaire*, Edition du Symbolisme, Paris 1935.

Wolfe, B. H., *The Devil's Avenger: A Biography of Anton Szandor LaVey*, Pyramid Books, New York 1974.

Woodroffe, J., *Śakti and Śakta*, Ganesh, Madras 1975.

Wright, L., "Sympathy for the Devil," *Rolling Stone*, 5 September, 1991.

Yates, F. A., *The Rosicrucian Enlightenment*, Routledge & Kegan Paul, London 1972.

———, *The Occult Philosophy in the Elizabethan Age*, Routledge, London 2000.

Yeats, W. B., *A Vision*, revised edition, Macmillan, London 1962.

Yronwode, C., "Paschal Beverly Randolph and the Ansairetic Mysteries," www.luckymojo.com.

———, *The Reverend Hargrave Jennings and Phallism*, www.luckymojo.com.

Zephyros, Frater, "The Ophidian Current," www.groups.msn.com/TheMage/theophidiancurrent.msnw.

Zimmerman, J. E., *Dictionary of Classical Mythology*, Harper & Row, New York 1964.

Znamenski, A. A., *The Beauty of the Primitive: Shamanism and the Western Imagination*, Oxford University Press, New York 2007.

Index

Abraxas, 117, 118–119
Adler, Margot, 77, 204, 225
Aethyrs, Thirty, 91
Agrippa, Cornelius, 145
Ahnenerbe, 220
Ain Soph Aur, 8–9, 10
Aiwass (Aiwaz), 84, 90, 116
Akashic records (Theosophy), 132
Alchemy, 6, 14–17
Alien, designs for (H.R. Giger), 268
Alliette, Jean-Baptist, *see* Etteilla
Altar, magical, 66
Altars, satanic, 209
Altered states of consciousness,
    119–123, 253, 257
Anderson, James, 25
Andreae, Johann Valentin, 29, 30, 33
Andrews, Lynn, 235
Anger, Kenneth, 153, 208
Antinomianism, 81, 116, 123, 125
Aquino, Michael, 5, 6, 116, 117, 120, 210,
    211–213, 215–217, 222, 223
Archangels, 58
Archetypes (Jung), 222–223, 232, 233,
    234
Archetypes, dark, 267–271
Argenteum Astrum (Aleister Crowley),
    77, 90–91
Ars Magica, 266
Ashcroft-Nowicki, Dolores, 77, 133, 134

Assiah, 11
Atavistic resurgence (Austin Osman
    Spare), 138, 150, 152
Atziluth, 11
Automatic drawing (Austin Osman
    Spare), 149–153
Automatic drawing (Rosaleen
    Norton), 154

Bailey, Alice, 175
Baphomet, 95
Bardon, Franz, 64
Barton, Blanche, 206
Bataille, Georges, 118, 123, 125
Bednarowski, Mary Farrell, 199
Bell, magical, 69
Beltane, 186–187
Bennett, Allan, 78, 82, 83, 112
Bergson, Moina, 47, 48
Berridge, Edward, 46
Bertiaux, Michael, 6, 226, 244–250
Besant, Annie, 180
Besant-Scott, Mabel, 180
Bharati, Agehananda, 109, 114
Blackwood, Algernon, 47
Blain, Jenny, 242–243
Blavatsky, Helena P., 46, 78, 175
Body of light, magical, 64, 120
Bogdan, Henrik, 93, 100
Bolen, Jean Shinoda, 231, 233–234

Bone, Eleanor, 196
Bone, Gavin, 198
Book of Lies (Aleister Crowley), 92, 98
Book of Shadows, Wiccan, 193
Bourne, Lois, 196
Brahman, 109, 111
Brand, Stewart, 262
Briah, 11
Brodie-Innes, John W., 47, 56, 69–70, 120,
    121–122, 128
Brotherhood of Eulis, 100, 104
Buckland, Raymond, 77, 184
Budapest, Zsuzsanna, 77, 200–202,
    205
Budge, E.A. Wallis, 64
Bulwer-Lytton, Edward, 100
Burckhardt, Titus, 16–17
Burgoyne, Thomas H., 104
Butler, W.E., 133–134

Cakes of light (Aleister Crowley), 89, 98,
    106, 125
Campbell, Joseph, 230–231, 232, 233, 254
Candlemas, 186
Carroll, Peter J., 251, 252, 253, 254–255
Carter, Frederick, 135, 149
Castaneda, Carlos, 4, 234–237
Chakras, 110–111
Chaos magick, 79, 250–255
Christ, Carol P., 171, 203
Chthonic deities, 117–118, 125
Church of All Worlds, 264
Church of Satan, 117, 205,
    206–210
Church of Wicca, 264
Circle Sanctuary, 264
Circle, magic, 65–66
Collective Unconscious (Jung), 226–228
Colquhoun, Ithell, 59
Constant, Alphonse-Louis, *see* Lévi, Eliphas
Core shamanism (Harner), 241
Court de Gébelin, Antoine, 17–18, 20
Covens, Wiccan, 176
Crabtree, Vexen, 79–80
Creation, 10
Crotona Fellowship, Rosicrucian, 180
Crowley, Aleister, 4, 5, 36–37, 47, 55, 59, 64,
    65, 66, 69, 77, 78, 79, 81–92, 94–100, 106,
    107, 108, 115, 116, 117, 123, 125, 127, 131, 153,
    154, 175, 182, 183, 194, 211, 225, 250, 251, 271

Crowley, Rose, 83, 84, 91
Crowley, Vivianne, 172, 204
Crowther, Arnold, 182
Crowther, Patricia, 194, 196
Cup, magical, 67, 98
Curwen, David, 108
Cyberdelic computer movement, 262
Cybermagic, 273

Daly, Mary, 199
Dark magic, 80, 116
Dashwood, Sir Francis, 209
Davidson, Peter, 104
Davis, Erik, 263
De Leon, Moses, 7, 8,
De Mille, Richard, 236, 237
Death posture (Austin Osman Spare),
    143–145, 151
Dee, John, 29, 31, 91
Degrees, Masonic, 24
Dery, Mark, 259, 261, 262
Deveney, John, 93, 100
Dianic witchcraft, 201
Disc, magical, 68
Discordian Movement, 253
Dowse, Jem, 264
Dragon Rouge, 80–81, 116, 117, 124,
    125, 213
Drawing down the Moon (Wicca), 125,
    187–190
Druids, 187
Dungeons and Dragons, 265
Duotheism, Wiccan, 204

Ecstasy, magical, 143, 149, 151
Egyptian Book of the Dead, 64
Elementals, 58, 70, 71, 153
Eliade, Mircea, 105, 241
Elixir of life, alchemical, 33
Encausse, Gerard, *see* Papus
Enochian magic, 91
En-Sof, see Ain Soph Aur
Equinox of the Gods (Aleister Crowley),
    85, 86
Erzulie, voodoo goddess, 161, 170
Esbats, Wiccan, 184–185
Etteilla, 18–19, 20
Eulis! The History of Love (Paschal Beverly
    Randolph), 102
Evocation, magical, 66

Farr, Florence, 47, 48, 53–55,
  73, 75
Farrar, Janet, 195, 196–198
Farrar, Stewart, 196–198
Felkin, R.W., 56, 130
Feminism and Wicca, 199
Ferguson, John, 12
Ficino, Marsilio, 12, 13,
Firth, Violet Mary, *see* Fortune, Dion
Flowers, Stephen, 81
Fludd, Robert, 28–29
Flying Rolls (Golden Dawn), 69, 70, 72, 73,
  75
Form magazine (Austin Osman Spare), 135,
  149
Fortune, Dion (Violet Firth), 47, 64, 121,
  127–134, 154, 155, 175, 226
Foundation for Shamanic Studies, 237
Foxcroft, Ezechiel, 29
Fraternity of the Inner Light, 129, 131,
  132, 133
Freemasons, 23–27, 35, 128
Fuller, J.F.C., 91
Furst, Peter, 237

Gardner, Gerald Brosseau, 179–184, 194
Garrison, Omar, 109
Germer, Karl, 107
Giger, H.R., 267–271
Ginsburg, Christian, 10
Glover, Walter, 153
Gnosis, 5
Gnostic Christianity, 129
Gnostic Church in Haiti, 246
Gnosticism, 226, 229, 245, 248
God-names, 4, 247
God, 7, 11, 12–13, 15, 16, 26, 29, 32, 36,
  43, 44, 62, 64, 109, 123, 125, 139, 151,
  231, 225
Goddess spirituality, 5, 77, 171, 175, 198–204,
  271, 273
God-forms, magical, 63, 167,
  168, 225
Godwin, Joscelyn, 93, 100, 104
Goetia, 62, 124, 145
Gold, alchemical, 15–16
Golden Hind magazine (Austin Osman
  Spare), 135
Goldenberg, Naomi, 199
Gold-und Rosenkreuz Order, 25, 34–35, 36, 44

Gonne, Maud, 47, 48
Grant, Kenneth, 80, 86, 87, 107, 115, 116, 131,
  135, 140, 147, 163
Great Beast 666 (Aleister Crowley), 85, 87
Great Goddess (Wicca), 176, 177–178, 187,
  188, 199, 203, 259, 264
Great Rite, Wiccan, 183, 191–192
Greater Sabbats (Wicca), 176–177, 185
Greenlees, Gavin, 153
Guaita, Stanislas de, 36, 37, 39, 40
Guede, Voodoo god of the dead, 247, 248

Halloween, 185
Harner, Michael, 237–241
Hecate, Rosaleen Norton's relationship
  with, 158
Hellfire Club (Dashwood), 209
Hermes Trismegistus, 3, 12, 13, 18
Hermetic Brotherhood of Light, 93
Hermetic Brotherhood of Luxor, 93,
  100, 104
Hermetic Order of the Golden Dawn, 4, 5,
  6, 13, 21, 25, 35, 36, 41, 43–75, 83, 90,
  100, 119, 120, 122, 124, 127, 128, 129, 131,
  134, 226
Hermetic tradition, 12–14, 122–123
Hesse, Hermann, 226
Himmler, Heinrich, esoteric practices,
  219–220
Hine, Phil, 252, 253
Hiram Abiff, 26
Hockley, Frederick, 44
Holmyard, E.J., 15
Holy Grail, 46, 75, 98, 106
Holy Guardian Angel, 83, 116, 246
Horniman, Annie, 47, 53, 83
Houston, Jean, 231–233
Hrafnar community, 241
Hume, Lynne, 189, 192
Hunter, Edward A., 55
Hutchison, Michael, 264

Illuminates of Thanateros (IOT), 251
Imagination, mythic, 62
Imbolc, 186
Immortality, pursuit of (Temple of Set),
  222, 223
Initiations, Wiccan, 177, 189–192
Isis-Urania Temple (Golden Dawn), 49, 53,
  55, 56

Janicot (Rosaleen Norton), 161–163
Jean-Maine, Hector, 246
Jennings, Hargrave, 100, 101, 104
Johnson, Pamela Hansford, 91
Jones, George Cecil, 82, 83, 91
Jung, Carl Gustav, 112, 132, 171, 226–229
Jungkurth, Marcus M., 151

Kabbalah, 4, 6, 7, 8–12, 20, 34, 36, 37, 40, 108,
    123, 124, 127, 137, 163, 229, 245, 247
Karmas (Austin Osman Spare), 139, 145, 147,
    148, 151, 152
Kelley Edward, 91
Kellner, Carl, 93, 104
Kelly, Aidan, 182, 183
Kia (Austin Osman Spare), 137–138, 140, 143,
    145, 151, 252, 254
King, Francis, 49, 93, 112–113, 120,
    183
Knights Templar, 24
Koenig, Peter R. 92, 94, 104, 105, 106–107
Kundalini yoga, 108, 109–112, 115, 117

L'Ordre Kabbalistique de la Rose Croix, 37,
    39, 41
La Barre, Weston, 236
La Fontaine, Jean, 206
Lamen, magical, 68
Lammas, 187
Laurel, Brenda, 267
LaVey, Anton, 5, 80, 116, 117, 206–210, 214,
    221
Law, Ian, 150
Leary, Timothy, 261, 262
Left-Hand Path, 78–81, 112, 115–117, 122, 123,
    125, 127, 151, 157, 267
Leland, Charles G., 183
Lesh, Cheri, 201
Letchford, Frank, 139, 144, 148, 149
Lévi Eliphas, 19–21, 35, 36, 37, 62,
    100, 154
Lewis, James R., 208
Liber 777 (Aleister Crowley), 59–61
Liber Al vel Legis (Aleister Crowley), 85,
    86–87, 89, 90
Liberal Catholics, 246
Lilith (Rosaleen Norton), 158–159, 160
Lincoln Order of Neuromancers, 253
Lindsay, Norman, 153
Little, Robert Wentworth, 35, 36,
Logos, shamanic contact with the, 258

Lovecraft, H.P., 270
LSD, 262
Lucifer, Rosaleen Norton's relationship
    with, 159–161
Lughnassadh, 187

Machen, Arthur, 47
MacKenzie, Kenneth, 35, 44, 100
MacLellan, Gordon, 273
Mageia, 13,
Magic, high, 5, 13–14
Magical allies (Castaneda), 236
Magical correspondences (Golden
    Dawn), 59
Magical ritual and the senses, 62–63
Magick in Theory and Practice (Aleister
    Crowley), 62, 82
Mahatmas (Theosophy), 46
Maier, Michael, 33
Major Arcana (Tarot), 17, 20, 21, 37, 72–73,
    120, 122
Maslow, Abraham, 230
Masonic mythology, 25–26
Masonic rituals, 44
Materia prima, 16
Mathers, Moina, 54, 70, 71, 75, 128, 129, 130
Mathers, S. L. MacGregor, 35, 43, 46, 47, 51,
    52–55, 62, 66, 71, 83, 90, 130, 131, 175
Matus, don Juan, 235–236
May Eve, 186–187
McIntosh, Christopher, 24, 29, 33, 35
McKenna, Terence, 257–260
Medici, Cosimo de, 12
Medici, Lorenzo de, 12
Medina, Ramon (Huichol shaman), 236–237
Melton, J. Gordon, 93, 114, 115
Merkur, Dan, 122, 123
Microcosm, Four Points of the, 66
Middle Pillar, Kabbalistic, 72
Monastery of the Seven Rays, 247, 250
Moore, Vadge, 117, 118, 119, 123, 125
Moriarty, Theodore, 128, 129
Morris, Maxine, 194
Mudd, Norman, 92
Murray, Margaret, 175, 181
Museum of Magic and Witchcraft, Isle of
    Man, 183
Myerhoff, Barbara, 236, 237
Mysteria Mystica Maxima (Aleister
    Crowley), 92
Mythic imagination, 231

Names of God, 64
Names of power, Kabbalistic, 73
Necronomicon (H.P.Lovecraft), 268, 270
Necronomicon (H.R. Giger), 270
Neoplatonism, 226
Neo-Pythagorean Gnostic Church, 246
Neo-shamanism, experiential, 238–241
Neuburg, Victor, 91
Newton, Joseph Fort, 23
Norse sagas, 241, 242
Norton, Rosaleen, 5, 6, 127, 153–173, 175, 184

Oil, magical, 66
Online neopagan rituals, 264
Order of the Elect Cohens, 245
Ordo Templi Orientis, 80, 89, 92–100,
    107–109, 114, 183
Orridge, Genesis P., 252
Osiris, Frater, 96
Osmond, Humphry, 261
Otherworld, 273

Pan, worship of (Rosaleen Norton), 155, 156,
    157, 158, 171–172, 173
Panarion (Epiphanius), 105–106
Pandit, Madhav, 111
Papus, 20, 21, 37, 39,
    104, 245
Paracelsus, 28
Pasqually, Martinez de, 245, 246
Paxson, Diana, 241, 244
Peck, William, 47
Péladan, Joséphin, 36, 37, 39–40, 41
Pentacle, *see* Disc, magical
Phibionites, 105–106
Philosopher's Stone, 33
Pico, Giovanni, 13
Pistoia, Leonardo da, 12
Plaskow, Judith, 199
Prana, Hindu, 95
Pranayama, 112
Pylons (Temple of Set), 215

Qliphoth (Kabbalah), 107, 122, 124,
    163–165

Ra-Hoor-Khuit (Aleister Crowley), 86, 87,
    89,
Ramsay, Andrew Michael, 24, 25
Randolph, Paschal Beverly, 93, 100–104, 245
Reade, Winwood, 27

Rede, Wiccan, 178–179
Redgrove, H. Stanley, 16
Reeder, Sara, 264
Regardie, Israel, 5, 57, 226
Reification (Austin Osman Spare), 140
Reuss, Theodor, 92, 93, 94, 96, 104, 106
Richardson, Alan, 128
Rider-Waite Tarot deck, 21
Right-Hand Path, 78–79, 112, 122, 123
Rising in the planes (Golden Dawn), 71–72,
    122
Ritual grades (Golden Dawn), 49–51, 57–59,
    83
Ritual magic, symbols of, 65–69
Role-play, magical, 261, 265–267
Rosencreutz, Christian, 27–32, 51
Rosenroth, Knorr von, 34
Rosicrucians, 27–36
Rushkoff, Douglas, 263, 266–267

Sacred Magic of Abramelin the Mage, 53
Sacred psychology, 231–234
Saint-Martin, Louis Claude de, 245, 246
Samhain, 185
Sanders, Alex, 185, 192–196
Satanism, contemporary, 80
Scarlet Woman (Aleister Crowley), 85–86,
    87, 115
Scholem, Gershom, 7, 10
Schreck, Nikolas, 208
Schreck, Zeena, 117, 208
Second Life, 264
Secret chiefs (Golden Dawn), 36, 43–44, 46,
    49–52, 53, 56, 129
Self-actualization, 229
Seidr magic, 241–244
Self-deification, 81, 125, 218, 221
Self-hypnosis, 154, 154, 165–166
Semple, Gavin W., 137, 145
Sendivogius, Michael, 14–15,
Sephirah Yetzirah, 7
Sephiroth, Kabbalistic, 8–9, 11, 62
Servants of the Light (SOL), 133
Set, Egyptian God of the Night, 221–222
Sex magick, Thelemic 81, 84, 85, 87, 89, 90,
    92, 94–100, 103, 104, 105, 106
Seymour, Charles R. F., 131–132,
Shakti, 110, 111, 113, 115
Shamanism, 234–241, 273
Sherwin, Ray, 251, 252
Shiva, 110, 111, 113

Sigils, magical, 94, 127, 143, 144–147, 151, 168, 252
Siliar, Andrew, 272
Simpson, Elaine, 55, 73, 75
Sinclair, Lilith, 213, 214
Sky-clad rituals (Wicca), 183, 190
Smith, Pamela Colman, 21
Smith, Wilfred Talbot, 107
Societas Rosicruciana in Anglia (SRIA), 35, 43, 44
Solomon's Temple, 25–26
Spare, Austin Osman, 3, 6, 80, 92, 97, 99, 127, 134–153, 155, 250, 251, 252, 254
Spermo-Gnostics, 105–106
Sprengel, Anna, 46, 49, 55
Starhawk, 77, 171, 200, 202–203
Stella Matutina, Order of the, 56, 63, 130
Steppenwolf (Hermann Hesse), 272
Sterling, Bruce, 261
Superstition, 3
Sutcliffe, Richard, 78
Sutin, Lawrence, 112
Swaffer, Hannen, 148–149
Swedenborg, Emanuel, 245
Sword, magical, 68
Symonds, John, 87

Tantra, 93, 108, 109–114, 117, 131
Taoism, 250
Tarot, history of, 6, 17–21
Tarot, meditative, 72, 73–75, 120–121
Tattvas, Hindu elemental, 70, 120, 121
Temple of Set, 5, 116, 117, 120, 123, 125, 205, 206, 210–222, 223, 225
Temple of Set, Nazi connection with, 218–220
Tetragrammaton, 11, 67
The Book of the Law (Aleister Crowley), 85, 86
The Equinox (Aleister Crowley), 90
Thee Temple Ov Psychick Youth, 252
Thelema, doctrine of, 77, 80, 81
Thelemic sex magick, 5, 108, 112–117, 125, 153, 183, 250
Théon, Max, 104
Theosophical Society, 129, 246
Theosophy, 128, 132, 148
Tobler, Li, 270–271
Trance states, 69–75, 165–169
Tranchell-Hayes, Maiya, 128
Tree of Life, Kabbalistic, 6, 7, 8, 10, 20, 21, 40, 41, 49, 51, 59, 61, 65, 66, 72, 108, 123, 124, 127, 163, 229, 247
Triangle, magic, 66

Ugly ecstasies (Austin Osman Spare), 151, 152
Unio Mystica, 263
Urban, Hugh B., 93, 100, 252

Valiente, Doreen, 182, 183, 184, 185, 196
Vama-marga, Tantric, 78, 108
Vaughan, Thomas, 27
Vehm, 220
Virtual reality, 260, 261, 266, 271
Void moment, 99, 138, 143, 146, 147, 151, 252
Völva seeress (Seidr magic), 242–243
Voodoo magic (Bertiaux), 244–250

Waddell, Leila, 92
Waite, Arthur Edward, 10, 21, 36, 37, 38, 79, 175
Wand, magical, 67
Webb, Don, 213, 221
Wertheim, Margaret, 260, 266
Westcott, Wynn W., 35, 36, 43, 45, 49
Wewelsburg working (Michael Aquino), 220
Wheel of the Year (Wicca), 185–186
Whore of Babalon (Aleister Crowley), 85, 87
Wicca, 5, 125, 175, 176–198, 271
Wild, Leon, 222
Will, magical, 3, 4, 44, 62–63, 68, 82, 86, 138, 143, 144
Williams, Tom, 263
Williamson, Cecil, 183
Wilson, Monique (Lady Olwen), 184
Witchcraft, Gardnerian, 199
Witches, Alexandrian, 192
Wolfe, Jane, 107
Woodman, W. R., 35, 43, 49
Woodward, Alphonsus F.A., 44
World Memory, 132
Wright, Lawrence, 208

Xeper (Temple of Set), 212, 213

Yates, Frances A., 29, 32, 33
Yeats, William Butler, 46, 55, 56, 83
Yetzirah, 11

Zephyros, Frater, 108
Zohar, 7, 8, 137
Zos (Austin Osman Spare), 137–138, 143, 151